THE AMERICAN ISHERWOOD

T0338067

The American
Isherwood

James J. Berg and Chris Freeman, Editors

Foreword by Stephen McCauley

University of Minnesota Press

Minneapolis

London

A version of chapter 7 was published as "Isherwood the Multiculturalist," *Chronicle Review* 56, no. 18 (January 15, 2010): B13–15. Chapter 15 was previously published as "Huxley and Isherwood: The California Years," *Aldous Huxley Annual* 7 (2007): 1–12; reprinted with permission of Lit Verlag. An earlier version of chapter 18 was published as "'Fagtrash': Pulp Paperbacks and Cold War Queer Readers," in *Middlebrow Queer: Christopher Isherwood in America* (Minneapolis: University of Minnesota Press, 2013), 45–70. A version of chapter 19 was published as "'Christopher wasn't satisfied with either ending': Connecting Christopher Isherwood's *The World in the Evening* to E. M. Forster's *Maurice*," *Papers on Language and Literature* 48, no. 3 (Summer 2012): 302–31.

Published by the University of Minnesota Press
111 Third Avenue South, Suite 290
Minneapolis, MN 55401–2520
http://www.upress.umn.edu

Library of Congress Cataloging-in-Publication Data
The American Isherwood / James J. Berg and Chris Freeman, editors ; foreword by Stephen McCauley.
    Includes bibliographical references and index.
    ISBN 978-0-8166-8361-1 (hc) — ISBN 978-0-8166-8363-5 (pb)
    1. Isherwood, Christopher, 1904–1986—Criticism and interpretation.
2. Homosexuality and literature—United States—History—20th century.
3. Literature and society—United States—History—20th century.
I. Berg, James J., editor.   II. Freeman, Chris, 1965– editor.
    PR6017.S5Z628 2014 823'.912—dc23
                                                                2014028192

Printed in the United States of America on acid-free paper

The University of Minnesota is an equal-opportunity educator and employer.

20 19 18 17 16 15   10 9 8 7 6 5 4 3 2 1

For Dan Luckenbill and Peter Edgerly Firchow

"I must be anonymous until I discover a new self here, an American me."

—CHRISTOPHER ISHERWOOD, *My Guru and His Disciple*

CONTENTS

Outside the Frame

STEPHEN McCAULEY

Charm is among the most elusive and hard to define qualities a person can possess. It's also one of the rarest, but never mind. As with many other things in life—art, pornography, bad hair—most of us feel we know charm when we see it, even if we can't explain it in the abstract. One definition I especially like is Richard Avedon's. He describes charm as "the ability to be truly interested in other people." Coming from someone who made a career of taking pictures of others, there's perhaps an element of the self-congratulatory in this, but still, it's simple, direct, and gives you something concrete to strive for. While charm is frequently looked at as a parlor trick of sorts, often with mercenary intent behind it ("he tried to charm his way into her will," and so on), Avedon kicks it up to the level of admirable, altruistic virtue. His "charm" is not merely the ability to make the person sitting next to you feel like the most interesting person at the dinner table; it's truly finding him so.

If you subscribe to this definition, you have to conclude that Christopher Isherwood was among the most charming writers of the twentieth century and perhaps one of the most charming men. His ability to bring characters to life on the page with such stunning precision and economy is, of course, a triumph of his pristine style and impeccable taste—his unfailingly balanced sentences are never look-at-me showy, and he never veers into the territory of caricature, even in his more broadly drawn comic portraits. Still, the ability to render people on the page (fictional or not) with such depth and accuracy must be rooted in a passion for others, a habit of watching, listening, and understanding, without judging or getting in the way.

In the opening paragraphs of *Goodbye to Berlin,* Isherwood famously describes himself as "a camera . . . quite passive, recording, not thinking." The phrase "I am a camera" became the title of the first stage adaptation of the Sally Bowles section of that novel. This strikes me as typical of Isherwood's modesty and his complicated brand of self-effacement. Far from being the unthinking, passive, mechanical camera, he was a masterful photographer whose trained eye filters out the irrelevant and obvious details and captures the essence of an individual frozen in the middle of a revealing gesture. A bit like Richard Avedon, come to think of it.

Anyone, I suppose, might have noticed Mr. Norris's "unusually light blue eyes," but only the "truly interested" writer would have seen that they were "innocently naughty" like "the eyes of a schoolboy surprised in the act of breaking one of the rules." There are Sally Bowles's infamous emerald green fingernails; but more impressively, the fact that they draw attention to her stained hands, "dirty as a little girl's." These are artfully composed snapshots of characters, and, as with any memorable photograph, ones that leave us with a clear suggestion of the life lived outside the frame.

Like a photographer, Isherwood chose, in many of his most famous books, to stay in the room but partially hidden behind the camera. He never disappears, but the central drama of the scene frequently involves another character. Various screen and stage adaptations of his work have taken liberties with the source material in order to make the "Christopher" character more of an involved player. (Even screenwriter and director Tom Ford's controversial decision to change George's death from heart attack to suicide in his adaptation of *A Single Man* might be seen as an attempt to give the autobiographical main character more of an active hand in his own fate.)

This standoffish quality is an interesting paradox in a writer who wrote extensively, almost obsessively, about his own experience. In book after book, Isherwood encourages the reader to believe that even if the work is labeled fiction, it is, in fact, his life story. The opening lines of *Prater Violet* are, after all, "'Mr. Isherwood?' 'Speaking.' 'Mr. Christopher Isherwood?' 'That's me.'" It wasn't until *Christopher and His Kind* in 1976 that Isherwood stepped into the frame without disguise, untangled fact from fiction, and made it clear precisely how much he had fictionalized the events of his life and the people he met. (More than you might think, but probably less than the current flock of "memoirists.") But in that book, his most bluntly autobiographical, Isherwood writes about himself in the third person, almost as if he needs to make of himself an "other" in order to justify being "truly interested." Charm prevails.

I first read Isherwood on a train. I was living in New York at the time, trying, in a muddled way, to write a novel. I had to go to Boston to attend a funeral, and as I was rushing out to Penn Station, I grabbed a copy of *The Berlin Stories* from a friend's bookshelf. "You'll like it," my friend said. "But I want it back."

There was no Acela Express on the Northeast Corridor then to whisk you between New York and Boston. The trip was scheduled at close to five hours, and it often took significantly longer, with unexplained stops in the middle of Connecticut and long pauses in New Haven while the conductors switched from electric to diesel engines.

I took Amtrak back and forth between Boston and New York several times a month for about four years. The delays and discomforts rarely bothered me, mostly because it was my favorite place to read. The train was a quieter place then—no electronic devices and no one talking loudly into a cell phone—and when it ground to a halt far from any station, I was usually pleased. On that particular trip, I was especially delighted by the sluggish pace; I had time to read all of *Goodbye to Berlin*. I arrived in Boston late for the funeral, but feeling as if my appreciation of what made for great writing and a great novel had been altered.

At that point in my twenties, I was convinced that anything that was obtuse, floridly written, and that took itself Very Seriously must be *good*. If I found a book incomprehensible and stylistically off-putting, it was probably *great*. Many of my struggles with writing revolved around my self-imposed attempts at obfuscation.

Reading Isherwood was like having the cobwebs swept from the room. *Goodbye to Berlin* confirmed for me a number of things I'd suspected deep down but was too intellectually insecure to fully accept: that carefully delineated, fully realized, vividly drawn characters are the most crucial element of any good novel; that once you believe in a character—like him or not—the events of his life are more than enough "plot" to keep you reading; that big ideas are no stand-in for small, personal details; that the largest themes can emerge from the most inconsequential events; that clarity and precision, not obscurity, are the basis of the most elegant style. That the comic and the deadly serious can coexist comfortably, often in the same sentence.

I never returned my friend's copy of *The Berlin Stories,* and I still have it on my bookshelf. I've reread it—along with *Prater Violet, Down There on a Visit,* and *A Single Man*—multiple times. More important, it's a book I reach for and open when I'm feeling stuck in my own work and need a push. You can open any Isherwood novel at random and discover a paragraph so filled with wit, insight, and unaffected elegance that you're inspired to wrestle with words a little longer and strive for his level of excellence. When I'm teaching creative writing classes, I often use passages from Isherwood to illustrate the virtues of precision and the benefits of paying attention to the world and the people around you.

In the decades since discovering Isherwood, I've been shocked by the number of serious readers and talented writers I meet who have not. They've heard of him, of course, but his novels rarely show up on the syllabi of academic colleagues (although the film version of *A Single Man* has begun to), and it's a pleasant surprise (but still a surprise) to see the virtues of his prose extolled alongside those of Flaubert, Henry James, and Stephen Crane in a book like James Wood's excellent *How Fiction Works.*

You'd think it would be otherwise. His portrait of prewar Berlin is probably the most vivid in English literature. He was writing about homosexual characters at a time when few literary novelists were. He was many decades ahead of his time in blurring the lines between fact and fiction, something that's taken for granted in the contemporary memoir.

I've never fully understood this, although I do have a number of theories. The literary establishment seems to be drawn to writers who announce their importance in loud, long books that demand to be taken seriously, whether they've earned it or not. Isherwood's polite self-effacement doesn't fit comfortably into that mold. His writing on love and sexuality is masterful, but prior to *A Single Man,* probably too reserved to satisfy those who read through the lens of identity politics. (Isherwood's description of love and relationships in the final pages of *Prater Violet* is among the most beautiful I've read, even if genders are carefully unspecified.) There's a lightness of tone that runs through most of his fiction that might be interpreted as effete and might confuse those who need to be hit over the head with Seriousness. And there's an insistence upon presenting people as the flawed, fascinating creatures they are, without raining down harsh judgment.

Maybe too many readers underestimate the power and are suspicious of Isherwood's charm. A risky miscalculation, as you're about to find out.

An American Outsider

JAMES J. BERG AND CHRIS FREEMAN

What I know is what I am.

—CHRISTOPHER ISHERWOOD, *A Single Man*

One of Christopher Isherwood's most memorable characters, George, his "single man," is a college professor whose life has certain significant parallels with his creator's life: fifty-eight years old, gay, Los Angeles transplant from England, Santa Monica resident, lover of literature and handsome young men. But George was also a hypothetical creation—and the hypothesis was, "what would life be like after a longtime partnership has ended?" In fiction, George's lover Jim dies suddenly in a car crash; in real life, Christopher and his lover Don Bachardy were having major relationship troubles.

Despite these autobiographical resonances, one significant irony is that Christopher Isherwood never wanted to be a college professor. He got himself expelled from Cambridge University after his first year. About twenty years after relocating to the United States and well into his distinguished writing career, however, he did what many writers do: he accepted a series of visiting appointments at universities and colleges. As a visitor to campus, he was both an outsider and an honored guest: a guest by virtue of his accomplishments, invited by the "real" academics, an outsider because he lacked the credentials offered and required by universities. His stays varied by length, by assignment, by title; some appearances were billed as lectures, others as readings; he taught classes on modern literature and gave seminars on creative writing; he invited friends like Aldous Huxley, Stephen Spender, and W. H. Auden to visit his classes.

There is much to learn about the man, his work, and his life from his teaching and his more formal presentations. He delivered his most comprehensive lecture series, called "A Writer and His World," at the University of California in Santa Barbara in the fall of 1960. The talks were recorded and transcribed and later broadcast on the radio. To construct the Santa Barbara lectures, Isherwood prepared notes, selected passages of his own and other writers' works to read and discuss, and, of course, he worried about his reception by an audience of undergraduates. That is to say, he behaved very much like a college professor.

The Santa Barbara lectures were primarily for students, but they were also open to the public. The university moved his final performance off campus to the Lobero Theater, expecting and receiving a larger audience. Isherwood used the occasion as a summing up of what he cheekily called "the absolute cream of my wisdom," delivering in his "Last Lecture" elements of his philosophy of his life as a writer.

His first tenet is that every writer must be an outsider, but not merely as a matter of opposition. For him, the writer is a valuable member of the community as "a truly cooperative and social outsider . . . sometimes assenting, sometimes dissenting, but always, one hopes, in some way illuminating the problem under discussion."[1] Isherwood saw himself as an outsider in many ways. He was an Englishman living in Los Angeles, Vedantist, pacifist, homosexual. He used these circumstances to define a subject position in relation to issues he wrote about: his own past, England, Los Angeles, religion, the movies, the present, the future.

The "Last Lecture" can be seen as Isherwood's version of "What I Believe" (1938), the essay in which E. M. Forster laid out what he called his "reflections as an individualist and a liberal" as the political forces in Europe moved inexorably toward World War II. Isherwood ends his last lecture with a lengthy quote from Forster's conclusion:

> The memory of birth and the expectation of death always lurk
> within the human being, making him separate from his fellows, and
> consequently capable of intercourse with them. Naked I came into
> the world, naked I shall go out of it! And a very good thing too, for
> it reminds me that I am naked under my shirt, whatever its colour.
> (Isherwood, *Isherwood on Writing*, 142)

In using Forster to close his own lecture, letting Forster's final statement be *his* final statement, Isherwood is paying homage, acknowledging the lasting influence Forster had on him as a writer and a man.

Like Forster, Isherwood believed foremost that a writer must be an individual, and the writer must first write from his own experience and perspective. "Because, after all, what else does he really have? . . . What he knows is his own experience, not somebody else's—that is only filtered through his own experience" (ibid., 130). This is clearly Isherwood's practice as well as his theory. He also identifies himself in the lecture as an existentialist, "not in any terribly complicated meaning of the word, but simply somebody who believes in his own experience. I believe the most that anybody can do is to follow his experience, to try to understand what it means, to try not to lie to himself about its meaning, and that is all" (140). Isherwood found inspiration and material in his own life, which he recorded meticulously in his diaries, and in trying to make sense of his life and world. Of course, these things are always complicated. Isherwood's solution was simplification, to zero in on something he could try to articulate. This was his lifelong project, and considering this aspect of his work is the subject of many of the essays in this volume.

Here is perhaps where Isherwood connects most significantly to Forster, his friend and mentor. Both refused grandiosity, both used humor for self-deprecation, and both of them ultimately represent the "antiheroic hero." Isherwood identified Forster as such in *Down There on a Visit* (1962), arguing that this type of hero rejects the grand gestures of the traditional tragic hero—the self-sacrificing move to save others that ends up being an act of aggression against others. "While the others tell their followers to be ready to die, he advises us to live as if we were immortal."[2] For Isherwood and for Forster, living as if they were immortal meant getting on with their work, continuing with their writing and searching.

One of Isherwood's fundamental beliefs about writing was that you just had to do it: "the thing to do is to *get something down on the paper*, and then you have something to work on" (*Isherwood on Writing*, 135). Isherwood's most assiduous occupation was his near-daily diary keeping. If we had to pick one major development related to Isherwood in the last fifteen to twenty years, it would be the publication of his diaries. Edited by Katherine Bucknell and published in three volumes, the diaries provide the most complete record of Isherwood's life (or perhaps any writer's life), covering 1939 to 1983. The published diaries have revealed more about Isherwood than many people would have liked to know, and they have sparked considerable controversy. Isherwood's sexual candor, his tendencies toward drunkenness, hypochondria, occasional displays of racism, anti-Semitism, and misogyny have all been criticized. One could ask whether these volumes provide too much information, whether some editing would have been a kindness to the writer. However, these are the very things that make Isherwood so painfully human, and so much a man of his time. The diaries of the 1970s, published under the title *Liberation* (2012), provide the most satisfying experience for the reader: the end-of-life sadness, sense of accomplishment, happiness with his love for Bachardy.[3] What we get finally is Isherwood still teaching. The million-plus-word diaries may end up being Isherwood's greatest contribution to literature and culture.

Twenty years ago, the emerging field of gay studies seemed to be ignoring Christopher Isherwood. Modernist studies seemed more interested in his friend and sometime lover, W. H. Auden; and Isherwood was getting little traction in the rising genres of memoir and creative nonfiction, forms that he had pioneered. *The Isherwood Century* (2000) was our attempt to account for Isherwood's place in the twentieth century and to consider his legacy.[4] That project helped catalyze and bring together what has turned out to be an engaging, growing community of scholars working on Isherwood and related topics.

When we edited that book—the first ever collection of essays on Isherwood's life and work—the newest material available was the first volume of the *Diaries,* covering 1939–60, but most of the 1950s was missing from that book.[5] *The Isherwood Century* was our attempt to bring him out of the shadow of the "Auden generation" and to figure out his place in modernism and in the emerging canon of gay literature. That volume discussed Isherwood's work in terms of Anglo-American writing, documentary fiction, memoir, modernism, California, and spirituality. It was necessary to us then, as it is now, to include consideration of Isherwood's life with his partner Don Bachardy, their life together in Santa Monica, and their working partnership.

Most of Isherwood's work is now back in print, thanks largely to the University of Minnesota Press; a full-fledged biography by noted scholar Peter Parker was published in 2004; a very fine documentary, *Chris & Don: A Love Story,* was released to critical acclaim in 2007; and two film adaptations have been seen in wide release, *A Single Man* in 2009 and *Christopher and His Kind* in 2011. So much of this new creative and scholarly work has been facilitated by the acquisition of Isherwood's papers by the Huntington Library in 1999. Once the vast archive was carefully cataloged by Sara (Sue) Hodson—who writes about that treasure trove of manuscripts, photos, correspondence, and ephemera in her essay for this book—scholars have been able to use the material to enhance their work. The acquisition also enabled the Huntington to establish, along with the

Christopher Isherwood Foundation, annual fellowships to help scholars who want to work in the archive. Isherwood fellowships have been instrumental in the work of several scholars in this collection, including the late Peter E. Firchow, Jamie Carr, Rebecca Gordon Stewart, Mario Faraone, and Lois Cucullu. In fact, whole volumes have been produced comprised almost entirely of material in the archive, including *Letters between Forster and Isherwood on Homosexuality and Literature* (2008), edited by Richard E. Zeikowitz; *Kathleen and Christopher: Christopher Isherwood's Letters to his Mother* (2005), edited by Lisa Colletta, who has a new essay in this book; and *Isherwood on Writing*.

The American Isherwood picks up where *The Isherwood Century* left off. The essays here focus primarily on Isherwood's life and work after 1939, after his emigration to the United States. In addition, they make extensive use of this newly available material, including letters, images, unpublished diaries, and drafts. Our goal is simple: to bring together new knowledge that establishes Isherwood's place in the twenty-first century.

The book is organized into three sections. The first examines Isherwood's masterpiece, *A Single Man*, as it relates to his life with Bachardy, as response to and influenced by Virginia Woolf's *Mrs. Dalloway*, and as a document of the early 1960s in his adopted home, Los Angeles. The second part considers Isherwood's work and his legacy in terms of his spiritual life, bringing to bear new understanding of Isherwood's study of Vedanta, his relationship to his guru, Swami Prabhavananda, the tensions inherent in practicing Eastern religion in the American West. The final section focuses on Isherwood's work in the context of friends and colleagues, notably Edward Upward, Forster, and Aldous Huxley; celebrity culture in Hollywood; and the reception of gay-oriented writing in Cold War America.

One of Isherwood's longest-lasting friendships was with school chum Upward. In 1939, shortly after Isherwood's immigration and conversion to Vedanta, Upward wrote to Isherwood with the bluntness only a close friend can. A Marxist, Upward was harshly critical of Isherwood's new-found pacifism and his Eastern religion. Benjamin Kohlmann's essay, in the third section of this book, discusses this difficult but significant exchange between these two intimately connected men. Kohlmann argues that Upward's biggest concern was the possibility that these new commitments might interfere with Isherwood's work, which Upward understood quite well: "Your strength as a writer has always been and always will be in your ability to see and understand persons and things." His hope for

Isherwood was that he would "be able to write about what interests you the most—real persons and things."

Upward's concerns were valid, in that Isherwood struggled to bring together his new faith with his occupation. He eventually overcame that difficulty, and his work for the following forty years reveals the accuracy of Upward's assessment of his friend's talent: the things that interested Isherwood continued to be his own life and experiences, and his writing is his attempt to make sense of it all. As Isherwood explained in a lecture in 1960, "I write in order to find out what my life means and who I am, to find out if there's meaning in the external world, and then, I suppose, if I decide that there isn't, to impose a meaning of my own" (*Isherwood on Writing*, 54).

Notes

1. Christopher Isherwood, *Isherwood on Writing*, ed. James J. Berg (Minneapolis: University of Minnesota Press, 2007), 132.

2. Christopher Isherwood, *Down There on a Visit* (1962; reprint, Minneapolis: University of Minnesota Press, 1999), 162. See also *The Sixties: Diaries, Volume Two: 1960–1969*, ed. Katherine Bucknell (New York: Harper, 2010), 152.

3. Christopher Isherwood, *Liberation: Diaries, Volume Three: 1970–1983*, ed. Katherine Bucknell (New York: Harper, 2012).

4. James J. Berg and Chris Freeman, eds., *The Isherwood Century: Essays on the Life and Work of Christopher Isherwood* (Madison: University of Wisconsin Press, 2000).

5. Christopher Isherwood, *Diaries, Volume One: 1939–1960*, ed. Katherine Bucknell (New York: Harper, 1996).

A SINGLE MAN AND LOS ANGELES
CULTURE IN THE 1960s

She is trained in the new tolerance, the technique of annihilation
by blandness.

—CHRISTOPHER ISHERWOOD, *A Single Man*

The American Isherwood begins with the author's best work and most
productive decade, *A Single Man* and the 1960s. Many readers and scholars consider the short novel his masterpiece, and Isherwood himself was
not shy about using that term for it: "I am almost certain that it is my
masterpiece; by which I mean my most effective, coherent statement, artwork, whatever you want to call it."[1] Written in the middle of Isherwood's
American period, in 1962–63, the novel is his first to focus on a homosexual protagonist, George, a college professor. This alone would put it
in the forefront of gay literature of the twentieth century. That George's
sexuality is not a problem for him, that it is rather matter-of-factly presented, makes *A Single Man* a pioneering work. Taken as a whole, it is
quintessential Isherwood, encompassing all of the themes and concerns
he wrote about in his career: the role of the outsider, the value and meaning of experience, the importance of personal relationships, and the need
for spiritual sustenance.

In a forthright depiction of a well-adjusted gay man grieving for a
lost partner, Isherwood illustrates what his friend the psychologist Evelyn
Hooker found in her research: that gay men are no more or less happy
than straight men. This rather affirmative portrayal of a gay protagonist
was not wholly embraced by critics at the time. But Isherwood didn't

seem to mind. As he noted in his diary in the fall of 1964, "Despite the sour reception of *A Single Man* in this country, I still feel very good about it. Not so much as a work of art but as a deed. I feel: I spoke the truth, and now let them swallow it or not as they see fit. That's a very good feeling, and this is the first time that I have really felt it" (*The Sixties,* 341).

One of those truths was that gay people can indeed have happy lives, which is addressed here by Lois Cucullu, who argues that Isherwood was portraying the "happier year" that E. M. Forster envisioned in his posthumously published gay novel *Maurice* (1971). Cucullu details the complicated gestation of *Maurice* and the significant role Isherwood played in its development and publication. Maurice and his lover Alec escape to an imaginary greenwood, where Forster envisioned them in a future that would allow men like them to live and love openly together. Cucullu shows that Isherwood actually lived in that future with his lover, Don Bachardy, in the greenwood of Santa Monica, California. However, Isherwood's novel takes place not in a mythical island of serenity, but in a real world of neighbors, colleagues, and freeways. The world around George often sees homosexuals as a blight, devalues their relationships, and pretends to a tolerance that would "annihilate by blandness." It is against these forces that George battles this day and every day, as, no doubt, did his creator.

Looking at the novel through the lens of Isherwood's relationships with Forster and Bachardy, Cucullu relies on solid scholarly detective work. She is supported by the compelling documentary *Chris & Don: A Love Story.* Released in 2007, this film by Guido Santi and Tina Mascara portrays the thirty-year Isherwood–Bachardy relationship through home movies, interviews with Bachardy and others, and extracts from Isherwood's writing. In an essay written especially for this volume, the award-winning filmmakers discuss the genesis of their project, the audience reception, and their continuing friendship with Bachardy.

A trio of essays examine *A Single Man* from different vantage points. Carola M. Kaplan spent most of her academic career working on modernism before she retrained as a psychoanalyst. She wrote one of the first dissertations on Isherwood in the early 1970s. Her previously unpublished interview with him appears in our earlier book, *The Isherwood Century.* Kaplan's new essay traces the development and revisions of *A Single Man* using archival material from its earliest draft, which he called "The Englishwoman," the second draft as "The Englishman," to the final version. Kaplan notes that Isherwood began the novel with the question of his relationship with Bachardy in mind: the couple experienced a period of difficulty and strain in the early 1960s. Kaplan analyzes the issue of grief in the novel to show how Isherwood used George's grief as a way to work through his own feelings of separation and loss.

Jamie Carr, author of *Queer Times: Christopher Isherwood's Modernity*, also addresses grief in *A Single Man*, considering it alongside a novel that inspired it, Virginia Woolf's *Mrs. Dalloway*. Carr examines the relationship between the two novels through the characters of Septimus Smith and George, both of whom are mourning an "unspeakable loss." For Smith, that loss is the death in battle of a beloved fellow officer; for George, the loss is the death of his partner, Jim. Both characters experience rage against a society that does not acknowledge their loss and demands that they grieve in silence. Septimus does not survive; George might.

William R. Handley, whose expertise is the literature of the American West, also invokes *Mrs. Dalloway* and adds the visual arts to his consideration of *A Single Man* in the context of 1960s Los Angeles. He argues that the city is as integral a part of Isherwood's novel as London is of Woolf's. For Handley, the novel's sense of loss stems from George's relationship to the postmodern city of L.A., with its "missed connections, social alienation, and impending doom." The spiritual and political leanings of the two authors impel them to show how both writers use plot and narrative to connect nature, humans, and technology. Handley includes a discussion of contemporary paintings of the Los Angeles landscape to illustrate how the conventions of fiction and narrative are used to show the relationships between humans and their environs.

The final two essays in this section examine the 2009 film adaptation of *A Single Man*, directed by Tom Ford with a screenplay by Ford and David Scearce. Kyle Stevens approaches the film as Ford's reinterpretation of Isherwood's novel—at once a portrayal of a gay man in the 1960s and an artifact of the more open era of 2009. The film emphasizes George's grief and isolation, inserting a new subplot that has George plan, rehearse, and attempt suicide. For Stevens, this plot is not a part of the homophobic twentieth-century tendency in film and fiction to end with a dead homosexual but rather a self-aware and self-willed decision by Ford to allow George to end his suffering on his own terms.

We are reprinting here an essay we published not long after the film's premiere. Our argument is rather critical of the way Ford has depicted Isherwood's Los Angeles. We believe the film misses much of what fascinated Isherwood about his place and his time—the same sense of L.A. that Handley addresses. For Isherwood, it was important that George choose life as a single man, that his gay character not kill himself at the end of the novel. Indeed, Isherwood's protagonist, his antiheroic hero, is fully committed to life in the present: "George clings only to Now. It is Now that he must find another Jim. Now that he must love. Now that he must live."[2] This ending consciousness for George is every bit as important for Isherwood as it was for Forster to have his two men live happily at the end of *Maurice*.

Notes

1. Christopher Isherwood, *The Sixties: Diaries, Volume Two: 1960–1969*, ed. Katherine Bucknell (New York: Harper, 2010), 291.

2. Christopher Isherwood, *A Single Man* (1964; reprint, Minneapolis: University of Minnesota Press, 2001), 182.

1

A Single Man and the American Maurice

LOIS CUCULLU

In the documentary film *Chris & Don: A Love Story* (2007), home movies show a young-looking Christopher Isherwood and a boyish Don Bachardy in swimsuits at Will Rogers State Beach in the early 1950s.[1] That footage operates in the film as the locus of the pair's trysting. Out of their surfside camaraderie on a sunny beach grew a friendship that turned amorous and lasted until Isherwood's death in 1986. I begin with this romantically charged "beach" sequence that grounds the film's love story to make a larger claim about E. M. Forster's 1913 homosexual novel *Maurice* and its publication history. Contrary to Lytton Strachey's often cited 1915 critique that expressed doubt about whether the relationship between the two lovers, Maurice Hall and Alec Scudder, would last half a year, much less a lifetime, I suggest that such a relationship could and did last. It did so despite differences arguably greater than the fictional pair Maurice and Alec faced—differences of birthright, education, status, generation, and age, not to mention the challenge of the rabidly homophobic climate of Cold War America. The greenwood into which Maurice and Alec disappear at the conclusion of Forster's novel turns up four decades later and an ocean and continent away on a gay beach in Southern California.[2] Not only does Forster's *Maurice* make Chris and Don, the gay couple, and *Chris & Don,* the film, imaginable, but, importantly, without Isherwood's categorical support of Forster's manuscript, *Maurice* may never have been published. Indeed, during the same time frame in which Isherwood and Bachardy are sharing a beach near Santa Monica, in October 1952, Forster writes to Isherwood: "would you be willing to have a copy of *Maurice* on condition that it isn't published until I died, and was only published by you in the U.S.A.?"[3] Absent this behest and

Isherwood's acceptance, it was far from certain in the early 1950s how the novel *Maurice,* as literary text and cultural object, would end. Aside from the novel's plot, that it might wind up in a dustbin or consigned to a closed archive were distinct possibilities. Forster's offer of the manuscript and the friendship that stood behind it make *Maurice* every bit an American story, one that bears notably on Isherwood's own overtly gay novel, the elegiac *A Single Man.* Taken together, the two novels lend *Chris & Don* added poignancy and greater relevance. The ambit of this essay, then, is to shed light on four key moments of Isherwood and Forster's entwined relationship and publications: (1) Forster's manuscript of *Maurice* and the friendship between Forster and Isherwood; (2) Forster's 1952 gift to Isherwood of the exclusive rights to publish *Maurice* in the United States; (3) the 1971 posthumous publication of *Maurice* both in the United States and in Great Britain; and (4) Isherwood's 1964 novel *A Single Man.*

To begin, if we accept Forster's "Terminal Note" to *Maurice* written in 1960, then the genesis of his novel arises from a near-mystical exchange the novelist recalls of a visit to Edward Carpenter and his longtime partner George Merrill at Milthorpe in 1913. In Forster's words, Merrill touched his backside, as apparently Merrill was wont to do, with the instant effect that the touch "seemed to go straight through the small of my back into my ideas, without involving my thoughts."[4] Shortly thereafter, on September 13, 1913, according to Forster's "Locked Journal," he set to writing a novel of erotic male passion that he resolved would not end tragically.[5] As the eighty-one-year-old Forster subsequently explained in his note to *Maurice:* "A happy ending was imperative. . . . I was determined that in fiction anyway two men should fall in love and remain in it for the ever and ever that fiction allows, and in this sense Maurice and Alec still roam the greenwood" (250).

Although Forster never abandoned his objective of Maurice and Alec roaming the greenwood, he did waver over publication. In 1914, the cause in great measure was the pall cast by the 1885 Labouchère Amendment that had criminalized sexual relations between men. Most scandalously manifest in the trial, conviction, and imprisonment of Oscar Wilde for "acts of gross indecency" in 1895, it is useful to recall that Wilde's ultimate disgrace was first prompted in the libel suit by opposing attorney Edward Carson's suggestions of the homosexuality manifest in Wilde's *The Picture of Dorian Gray.* Carson's indictment in a legal proceeding of the artist based on his creative work, thus effectively outing Wilde, served as a stark cautionary tale that resonated well into the new century. Adding to this pall was the conflagration into which Europe had descended in 1914 that further intensified the climate of intolerance as well as Forster's hesitancy. This intolerance was all tóo patent in the scandal that greeted the publication of D. H. Lawrence's sexually explicit novel *The Rainbow.* The novel's representation of uninhibited sexuality drew hostile reviews that denounced *The Rainbow* for subverting common decency and undermining the nation's war effort, thus foreshadowing the scandal over Maud Allen's performance of Salomé that led to the notorious Billing's libel suit in 1918 on similar grounds. Inflamed public opinion became in 1915 the catalyst for the trial of Lawrence's novel and its eventual banning.[6] We may gauge Forster's own unease at this jingoistic atmosphere in his defense of Lawrence's novel. In a letter composed as he was to embark on his Red Cross assignment in Egypt, Forster wrote to Henry Newbolt, the highly regarded barrister, editor, and poet famous for his patriotic verse who had the ear of more than one Whitehall official. Writing in Lawrence's defense, Forster declared: "I feel myself that the right to literary expression is as great in war as it was ever in peace, and in far greater danger, and I write on the chance of your being willing and able to protect it" (July 11, 1915, Beinecke).[7] Adding to these legal and wartime impediments was Forster's own ambivalence at the outright sentimentalism present in *Maurice* that his fellow modernists were pronouncing déclassé by 1914. Following the great popular and critical success of *Howards End,* Forster worried whether his fellow writers might not pan such an openly passionate work. Taken as a whole, the homophobia, criminality, censorship, and banishment Forster would certainly have confronted had he published *Maurice* took their toll. Factoring the effect publication and scandal would have had on his mother, who was still living, and, later, on his lover Bob Buckingham, a member of the police force who would go on to marry and have a son, only exacerbated Forster's reservations. All these encumbrances, plus Forster's uncertainty over the literary judgment of his peers, argued against publication.

Despite these impediments, however, Forster continued working on the manuscript, even passing a typescript discreetly around to his circle of friends and writers in the midst of composing it, and afterward for some fifty years. All the while, he and his readers were aware of the difficulties that would ensue were the typescript to land in the wrong hands or become public. Forster also passed the text around selectively, withholding it, for example, from Virginia Woolf but loaning it to the painter Duncan Grant.[8] It wasn't, therefore, out of the ordinary for the novelist to offer *Maurice* nearly two decades later in the 1930s to new acquaintance Christopher Isherwood. Having admired the younger writer's *The Memorial,* which was published by Hogarth Press in 1932, Forster had arranged an introduction to Isherwood through mutual friend William Plomer that same year.[9] Shortly thereafter, in 1933, he offered Isherwood a copy of *Maurice* to read. Representing the up-and-coming generation of British writers, the younger Isherwood was, like Forster, homosexual and more openly so, and, like Forster, possessed a Cambridge connection. Isherwood had, however, defied his affiliation by lampooning it in his writing and then withdrawing from the university in 1925. The more bourgeois Forster, on the other hand, remained and would continue to remain under the thrall of the Oxbridge romance, which, under the impress of a classical studies curriculum, had proffered the bonus of legitimating homophilia and eroticizing collegial socialization, albeit covertly, for Forster's generation.[10] Notwithstanding differences of generation, class, and temperament, the two became close friends, evident in the gradual shift in salutations of Forster's letters from the formal "Dear Isherwood" of 1933 to "My dearest Christopher" by 1938. What bound their friendship was their shared interest in writing, not the least being Isherwood's advocacy of the manuscript *Maurice.*

According to Isherwood, the first question Forster wanted answered about *Maurice* was "Does it date?" As Isherwood later recalled, he candidly replied to Forster what is perhaps his most judicious and forthright piece of advice: "Why *shouldn't* it date?"[11] What is significant in this exchange and proved constant in the years to come is Isherwood's assurance that the novel's topic and frank sentimentality did not harm Forster's literary reputation. Isherwood's encouragement thus allayed the novelist's fears that publication imperiled his legacy as a writer. Forster's letter to Isherwood of April 27, 1933, tellingly makes the point: "I've some other stuff to show you some time," Forster writes, "thought it better than *Maurice* until recently, but began to have my doubts; as you say, why shouldn't one date?"[12]

Of the novel, Isherwood later admitted, "its antique locutions bothered him, here and there," but as he went on to observe:

> the wonder of the novel was that it had been written when it had
> been written; the wonder was Forster himself, imprisoned within the
> jungle of pre-war prejudice, putting these unthinkable thoughts into
> words. Perhaps listening from time to time, to give himself courage,
> to the faraway chop-chop of those pioneer heroes, Edward Carpenter ·
> and George Merrill, boldly enlarging *their* clearing in the jungle.
> (*Christopher and His Kind,* 126; emphasis in original)

Comparing it with Forster's other works, Isherwood put the matter squarely: "it was both inferior and superior to them: inferior as artwork, superior because of its purer passion, its franker declaration of its author's faith." Yet his defense of *Maurice* continued unabated, for which he earned Forster's gratitude. As the older writer expressed it in a letter on August 28, 1938:

> It certainly is a comfort to know that my work is respected by someone whom I respect and [am] as fond of as you. It confirms my belief that life is not all nonsense and cruelty—the inversion of Victorian complacency—but has hard spots of sense and love bobbing about in it here and there. (Zeikowitz, *Letters between Forster and Isherwood*, 75)

With such encouragement, Forster debated again over publication of *Maurice*. In the same letter, he conceded:

> I wish it could be published, especially after getting your letter. But it isn't so much my mother now—it's Bob. Everyone connects him with me, and this Dover muddle showed me how careful I must be not to bring bother or harm his way. My *"Life"* if briefly and blazingly written, might be worth doing after my death, but that's ruled out too while he lives. (Ibid.)[13]

Isherwood, among the first generation of influential twentieth-century British writers, had the foresight not to disparage the emotional content of the novel but to recognize the work's courage and to find value in its honest sentiments that seemed indispensable to its groundbreaking content. "Almost every time they met, after this," Isherwood later recalled, "they discussed the problem: how should *Maurice* end? That the ending should be a happy one was taken for granted; Forster had written the novel in order to affirm that such an ending is possible for homosexuals" (*Christopher and His Kind*, 127).

Forster and Isherwood's friendship was reciprocal but not without its differences. After Isherwood, along with W. H. Auden, emigrated to the United States, he was roundly castigated publicly and privately for deserting his country in a time of impending catastrophe. His motives were certainly complex. They clearly included his failure in the 1930s, graphically chronicled in *Christopher and His Kind*, to get his German friend and lover Heinz Neddermeyer safely out of that country and away from conscription into the Nazi military. It also included his growing realization, as he would recount in his diary, of being at heart a pacifist, regarding his pacifism as part of his father's legacy to him and his own expression of spirituality (*Diaries*, 1:5). His decision also stemmed from the marginalization and stigma of being homosexual, from which came his inherent distrust of authority and institutions. As he explained in *Christopher and His Kind:*

> As a homosexual, he had been wavering between embarrassment and defiance. He became embarrassed when he felt that he was making a selfish demand for his individual rights at a time when only group action mattered. He became defiant when he made the treatment of the homosexual a test by which every political party and government must be judged. His challenge to each one of them was: "All right, we've heard your liberty speech. Does that include us or doesn't it?" (334)

Forster's support of Isherwood coheres with the principles of his 1938 essay "What I Believe." Here Forster had asserted: "if I had to choose between betraying my country and betraying my friend, I hope I should have the guts to betray my country."[14] Yet, we may glimpse the limits of Forster's position and the difference in their generations expressed in Isherwood's diary response to the older writer's view of the war:

> Dear Morgan, how can you write, "'Cracow' has become for me the symbol of Nazi bullying on the continent, and I can hardly see the name without trembling with rage?'" I should like to read aloud to you the scene from *Howards End*, when the boy dies of heart failure and Miss Avery comes out of the house with the sword. It was you who taught us the futility of hate.
>
> When "peace" returns, let me never again forget that suffering is always with us. This war is not unique. During the gayest periods of my life, people were being killed and starving and dying in agony. When you are personally involved, don't be provincial and exclaim, "*This* is the Big Thing!" That kind of talk is for journalists and businessmen, who rate the bombing of London above the bombing of Chungking because the real estate is more highly insured." (*Diaries*, 1:137)

With the ending of World War II and his mother's death, in March 1945, Forster began thinking seriously once more about publication as he continued revising the concluding chapters of the novel. As he concerned himself with how the pair of lovers were to come together and show their bond, he wrote Isherwood during a visit to England, the younger writer, by then, firmly transplanted to Los Angeles: "What I am really writing about though is *Maurice*," Forster explained. "I should very much like a talk alone with you during the next week or so. I am ashamed at shirking publication but the objections are formidable. I am coming up on Tuesday for a night or probably two. Wednesday morning should be all right" (Zeikowitz, *Letters between Forster and Isherwood,* 144). These discussions led to further revisions of the novel and another retyping of the manuscript. During this postwar period Forster made the critical decision to publish the novel, but only after his death.

In October 1952, just a few months before Isherwood and Bachardy would be introduced on a beach near Santa Monica, Forster writes Isherwood with his proposal of making Isherwood a gift of *Maurice* in order that he would see to its being published in the United States on the author's death. As Forster explained the particulars, his friend and literary executor W. J. H. (Jack) Sprott, Cambridge graduate and lecturer at Nottingham University, would retain the copyright to the novel, but Isherwood would have exclusive rights to bring the novel out in the United States. On October 15, 1952, Forster wrote Isherwood formally of their agreement, with specific provisions:

> As agreed, I write a formal letter to confirm my gift to you of one of the typescript copies of *Maurice.*
>
> It is your property, and I assign you the right to arrange for its publication in the U.S.A. after my death. You have the right to sign the necessary contracts and to receive all royalties and other payments.
>
> By the terms of my will, all my MSS and literary rights become the property of my executor, Professor W. J. H. Sprott, or of the executor acting in his place. Professor Sprott has, however, written you a letter which you will receive at the same time as this one, and you will see from it that he fully approves of the arrangement between you and myself, and formally undertakes to respond to it.
>
> He does however make two stipulations. (i) If the book is not published in the States within three years after my death, all U.S. publication rights must revert to him. (ii) You must not publish or attempt to sell the book in Great Britain: if you did this my executor would be entitled to take action against you.
>
> I have had a talk with Mr. Monroe Wheeler. If for any reason you do not wish to publish, he is willing to act in your place. In that case all U.S. rights would pass to him and he would be entitled to sign contracts and to receive royalties, etc. (Ibid., 152)

Although not specified in the formal agreement, Forster, in a separate letter to Isherwood of October 15, 1952, indicated that were he or Wheeler unable to publish, then Wheeler's partner, the American expatriate writer and later president of the American Academy and Institute of Arts and Letters Glenway Wescott, would proceed with publication.[15] In addition, Forster sought not only Sprott's consent but that of his lover, Bob Buckingham, as well. Forster made clear: "Bob has been fine over it. "Do you want it published?"—Yes—Then I'll see it is" (ibid., 153). Forster then arranged, via Wheeler who was visiting England, to deliver a typescript copy of *Maurice* covertly to Isherwood for safekeeping. When the typescript was finally secure in Isherwood's hands, Forster wrote him effusing: "always generous, praising and helping me, always believing in what *Maurice* tried to do. Dear Christopher oh you have been a good friend." And ended with, "I am more glad than ever that the typescript is with you and that Jack Sprott has behaved so well" (154).

The comment that Sprott had behaved well, as Forster characterized it, hints at the magnitude of the step that the aging author had taken. It was critical on at least two fronts. First and foremost, granting Isherwood, a staunch advocate of *Maurice,* the rights to publish in the United States provided Forster insurance that the novel would in fact be published on his death. Given its forthright depiction of homosexual liaisons and passion, especially at Cambridge where Forster continued his long association, and given the pressure that might be brought to bear on his literary executor, also a Cambridge man, Forster worried that the novel might be left to languish on his death. In his last twenty-five years, Forster enjoyed a virtual sinecure at Cambridge, as resident and honorary don of King's College. Moreover, in the 1960s, he came to worry over his executor Sprott's ability to act in his best interests when it became clear that his longtime friend suffered from alcoholism (Furbank, *E. M. Forster,* 2:305). It is also worth noting that D. A. Parry, vice-provost of King's College, would serve with Sprott as trustees of Forster's estate. This connection raised the possibility that Parry's institutional influence might come to bear inordinately on decisions Sprott made about Forster's literary estate after his death. Isherwood was their counterweight and leverage against any reluctance on *Maurice*'s behalf. After all, Isherwood had not only proved himself Forster's trusted friend and *Maurice*'s ally but had also shown his mettle before in the face of imposing institutional forces.

Second, appointing Isherwood was also significant in that Forster appears to have set aside his qualms about the effect of publication on his literary reputation, not just over its outright depiction and promotion of gay life and love but its romanticizing of the pair's relationship. That Forster's confidence was never absolute is plain in his handwritten note at the top of the 1960 typescript: "Publishable—but worth it?"[16] Another

of Isherwood's generation, whose literary reputation would arguably sur-
pass Forster's in time, seems to have lobbied against *Maurice*. Auden, like
Isherwood a naturalized U.S. citizen, had apparently argued against publication in 1952, according to Glenway Wescott, who was, incidentally
instrumental in bringing Forster to New York for the Blashfield lecture
at the National Institute of Arts and Letters in 1948 and then pivotal in
assisting Isherwood with the U.S. publication of the novel. In the draft
of a reminiscence of Forster following his death, Wescott quotes Auden
anonymously:

> "It probably won't ever be published; it oughtn't to be. Even post-
> humously it would do Forster's reputation more harm than good. It
> might be taken to throw light on his own life and love relationships,
> which must be kept quiet if possible, having nothing whatever to do
> with his literary art. It isn't worth publishing. It is too personal and
> boring and frivolous and old-timey."[17]

On June 7, 1970, a sixty-five-year-old Isherwood received the news of
Forster's death at ninety-one in a telephone call from a United Press reporter in New York. When he had last visited Forster in March, it was
clear that Morgan was failing. Yet, as Isherwood recalls, when he spoke
of *Maurice*, "he showed pleasure and he told me he was glad to think of
all this again and wished he could write another such story."[18] Sadly sharing the news of his death with Bachardy, Isherwood acknowledged that
Forster had "had a very happy life, he was very lucky." And Bachardy,
comforting Isherwood, averred that he had too. What consoled him was
that Forster had died in Coventry at the Buckinghams' home: "he didn't
die alone in that big chilly bedroom in the college; he was snug and warm
and tucked up and looked after by May and Bob" (*The Sixties*, 83).

   In the year following Forster's death and despite the thorny publication rights and an interval of some sixty years, *Maurice* was published
simultaneously in 1971 in Great Britain and the United States. The con-
tracts, text, cover, proofs, and date of publication were in due course
agreed upon and coordinated by all parties. In hindsight, the consensus
to publish is rather astonishing in light of this provocative novel's history. The reasons are numerous. Primary among them is surely Forster's
1952 granting Isherwood legal entitlement to publish the novel in the
United States. That prospect, known and agreed to by all parties, deci-
sively changed the ground rules for the novel in 1952 and guaranteed
its future in print, at least in the United States. By Forster's death in

1970, the climate for publication had changed for the better. The author's British representatives, therefore, hardly fancied Americans stealing their thunder by having an expatriate writer and a U.S. publisher bring out a posthumous novel by one of England's internationally recognized luminaries, no matter how provocative the subject matter, and, on top of that, reap considerable profits in the bargain. These realities point to a second but no less critical reason, the financial incentive. This incentive involved not just the literary executor Sprott, who was to be the recipient of the proceeds from Forster's estate while he lived, but also Cambridge, which would accede to them on Sprott's death. The financial incentive also involved the publication of the American *Maurice.*

All of this fell to Isherwood, who had to negotiate the what, when, and how of publication as well as negotiate with his British counterparts that now included, besides Sprott and Parry, P. N. Furbank, who undertook the final editing of *Maurice* and whom Forster had charged to write his official biography. Matters were further complicated for Isherwood by the fact that he was in the midst of completing what for him was a very personal project, the prodigious biography of his parents, *Kathleen and Frank.* As to *Maurice,* concern quickly arose over the final editing of the manuscript. Isherwood's copy, which he kept in a vault, dated from the 1950s and did not take into account the changes that Forster had made in 1960 in which he had concluded the plan of the closing chapters in which Maurice and Alec commit to one another in the boathouse at Penge, thus leaving out the epilogue that Isherwood and others had thought ineffective and unnecessary. There was also Isherwood's insistence that Bob Buckingham should give his consent to publication, which, despite Forster's confidence, became problematic in the end.[19] Moreover, that Forster's note must be included at the conclusion of the novel and that Furbank's introduction must not were further stipulations Isherwood demanded. In his diary, he records that he had even encouraged Wescott to write a foreword to the novel knowing that if he, Isherwood, were to, he would offend Furbank. "Furbank's foreword, alone," noted Isherwood, "simply isn't right for America, it is too inner-circle" (*The Sixties,* 124). Therefore, in the end, the published American *Maurice* stands unadorned, without preface or preamble to Forster's story of gay love, and concludes with his 1960 "Terminal Note."

As to the publisher, while Arnold remained Forster's British publisher, there was no such certainty in the United States as to which press would print the novel. There had been enough talk in the trade circulating about an unpublished Forster novel that those savvy in the publishing industry started making inquiries even as Forster's obituaries began to appear. Despite the novel's content, a handful of the most respected U.S. publishers vied for the rights to the novel, including Holt, Harper, Prentice Hall, Norton, and, of course, Harcourt Brace, Forster's U.S. publisher in his lifetime. All reckoned that the likely return on a novel by an author of Forster's stature would be considerable. Yet, if Harcourt Brace had succeeded in gaining the contract and "just imported sheets from Arnold," as Monroe Wheeler shrewdly warned Isherwood in the summer of 1970, then "in that case the estate will get all or almost all of the royalties; in any event the income here will be minimal."[20] With that prospect in view, Isherwood, with Wescott's help, secured literary agent Ivan von Auw of Harold Ober and Associates to represent Isherwood's American interests. Under von Auw's astute handing, Norton eventually secured the U.S. contract with the handsome advance of $135,000. This proved a good investment as Norton has profited in turn ever since. History, it would seem, was on *Maurice*'s side, and publishers, such as E. A. Hamilton at Arnold and George Brockway at Norton, understood the financial ramifications from the start. When it came to publication, *Maurice*'s "greenwood" acquired a distinctly pecuniary hue.

Yet, even from a financial perspective, there arises another American connection involving Isherwood that further distinguishes the American *Maurice*. In arranging for Isherwood to receive a copy of *Maurice* and the formal documents of agreement, Forster wrote Isherwood:

> I know that you won't like receiving any money from sales and will refuse to accept it, but it is the simplest that the owner of the MS and rights should receive; otherwise such complications. What I would like is for the money to be kept in America for people from here who want to visit America and can't: Bob specially in my mind. Alternately, to help any one who is in trouble. Would you mind receiving it now? (Zeikowitz, *Letters between Forster and Isherwood*, 153)

To Wheeler, visiting in London and acting as intermediary between Forster and Isherwood, Forster wrote the same day of his intentions. Explaining that Isherwood would not want to benefit personally from sales of *Maurice*, Forster told Wheeler of his wish to have Isherwood use any proceeds from the novel to create a fund to support visits of English writers to America, "visiting Bobs" as he called them (ibid.). Thereafter the future legacy became informally known as "The Visiting Bob Fund" (August 1, 1970, Wescott letter to Isherwood, Beinecke).

And this idea of supporting "visiting Bobs" is in fact what transpired.

Rather than accepting the advance for the novel and the royalties, which have been considerable and have continued unabated since 1971, Isherwood, with the assistance of Wheeler and Wescott, transferred all rights and royalties to the National Institute of Arts and Letters in New York for the establishment of an E. M. Forster Award. That award, as Forster had hoped, has since been given to support an English writer visiting America.[21] Forster's gift to Isherwood thus became a means to bring other British writers and artists to America. Counted among its many recipients have been Margaret Drabble, Seamus Heaney, Julian Barnes, Jeanette Winterson, and Timothy Mo.

In his 1972 review of the novel for the gay magazine *California Scene,* Isherwood continued his advocacy of *Maurice* against charges that Forster had long anticipated. On the critique of its sentimentality, Isherwood countered: "We are terribly afraid of what we call sentimentality—the rash, incautious expression of feeling. Yet that kind of sentimentality is something most of us need to practice today." On its bias, Isherwood affirmed that the novel was partisan: "And why shouldn't it be? Forster was attacking the laws and taboos and prejudices which made life miserable for his minority, the homosexual minority, in 1914. Many of those laws, taboos and prejudices still exist. In this sense, *Maurice* cannot, alas, be called out of date."[22] On the subject of *Maurice*'s continued relevance, Isherwood's remark targeted a much broader audience.

There is in this reciprocity of Isherwood championing Forster's manuscript and Forster bequeathing it to Isherwood for U.S. publication yet another aspect that speaks to treating *Maurice* as an American story—and that is the writing and publication in Isherwood's lifetime, some would say at the height of his celebrity, of his own gay novel *A Single Man.* That it appears in 1964, the decade between Forster's 1952 behest and Isherwood's success in seeing *Maurice* through to publication in 1971 is significant. Like Forster, Isherwood struggled greatly over how to be true to himself as a gay man and as an artist. As Katherine Bucknell, editor of Isherwood's diaries, points out in her Introduction to volume 1:

> Earlier in his career, it was not possible for him to write forthrightly about a homosexual character, and particularly not about himself as a homosexual. When he was writing *Mr Norris Changes Trains* he "wasn't to admit that the Narrator was homosexual," first because he feared to create a scandal, and second, because he did not want to shift the reader's attention away from Mr. Norris. The reader, he argued, would have been distracted if the narrator had been "an avowed

homosexual, with a homosexual's fantasies, preferences, and prejudices." . . . Thus, he left the narrator without explicit sexuality because
he "dared not make the Narrator homosexual. But he scorned to make
him heterosexual." (*Diaries*, 1:xxx)

For many, the answer to this struggle plays out in *A Single Man*. Originally
begun as "The Englishwoman," Isherwood soon realized that his topic
was about neither the English nor a woman, though both of course figure
importantly in this narrative of loss and longing. That realization and
the title in fact came at the suggestion of Bachardy, who seems to have
sensed from Isherwood's description the central dilemma of the novel
(*The Sixties*, 223, 283).

The action of *A Single Man* takes place over less than twenty-four
hours in 1962 Los Angeles, in winter, just before the Christmas holidays
and just after the Cuban missile crisis. The novel unfolds under the specter, then, of a nuclear war on one hand and in the heyday of nuclear family conformity on the other—and, just as significant, before the bohemian
revolt of Haight-Ashbury and of the gay rights uprising of Stonewall that
would erupt later in the decade. At the close of one era and the opening of
another, Isherwood's novel mourns what its central protagonist George
cannot publicly and outwardly mourn—the death of his lover Jim—in
that most mundane of modern calamities, a car accident. More ironic still,
it happens not on one of the notorious freeways of Southern California,
but while Jim is visiting family in the Midwest. Thus George, alone and
at a distance, cannot claim the body of his lover even in death. Nor can
he openly grieve Jim's death to his colleagues at the university where he
teaches, nor to his neighbors who have transformed the once bohemian
neighborhood over the course of the 1950s into a proto-suburban development, staunchly heterosexual and conformist, and utterly committed
to the breeding and rearing of offspring as if it were the surest biological
deterrent to a postwar Communist invasion.[23]

The novel mourns as well the failed intimate expressions of sorrow
and condolence. George, the unacknowledged lover, declines the invitation to the funeral in Ohio that Jim's uncle extends to him as "the room-
mate." Even George's close friend and compatriot Charlotte is unable
to grant George's loss the same gravitas and intensity as her own over
the desertion first by her husband Buddy and more recently by her son
Fred. Much later in the night and novel, when, with his student Kenny
Potter, George risks talking about Jim, Kenny's complete lack of interest
strands George once more in his grief. It is as if Isherwood's *A Single Man*

was intent on exposing in 1962 the limits of the greenwood into which Maurice and Alec had ventured at the end of Forster's novel to live happily ever after. Indeed, if we examine closely the house George and Jim take as their home, it resembles something of the utopic space Forster had imagined for his two lovers:

> George and Jim saw the yellow sign ["Children at Play"], of course, the first time they came down here, house-hunting. But they ignored it, for they had already fallen in love with the house. They loved it because you could only get to it by the bridge across the creek; and the surrounding trees and steep bushy cliff behind shut it in like a house in a forest clearing. "As good as being on our own island," George said.[24]

This forested island, this "greenwood" refuge that provides the couple such plenitude, is also the island that separates and excludes them from their environs and from full participation and recognition in the larger world they inhabit. For Isherwood's novel, it is not so much a question of the steadfastness of the two lovers that Strachey had predicted would not hold up for Forster's pair in *Maurice*—after all, in *A Single Man,* Jim had run off with Doris to Mexico only to run back to George repentant over his misguided peccadillo. It is rather a question of this sequestered "greenwood," of this limited space alone sustaining George and Jim as a couple. In keeping with the novel's theme of Tithonus, however alluring this greenwood escape might appear, it is a flawed eternity—and not the least for the dystopia of greater Los Angeles that appears to engulf it.

George chronicles this fallen world in his architectural survey of the postmodern metropolis that is L.A. George's city includes the highrise apartment complex under construction that will soon menacingly lord over the landscape; the university factory, which employs him as a teacher, that mechanically cranks out workers equipped only with the merest transitory technical skills to maintain themselves; the overabundant supermarket with its pretense of "suspended insecurity"; and, in between, the freeways, motels, and hospitals to treat the populace's chronic mobility—motels for temporary and hospitals for terminal egress with the freeways functioning as their supply lines. Opposing these monuments of late modernity are those modest and incremental sanctuaries George also traverses—the gym, the classroom, the beachfront bar, and, of course, the beach itself at night adjoining the immensity of the ocean, where intimacy and human exchange are still possible. There is in this novel the realization of how shrunken the greenwood and how impoverished and menacing its environs have become in this American Babylon of the eternal "now."

Of the many contexts in which to consider these two groundbreaking novels, *Maurice* and *A Single Man,* reading them together and in tandem with their publication history gives us an appreciation of the great stakes and extraordinary costs involved over the course of the century in which Forster first imagined his novel of requited male love. If it was a milestone for him to fictionalize a happy gay couple, and, with Isherwood's support, to publish this work finally as a novel, even if after his death, it was no less a milestone for Isherwood, not content to commemorate a similar couple's bond, but to insist in his novel on mourning publicly and privately their loss. In this way, Isherwood demanded not just a happy ending for the pair but on ending their isolation in Forster's "greenwood."

In retrospect, we can at least assert that by the time that *Maurice* is published in 1971 the coerced ostracism and out-and-out hostility observed in *A Single Man* are lessening—no small triumph for Isherwood's novel. And one unexpected but unmistakable sign of this change may be found in the unlikeliest of places—that most middlebrow of American cultural enterprises, the Book-of-the-Month Club. Clifton Fadiman, in his reader report, would recommend *Maurice* for selection, an unthinkable prospect in 1952 or 1964.[25] As Fadiman expressed it:

> In 1960 Forster recognized that the public attitude toward homosexuality had changed—"from ignorance and terror to familiarity and contempt." By the time of his death the official English attitude had again shifted, and the public reaction of "contempt" had notably relaxed in favor of a more civilized view. Today in England homosexual interchange between consenting adults, provided they commit no public nuisance, is no longer a crime.

And he continued:

> As stated, a posthumous novel about homosexuality by a great homosexual writer is news. But if were no more than that, there would be little reason for offering it to our members. And it is more than that. It is an interesting, often moving, book apart from the sensational circumstances of its publication. And it goes without saying that it will be required reading for all Forster admirers.[26]

Fast-forward some four decades, and the film *Chris & Don* responds to both Forster's and Isherwood's fictional dilemmas in the documentary memorializing Isherwood and Bachardy's life together. There may be those who remain unimpressed by the novel *Maurice,* who scoff at the utter romanticism of fictional lovers Maurice and Alec, just as there are those who may consider *Chris & Don* a similar exercise in sentimentality.[27] Still, it is no less true that *Maurice* made imaginable lives that had long been circumscribed under legal proscriptions and social ostracism. Surely, Isherwood's and Bachardy's are two such lives, even if we discount the great coincidence of the pair coming together on a Santa Monica beach as the manuscript of *Maurice* is making its way from England to America. Likewise, *Chris & Don: A Love Story* justly celebrates the lives of these two men as lovers, as artists, and as public figures. And significantly, it most publicly and poignantly mourns with one the heavy loss at the death of the other.

Notes

I wish to express my gratitude to Sara S. Hodson, curator of literary manuscripts, and the staff of the Huntington Library for their great assistance with the Christopher Isherwood Collection. I also thank the Provost and Scholars of King's College, Cambridge, and the Society of Authors as the literary representatives of the E. M. Forster estate for permission to quote from his work. I am also indebted to Virginia Dajani, executive director of the American Academy and Institute of Arts and Letters, for her help in researching Isherwood's and the Institute's roles in the publication of *Maurice* and the establishment of the E. M. Forster Award. No less am I indebted to the curators and staffs of the rare books and special collections at Yale's Beinecke Library, Princeton's Firestone Library, and Columbia's Rare Book and Manuscript Library. None of this research would have been possible, however, without the generous grants provided by the Graduate School and the College of Liberal Arts of the University of Minnesota, for which I extend a sincere thank you.

1. P. N. Furbank, *E. M. Forster: A Life,* 2 vols. (New York: Harcourt, 1978), 2:15.

2. It is interesting to note Isherwood's early mention of Bachardy in a typed letter to his friend Glenway Wescott of November 2, 1953, about plans for a short Christmas visit to New York with Bachardy in which Isherwood is hopeful that Wescott will find "the boy" as adorable as he does (November 2, 1953, Glenway Wescott Papers, Beinecke Rare Book and Manuscript Library, Yale University; hereafter, Beinecke).

3. Richard E. Zeikowitz, ed., *Letters between Forster and Isherwood on Homosexuality and Literature* (New York: Palgrave Macmillan, 2008), 151.

4. E. M. Forster, *Maurice: A Novel* (New York: Norton, 1971), 249. Unless otherwise stated, citations of *Maurice* refer to the Norton edition of the novel.

5. E. M. Forster, "The Locked Journal," E. M. Forster's Papers, King's College Modern Archives, Cambridge University.

6. On Lawrence's novel and its trial, see Adam Parkes, *Modernism and the Theater of Censorship* (Oxford: Oxford University Press, 1996), 21–32.

7. Used with permission of the Provost and Scholars of King's College, Cambridge, and the Society of Authors as the literary representatives of the E. M. Forster estate. Forster would subsequently lend his support in the censorship trials on behalf of Lawrence's *Lady Chatterley's Lover* and Radclyffe Hall's *The Well of Loneliness*.

8. For a discussion of those who read the novel, see especially Philip Garner's introduction to the Abinger edition of *Maurice* that builds on P. N. Furbank's 1978 biography, *E. M. Forster* (Abinger edition, ed. Philip Gardner, vol. 5 [London: Andre Deutsch, 1999]). As late as 1960, Christopher Isherwood records loaning his typescript to the actor Charles Laughton to read (*Diaries, Volume One: 1939–1960*, ed. Katherine Bucknell [New York: Harper, 1996], 857–58).

9. In 1932, revisions of the novel had prompted Forster to have the manuscript retyped. In the 1932 manuscript, the "Epilogue" that shows the pair of lovers as woodcutters is dropped.

10. Furbank's biography captures the allure of Cambridge and Forster's attachment: "Nowhere outside England has there been an institution like Victorian Oxford and Cambridge—that Cockaigne or 'great good place' for the sons of the professional middle classes. Forster fell in love with Cambridge himself, though not in any tragic sense. Cambridge transformed him, and he always acknowledged his debt" (*E. M. Forster,* 1:49). Forster expresses this sentiment in his 1941 reminiscence "Cambridge" in *Two Cheers for Democracy* (New York: Harcourt, 1951), 348–53.

11. Christopher Isherwood, *Christopher and His Kind* (New York: Farrar, Straus and Giroux, 1976), 126; emphasis in original.

12. Richard Zeikowitz, ed., *Letters between Forster and Isherwood on Homosexuality and Literature* (New York: Palgrave Macmillan, 2008), 20–21.

13. The "muddle" refers to the awkwardness over Joe Ackerley's untimely dislodgment during a stay in Dover. The town, according to Furbank, had become a favorite port of call for Forster and his circle between the wars, until "Ackerley's activities had finally been too much for the 'Holy Ladies,'" as the two women were called who ran the boarding house where Ackerley and Forster customarily stayed, and he was asked to leave. The result, as Furbank quotes Forster: "'Dover is, alas, henceforward a Closed Port'" (Furbank, *E. M. Forster,* 2:226).

14. E. M. Forster, "What I Believe," in *Two Cheers for Democracy* (New York: Harcourt, 1951), 67.

15. Forster explained: "I've asked Monroe [Wheeler] if he would see to the thing if you couldn't. He said he would. If neither of you acts, I would be grateful if Glenway [Wescott] would take over, but have put Monroe's name in the formal letters, since we had talked about it" (Zeikowitz, *Letters between Forster and Isherwood*, 153).

16. E. M. Forster, *Maurice: A Novel*, Introduction, by P. N. Furbank (London: Edward Arnold, 1971), xi.

17. See Wescott, draft of "Forster in New York and New Jersey," September 1971, Beinecke. When Furbank asked Isherwood in 1970 how intimate Forster and Auden were, Isherwood replied: "I said not very, and added, that Wystan had always found it difficult to be intimate—he's shy in that way" (Christopher Isherwood, *Liberation: Diaries, Volume Three: 1970–1983*, ed. Katherine Bucknell [New York: Harper, 2012], 73).

18. Christopher Isherwood, *The Sixties: Diaries, Volume Two: 1960–1969*, ed. Katherine Bucknell (New York, Harper, 2010), 22.

19. See Wendy Mofatt's discussion of Bob and May Buckingham's response to publication as well as the specifics of Forster's will: Wendy Mofatt, *A Great Unrecorded History: A New Life of E. M. Forster* (New York: Farrar, Straus and Giroux, 2010), 322–23.

20. Wheeler is quoted in a letter from Wescott to Isherwood, in which Wescott goes on to state: "I don't think he trusts the English faction, that is, the estate, to move expeditiously, with perhaps too many cooks for the broth. He suggests your being prepared to publish independently in good time before the expiration of the three year term, as EMF suggested" (August 26, 1970, Beinecke).

21. The National Institute of Arts and Letters (1898) and its associated organization the American Academy of Arts and Letters (1904) combined in 1976 into the single entity American Academy and Institute of Arts and Letters. Wescott and Isherwood were members, the former serving as president from 1959 to 1962. Forster was named an honorary foreign member following his address there. As noted in the history of the organization, the upsurge in book sales following the Merchant–Ivory film of the novel increased the royalties supporting the award so that it continues to fund "visiting Bobs" to this day (John Updike, ed., *A Century of Arts & Letters* [New York: Columbia University Press, 1997], 262n30). Royalties received from Norton in 1988, according to Academy records, were in excess of thirty thousand dollars (American Academy and Institute of Arts and Letters, New York).

22. Christopher Isherwood, review of *Maurice* by E. M. Forster, *California Scene* (January 1972): 14.

23. At the Huntington conference in 2000, "Christopher Isherwood: Private Faces," and in the film *Chris & Don*, Bachardy stated that Isherwood's personal reason for writing the novel was the prospect that Bachardy might leave him.

My reading does not discount this motive but rather concentrates on the novel's engagement with loss in a society that still criminalized and stigmatized homosexuality. [See the essay by Carola M. Kaplan in this volume for more on that aspect of A Single Man.—Eds.]

24. Christopher Isherwood, A Single Man (1964; reprint, Minneapolis: University of Minnesota Press, 2001), 19–20.

25. That Fadiman would recommend Maurice is an interesting phenomenon in itself when we consider what Janice Radway had to say about her own membership to the club in the same time period: "three years into graduate school, I had learned to disparage the club as a middle-brow operation offering only the come-on of free bestsellers to people who wanted only to be told what to read in order to look appropriately cultured" (Janice Radway, A Feeling for Books: The Book-of-the-Month Club, Literary Taste, and Middle-Class Desire [Chapel Hill: University of North Carolina Press, 1999], 1).

26. Clifton Fadminan, "Reader's Report on Maurice," Columbia University Rare Book and Manuscript Library, 2.

27. For such a disparagement of Maurice, see Cynthia Ozick's 1983 essay "Morgan and Maurice: A Fairy Tale," in Art and Ardor: Essays (New York: Knopf, 1983), 61–79.

2

Labor of Love

Making *Chris & Don*

TINA MASCARA AND GUIDO SANTI

Chris & Don: A Love Story is a feature-length documentary film focusing on the thirty-year relationship between Christopher Isherwood and Don Bachardy. The film was four years in the making and solidified our partnership as filmmakers and our relationship as a couple. We met a few months prior to beginning this project, so in a sense, we adopted Chris and Don as role models, and we were inspired by their commitment to each other and, above all, to their work and creativity.

Don was our muse in deciding to embark on this journey because he is unlike anyone we've ever known, and we felt his life was compelling and would be an interesting subject for a film. His persona is undeniable and anyone who has ever met him can attest to that. He's riveting, creative, witty, entertaining, and a natural raconteur, and, luckily for us, he's comfortable in front of a camera. Naturally, we wanted our film to be told from his point of view, using his voice and recollections, thus taking the viewer on a historical journey without utilizing third-person narration, as is customary in a lot of television documentaries. Don was very open and honest; he never deflected a question or denied us access to any material we deemed pertinent to the film. He let us use his diaries, his love letters, and his drawings. He opened the doors to a flood of information that, even now, several years after the release of the film, we are still processing. Most of all, he gave us access to this beautiful 16 mm footage, shot in the 1950s, of him traveling around the world with Chris.

This priceless material gave us a unique insight into their life. We see them on a boat going to Tangier and vacationing in Venice, London, and Paris. We see them in the company of film stars and important literary friends; we see them in their most intimate and personal moments.

Imagine how we felt cutting this material into our documentary: we were in awe, not only because of the people in it, but because the film was in pristine condition with very vibrant colors. They shot it in Kodachrome, which had a very saturated look. The irony is that Don kept this priceless footage in a cabinet, facing the ocean, but, after fifty years, it was still in perfect condition.

We were so fortunate to work with Don. Over the years, he has become a dear friend, and we love spending time with him. Once every week or two, we go out together for dinner and a movie. It is always a new experience. Don says so many interesting things about the present and the past that we wish we were still filming. In a sense, our film is not finished because our fascination with the man and the artist is not over yet. On a recent night out, Don recounted some of the film directors he has painted over his career. There were so many! He told us a series of anecdotes that could have added another interesting chapter to our *Chris & Don* experience. Don has met and painted thousands of people. He has looked at them so closely and remembers particular details about their faces, mannerisms, and conversations. There is no one else like him and we feel very lucky that we were able to document a part of his life story.

Chris & Don involved a lot of preparation and money, and, as we mentioned earlier, it was many years in the making. At first we tried applying for grants, but the process was taking an incredible amount of time, so we just decided to go ahead and start filming. It seemed like a manageable task, as we were both filmmakers, so jumping into production was the easy part. We didn't have much of a budget but managed to buy a camera and some other equipment, mainly sound and editing software, and started production in a very independent way. Before our co-endeavor working on *Chris & Don,* we had always hired editors to cut our projects. However, on this film, we learned to use Final Cut, an editing system, and cut the film ourselves. We immersed ourselves into the process of logging and digitizing hundreds of hours of footage and transcribing the interviews to come up with a workable blueprint, which we followed to create our first edit. The editor in a documentary is essentially the storyteller, so even if we had an idea of the story, it became clearer as we started cutting. The process is very much like sculpting clay. Money is wonderful, but we always say, if we had secured grant money early on, we would not have made such a personal, intimate story. The lack of funds in our situation forced us to invest ourselves completely—body, mind, and spirit—to come up with creative ways to implement our vision. In the beginning, we worked whenever we had time, usually on weekends or

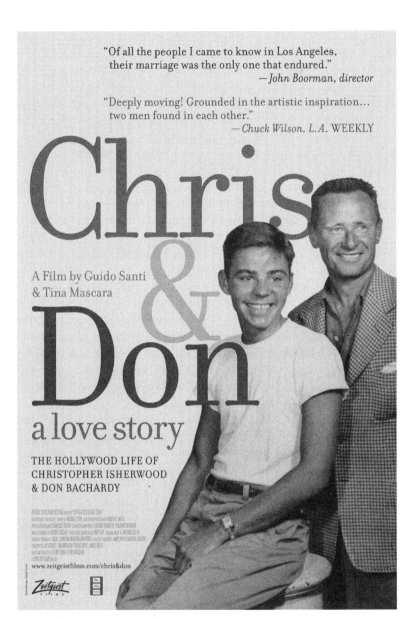

"Of all the people I came to know in Los Angeles,
their marriage was the only one that endured."
— *John Boorman, director*

"Deeply moving! Grounded in the artistic inspiration...
two men found in each other."
— *Chuck Wilson, L.A.* WEEKLY

A Film by Guido Santi
& Tina Mascara

Chris & Don

a love story

THE HOLLYWOOD LIFE OF
CHRISTOPHER ISHERWOOD
& DON BACHARDY

www.zeitgeistfilms.com/chris&don

Chris & Don: A Love Story, a film by Guido Santi and Tina Mascara (2007).
Zeitgeist Films release.

during holidays. Sometimes we had friends helping us; other times it was just us, with Tina doing sound and Guido filming with the camera. We would alternate asking questions to the people we interviewed.

We worked closely together every step of the way; we traveled to Ireland to film John Boorman, to Paris to speak with Leslie Caron, and to many other locations, including England and Los Angeles. Going to places like London was a logistical nightmare, as we didn't have additional hands to help us carry equipment, so finding subway routes with "lifts" was our main priority in scheduling appointments with our subjects. We would study subway maps and get off at stops with elevators just to avoid the flights of steps, even if it meant going out of our way. Also, some of our interviews didn't pan out as originally planned, as was the case when meeting with David Hockney. We arranged our schedule to be in London at a day and time set by David's assistant; however, when we called the morning of the interview to reconfirm, we learned that David had come down with a bad cold. The interview was pushed to later that day, then afternoon, and eventually canceled. We sat all day in a Starbucks close to David's studio, waiting for word. It was cold, damp, and rainy and we were encumbered with equipment. We were really disappointed because we felt that David's interview would have given us tremendous insights into Chris and Don's relationship as he has been their lifelong friend and had documented their relationship in his paintings. We had always planned to reschedule the interview with him and return to London, but as we got deeper into the editing process, we realized we had enough good material and talking heads to bring our story to conclusion. Also, this was long before we got completion funds and we were strapped for cash. These are some of the types of obstacles we encountered; however, we did not want the lack of funds or crew to be a hindrance in any way as we were committed to making the best film possible.

We interviewed Don about nine times over a period of two years. It was a necessary process because we decided from the very beginning that the film had to be told in his voice and from his point of view. He was the protagonist and this was mainly his story, but, of course, Chris was a central part of it. We wanted it to be an intimate, personal portrait of his relationship with Chris. We wanted to present their story more as a memoir, a private diary, rather than a more traditional documentary. After all, both Chris and Don kept diaries throughout their lives, and that seemed to us the best way to achieve what we wanted. Chris's voluminous diaries became our starting point in the film, with Michael York's brilliant interpretation recalling his first impression of Don. And, as Don recounts in the film, he started reading Chris's diaries immediately after Chris died, beginning with the most recent volumes and working his way back to the beginning, when they first met. Chris's diaries also come back in the end, so they serve as the bookends and the spine of the story. They allowed us to bring Chris's voice alive in the film, to show his point of view, and to create the perfect juxtaposition to Don's narration. Also, because the film spanned more than one hundred years of history and included two biographies, starting in 1904 with Chris's birth, we had to license archival footage from various broadcasters and distributors, which is shockingly expensive, costing thousands of dollars a minute. We knew we had to include some archival footage because it gave the viewer a historical context to the lives of these two men, but we only allowed ourselves to use it sparingly, knowing that we'd eventually have to pay for it. We also used some archival material without licensing it because of fair-use practices in documentary films, which allow the use of copyrighted material for criticism or commenting. Fair use is the necessary balance between strict copyright law and the freedoms of the First Amendment, so we hired a law firm specializing in the fair-use doctrine to help us understand when it was appropriate to invoke this right. In the end, even with utilizing fair-use material, licensing footage for *Chris & Don* was our single biggest expense.

About two and a half years into the project, we felt ready to put together a rough cut, which we showed to Don and to James White, who eventually became one of our producers. The cut was very patchy, but the overall structure was there. They were able to understand what we were going for. We were afraid that Don might have a negative reaction to what we showed him, but, fortunately, he liked it a lot. This was the very first time we thought that maybe we had something valuable, something good.

During one of our meetings, Don shared with us a number of cards and letters Chris and Don had exchanged over the years. Some of them contained drawings of kittens and horses that they did of each other using their animal personas. Don was Kitty, a white furry kitten, and Chris was Dobbin, an old horse. They were characters created out of fun that added a certain degree of playfulness to their relationship. They wrote letters to each other as Kitty and Dobbin, and created imaginary adventures in their animal personas, which sometimes reflected the real problems they were facing in their life together. It was a language of love that allowed them to stay close and connected even when the relationship was going through its most rocky time. We were particularly touched by the letters they wrote to each other when Chris moved temporarily to San Francisco to teach and Don was left alone in the house. They were seriously considering breaking up, but they never stopped writing to each other. We knew we wanted to include these letters in the documentary but didn't have the right footage to express the idea of love and playfulness these letters inspired. It was difficult because by then we'd used all the archival material that we had, and we were running out of options. Tina had the idea to animate the character drawings in the cards and create a couple of situations to go along with Don's and Michael York's narration of the letters. We were enthusiastic about the possibility and began searching for the right people to do the job.

We found them almost immediately in Katrina and Kristina Swanger, two very talented sisters, who at the time were studying at College of the Canyons, where Guido was teaching. They understood perfectly well what we wanted, and in a few weeks they animated the short scripted scenes that we gave them. We loved the drawings they did because they resembled the originals done by Isherwood, who was not good at drawing at all. They were imperfect and slightly off scale, which made them all the more endearing and funny. It was important to maintain this aspect in the animation because having a good sense of humor is apparent in Chris and Don's relationship.

One of the last hurdles to overcome was finding the right composer to bring unity to our film, which included various parts. There were the two biographies, Chris's life before Don, Don's struggle to become an artist, and Don's life after Chris, all of which were encompassed in the greater theme—their love story. Music in a film can never be underestimated, because it heightens the emotional elements, which are vital for viewer participation. We had always wanted to make a film that people could connect to, so settling for anything less than the best was never an option for us; however, finding the right person took time. At first we worked with friends who are talented musicians, but had little experience with film score and composition. We wasted months and became increasingly frustrated as we waited to hear anything that could bring to life our story. One day as we were leafing through a documentary magazine, we read about Miriam Cutler, a composer working in Los Angeles who had scored a lot of critically acclaimed documentary films. We met with her, listened to some of her music, and instinctively felt she was the right person to work on our film. She is an incredibly busy professional, and it just so happened one of the films she had been scheduled to work on fell through, so she had an opening in her full schedule to work with us.

We hired her immediately. She came through for us and produced a score that brought *Chris & Don* to a whole new level.

By this point, the film was finished, but we didn't really know what we had until we got it into the Telluride Film Festival. Suddenly, everything became more real to us. Telluride is one of the best festivals in the world. Being selected there gave us hope that the film might eventually find distribution and be seen by a broader audience. It was an important moment for us because it was our film's debut. Of course, we wanted people to like it, especially after having invested so much time and energy into seeing it to completion. We were at every screening and always sat in the back, trying to be as inconspicuous as possible, as we watched people's reactions. We could feel the audience, and it was almost like being inside their skins, watching the movie, not as us, but as them. There's a moment near the end of the film in which Don talks about painting Chris as he was dying. It's a poignant moment because Don recounts painting Chris until his last breath and continuing to paint him even after his death. In the first screening, we remember hearing people in the audience crying. For us, this was a relief because it meant they had stayed with us through the ninety-minute journey, they had given the movie a chance, and they were engaged. At the end of the film, the lights went on and there was great applause.

Even though Telluride was one of our best festivals, our documentary wasn't well attended. The venue was new and off the beaten track, and the time slots we were given to screen our film competed with some of the best films made that year, films that had just debuted at Cannes with directors and actors in house for their screenings, the likes of Julian Schnabel, Sean Penn, and Daniel Day-Lewis. Having said that, our screening did yield two very special guests, Gerald Peary, one of the most respected critics in the United States, and his wife, Amy. After the film was over, they both were very enthusiastic about our documentary, saying it was "nearly perfect." We probably wouldn't have believed him if not for the fact that he mentioned *Chris & Don* in a review he did of the festival for the *Boston Phoenix*.

Most of our early reviews were quite good. The very first reviews we had appeared in *Variety* and the *Hollywood Reporter* and both were positive, especially the one by Kurt Honeycutt in the *Hollywood Reporter*. Those reviews helped boost our confidence in the film, which at that time we needed badly. When you work on a project for so long, and in isolation, as we did, you start losing perspective, and each day becomes a fight to overcome negative thoughts. We had quite a few of those days.

Before the film had its first screening, we showed it in our apartment to a select group of friends, mostly filmmakers. It was a test screening that turned out to be a bad experience for us because nobody really liked it. Everyone had ideas about how to change it and make it better, although we made it clear from the very beginning that the picture was finished, or "locked," as you say in film jargon. It took us weeks to shake off the feeling of disappointment we had, but in the end we didn't change a single frame. So, a few months later, when positive reviews started to pour in, we felt glad that we'd stuck to our guns. The film became a critical success, and naturally that made us quite happy, not just for ourselves but for Chris and Don as well. We will never grow tired of saying that we made this film with heart because we believed, and still do, that their story was exceptional and so was the love they shared. Even now, when the film receives praise or gets a positive review on the Internet by some critics or viewers, we feel proud to have contributed somehow to the legacy of their life together.

After the film had its theatrical run, we began receiving a few invitations from some very reputable schools such as USC, California Institute of the Arts, Johns Hopkins, and Cornell University. We immediately embraced this as a new opportunity to expand our audience to college and university students, an age group that usually doesn't go to see documentary films. We thought it was great that our film was utilized as a teaching tool in a variety of classes in subjects such as gender studies, American literature, history, and documentary filmmaking. Showing the film and talking to the students afterward has been a great experience for us. At first we thought younger audiences would not be interested in a story of two artists, two gay men who shared a life together that spanned almost a century. But maybe because the documentary was never intended to be didactic in the first place and focused more on the emotional aspect of their relationship rather than the historical and literary aspects of it, the response we received from younger audiences was always positive. What was most appealing to the students was the deep love and commitment Chris and Don showed for each other, the way they managed to stay together for such a long time. What they learn from the film is that there were people before them who were not afraid to defy the time in which they lived; who paved the road for a better understanding and acceptance of gay relationships; who believed that people shouldn't be judged for their sexual orientation or preferences, but had the right to love whoever they wanted and how they wanted. Chris and Don were these people. They lived by their own rules because there were no rules in the 1950s about how a gay couple should live. If anything, they were avoided and even ostracized by people who thought their age difference was too much to handle. Even in the case of their dear friend Evelyn Hooker, who was one of the first psychologists to study the behavior of gay people: she rented Chris and Don a cottage house, but after a while she became self-conscious of their presence and of what the neighbors might think of them, and asked them to leave. They certainly looked odd to many people because Don looked so much younger than his age, although he was legal.

Because their story covers the span of a hundred years, from Isherwood's birth at the turn of the century to the present days with Bachardy still living and working at their house in Santa Monica, the film offers also a look into other themes and topics, such as pacifism, the intellectual melting pot of writers and artists of various kinds coming from Europe to Los Angeles in the 1930s and 1940s, gay rights in the 1960s, and the art of portraiture, to mention a few. Chris and Don not only lived those times as protagonists but they also recorded the people, the changes, the trends, and the ideas that populated those years. They did it with artful details and talent in their different forms—Isherwood in his novels and diaries and Don in the thousands of portraits he did over the years.

When we started the project, we remember Don saying he approved of us making a film about him and Chris because he knew we didn't have an agenda in mind. He was afraid a gay filmmaker would have been more inclined to put more emphasis on the political aspect of their story rather than just tell their story as it was. We can't say whether Don was right or wrong in his apprehension, but certainly we approached the story with open minds. We loved their story, and as filmmakers we were committed to tell it in the most direct way. Chris and Don's life inspired us and continues to inspire us—in particular, the commitment to their work and the discipline with which they pursued it. For years, they had the same routine every day; they would wake up, go for a swim, have breakfast, work together on a script or a project, and then Don would go to his studio to paint and Chris to his, to write. At night, they would either see friends or go to the movies. It sounds like a perfect life to us because both of us are artists and always in search of a balance in our lives. Chris and Don lived their lives (and Don continues living his) with intention, fully engaged in every moment of it. They lived with almost a Zen-like attitude, knowing that the process, the journey of living, was more important than its final goal or destination, an idea they possibly adopted from Vedanta. They used words and colors to fix, on paper or on a canvas, the people they met, the experiences they had, as well as the moments of exhilaration or sorrow they both felt at times. They did that always with the honesty of a photographic camera.

That may be also part of the reason why some people have reacted unfavorably to some of Chris's writing or felt disappointed by Don's painting: because their work was never intended to be flattering or nice, quite the contrary. If you take a snapshot of life, in a particular moment at a particular time, that snapshot may not necessarily show you what you would like to see or read. That snapshot doesn't define you but at the same time is part of who you are; it is not a definite statement on life or people, just a temporary one. Like the last paintings Don did of Chris when he was dying: those paintings, which document in painful detail Chris's deterioration day by day until his last breath and beyond that, because Don kept painting Chris for a whole afternoon after he was dead, are the most poignant example of that honesty they applied to their lives. Don painted Chris with participation and detachment; he shared Chris's pain but he was also able to observe it at a distance. They went through the experience of death together as if to show us, once again, that the process, the journey, was more important than the final goal. We believe this is an exemplary lesson for anyone who wants to be an artist.

The timing of the film with the political debate on gay marriage was purely coincidental. The film was released in the theaters right when Californians were asked to vote on Proposition 8, which overturned the California Supreme Court's ruling that same-sex couples have a constitutional right to marry. We didn't have any control on the release dates, but we benefited from what was happening because people were talking about gay marriage and gay relationships, and Chris and Don certainly had one of the longest and best-documented relationships in the history of the LGBT community. They had their ups and downs, like anybody else, but they stayed together until the end. Chris and Don were not political activists, although they always supported their community and never shied away from interviews and public support of gay causes. They didn't need to be overtly political because their life together was already a political statement in itself. They were a couple who lived in an openly gay relationship for more than thirty years. They didn't march in the street but were always available to help anyone who asked. As Don says in an interview, which is part of the film DVD extras, they were always in favor of gay unions, although he adds very candidly that he never felt the need of an official "sanctification" of his relationship because he didn't need anyone's approval for loving a man, for loving Chris, especially if this

This undated photograph presents a relaxed Isherwood. Photographer unknown. Courtesy of Don Bachardy.

approval was coming from a society that always opposed their lifestyle as morally wrong and sinful. We understand Don's position as we feel more and more surrounded by bigotry and disinformation in our society. It was important to us that their story would speak to anyone, gay or straight, men or women, old and young. We hope that the film helps to break some stereotypes in people's perception of same-sex relationships.

Making *Chris & Don* was for us a labor of love. We met Don and fell immediately in love with him and his story. Without him at the center of our narration, it would not have been possible to make the film. Since the unexpected success of our film, documentaries have taken more of the central stage in our lives. We keep developing new projects and have recently completed *Monk with a Camera,* a feature-length documentary about the life and journey of Nicholas Vreeland, a Westerner who gave up his worldly life and passion for photography to become a Tibetan Buddhist monk. We shot the film in India and New York with the same commitment and attitude as with *Chris & Don.* What attracts us is the possibility to produce, shoot, and edit the project on our own, with a few collaborators, without the burden of a large production. Plus, the technology today is so advanced that all you need to start is a decent consumer camera and good editing software; the rest is up to you and your ability to find a good and powerful story to tell. And this is how we started to shoot *Chris & Don.* At first, it was only us, and then our dear friend and director of photography Ralph Smith and a few other collaborators joined our production. There was no pay involved, everyone donated their time, usually the weekends, and worked for free. Whatever money we were able to raise during production was eventually used for postproduction costs, to pay for special film processing and archival material. The main drawback was that it took us years to complete the film, but the time we had at our disposal also gave us the chance to do the best possible job.

We were very fortunate with *Chris & Don* because we had a powerful story, some beautiful 16 mm footage, great interviews by all the people who appeared in the film, charming animation, and a lovely jazz score. We couldn't wish for anything better. The film was launched at Telluride, and a few months after that it had its Los Angeles premiere at the AFI Film Festival. A couple of weeks after that, we got picked up by a very reputable art-house distributor, Zeitgeist Films. Emily Russo and Nancy Gerstman at Zeitgeist pretty much did the rest: they released the film theatrically in all the major cities in North America, sold the TV rights to the Sundance channel, and released a beautifully designed DVD.

Years after its original premiere, we came to the realization that the film has a life of its own, through DVD rentals, on-demand, and sales requests from foreign territories. It is fascinating because we've met so many people who have seen the film. It is the highest possible satisfaction not only for us, but also for Chris and Don. We are glad that people watch and love their story.

3

Working through Grief in the Drafts of *A Single Man*

CAROLA M. KAPLAN

During a particularly turbulent period in his relationship with Don Bachardy, in which a breakup seemed imminent, Christopher Isherwood wrote multiple drafts of the novel that was to become *A Single Man.* In these drafts, he recounts a journey from shock to resignation, as he contemplates the loss of his beloved life partner. Engaging in an artistic process that parallels the psychoanalytic process Sigmund Freud alludes to in "Remembering, Repeating, and Working Through," Isherwood proceeds from pain and incomprehension through an increasing understanding of personal crisis and novelistic potential to ultimate insight and artistic realization. In contemplating the loss of love, Isherwood recalls and works through multiple previous losses—the loss of innocence, of homeland, of youth. And he thereby comes to confront the ultimate loss, that of life itself.

But what does it mean to say that Isherwood "worked through" his feelings of abandonment and grief over loss? Indeed, Freud himself never explained the procedure. He merely posits, in "Remembering, Repeating, and Working Through," his essay account of the "talking cure," that the process requires bringing to awareness "forgotten" unpleasant experiences that one has never analyzed but that one instead evokes through repetitive behavior, enacting over and over the traumas that impaired one's thinking in the first place and that continue to impede one's progress toward a better life.

As Freud observes, "the patient does not *remember* anything of what he has forgotten and repressed, but *acts* it out. He reproduces it not as a memory but as an action; he *repeats* it, without, of course, knowing that he is repeating it."[1] In order to "work through" current difficulties, Freud maintains, the sufferer must overcome his resistance to dealing with painful buried memories and bring up to consciousness, that is, remember, that which he has come to repeat. The question is, how does one go about remembering in order to work through? Although Freud never specifies how "working through" is to be done, what he does suggest is that it is a process made possible by the relationship between the analyst and the patient. And indeed, over the decades of the twentieth century, the psychoanalytic understanding of how patients change shifted from an emphasis on insight based on interpretations provided by the psychoanalyst, to an emphasis on the healing powers of a trusting, intimate relationship between analyst and analysand. Through the research of the past two decades, particularly that of the Boston Change Process Study Group, we have come to know much about the procedural or unconscious knowledge that governs our interactions with intimate others and the relational components that foster therapeutic change. What enables us to change, we now understand, resides in interpersonal exchanges that alter our "implicit relational knowing," our way of being with others. These exchanges can result in "now moments" or "moments of meeting," in which two subjectivities come together in new understanding. Such heightened moments, whether between patient and analyst, parent and child, or lover and lover, reorganize not only the relationship between the participants, but, more importantly, each person's habitual and unconscious understanding, that is, his or her implicit procedural knowledge or way of acting and interacting with others. The distinct qualities and consequences of these moments characterize "a sequencing process" referred to as "moving along." As the psychoanalyst and infant development specialist Daniel Stern notes about emotional or affective communication, it is these changes in the intersubjective relational realm that have lasting therapeutic effect.[2] In short, cumulative changes in implicit relational knowing facilitate the process of moving along that ultimately results in "working through."

The implicit relational knowing that a writer has experienced in his intimate relationships forms the basis of his relationship with his imagined reader, the intimate other who will receive and respond to the literary work and to the author implied in it. From original conception through subsequent drafts, the writer's choices are shaped by his desire for the imagined reader's approval of his accuracy, honesty, skill, and insight into human experience. For Isherwood, this concern was acute because his writing was in general autobiographical, inviting connections between his work and life. Isherwood's sense of connection with his reader was further magnified by the fact that his imagined first reader, whose approval he most coveted, was Don. But Don was not merely the imagined reader: he was also the consultant in the process of creation. Isherwood confided in him his writing difficulties, discussed his artistic choices, and sometimes adopted Don's suggestions. Paradoxically, then, Isherwood's chief personal resource in working through his pain, confusion, and insecurity over the possible loss of Don was Don himself. As much as Don caused Chris anguish and jealousy with the threat of leaving, emotions that impelled Chris to undertake the novel that was to evolve into *A Single Man*, it was also Don who encouraged him to understand what the emerging work was really about—and thus he helped Chris to move along in both his life and his writing.

Don's ability to help Chris in this way was based on the implicit relational knowing that underpinned the relationship they had developed together over the years. Thus, even in the 1962 entries in Isherwood's diary, *The Sixties,* which chronicles the most troubled period in their life together, Chris's despair is tempered by hope. To be sure, Isherwood chronicles their frequent quarrels, in which Don complains about his lack of freedom and Chris's possessiveness, while Chris struggles with jealousy and the fear of losing Don. Yet this year also shows many reconciliations and "moments of meeting."

Early in the year, Chris determines to help Don as he struggles to paint by buckling down to his own work, a resolve that spurs Chris to work on his new novel, "The Englishwoman," the first version of *A Single Man*. At this time, he notes his short-lived "harmony with Don," although by mid-June, he laments: "Don is in a flap. Have I ruined his life? Or not? Or what?"[3] Yet, less than a month later, he states: "we are happy together as almost never before; never, at any rate, since the earliest time, and that was in such a different way" (205). This recollection of their earliest time together may have been the catalyst for the ending of "The Englishwoman," in which a barely disguised Chris, writing in the first person, records the hopeful beginning of a love affair with a young student named Colin. However, by August, "a bad month, for both of us" (215), Chris records with "deep, deep gloom" that his problems with Don are "still acute" (214).

September brings a crucial "moment of meeting," in which Chris, bogged down in the writing of the novel, confides his discouragement to Don, who helps him to a breakthrough. Before this exchange, Chris was feeling "stuck":

> Yesterday I reread my novel, the fifty-six pages I've written so far. I am discouraged; very little seems to be emerging. . . . I do not have a plot

and I don't even know what I want to write a novel about. . . . no,
that's not quite true. I want to write about middle age, and being an
alien. And about the Young. And about this woman. The trouble is,
I really cannot write entirely by ear; I must do some thinking. (221)

A few days later, it is Don who helps him to think about the novel in
a different way: "This morning we went on the beach and discussed
The Englishwoman, and Don, after hearing all my difficulties with it,
made a really brilliant simple suggestion, namely that it ought to be *The
Englishman*—that is, me. This is very far-reaching" (223).

What Isherwood reports here is what Daniel Stern would consider
a quintessential "moment of meeting."[4] Such a moment of intimate encounter facilitates a positive change in communication between two subjectivities. As with all such moments, it is spontaneous and "improvisa-
tional" and it takes place "in the domain of implicit knowledge" about
what to do, think, and feel in their specific relationship" (300). Further,
"it is characterized by both participants interacting in a way that creates
a new implicit understanding of their connection and permits a new 'way-
of-being-with-the-other.'" In such a moment of meeting, the relationship
changes, as the participants recognize that "something of importance,
bearing on the future, is happening" (302). Indeed, this moment proved
to be the turning point in the evolution of the novel. And it was, I believe,
a turning point as well in the evolution of their relationship.

A month later, Chris exults: "I feel that my novel is developing in a new
way, as a much simpler structure, a day in the life of this Englishman"
(*The Sixties,* 236). And Don, the secret sharer of his creation, continues
to encourage him, as Chris notes:

> Yesterday, I showed Don the first twenty-eight pages of this second draft
> of my new novel. He was far more impressed, even, than I had hoped.
> He made me feel that I have found a new approach altogether; that, as
> he put it, the writing itself is so interesting from page to page that you
> don't even care what is going to happen. That's marvelous and a great
> incentive to go on with the work, because I always feel that Don has a
> better *nose* than almost anyone I know. He sniffs out the least artifice or
> fudging. He was on his way out after reading it, and then he came back
> and embraced me and said, "I'm so proud of old Dub." (246)

These moments of meeting, in which Don first helps Chris to develop
what is potential in the novel and, later, to persist in his new approach,
serve to keep Chris working steadfastly on what was to become his best
fictional work, as well as sustain his hope that he and Don can move be-

yond their impasse and heal their relationship. At the end of 1962, when Isherwood was into the second draft, his diary entry is cautiously optimistic: "A bad year with Don. And yet, despite all omens, I still believe we may get through this phase to some new kind of happiness together" (255). Indeed, the coming to fruition of *A Single Man*, with Don's suggestions and encouragement, nurtured their collaboration (already begun with several unproduced screenplays) that would later blossom most fully in the teleplay of *Frankenstein* and the screenplay of *A Meeting by the River*.

Although these sudden revelatory moments with Don were highlights of Isherwood's personal and artistic journey that led to *A Single Man*, his diary discloses that the ideas that resulted in the novel in fact had a slow germination. Isherwood's original idea was for a novel that dealt with a father–son relationship, as recorded in a November 1961 diary entry: "I keep thinking of a possible father–son novel, about Don and me, more or less. What puts me off, at present, is fear of being sentimental, and also the mistrust of presenting one relationship in terms of another. But the answer to this latter objection is: why do you have to think in categories of relationships at all? Why not simply describe *a* relationship?" (134–35). In this statement is the germ of an important idea in *A Single Man*— the idea of the fluidity and interchangeability of relationships. This entry shows a step en route to the development of an important theme in the novel, that what is important between two people is not the specific nature of the relationship but the connection between them, which is everchanging. Indeed, the various drafts of the novel demonstrate ever more clearly the indefinability of relationships and the inadequate categories that designate them. As a case in point, toward the end of *A Single Man*, George and Kenny's relationship changes, in a role reversal, from teacher with student or mentor with mentee to willful child with patient nanny, as a drunken George prompts Kenny to take charge of him.

In early 1962, when the crisis between Chris and Don grew most acute, Isherwood recorded in his diary another idea for a novel, one that contains some of the specific material that would find its way into *A Single Man*. This idea for a novel dealing with a relationship comparable to his and Don's, that between a middle-aged professor and his young student, is much more fully elaborated than the father–son germ of a novel recorded a few months earlier. Under the heading "Some raw material for a novelette" (160), this treatment begins with an ego-salving fantasy of a middle-aged professor pursued by an attractive male student. The student brings the protagonist, a thinly disguised Isherwood in the role of professor, the manuscript of a novel with a homosexual theme. When the professor encourages the student to make the sex scenes more explicit, he does so; then he tells the professor he would like to have sex with him. In a graphic scene (more explicit than anything Isherwood published), the professor and student enjoy great sex, after which the professor congratulates himself for initiating the young man so satisfactorily. As he muses: "He has been privileged to assist at a rite of spring, as it were. He tells himself that Y. will never be able to forget him. He will have been the first. And Y. will never quite be able to recapture that thrill again" (ibid.). But although this scenario, at its inception, may have offered Isherwood consolation for his bruised ego and jealousy over Don's relationships with others, the realistic writer in Isherwood cannot let the treatment rest in fantasy. At the finale, the professor discovers that the experience was more memorable to him than to the young man, who passes up an encore in favor of a party at the home of his parents, whom he joins on their European tour. Thus, the novel ends in rejection and the professor's sour reflection "that the Young are the Young are the Young, but that the Old, thank goodness, are tough—as they need to be" (166).

Interestingly, when Isherwood reworked this material in the first version of *A Single Man,* "The Englishwoman," he fashioned a draft with some of the retrospective quality of *Down There on a Visit,* as if he needed to clear his desk—and to distance himself somewhat from his current problems—before moving on. Although "The Englishwoman" is told in the first person by a narrator named Chris, it is the draft farthest removed from dealing with Isherwood's life crisis. In this version, the writer-narrator, a visiting professor at L.A. State, strikes up an acquaintance with Colin, a British-born student in his class, who invites him home to meet his mother, a fan of Isherwood's fiction. Isherwood's original plan for the novel, as recorded in his writing notebook, was "to show America through British eyes," noting, "By keeping my viewpoint, I can do this bifocally—showing how America seems to the Englishwoman and how it seems to me." In other words, the novel will center on "the Englishwoman herself, and her world," contrasting her "nostalgia" and longing to return to England with Chris's ambivalence about whether to stay in America or return.[5]

Yet, as the draft unfolds, it centers not on the Englishwoman but on Chris's developing relationship with the son. As Isherwood outlines it, in his writing notebook: "I discover that Colin probably wanted me to meet his Mother because he is having a problem with her, and he hopes I'll take his side and help him to solve it. He wants to get away from home." Reacting against "the British half of his parentage because of the way it is presented to him by his Mother," Colin storms out of the house and Chris follows him. They spend the rest of the day together, first at Chris's house, then at the beach. And Charlotte, "realizing sadly that Colin doesn't even want her around, decides to return to England and live with her sister. Her going away is like a death to her, and yet it's a kind of relief, because she hasn't been happy here." Colin, Chris discovers, has plans for their future together. He is eager to become part of Chris's life by helping him in any way he can—and Chris tests him by giving him the tedious job of pasting his articles and newspaper clippings into scrapbooks, which Colin does meticulously. Then they go swimming in the ocean, where a drunken Chris is downed by a huge wave and rescued by Colin who, "like a Nanny," carries him safely home.

Clearly, through the figure of Colin, Isherwood recapitulates the trajectory of his youth—a renunciation of England, an escape from Mother, and a repudiation of heterosexuality. From this initial wish-fulfillment narrative of middle-aged professor pursued by an attractive young man, Isherwood will move on to a larger consideration of his loneliness, his alienation, and his sense of "exile."

Although the coming together of Chris and Colin contains elements of Chris's early relationship with Don, it avoids any hint of later difficulties—and so, in psychological terms, is more a repetition than a reconsideration. But this treatment does enable Isherwood to play out the fantasy of having a partner more eager to please than Don—an option he rejects, in a subsequent diary entry, in which he writes about Don: "He is terribly complicated, nervous, talented, affectionate, frank yet quite capable of telling the most drastic lies—and, let me face it, I like him that way. I think I want someone to look after me and wait on me hand and foot—but I don't or I should get one—it isn't difficult. So I really should make it a rule never to complain in that cold elderly way because he won't do just exactly what I want" (260–61).

The second draft, "The Englishman," although told at a greater distance (in a third-person narrative of a protagonist who shares Isherwood's middle name, William), confronts more directly Isherwood's ambivalence and indecision in leaving England behind to embrace his adoptive country (Huntington Library, CI 1061). It also presents at the center of the narrative a homosexual partnership, for the first time in Isherwood's fiction—as well as explores the grief resulting from the loss of such a relationship. By introducing into the narrative the death of William's lover, Tom, Isherwood attempts to deal, in a distanced way, with the possibility of losing Don.

The plot of "The Englishman" is much the same as that of the later *A Single Man*. It explores the events of a single day in the life of William, a middle-aged English professor, who wakes and breakfasts; drives to campus; teaches a literature class; chats with Colin, an attractive student; visits his partner's former female lover, dying of cancer, at a hospital; goes to the gym; shops for dinner at a supermarket; changes his mind about the dinner invitation he'd turned down; eats dinner with his friend Charlotte at her home; visits a neighborhood bar where he runs into Colin, with whom he drinks, swims in the ocean, and returns to his house. He offers Colin his spare bedroom in which to enjoy sex with his girlfriend; is disappointed to find that Colin considers him a dirty old man; and, after some flirtatious talk, he passes out and awakes to find Colin gone. "Little teaser," he ruefully reflects about Colin, but without rancor.

This much more fully developed version of the novel presents William with an array of life choices, which he considers but rejects. For example, he briefly considers, then rejects, a companionate marriage with a female colleague and fellow British exile, Cynthia Leach, "because, Tom or no Tom, loneliness is not the worst that can happen to anyone, and two lonelinesses do not make a togetherness."[6] And Isherwood's writing notebook reveals that he considered but rejected a number of other narrative choices. For whatever reason—perhaps because this would have come too close to Isherwood's own experience with Don—Isherwood also considers but rejects the idea of making his partner's dying former lover a man, rather than a woman. In his notebook, he posits: "There is a youngish man dying of cancer who has, maybe, had an affair with William's friend. He is therefore a kind of duty to William, an ex-object of jealousy and a memento mori."

Further, Isherwood considered but rejected the idea of presenting an actual sexual encounter between William and Colin. Not only was Isherwood aware that he might alienate otherwise sympathetic readers, who would balk at the violation of the boundary between teacher and student (*The Sixties*, 161), he was also aware that sex in itself would not necessarily alleviate William's loneliness and isolation. As he notes: "Above all else, William is an observer. I would carry this to such lengths that I think he could even have sex with somebody (Colin?) somewhere in the book and remain quite unattached. His real sex life should be in his masturbation fantasies."

Finally, for the last draft of the novel, Isherwood considered but rejected the possibility of his protagonist's making a life in England with Charlotte. In his notebook, Isherwood has his protagonist, now named

George, consider returning to England with Charlotte and their running a pub together, an idea that he and Jim had toyed with before Jim's death: "It could be equally well a project for George and Charlotte and therefore a *reason* for them to live together."

Significantly, Don was actively involved in Isherwood's final revision of the novel into *A Single Man*. It was Don who suggested to Chris the introduction of a lost lover in William's life. And Don, whom Chris termed a "wizard at name finding," came up with the names for the characters Kenny and Doris (*The Sixties*, 289). Most significantly, Don helped Chris realize that the title "The Englishman" "didn't seem right, because the fact that George is English is not the most important thing about him." Then Don came up with *A Single Man,* which Chris "knew instantly" was the perfect title (283). All this while, Chris and Don's relationship continued to be turbulent. On June 2, 1963, Isherwood reports in his diary that he is at page 77 of the second draft, "bringing it up to the beginning of the big scene with Charlotte. I do so want to get all this work squared away before I face a complete break with Don—if there has to be a break" (277). Then, a few days later, Isherwood reports, "Don says he can't make his case against me stick. He asks forgiveness. I forgive . . . and so we go on" (ibid.).

In *A Single Man,* Isherwood succeeds in working through his personal difficulties by means of George, a composite figure who is and is not a self-portrait. Through a series of small realizations, his sense of himself refracted, augmented, and finally clarified by his various encounters with others, George sheds some of the small complaints and estranging bitterness that obscure his day. And, in doing so, he comes to embrace the larger grievances—and thus the community—he shares with the minority to which he is happiest to belong, the minority of the living.

In part through his discussions with Don, Isherwood became clearer about the "inwardness" of his material (*The Sixties,* 247). In this way, his final version became more focused and more spare than "The Englishman." Perhaps his most significant revision was in the characterization of "The Englishwoman," Charlotte or Charley. In "The Englishman," his feelings toward Charley are more ambivalent than in *A Single Man:* although he enjoys the "perfect unselfconscious way of their sitting down together" as a kind of "sacrament," he feels she violates it by telling him of her unhappiness, which makes him feel "trapped, compromised, cornered." But then he recognizes that he is reenacting with her his old difficulties with his mother ("The Englishman," 43). Further, in "The Englishman," William shares Charlotte's nostalgia for England. But in *A Single Man,* this longing for the past is almost entirely displaced onto Charley: As George tells Charley, "You won't find the past in England. Or anywhere else, for that matter."[7] And he deplores her decision to return to England to live with a sister who detests her, as "drooling masochism" (142).

Finally, in *A Single Man,* Charley is less attractive and less perceptive than in the previous version. In "The Englishman," she is a "small and quite slender" woman with "something charming and good-humoredly battered about her looks," who "always jokes on herself." In *A Single Man,* she merely looks "battered" and "untidy": "Her poor cheeks are swollen and inflamed"; her costume "emphasizes her lack of shape" and, when she is kidded, she doesn't "get the point" (121). Because George sees Charley as pathetic and lovable, if deluded, he treats her with indulgence, affection, and tenderness. In this final version, the protagonist can afford to be—and is—warmer toward Charley, because he sees more clearly and without rivalry the differences between their two perspectives.

In *A Single Man* Isherwood depicts a protagonist who is able at last to answer the questions Isherwood posited for him (and for himself) in his writing notebook: "Do you regret having come to America? Is life in America tolerable? Do you want to go back to England to die? How are you going to bear the rest of your life?" George's answer: to stay in America because "This is where he found Jim" (182). And to look to the future with hope: "He believes he will find another Jim here. He doesn't know it, but he has started to look already" (ibid.).

As Isherwood, in revising the novel, downplayed his protagonist's estranging Englishness, many of his eccentricities, and most of his pet peeves, he shaped *A Single Man* into a "one day in the life" prose poem, emulating one of his favorite works, Virginia Woolf's *Mrs. Dalloway,* which he had recently read and praised as "prose written with absolute pitch, a perfect ear. You could perform it with instruments" (*The Sixties,* 217). As he revised the drafts of what would become *A Single Man,* he acknowledged this debt: "This novelette is, before all else, a sort of Virginia Woolf poem about life, specifically about male middle age" ("Writing Notebook"). In order "to avoid plottiness," he removed extraneous detail in favor of sustained mood: "Because it is a poem, even in a sense a musical composition, it should be continuous in feeling" ("Writing Notebook").

As in *Mrs. Dalloway,* the development of Isherwood's protagonist is effected through his encounter with a foil character, Charlotte, who suggests to him his direst possibilities. Just as Septimus Smith must commit suicide so that Clarissa may live, so Charlotte, in her retrograde thinking and masochistic inertia, impels Chris/William/George to leave the past behind and get on with his life. Over the drafts, Isherwood more and more clearly develops the character of Charlotte as foil—and he thereby enlarges the dimensions and the resonance of his protagonist.

After reading *Mrs. Dalloway,* Isherwood asked himself: "Could I write a book like that and keep within the nature of my own style? I'd love to try" (*The Sixties,* 217). *A Single Man* is the triumphant answer to that question.

But the novel was more than an artistic triumph. It was a personal triumph as well. It records and works through Isherwood's deepest fears—of losing his beloved partner, of remaining an exile, of dying alone in a foreign land. As a result, Isherwood emerged from his crisis with Don more confident as a man and as a writer and more hopeful that he and Don could forge a future together—a future that was in fact to last two more decades to the end of Isherwood's life. Through the implicit relational knowing that undergirded Isherwood's relationship with Don and Don's relationship with him, their life collaboration fostered an artistic collaboration that renewed their partnership. Thus did Christopher, aided by Don, turn life into art. And thus did Christopher and Don, in recommitting to each other, change art back into life.

Notes

1. Sigmund Freud, "Remembering, Repeating, and Working Through" (1914), in *Standard Edition of the Collected Psychological Works of Sigmund Freud,* trans. James Strachey (1958; reprint, London: Hogarth Press, 2001), 12:148.

2. Daniel N. Stern et al., "Non-Interpretive Mechanisms in Psychoanalytic Therapy: The 'Something More' Than Interpretation," *International Journal of Psycho-analysis* 79 (1998): 903.

3. Christopher Isherwood, *The Sixties: Diaries, Volume Two: 1960–1969,* ed. Katherine Bucknell (New York: Harper, 2010), 173, 198.

4. Daniel N. Stern, "The Process of Therapeutic Change Involving Implicit Knowledge: Some Implications of Developmental Observations for Adult Psychotherapy," *Infant Mental Health Journal* 19.3 (1998): 300–308.

5. Christopher Isherwood, "Writing Notebook," Huntington Library (CI 1158) 131.

6. Christopher Isherwood, "The Englishman," Huntington Library, 1962, (CI 1061) 31.

7. Christopher Isherwood, *A Single Man* (New York: Simon and Schuster, 1964), 141.

4

Writing the Unspeakable in
A Single Man and *Mrs. Dalloway*

JAMIE CARR

When asked in a 1973 interview by Carola M. Kaplan if he had Virginia Woolf's *Mrs. Dalloway* in mind while composing *A Single Man*, Christopher Isherwood affirms, albeit briefly, this novel as one influence on his narrative form.[1] In his diary in the early 1960s, however, he unquestionably praises Woolf's novel as "one of the most truly beautiful novels or prose poems or whatever that I have ever read. It is prose written with absolute pitch, a perfect ear. You could perform it with instruments. Could I write a book like that and keep within the nature of my own style? I'd love to try."[2] That Isherwood was rereading *Mrs. Dalloway* while beginning to compose *A Single Man* suggests a more profound connection between his and Woolf's work than his later remark indicates. Although Woolf had been critical of Isherwood's generation of writers in the 1930s for their explicitly politicized art, and he alternatively referred to her as an ivory-tower effete, each also held high regard for the other. Strikingly, like Woolf's coupled characters, the eponymous Clarissa Dalloway and the "shell-shocked" soldier Septimus Smith, the two writers shared a political aesthetic philosophy that has yet to receive adequate scholarly discussion.

Like *Mrs. Dalloway*, *A Single Man* follows the consciousness of a middle-aged character reflecting on life and death, love and loss over the course of a single day. Each consciousness, conveyed through a combination of modernist stream-of-consciousness narration, interior monologue, and free indirect discourse, is effectively shown to be shaped by the exterior world—the historical moment; the national context; and encounters with others, however ephemeral or deeply rooted, life-affirming or oppressive these connections might be. In *Mrs. Dalloway*, Clarissa's consciousness is impacted by the death of the lower-class soldier who is nevertheless silenced by her milieu—a class that does not want to hear about the traumas of a war it deemed this man's duty to fight. Isherwood's novel is similarly set in a conservative postwar climate, in this case the Second World War. Here it is the death of his lover that pervades George's consciousness—that and the attitudes of a society that oppresses homosexuals in midcentury America. In this experience, George shares more in common with Woolf's traumatized soldier, Septimus Smith, however. Septimus's trauma is directly linked to the death of his officer, Evans, and to the suppression of his grief over this loss.

Woolf's subtle exploration of same-sex mourning appears to have been particularly poignant for Isherwood as he was writing *A Single Man*. As Don Bachardy mentions in an interview, Isherwood may have at this time been imagining the loss of his own partner—the loss of Don—during a difficult period in their relationship.[3] Woolf's novel also recalled to Isherwood's mind an earlier loss in his life. His rereading of *Mrs. Dalloway*, which was on his reading list on April 30, 1962, sparks the memory of his father's death in the First World War. Just over a week later, on May 9, 1962, he records for the first time the anniversary of this loss: "May 9: The day Daddy was killed in France—or was it? I have forgotten. Is this awful? No—not particularly. But at least I'm remembering him today" (*The Sixties*, 186). In that same diary entry he notes that he is "on page 16 of the new novel. I still don't know what to think of that" (ibid.). This "new novel" would become *A Single Man*, a work that, like *Mrs. Dalloway*, is permeated by mourning. Although George may have met his beloved Jim in military uniform just after the end of the Second World War, *A Single Man* is not about the traumas or memories of war and loss. George's psyche is nevertheless affected, like Septimus's, by the suppression of his grief for an "unspeakable" love and his rage toward a society that demands this silencing.[4]

Indeed, what is most noteworthy in the correspondence between *Mrs. Dalloway* and *A Single Man* is their related effort to articulate truths about the prohibitions against publicly mourning the loss of a same-sex love object. The exclusionary tactics Woolf and Isherwood identify circulate in particular around same-sex desire, a desire that cannot be uttered by Septimus in 1920s England and can only publicly be named, ironically, as the "unspeakable" by George in 1960s America. In opposition to this silencing, both Isherwood and Woolf give voice to their otherwise silenced characters. Creating a counterdiscourse to the exclusionary practices of "normative" mourning, Isherwood further establishes a connection between George's experience of loss and the reader's.

When Woolf conceptualizes the thematic content of *Mrs. Dalloway,* she comments that she wants Clarissa and Septimus to convey truth and social critique. Her working notes for the novel express this focus: "Sanity and insanity. Mrs. D. seeing the truth. S. S. seeing the insane truth."[5] Later she remarks in her diary that she wants "to criticize the social system and to show it at work at its most intense."[6] Some of Woolf's reviewers found the otherwise well-reviewed novel too "sensitive," suggesting perhaps a backlash against its critiques or discomfort with "the insane truth" Septimus attempts to communicate.

Isherwood's conception of *A Single Man* accomplished what he saw as a similar "deed" to speak the truth. Although the novel received, in his words, a "sour reception," he "still [felt] very good about it" (*The Sixties,* 341). Indeed, he declares in his diary, "I feel: I spoke the truth, and now let them swallow it or not as they see fit" (ibid.). But whereas Woolf's truths evince an *implicit* critique of the silencing of same-sex desire and grief (but explicitly of the medicalization of "the mad" and the will to impose power over others), Isherwood's truth *explicitly* censures society's creation of and fear of "Others," most specifically homosexuals. It is this frankness that compels Katherine Bucknell to claim, rightly so, that Isherwood's "narrative is subtle, exact, unafraid, and powerful" (ibid., xviii). In an era marked by the increased surveillance and suppression of homosexuals, *A Single Man* was, and remains, a work of courageous— and singular—expression.

The connections between Woolf and Isherwood may at first glance seem somewhat tenuous. At the end of the 1930s, Woolf was publicly critical of Isherwood's generation of leftist writers. In her well-known 1940 essay "The Leaning Tower," Woolf accuses "[Cecil] Day Lewis, [W. H.] Auden, [Stephen] Spender, Isherwood, Louis MacNeice and so on" for what she sees as their class hypocrisy. Although they feel anger about the exploitation of the working classes, their writing is merely reactionary toward their own class, a background that affords them the very privilege of a life of writing. They thus express, she contends, feelings of "discomfort; next self-pity for that discomfort; which pity soon turns to anger—to anger against the builder, against society."[7] As if proving Woolf's point for her, this essay brought much reaction from several of those 1930s writers, and, as Isherwood remarks in his memoir *Christopher and His Kind,* they used her conversely "as an enemy image of the ivory-tower intellectual."[8]

Still, despite her critique, Woolf acknowledges in her diary a fondness for this particular young author when she meets him for the first time in

1937: "I[sherwood] rather a find: very small red cheeked nimble & vivacious," she cheerily records.[9] He is "a most appreciative and merry little bird," she finds, when Isherwood tells her that he likes her books—which, she admits, "put some colour into my cheeks." Woolf records here that Isherwood goes on to say that she and E. M. Forster are "the only living novelists the young . . . take seriously" (59). She notes, too, her praise for Isherwood, discerning that he is "a real novelist, I suspect; not a poet; full of acute observations on character & scenes. Odd how few 'novelists' I know: it wd. interest me to discuss fiction with him" (ibid.). Significantly, after this first meeting, Woolf finds Isherwood to be "one of the most vital & observant of the young" (ibid.). Although she did discuss writing with Isherwood's close friends John Lehmann and Stephen Spender, history interfered with the two novelists—who met only "half-a-dozen times"—ever discussing fiction.[10] Woolf was certainly well aware of Isherwood's work, however, as her Hogarth Press, under the editorship of Lehmann, published three of Isherwood's novels, *The Memorial* (1932), *Mr Norris Changes Trains* (1935), and *Goodbye to Berlin* (1939), as well as his short story "Sally Bowles" (1937) and his memoir *Lions and Shadows* (1938). And Isherwood was clearly an astute reader of Woolf as his work engages with her aesthetics over the course of his writing life.

Not only does *A Single Man* take its structure and sociopolitical content from the precedent set by *Mrs. Dalloway*, but Isherwood's early novels *All the Conspirators* (1928) and *The Memorial* also borrow their formalist modernist styles from Woolf. Isherwood admired her technique as he later reread *Mrs. Dalloway*, contrasting it to its own "predecessor," James Joyce's *Ulysses* (1922)—as Woolf herself had done. "It is a marvelous book," he writes of Woolf's novel:

> [her] use of the reverie is quite different from Joyce's stream of consciousness. Beside her, Joyce seems tricky and vulgar and cheap, as she herself thought. Woolf's kind of reverie is less "realistic" but far more convincing and moving. It can convey tremendous and varied emotion.
> (*The Sixties*, 219)

Well before feminist critics would rescue Woolf in the 1970s from a predominantly male literary canon authored by the New Critics, Isherwood recognized her literary value and significant contribution to modernist literature. She was a "great and original talent," he wrote in tribute to her upon her death, one of the few public pieces he felt he could write after his departure from England at the start of a Second World War. "I am happy to think she is free of [this world]," he continues, before everything she loved has been quite smashed. If I wanted an epitaph for her, taken from her own writings, I should choose this: "It was done; it was finished. Yes, she thought, laying down her brush in extreme fatigue, I have had my vision." (Quoted in Rosenbaum, *The Bloomsbury Group*, 414)

If Woolf's style appealed to Isherwood, so too did her politics. He was singular in his reading of "The Leaning Tower." Unlike others of his generation, Isherwood's response to Woolf's indictment—informed by critical reflection rather than reaction—appears not in an equally polemic article but rather in his first novel since leaving England, *Prater Violet* (1945). As in Woolf's essay, the left bourgeois artist is criticized in this novel for scapegoating his own class in embarrassment over his class positioning and consequently for writing propaganda rather than art. *Prater Violet*, like *The World in the Evening* (1954) that follows it, in which Woolf appears in the figure of the novelist Elizabeth Rydal, elaborates on Woolf's aesthetic style of formulating political critique from the perspective of the "microcosm." Rather than explicitly engage historical politics in her novels, Woolf, like Isherwood's Rydal, "tried to reproduce them in miniature, the essence of them," namely, violence, misogyny and homophobia, the oppressive social practices of everyday life.[11]

In naming her essay "The *Leaning* Tower"—suggesting not only class, political, and artistic positioning—Woolf intimates, perhaps, a vantage from which the 1930s writers should be writing. "Leaning" connotes a "tendency," to cite a synonymous term made prominent by queer theorist Eve Kosofsky Sedgwick, a position that is athwart, not "straight," which is "queer."[12] Feminist literary critic Shari Benstock suggests that Woolf was critical not only of the hypocrisy of this group of writers but also of the putative "secret heart of [their] poetry," with its "component elements of public school homosexuality and reaction against bourgeois values."[13] It may rather be the case that Woolf was encouraging them to theorize this aspect of their social lives, a call to which Isherwood was already responding. Indeed, Erin Carlston perceives a shared politics in the social positions these writers occupied as a woman and as homosexuals in 1930s Europe. In *Thinking Fascism: Sapphic Modernism and Fascist Modernity*, Carlston notes:

The homosexual or bisexual members of the Auden group . . . shared Woolf's understanding that the "private" realm of sexuality is inherently political, and that the regulation of sexual expression is one of the critical functions of patriarchal structures of domination. . . . They realized, as she did, that to be disloyal to patriarchy—by flouting the paradigms of compulsory heterosexuality . . .—is ultimately to be disloyal to the *patria*, to call into question the terms of one's membership in the national community.[14]

Just as Woolf had compared the British patriarchy to fascism for its ideological oppression of women, Isherwood critiqued English constructions of masculinity and the power of the state, church, medicine, and family to normalize sexuality, an ideology he referred to as "fascist filth." Given these similar outlooks, Hermione Lee can thus claim in her biography *Virginia Woolf* that upon Isherwood and Auden's departure from Europe in 1939, "She did not join in the general war-cry against them as queer traitors."[15] Woolf wrote against oppressive heterosexist attitudes when she coupled the politics of women and gay men not only in *Mrs. Dalloway* but also in her late novels *The Years* (1937) and *Between the Acts* (1941), a theme Isherwood likewise takes up in *The World in the Evening*. If Isherwood did not later outwardly identify his shared politics with Woolf, he was clearly moved by her work, as his praise of *Mrs. Dalloway* illustrates and which becomes apparent in *A Single Man*.

In *Mrs. Dalloway*, Woolf critiques the power of doctors to institutionalize and therefore silence Septimus, the shell-shocked soldier who attempts to speak the truth both about the violent effects of war and about the suppression of same-sex affection and grief over this loss. Scholar Elaine Showalter has effectively outlined the hostility shell-shocked soldiers received in Great War–era Britain. Perceived as a form of war resistance and a deliberate retreat from masculine duty, traumatized soldiers were often ignored, denied adequate psychological treatment, and ridiculed as cowards, as Woolf effectively illustrates in her novel. *Mrs. Dalloway* brings the issue of sexuality to bear on "masculine duty," which requires the suppression of feelings for those of one's own gender.[16] The grief Septimus might feel over the loss of another man is not socially acceptable, and it is this proscription that is socially traumatizing.

It is precisely through the war, however, that Septimus develops affection for Evans. Although he volunteered for the war to protect an icon of English identity, Shakespeare, what Septimus comes to realize upon his return home is that "love between man and woman was repulsive to Shakespeare."[17] He and Evans—who was "undemonstrative in the company of women"—"had to be together, share with each other, fight with each other, quarrel with each other" (84). But this relationship is not allowed expression, and Septimus, well trained in the rituals of normative masculinity, does not or cannot mourn when Evans is killed. Indeed, he "congratulated himself upon feeling very little and very reasonably. The War had taught him. It was sublime" (ibid.). Septimus loses this relationship just before the Armistice, only to marry just after when, ironically, "the panic was on him—that he could not feel" (85).

The novel implicitly links Septimus's inability to acknowledge his feelings for Evans to his shell-shocked or traumatized existence. Writing on soldiers' experiences during the Great War, Sigmund Freud identified trauma in his 1914 essay "Remembering, Repeating, and Working Through" as a response to an event that cannot be incorporated into the psyche and so is repressed or "forgotten"; it is that which cannot be represented—or spoken.[18] Unable to be integrated into a narrative the mind can process, the event can only be known belatedly and expressed indirectly. It appears in acts compulsively repeated, not willfully remembered, and thus has a "ghostly quality" that interrupts the present with the past. Woolf clearly correlates the discourse of shell shock with the discourse of masculinity and the proscriptions against "feel[ing] too much for a man," as Showalter discusses ("Male Hysteria," 193). What must be forgotten, yet cannot be, is Evans.

Evans consequently appears to Septimus throughout the novel as a ghostlike presence. Walking through Regent's Park with his wife Rezia, Septimus "sees" Evans: "There was his hand; there the dead. White things were assembling behind the railings opposite. But he dared not look. Evans was behind the railings!" (24). Septimus cannot will these appearances and so feels anger when Rezia interrupts this image. He does not want to let Evans go. Later Evans *speaks* to Septimus from behind a screen in the couple's apartment. It is at this moment that "the great revelation took place": Septimus realizes that "Communication is health; communication is happiness, communication—" (91). Woolf's use of aposiopesis, breaking off Septimus's utterances in the midst of his truth telling, narrativizes his silencing; he knows what it is he cannot speak.

Septimus's silencing is made more emblematic through his impending institutionalization and eventual suicide, which his doctors read as "cowardly"; they cannot hear Septimus's "great revelation," though it is communicated to Clarissa and to the reader. When Clarissa hears of this man's suicide, she is compelled to reflect on love—*his* as well as her own. She wonders: "But this young man who had killed himself—had he plunged holding his treasure? 'If it were now to die, 'twere now to be most happy,' she had said to herself once, coming down in white" (180). Clarissa here alludes to her memories earlier in the novel when she recalls being at Bourton as a young woman with Sally Seton. She feels for Sally the intensity of heterosexual love:

> "If it were now to die 'twere now to be most happy." That was her feeling—Othello's feeling, and she felt it, she was convinced, as strongly as Shakespeare meant Othello to feel it, all because she was coming down to dinner in a white frock to meet Sally Seton! (34)

Clarissa's treasure is a kiss she shares with Sally after which "she felt that she had been given a present, wrapped up . . . a diamond, something infinitely precious" (35). Like the doomed figures of her allusion, however, Clarissa's love for Sally is infiltrated by the outside world. Here, impressed upon by heteronormative society, Woolf's character is not able to express or act upon this love.

Clarissa thus wonders whether others have likewise forced Septimus's soul or, *"had he plunged holding his treasure?"* If Clarissa's mourning for Septimus, neither the ritualistic grief of the Victorian era nor the consolatory grief of war commemoration, nevertheless finds closure— "She felt glad that he had done; thrown it away" (182)—the novel does leave Septimus's grief unresolved. Clarissa intuits his suffering, sustains it through her question. Through this "doubling," Woolf fully connects Septimus's death to society's unwillingness to sanction same-sex love.

Woolf's representation of *Septimus's* mourning—a mourning resistant to closure yet that ends in suicide—compels the question of the relation between mourning and madness (or melancholia). Around the time that Freud published his work on trauma, he produced his now classic work on mourning and melancholia. Both texts were shaped by the experiences of the Great War. Freud regarded mourning as a "normal" process of working through grief by withdrawing one's attachment to the lost object.[19] Melancholia he considered a pathological form of grief in which one undergoes "an extraordinary fall in . . . self-esteem, an impoverishment of . . . ego on a grand scale" (155). Although Woolf did not begin reading Freud until the close of the 1930s, she was well aware of the pathologized discourses of grief that preceded him. Susan Bennett Smith points to links made between grief and madness in the first decade of the twentieth century by Dr. George Savage, one of Woolf's own doctors.[20] In *Mrs. Dalloway*, Woolf counters theories that mourning leads to madness by illustrating instead that it is the *proscriptions on mourning* that lead to "madness," thus Septimus's last words of defiance as he leaps from the window: "I'll give it you!" "It was their idea of tragedy, not his," he thinks moments before (146).

By the 1930s, the "Auden generation" was certainly well versed in Freudian discourse. Whether or not Isherwood himself had direct knowledge of "Mourning and Melancholia," his representation of grief in *A Single Man* advances an understanding that mourning a loved one is without end—though for Isherwood, unlike for Freud, this sustained mourning need not be pathological. And unlike in Woolf and the particularized case of the traumatized soldier, society's proscriptions do not lead to madness but to anger and, ultimately, to empathy. Resistant throughout his body of work dealing with pathologized views of homosexuality, Isherwood forwards in this novel a truth about the silencing of same-sex mourning and at the same time portrays an experience of grief that is common to all.

Although scholars acknowledge the loss George has experienced in *A Single Man,* analysis of this loss tends to remain less thematically important than the novel's Vedantist views of eternal existence. Brian Finney, for example, points to the novel's "elementary presupposition which the Vedantist shares with anyone who believes that life of some sort continues after death—that the everyday conception of the self is an illusion";[21] and Claude Summers argues in his recent comparison of Isherwood's novel with Tom Ford's 2009 adaptation that "Isherwood's great theme is the transience of mundane existence when seen from the perspective of eternity."[22] David Garnes points instead to the novel's affirmation of life, viewing George as a "vital and passionate being."[23] And although its predecessor opens with a love of life, ends with the celebration of Clarissa's existence at its close ("For there she was" [190]), and offers a consolatory sense that people continue on in each other's memories after death, *A Single Man* is throughout marked by loss and ends with the imagined death of its protagonist. The reader is thereby confronted with the reality of loss—it is without resolution.

As with *Mrs. Dalloway,* Isherwood's reader encounters the protagonist on an ordinary day; George is an Everyman. The novel's opening thus poses an ambiguity for the reader: whose voice is narrating and whose life is being narrated? "Waking up begins with saying *am* and *now,*" the narrative voice begins. As this being gains consciousness, it is able to recognize "*I,* and therefrom deduced *I am, I am now*" (9; emphasis in original). With whom is the reader meant to identify, the narrative voice or the observed object, and are these the same entity? As the novel moves seamlessly between its narrative omniscient voice and interior monologue without the shifting perspectivism of Woolf's novel, the reader becomes intimately connected to George.

Despite its opening narrative of an emerging consciousness just waking, *A Single Man* is nevertheless more concerned with dissolution. The narrating consciousness soon realizes that every "now" it has experienced is "obsolete," about to pass on. What lies ahead is death, thus the *twitch* of the "vagus nerve," that core nerve of life that brings voice and sound and connects brain to heart to lungs. The novel's consciousness moves from the pronoun "I" to "it" to "he," a simultaneous gain and loss of individual and social identity reflected in the mirror in an image that retains "the face of the child, the boy, the young man, the not-so-young man—all present still, preserved like fossils on superimposed layers, and, like fossils, dead" (10). The recognition of the self that the *"I am"* expresses exits as the ambiguous pronoun "it" appears. It is only when the reader learns the name of this consciousness, George, that identification can take place. Thus the displacement from "it" to *"he"*—a gendered product and performance that "others must be able to identify" and whose "behavior must be acceptable to them" (11).

Yet George's behavior is not acceptable to others. Living in a house in the California suburbs in 1962, formerly with his partner Jim, George's neighbors fear that he will no longer "be ignored, explained away"; he is "the unspeakable that insists, despite all their shushing, on speaking its name" (27). Not fully considered human, George is a "monster" whose "unspeakable" identity has been created by statistics, psychology, therapy, and so-called liberal tolerance to exclude him from the majority as "Other." Isherwood creates ambiguity over whether this annihilation is figurative or literal, however. In a tone mocking the thoughts of his neighbors, George states a truth for same-sex couples in 1960s America: "this kind of relationship can sometimes be almost beautiful—particularly if one of the parties is already dead, or, better yet, both" (28). Only in death can such behavior be deemed "acceptable" to heteronormative society.

The cruel irony of the neighbor's attitudes, however, is that "Jim is dead. Is dead" (13), and it is this loss that gives gravity to the other reflections on death and loss in the novel. Jim has died in a car accident, yet George cannot publicly mourn him. He understands that Mrs. Strunk who lives across the little bridge that separates his house from his suburban neighbors "would enjoy being sad about Jim! But, aha, she doesn't know; none of them know" (28). George triumphs in keeping secret Jim's death so that his neighbors do not triumph *over* this death. He chooses to preserve his relationship with Jim and the memory of Jim's life. In response to his neighbor's questions, George tells Mrs. Strunk "that Jim is fine" (29). The alternative is to subject their relationship to further scrutiny, to psychologizing, to "exorcism," indeed, to the eradication of their life together (ibid.).

The anger George feels is never fully outwardly articulated, however, at least not by George. Just as his sexuality cannot be "spoken" in mid-century suburban America, George's rage over his treatment cannot be uttered either—both must remain private, an expression of his fantasies (an imperative Isherwood resists through the very writing of this novel). Enraged by mainstream media's articles on "sex deviates," for instance, George can only imagine revenge against the editors who publish stories that foster fear of homosexuals. His daydream of settling scores extends as well to the police who raid gay bars and to the "ministers who endorsed the campaign from their pulpits," all of whom "understand only one language: brute force" (38). Through "their words, their thoughts, their whole way of life," they "willed" the annihilation of Jim's existence, George thinks (40). If Isherwood enacts the reality of George's silencing through interior monologue, he nevertheless voices a pointed critique of the conservatism of the Cold War era, during which, according to historian John D'Emilio,

> Homosexuals and lesbians found themselves under virulent attack: purges from the armed forces; congressional investigations into government employment of "perverts"; disbarment from federal jobs; widespread FBI surveillance; state sexual psychopath laws; stepped-up harassment from urban police forces; and inflammatory headlines warning readers of the sex "deviates" in their midst.[24]

It is these very institutional forces—psychiatry, the police, government, and mass media—that George condemns privately at a moment when it was dangerous to do so publicly, as Isherwood well knew. One hears in George's voice, then, the pleas of his author: "What is this life of ours supposed to be *for*," he asks; "Are we to spend it identifying each other with catalogues . . . ? Or are we to try to exchange *some* kind of a signal, however garbled, before it's too late?" (174; emphasis in original).

Throughout the novel, Jim resurfaces in George's present just as Evans appears to Septimus, though not as a return of a repressed mourning. Instead, their life together is composed for the reader. What materializes is a deeply connected, committed, and loving relationship, the memories of which are intricately woven into George's interiority, threaded through his domestic space, across the landscape and into the lives of others. George needs these memories to imagine a possible future, to know that amid the hatred, "he must love . . . he must live" (182).

Yet, the question of George's survival becomes ambiguous as the novel reaches its close, as George returns to his bed at the end of his long day for the loss of consciousness everyone experiences through sleep. It is this loss, however, that assures George's connection to others—"that consciousness which is no one in particular but which contains everyone and everything, past, present and future, and extends unbroken beyond the uttermost stars" (184). This dissolution is met with the real or imagined death of this body, such that the loss of George remains with the reader. There is no other character upon whom to displace grief, no other character whose mourning might be consolatory and with whom the reader might identify. It is grief that survives, then, in answer to the question George contemplated earlier in the day: "what exactly it is that survives?" (15). It is no wonder that Isherwood had at one time considered calling the novel "The Survivor." Isherwood sustains loss to connect wholly the protagonist/narrator and the reader; we experience the loss of a voice we have come to know.

Isherwood's particular strand of frankness, writing a novel with a gay male protagonist explicitly critical of the society that would shun him, lends a difference in pitch to A Single Man from the novel that precedes it and so conveys the nature of Isherwood's style. Had Woolf lived long enough to read Isherwood's novel, she would likely have taken issue with the scatological imagery she found abhorrent in Ulysses, but she would also likely have commended Isherwood's keen observations and truthful portrayal of same-sex desire, just as she had stood in support of Radclyffe Hall's lesbian novel, The Well of Loneliness, when it was brought to trial for its explicit subject matter in 1928. In their efforts to speak the truth in Mrs. Dalloway and A Single Man, Woolf and Isherwood convey a shared political aesthetic philosophy that literature can articulate a counterdiscourse to the social proscriptions against same-sex desire and public mourning when this love is lost. If Woolf provided Isherwood with inspiration, it was nevertheless one of subtle intonation and implicit expression. Such subtlety was not Isherwood's style in the years following his departure from a repressive England and fascist Europe. It would be left to him to render this critique explicit.

Notes

1. See Carola M. Kaplan, "'The Wandering Stopped': An Interview with Christopher Isherwood," in The Isherwood Century: Essays on the Life and Work of Christopher Isherwood, ed. James J. Berg and Chris Freeman (Madison: University of Wisconsin Press, 2000), 272.

2. Christopher Isherwood, *The Sixties: Diaries, Volume Two: 1960–1969*, ed. Katherine Bucknell (New York: Harper, 2010), 217.

3. See Armistead Maupin, "The First Couple: Don Bachardy and Christopher Isherwood," in *Conversations with Christopher Isherwood*, ed. James J. Berg and Chris Freeman (Jackson: University Press of Mississippi, 2001), 193.

4. I bring Isherwood's memory of his father into the discussion here to elucidate the focus on mourning that *Mrs. Dalloway* motivated. A further reading of the connection between this memory and the Septimus/Evans relationship is Stephen da Silva's observation that "the father–son connection for Isherwood is inherently homoerotic." See Stephen da Silva, "Strategically Minor: Isherwood's Revision of Forster's Mythology," in Berg and Freeman, *The Isherwood Century*, 191.

5. Virginia Woolf, "The Hours," in *The British Museum Manuscript of Mrs. Dalloway*, ed. Helen M. Wussow (New York: Pace University Press, 2010), 412.

6. Virginia Woolf, *The Diary of Virginia Woolf*, vol. 2, *1920–1924*, ed. Anne Olivier Bell (San Diego: Harcourt Brace Jovanovich, 1978), 248.

7. Virginia Woolf, "The Leaning Tower," in *Folios of New Writing* (London: Hogarth Press, 1940), 171.

8. Christopher Isherwood, *Christopher and His Kind* (New York: Farrar, Straus and Giroux, 1976), 114.

9. Virginia Woolf, *The Diary of Virginia Woolf*, vol. 5: *1936–1941*, ed. Anne Olivier Bell (San Diego: Harcourt Brace Jovanovich, 1984), 59.

10. S. P. Rosenbaum, *The Bloomsbury Group: A Collection of Memoirs and Commentary* (Toronto: University of Toronto Press, 1995), 413.

11. Christopher Isherwood, *The World in the Evening* (1954) (Minneapolis: University of Minnesota Press, 1999), 119.

12. See Stephen Barber, "Lip-Reading: Woolf's Secret Encounters," in *Novel Gazing: Queer Readings in Fiction*, ed. Eve Kosofsky Sedgwick (Durham, N.C.: Duke University Press, 1997), 401–43.

13. Shari Benstock, *Women of the Left Bank: Paris, 1900–1940* (Austin: University of Texas Press, 1986), 407.

14. Erin Carlston, *Thinking Fascism: Sapphic Modernism and Fascist Modernity* (Stanford, Calif.: Stanford University Press, 1998), 181.

15. Hermione Lee, *Virginia Woolf* (New York: Alfred A. Knopf, 1997), 694.

16. See Elaine Showalter, "Male Hysteria: W. H. R. Rivers and the Lessons of Shell Shock," in *The Female Malady: Women, Madness, and English Culture 1830–1980* (New York: Pantheon, 1985), 167–94.

17. Virginia Woolf, *Mrs. Dalloway* (1925), ed. Mark Hussey (Orlando, Fla.: Harcourt Brace Jovanovich, 2005), 87.

18. Sigmund Freud, "Remembering, Repeating and Working Through (Further Recommendations on the Technique of Psycho-Analysis II)" (1914), in *The Standard*

Edition of the Complete Psychological Works of Sigmund Freud, trans. James Strachey (London: Hogarth Press, 1958), 12:150.

19. Sigmund Freud, "Mourning and Melancholia," *Sigmund Freud: Collected Papers,* trans. Joan Riviere (New York: Basic Books, 1959), 4:154.

20. See Susan Bennett Smith, "Reinventing Grief Work: Virginia Woolf's Feminist Representations of Mourning in *Mrs. Dalloway* and *To the Lighthouse,*" *Twentieth Century Literature* 41.4 (Winter 1995): 310–27.

21. Brian Finney, *Christopher Isherwood: A Critical Biography* (New York: Oxford University Press, 1979), 251.

22. Claude J. Summers, "*A Single Man*: Ford's Film/Isherwood's Novel," *GLBTQ: An Encyclopedia of Gay, Lesbian, Bisexual, Transgender and Queer Culture* (February 1, 2010; accessed August 4, 2011), http://www.glbtq.com/sfeatures/asingleman.html.

23. David Garnes, "*A Single Man*: Then and Now," in Berg and Freeman, *The Isherwood Century,* 201.

24. John D'Emilio, "Gay Politics and Community in San Francisco since World War II," in *Hidden from History: Reclaiming the Gay and Lesbian Past,* ed. Martin Bauml Duberman, Martha Vicinus, and George Chauncey Jr. (New York: NAL/Dutton, 1989), 459.

5

A Whole without Transcendence

Isherwood, Woolf, and the Aesthetics of Connection

WILLIAM R. HANDLEY

A "single" self is the starting point for the seemingly narrow canvas of what Christopher Isherwood referred to in his diary as his "novelette," *A Single Man*. I say "seemingly narrow" because the novel begins and ends in a single day with George, a character who can be taken to represent, when read in conjunction with Isherwood's diaries, the author's experiences, prejudices, and perceptions. Yet *A Single Man* is a more encompassing novel than either its title or the critical commentary on it suggests. Now an indispensable text in the canons of gay literature and of Los Angeles fiction, *A Single Man*'s interest extends beyond these important literary histories.

A profoundly environmentalist imagination is on display in this novel of mourning, missed connections, social alienation, and impending doom. The book's pervading sense of displacement and terminal loss (which Tom Ford's 2009 film reductively misrepresents as George waking up planning to kill himself) would seem to contradict the Vedanta philosophy Isherwood believed in, a metaphysics that asserts there is only one reality and that physical separation and temporal distinctions are illusions. David Garrett Izzo writes that "Isherwood the Vedantist believed that human-devised constructs of duality and time do not actually exist; there is no separation from, nor distinction between, twenty-four hours or twenty-four years."[1] Hence the microcosm of one day in George's life is also "the macrocosm of all his days." By this metaphysical logic, the novel would show us more than a single man's whole life in a single day, yet it does so in a manner that throws into negative relief Isherwood's sense of one reality. In what is perhaps his best work of fiction, Isherwood's environmentalist imagination illuminates the social, political, economic, personal, and natural conditions of a post–World War II and Cold War Los Angeles that are inseparable from each other and from George's experience during his day: they permeate everything from the city's built and natural environments to the recesses of George's psyche.

Around the same time that Isherwood wrote in his diary, "I seriously believe that I am, beyond all comparison, nastier and madder than ever before in my life," he declared this novel his "masterpiece" (as Auden later did also) and described it as his "most coherent statement."[2] The coherent statement the novel makes—a narrative in which "a single man" is fractured within himself and severed from both his dead lover and the world around him—is about the social and spiritual danger of dualisms that both construct and threaten lived reality at a time when the world was divided between two nuclear superpowers that had accepted a policy of mutually assured destruction (known as MAD). That policy inevitably involved the whole world and hence demonstrated—without anyone having to resort to metaphysics—Isherwood's Vedanta belief in nonseparability, or "pure nondualism": the belief that anything can be understood only in relation to everything else.

In Isherwood's diary as well as in his novel, there are references to the Cuban Missile Crisis and the threat of nuclear war: these historical conditions invade the thoughts of both George and his student, Kenny. But A Single Man is no more a political novel than it is a religious or spiritual one. If A Single Man has to do with politics or spirituality, it is realistically about their failure. While Isherwood often expresses in his diaries feelings of defeat that are echoed in A Single Man, this is not a novel of despair and hopelessness. As in Ralph Waldo Emerson's essays, the recurrent focus on what socially fails suggests what coheres behind appearances: a sense of metaphysical Oneness that the realities of cause and effect within time and space—the core interests of narrative art—would seem to contradict.

By contrasting A Single Man with the novel that inspired it, Virginia Woolf's Mrs. Dalloway, and by analyzing paintings of Los Angeles by James Doolin, I explore how aesthetic forms that aim to be both realistic and experimental can help us productively imagine social and political reality and the ethical relation between ourselves and the environment—without having to subscribe to any metaphysical assumptions, such as Vedanta or Emersonian transcendentalism. Through the lens of a single man, Isherwood challenges his readers, in a manner that metaphysical systems of thought also do, to understand the relation of all of the parts to a larger whole—both the larger whole of the novel and the world it represents. The aesthetic problem of understanding and interpreting the relations of the parts to the whole in Isherwood's novel aligns with the philosophical misapprehension—or crisis of ideas—that underlies a civilization's inability to understand and address what threatens civilization itself.

Isherwood understood the inseparability of the personal and the political. He came to Los Angeles on the eve of what became a cataclysmic war, after his lover Heinz Neddermeyer was conscripted into Hitler's army. World War II and the Cold War that followed were proof enough to Isherwood that history would never conform to metaphysics. But neither could his art. As a writer, he was an inveterate realist, even rendering his most subjective feelings with a clinical detachment, and nowhere more so than in the figure of George, a character who resembles him in many ways while seeming to lack Isherwood's powers of self-observation.

In fact, Isherwood resembled his character enough to worry a couple of his friends. Edward Upward, Isherwood writes, "wouldn't mind if George were further disguised, that is, made less like me."[3] Gavin Lambert, Isherwood records, "is concerned about George's identity. He feels that George's way of speaking and his attitude to his college job are so absolutely me that one cannot accept him as an independent character. This may well be true. But I'm not sure that anything can be done about it." But in a later interview, Isherwood said, "I feel that if I were really George, I would kill myself. Poor devil, what has he got? Nothing! And for me, sitting here in all the snugness of my life, it's terrible to be told that I am George!"[4] Yet, as he was writing the novel he recorded that he was reading through his diary "for possible bits" he could use: "Oh my God, it is so depressing! The sheer squalor of my unhappiness" (*The Sixties*, 264). And a few days later: "I have been reading through all these diaries and feel absolutely toxic with their unhappiness" (265). The disconnections among Isherwood's unhappiness, his spiritual beliefs, and the artistic success of this novel are suggested in a passage in the diary on September 19, 1963: "In case *A Single Man* is later thought to be a masterpiece, may I state that it bores me unutterably to reread? Going through it is really a grind" (290).

From Plato to Melville, from Whitman to Ginsberg, from Woolf to Morrison, writers have attempted to reconcile metaphysics with narrative art, to pit them against each other, or even to try, mystically, to enact metaphysics through language. Isherwood never attempted to write a novel that largely conformed to his metaphysical beliefs. *A Meeting by the River* is, in part, his dramatization of the intimate differences between belief and art. Isherwood expounded on his religious beliefs in his autobiography *My Guru and His Disciple* and in his biography *Ramakrishna and His Disciples*. Although *A Single Man* is not an overt statement of his philosophy, it can be read as demonstrating a social and spiritual need for Vedanta's core principle that there is one reality without division. As in *Mrs. Dalloway,* its inseparable threads have nothing to do with conventional plot and everything to do with the relation of each thread to all the others. In her introduction to *Liberation,* the final volume of Isherwood's diaries, Katherine Bucknell describes a quality in them that I would argue is also true of Isherwood's aesthetic sensibility, one in which "every thread" touches upon, reinforces, and contrasts "with every other thread, so that the rich cloth of his own life also portrays the fleeting sensibility of his time."[5]

One way Isherwood weaves threads in the novel is by creating homologies among nature, human beings, and technology, especially the homology between "this live dying creature" that is George's body and the growth and decay of Los Angeles.[6] Called "it" at this early point in his day, George looks at his face in a mirror: "it sees many faces within its face—the face of the child, the boy, the young man, the not-so-young man—all present still, preserved like fossils on superimposed layers, and like fossils, dead" (10). Later in the novel, the narrator describes how Los Angeles will die of overextension, when only a few years earlier George had felt he was in the midst of "primitive, alien" nature in "the half-light of dawn" as he witnessed coyotes "bounding . . . with great uncanny jumps" (111). What is "uncanny" is at once alien and familiar, strange for its hidden familiarity. George both identifies with and feels alienated from other minorities, and even from his own recognizable body. Homologies such as this between George and the city he lives in, both having undergone defamiliarizing change almost simultaneously, encourage a reading of narrative elements in tandem—not least because they come from a single character's consciousness and because this novel is not *this* novel when its thematic and other parts are treated separately. In a book that foregrounds seeming dualisms between youth and age, between past and present, between England and America, between Los Angeles neighborhoods and the ethnicities of its citizens, and between the body and the mind, the challenge is to read these differences and dualisms as inseparable, without falling into universal or metaphysical claims, if only because they share the same text and the problem of difference. This important novel in gay literary history is also about its setting in time and space: it is about Los Angeles, seen from an adopted, Far Eastern philosophical stance as disconnected from a singular, true reality.

A single self is also the starting point of Woolf's *Mrs. Dalloway*, which Isherwood reread before writing *A Single Man*. *Ulysses* in turn influenced Woolf's scheme for her novel. Titled after their main protagonists and sharing themes of separation and alienation, these works both obey and violate the three classical unities of drama derived from Aristotle's *Poetics:* the unity of a main action with no distracting subplots; the unity of place; and the unity of time (the story should take place within a day). James Joyce's early-twentieth-century Dublin, Woolf's post–World War I London, and Isherwood's Los Angeles vividly surround and inform Leopold Bloom, Clarissa Dalloway, and George. But, unlike the vast scholarship on *Ulysses* and *Mrs. Dalloway*, criticism of *A Single Man* often ignores or treats as accidental the city in which it is set. One can understand why: George, the novel suggests, is an unsuccessful transplant from England. Unlike George, Isherwood was quite at home in Los Angeles. Shortly after he finished *A Single Man*, Isherwood had to take a disrupting trip to Japan and recorded in his diary sentiments akin to his character's: "I feel dazed with unreality—which simply means unrelatedness. They have pulled me up by the roots . . . and dumped me down here. I can't be transplanted" (*The Sixties*, 306).

A paradox of all three novels is that their protagonists are so imbricated in a world they often feel separate from—and it is a paradox that Joyce had to exile himself to re-create his Dublin. Postwar Los Angeles inescapably informs *A Single Man*'s aims and meanings, not in spite of its recurring theme of rootlessness or its author's expatriate status but precisely in relation to them. Born of Isherwood's experience as an exile in a city he observed while intensely observing himself, *A Single Man* cries out for a connection to Isherwood's belief in one ultimate, nonseparable reality that he adopted through the study of Eastern religion in this western city. If the environment of Los Angeles is necessarily inseparable from our understanding of George and of Isherwood's belief in nonseparability or pure nondualism, what then is the reader to make of a title that seems to name an isolated part and that refers not at all to the environment?

Isherwood's novel itself seems to ask the reader to question its title. Lecturing to his students at the fictional San Tomas State College about Aldous Huxley's novel *After Many a Summer Dies the Swan*, George discovers they are unaware of the Greek mythic source behind the title's allusion to Tennyson's poem "Tithonus." He chides them: "I must say,

I don't see how anyone can pretend to be interested in a novel when he doesn't even stop to ask himself what its title means" (63). After an excursion into the myth of Tithonus, whom Zeus made immortal while denying him youth, such that he "gradually became a repulsively immortal old man" (65), George says, "'But before we go any further, you've got to make up your minds what this novel actually *is* about.'" "At first," Isherwood writes, "as always, there is blank silence. The class sits staring, as it were, at the semantically prodigious word. *About. What is it about?*" (66). The reader of the novel is suddenly sitting in that classroom, and Isherwood is asking her to make up her mind what *A Single Man* actually *is* about.

The reader might be forgiven for not having a ready and reductive answer, given that after he finished the first draft of the novel on February 3, 1963, Isherwood recorded in his "Writing Notebook" that he was "still not absolutely clear what this is about. If pressed I would have to call it a study in the psychology of middleage."[7] To several of its early reviewers, the novel was simply and appallingly about homosexuality: "feeble and disgusting," wrote the reviewer for the *Los Angeles Times* (Parker, *Isherwood*, 634). Many see it now as a pathbreaking gay novel; others see George as a kind of Everyman whose singularity makes him both individual and general, sharing in the problem of human separation. In an interview with Isherwood in 1965, George Wickes asked him if he felt the American critics had "very often missed the point" of the novel, adding, "To treat this as a homosexual novel is to overlook a much bigger subject." Isherwood replied, "What I have done in this particular novel is to write, among many other things, about minorities" (Berg and Freeman, *Conversations with Christopher Isherwood*, 44).

If we are interested in *A Single Man,* then, we too must ask what its simple but richly evocative title—which Don Bachardy proposed late into the drafting (*The Sixties,* 283)—is "about." A euphemism for a homosexual akin to "confirmed bachelor," which resonates with George's sense of alienation and paranoia about how others see him, the title suggests both particularity ("single") and universality ("a man"), something determinate and indeterminate. In describing a particular kind of human being—a homosexual—it nonetheless calls up the whole problem of identity and difference, of how a single man is different from but related to everything and everyone else around him—in a city and a nation composed of many minorities but with a powerful majority in the early 1960s. The relationship between the metaphysics of Isherwood's Vedanta philosophy (the belief that there is only one reality and identity is an illusion) and the realities of American democratic society (in which a *Pluribus* is not necessarily an *Unum*, let alone one nation under God) is one of the richest and most interesting underlying tensions in a novel that almost obsessively tracks the abstract or categorical labels of identity and the analogical language that negotiates difference and similarity. Isherwood ironically points to the failure of equality in American democracy through the faux-utopian moment when George is in the gym, a refuge of Whitmanian brotherhood, and thinks, "How delightful it is to be here. If only one could spend one's entire life in this state of easygoing physical democracy. . . . Nobody is too hideous or too handsome to be accepted as an equal. Surely everyone is nicer in this place than he is outside it?" (109).

There is, of course, a tradition in American literature that enacts these tensions, in Emerson and Whitman especially: can a metaphysics of unity be brought to bear upon a messy and divided plurality of citizens? And what literary form might that take? While Isherwood believed in the metaphysics of Vedanta—whose idea of the Brahman or Atman is akin to Emerson's Oversoul (indebted as it is to Asian thought rather than Christianity)—*A Single Man* is not a paean to democratic unity. As much as Vedanta had in common with Whitman's democratic transcendentalism, Isherwood might have called his book "A Leaf of Grass" if he had wanted to allude to Whitman. A narrative enactment of transcendentalist or dialectical unity did not interest him; the perception of reality did.

That the novel throws into negative relief Isherwood's metaphysical assumptions realistically suggests the difficulty of overcoming the self, as Vedanta and other forms of Transcendentalism challenge believers to do. It is ironic that Virginia Woolf, an atheist who held no metaphysical beliefs, created a narrative form in *Mrs. Dalloway* that Isherwood's novel does not attempt: the tunneling through and weaving together of multiple consciousnesses within a narrative voice that both disappears into and hovers over the characters it creates and listens to. I said that Isherwood's novel represents his beliefs *almost* only negatively, because there is one rare moment of the sort of omniscience that we see frequently in Woolf's novel. The narrative voice describes rock pools up the California coast. When the tide is out,

> Each pool is separate and different, and you can, if you are fanciful, give them names, such as George, Charlotte, Kenny, Mrs. Strunk. Just as George and the others are thought of, for convenience, as individual entities, so you may think of a rock pool as an entity; though, of course, it is not. . . . just as the waters of the ocean come flooding,

darkening over the pools, so over George and the others in sleep come the waters of that other ocean—that consciousness which is no one in particular but which contains everyone and everything, past, present and future, and extends unbroken beyond the uttermost stars. . . . the waters of the ocean are not really other than the waters of the pool. (183–84)

Influenced by Vedanta thought, this passage reads as if Emerson were describing his impersonal sense of nondifferentiability. Yet art relies on difference, and Isherwood's novel is obsessed with different social identities. The passage is an odd confessional moment in a novel that otherwise has nothing to preach.

Elsewhere and throughout much of it, the novel relentlessly depicts *not* nonseparability but separation and alienation, especially as effects of identity, politics, and war. One of George's students feels she cannot marry a Caucasian because her Japanese-American family was sent to an internment camp near the Sierra during the war; another is self-conscious that she is the only black student in his class; another, that the whole world is anti-Semitic—and George feels alienated from his neighbors onto whom he projects all kinds of homophobic assumptions: "Mr. Strunk, George supposes, tries to nail him down with a word. *Queer,* he doubtless growls" (27). One of George's colleagues has at various times "suggested they go and heckle a John Birch Society meeting, smoke pot in Watts with the best unknown poet in America, meet someone high up in the Black Muslim movement" (86). The same colleague tells him that some computer experts have argued that "it doesn't really matter if there's a war, because enough people will survive to run the country with" and that you should build a fallout shelter without letting anyone know what you're building, or else "if word gets around that you have a better type of shelter, you'll be mobbed at the first emergency" (87). In all of the older political crises from the twenties and thirties, each one of which "has left its traces upon George, like an illness—what was terrible was the fear of annihilation. Now we have with us a far more terrible fear, the fear of survival. Survival into a Rubble Age, in which it will be quite natural" for neighbors to gun down neighbors who don't have enough food stored, before they get dangerous (87–88). George traverses separate neighborhoods in the city throughout the day while hearing on his car radio about an array of threats, from Cuba to sexual deviants. And as the hours pass, he puts on various selves both to satisfy and to distance others with whom he interacts.

In a sardonic clue to the novel's underlying philosophy, Isherwood writes, "George cannot talk to another human being as if the two of them were alone when, in fact, they aren't. Even such a harmless question as 'What do you *honestly* think of Emerson?' sounds indecently intimate" (56). The pervasive paranoias and antagonisms both within George and on the airwaves reveal, like mutually assured destruction, the nonseparability of all things, and this sense of inseparability is demonstrated at the novel's end by how a tiny plaque that began forming years before in George will destroy all the outlying regions of George's body in one terrifying instant.

Like the novel it inspired, *Mrs. Dalloway* depicts a postwar society divided against itself. The alienated world in Woolf's novel is in dire need of following her friend E. M. Forster's injunction in the epigraph to his 1910 novel *Howards End,* "Only Connect." Both reflecting and defying a sense of alienation born of a crisis about the future of civilization, Woolf's narrative form makes connections and contrasts among characters and their thoughts, in particular by moving to another character's thoughts whenever Big Ben's chimes, slicing and dividing the day, impose uniformity. The shell-shocked war veteran Septimus Smith, cut off from his dead comrade Evans and from his wife, contemplates the kinds of radical and mystical connections that the narrative formally makes. He thinks, "leaves were alive; trees were alive. And the leaves [were] connected by millions of fibres with his own body. . . . All taken together meant the birth of a new religion."[8] Although she and her double, Septimus, never meet, Clarissa Dalloway is given similarly expansive thoughts about her connection to everything around her, even beyond her powers of perception:

> She felt herself everywhere; not "here, here, here" . . . but every-
> where. . . . So that to know her, or anyone, one must seek out the
> people who completed them; even the places. Odd affinities she had
> with people she had never spoken to . . . even trees . . . It ended in a
> transcendental theory which . . . allowed her to believe, or say that she
> believed (for all her scepticism), that since our apparitions, the part
> of us which appears, are so momentary compared with the other, the
> unseen part of us, which spreads wide, the unseen might survive, be
> recovered somehow attached to this person or that, or even haunting
> certain places after death . . . perhaps—perhaps. (232–33)

Whether or not Clarissa's sense of what might survive one's death is born of Woolf's atheism, it finds expression in the novel's narrative form (and not just because the novel survives Woolf). That form enacts what no one human being could have but which novels and films routinely attempt:

something like a godlike knowledge. Despite his beliefs, Isherwood did not represent the interpenetration of consciousnesses in his fiction. Woolf's faith in imaginative empathy, her deep sense of the interconnection between people and their environment ("even [with] trees") makes *Mrs. Dalloway* a novel not just about a party or one day in London, any more than *A Single Man* is about a day in Los Angeles. Woolf's deep trust in the artistic imagination makes her novel at one moment both unbelievable and moving. At the party, Clarissa is told just that a young war veteran has killed himself. With empathetic intuition, she understands accurately how he did it, and why. This kind of radical connection in the "real world" of Woolf's novel does not occur in Isherwood's novel of missed connections, despite the fact that he, unlike Woolf, believed in a metaphysics—which is given expression in the somewhat didactic yet moving moment about rock pools.

Another artistic representation of nonseparability across time and space that does not resort to metaphysics concerns the city in which *A Single Man* is set: four murals by James Doolin, completed in 1996 and set over two floors in Los Angeles's Metropolitan Transportation Authority building. They depict Los Angeles in four temporal frames: 1870, 1920, 1960, and after 2000. Another of Doolin's paintings, of a freeway overpass near downtown Los Angeles, was reprinted on the cover of Mike Davis's apocalyptic take on the city, *Ecology of Fear.* That both the MTA, presumably interested in the promotion of the city's development, and Davis, patently offended by what the MTA, the Department of Water and Power, and the LAPD created, would choose Doolin to represent the city in a sense speaks to what is so subtly ambiguous and compelling about Doolin's realistic paintings. In Doolin's four MTA murals, we might recognize sequential or linear images of progress in certain stages of development, from the pastoral to the global twenty-first century. But we are also encouraged to see what becomes, or rather has become, lost, starting with the colors green and blue, which are already besmirched in 1870 by train engine exhaust and in 1920 by the built environment and a dozen columns of smoke. The freeway system becomes visible in 1960, as does a thin layer of brown smog, and by "circa after 2000," the freeway system has become the city's exoskeleton. This is a visual story of both decline and growth, of a city's youth and age, and seen collectively, the murals make them seem to be happening simultaneously. The tension derives from the context of these murals' setting, in which these large images of past and future are spatially side by side and above and below each other. This arrangement

Four murals by James Doolin depict the city of Los Angeles in 1870, 1910, 1960, and circa after 2000. Courtesy of Koplin Del Rio Gallery, Culver City, California.

of the murals is impossible to see in their setting on two floors of the MTA building, but it is how Doolin intended them to be seen in relation to each other. The lines of concavity between these images of Los Angeles across time suggest contiguous space. Each image has a differently shaped frame, but collectively they are an image without a frame, as if seen from some Emersonian enormous eye: the view points north, south, east, and west, from some centered congruence of not just directional space but also of time. It is all happening now, was all happening then, and the future is the product of the past. A capitalist economy seems to accelerate time through the growth of the built environment—as Isherwood witnessed in Los Angeles both before and after the war that transformed the U.S. economy.

Doolin's mural of Los Angeles "circa after 2000" depicts a city that resembles dying embers that yet hold the promise of that beautiful, pollution-derived twilight, the promise of something to be born. This is the tension in Isherwood's novel that is played out not just on George's face: Los Angeles is both young and old, creative and destructive. George recalls driving in the past into the Hollywood Hills as a "venturing into the midst of primitive, alien nature." But on a drive he takes this day, he can feel nothing of that "long-ago excitement and awe" as he has to swerve to avoid other cars on blind corners. Even at the top of the hill, "they are building dozens of new houses. The area is getting suburban," and he becomes "oppressed by awareness of the city below":

> On both sides of the hills, to the north and to the south, it has spawned and spread itself over the entire plain. It has eaten up the wide pastures and ranchlands and the last stretches of orange grove; it has sucked out the surrounding lakes and sapped the forests of the high mountains. Soon it will be drinking converted sea water. And yet it will die. No need for rockets to wreck it, or another ice age to freeze it, or a huge earthquake to crack it off and dump it in the Pacific. It will die of over-extension. It will die because its taproots have dried up—the brashness and greed which have been its only strength. And the desert, which is the natural condition of this country, will return. (111)

George's perspective is similar to the vantage point Doolin depicts. What especially interests me about Doolin's murals is not just what we are seeing or how it illustrates what Isherwood describes, but *how* we are seeing it: in the circa 1870 mural, the only thing in the image that would permit a bird's-eye view is, well, a bird; in 1910 it is a balloon; in 1960 and circa 2000, it is airplanes, helicopters, and a blimp. (These are very small on these large murals and almost impossible to discern in the reproductions here.) In all of the murals, the viewer is impossibly positioned: these are fantasies of historical vision that recall Walter Benjamin's angel of history: spatializations of time from a sufficiently high perspective. Doolin's eye does not presume an Emersonian Oversoul, but it does seek to imagine time through space in a kind of simultaneous vision of historical change. Such representations envision the nonseparability of all parts of the whole, and there is no way to see a single man as simply single, unconnected to the whole picture. Yet the capacity for that vision derives from transportation technologies that have changed the color of the sky and the surface of the land. The famous earth shot from the moon is the culmination of this technological and visionary trajectory yet inseparable from the nuclear weapons to which rocket technologies had been harnessed during the Cold War—the potential destruction of the whole as negative proof of nonseparability.

That terrifying potential looms over Isherwood's novel. On the car radio, George hears a senator saying that "we should attack Cuba right now, with everything we've got. . . . The senator does not deny that this will probably mean rocket war" (37). George repeats back to his student Kenny what he has heard him say: "The past—no help. The present—no good. Granted. But there's one thing you can't deny; you're stuck with the future." Kenny responds, "I guess we are. What's left of it. There may not be much, with all these rockets—" "Death," George responds. "The future—that's where death is" (156–57). The homologies between George and the city he lives in are nowhere more apparent in this novel than here: George will die in the future, of course, but the rockets Kenny refers to that might spell death for civilization are being created in Los Angeles, a major reason the city is growing.

Isherwood's Los Angeles is clearly a post–World War II and Cold War city, whose creatively destructive energies and growth are indebted to a postwar economy that is transforming its social makeup. George's neighborhood of Camphor Tree Lane is a microcosm of this change:

> Maybe camphor trees grew here once; there are none now. More probably the name was chosen for its picturesqueness by the pioneer escapists from dingy downtown Los Angeles and stuffy-snobbish Pasadena who came out here and founded this colony back in the early twenties. . . . Their utopian dream was of a subtropical English village with

> Montmartre manners: a Little Good Place where you could paint a bit, write a bit, and drink lots. They saw themselves as rear-guard individualists, making a last-ditch stand against the twentieth century. (17–18)

Native to Asia, camphor trees have not made a successful transplant: the name evokes a false nostalgia for a rooted past. Escaping an already crowded western metropolis, Isherwood's pioneer colonists are bohemian throwbacks to a bygone era that is now changing all over again:

> The Change began in the late forties, when the World War Two vets came swarming out of the East with their just-married wives, in search of new and better breeding grounds in the sunny Southland; which had been their last nostalgic glimpse of home before they shipped out to the Pacific. . . . So, one by one, the cottages which used to reek of bathtub gin and reverberate with the poetry of Hart Crane have fallen to the occupying army of Coke-drinking television watchers. (18)

With his recurrent misogyny and heterophobia, George blames the wives for explaining to their husbands "that breeding and bohemianism do not mix" because "for breeding you need a steady job, you need a mortgage, you need credit, you need insurance." He imagines his students are equally locked into a heterosexual economy of production and reproduction: "What do they think they're up to, here? . . . preparing themselves for life which means a job and security in which to raise children to prepare themselves for life which means a job and security in which" (47). The campus's built environment reflects a relentless cycle of "destruction-reconstruction-destruction" with bulldozed hills and "tract upon tract" of dormitories that "are being opened up as fast as they can be connected with the sewers and the power lines." He imagines that ultimately "the campus will be cut off from the outside world by its own parking lots, which will then form an impenetrable forest of cars abandoned in despair by the students during the weeklong traffic jams of the near future" (43). (Anyone who lives in an urban area in the twenty-first century might think: that near future has already passed.) George, we are meant to infer, is like his environment: cut off from the outside world and from his taproots.

A Single Man is a worthy and original successor to the novel that inspired it, given these novels' deeply environmental sense of the inevitable, spiritually promising, and often tragic relation between any person and everything else. While *A Single Man* is less sentimental and mystical—that is to say, more realistic—than *Mrs. Dalloway,* both of these great novels are realistic in representing the failure of a collective relation between the subjective and the social. Inviting us to make connections between the title characters and the cities (and civilizations) they live in, they challenge us to understand the larger historical stakes of their literary worlds.

One such stake in *A Single Man* that I want to suggest in concluding this essay is how Isherwood delineates difference in sexuality with difference in economies and their consequent temporalities: the homosexual poet Hart Crane is linked with rearguard nineteenth-century pioneer individualism while the suburban heterosexual family is linked with a postwar economy of consumerism and pollution. (The street has two signs: one warning not to eat the watercress along the polluted creek; the other, "Children at Play.") My point is not about the historical accuracy of such a sexual and economic delineation but about how, as Jamie M. Carr writes in *Queer Times: Christopher Isherwood's Modernity,* the modernist concern with time and history meets up with a modern crisis of sexuality in Isherwood's work and, I would argue, also in Woolf's. Isherwood was attracted to Vedanta in part because it accepted his sexual orientation. But it also offered a metaphysics that contradicted time and space and hence made meaningless linear notions of progress associated with the heterosexual family. Influenced both by his Vedanta beliefs and by his unceasing realism, Isherwood's greatest novel makes a single, alienated man inseparable from the world around him. Set on one day in 1962 and written in the present tense, *A Single Man* reads as if it were written today.

Notes

1. David Garrett Izzo, *Christopher Isherwood: His Era, His Gang, and the Legacy of the Truly Strong Man* (Columbia: University of South Carolina Press, 2001), 223.

2. Christopher Isherwood, *The Sixties: Diaries, Volume Two: 1960–1969,* ed. Katherine Bucknell (New York: Harper, 2010), 291.

3. Christopher Isherwood, *Diaries, Volume One: 1939–1960,* ed. Katherine Bucknell (New York: Harper, 1996), 287.

4. James J. Berg and Chris Freeman, eds., *Conversations with Christopher Isherwood* (Jackson: University Press of Mississippi, 2001), 44.

5. Christopher Isherwood, *Liberation: Diaries, Volume Three: 1970–1983,* ed. Katherine Bucknell (New York: Harper, 2012), xiv.

6. Christopher Isherwood, *A Single Man* (1964; reprint, Minneapolis: University of Minnesota Press, 2001), 10–11.

7. Quoted in Peter Parker, *Isherwood: A Life Revealed* (New York: Random House, 2004), 618.

8. Virginia Woolf, *Mrs. Dalloway* (1925; reprint, Orlando, Fla.: Harcourt, Brace & World, 1953), 32–33.

Ford Does Isherwood

KYLE STEVENS

Explicating film scholar André Bazin, Colin MacCabe claims that "the cinema promotes a new form of adaptation in which the relation to the source text is part of the appeal and the attraction of the film."[1] I believe that such textual layers and multiple affective registers are especially significant in the case of *A Single Man*, Christopher Isherwood's 1964 novel about a man, George, mourning the death of his lover, Jim, adapted for the screen in 2009 by fashion designer Tom Ford. Between the two authors' two Georges—both of whom are thus present in the film—lies the emergence of the public struggle for gay and lesbian acknowledgment in American social and political milieus. In this essay, I will explore what *A Single Man* becomes for 2009, how it remembers gay identity in the early 1960s, and how it imagines the "epistemology of the closet" for its current moment's sexual politics—a pivotal moment when gay and lesbian citizens live between cultural acknowledgment and acceptance.

That is, I want to look at Ford's film through the lens of adaptation in order to think about how it thinks back on the novel, how it reflects its own historical moment, and what the intersection of those coordinates locates. Some actions from Isherwood's book make the leap from page to screen directly, such as the moment Jim and George canoodle on the couch reading. Other aspects of the novel, such as the context of paranoia yielded by the Cuban Missile Crisis and Cold War mentality, are given only a nod by the film, as in a hilarious cutaway shot to a "typical" family's bomb shelter. Still other aspects are retained with alteration, such as casting Latin American model Aline Weber as Lois, a character of Asian descent in the original story. Finally, there are countless events in and facets of the novel that do not appear in the movie, such as George's musings while driving and his descriptions of the layout of Los Angeles. Similarly, gone are the remarkably timely observations about higher education, such as when George laments the condition of students as "raw material . . . fed daily into [the university] factory" that would find echo that year during the Free Speech Movement at the University of California in Mario Savio's famous speech.[2]

Ford also injects myriad original elements, including a host of autobiographical details that invite reflection on the movie's authorship. Indeed, *A Single Man* may present a unique case in American film history: a debut work from an *already* famous, and famously gay, director (Ford also cowrote the screenplay and funded the project). Thus, the film is something of a hybrid: both Isherwood's story and Ford's personal tale. Ford's most significant—and contentious—decision was to have George intend to commit suicide. Given that gay characters in pre-Stonewall-era literature typically hid or wrestled with their desires before meeting a dismal fate, Isherwood's depiction of George as unashamed of his sexuality was decidedly forward-thinking. In the context of the early 1960s, then, and the novel is set in 1962, Isherwood's book can be construed as a conscious intervention into the literary history of the homosexual character type, a political argument that gays are neither perverse, nor mad, nor self-destructive.

Yet we might now see George's suicidal desire in Ford's film differently from Isherwood, for Ford's George's desire to kill himself does not stem from self-loathing. In fact, the film's political argument is not about gays' personal judgment, but about their public acknowledgment. While Jim's death motivates George's malaise and existential crisis in the novel, the movie suggests that George is equally upset by the denial of their love by those like their friend Charlotte and Jim's brother. Indeed, it is the devastatingly cold telephone conversation between Jim's brother and George, in which George is perfunctorily told of Jim's death and barred from the funeral because he is not family, that is the most moving moment in Ford's version.

Isherwood's book foreshadowed the sexual revolution and "permissive society" that arrived in the latter 1960s; Ford's emendation also proved slightly ahead of the times. A rash of suicides by young gay men occurred across America in 2010. Although suicide rates for queer youth have long been (and continue to be) disproportionately high, these suicides were different in that the devastating notes left behind did not just consist of shame and self-loathing, but contained accounts of horrific treatment by others. The issue garnered national media attention after Rutgers University student Tyler Clementi jumped off the George Washington Bridge (which was the third suicide of nine in the month of September alone).

These suicides were a shock to the many scholars and activists who believed that cultural visibility in mass media including film and television was the path to gay acceptance. Nevertheless, media attention to the 2010 suicides departed from past coverage (or lack of coverage) by portraying these teens as victims of bullies, homophobic laws, and anti-gay organizations. For the first time, mainstream media outlets assumed a relatively sympathetic audience when reporting on LGBT issues. Legally, the nation was freshly tolerant of homosexual acts: in 2003, a United States Supreme Court ruling, *Lawrence v. Texas,* struck down "all state laws criminalizing consenting sexual behaviors between adults."[3]

Yet cultural attitudes toward homosexual desire and sex acts ultimately say little about cultural attitudes toward gay and lesbian relationships, for to desire something is not necessarily to *care* about it. Accordingly, the heart of the political matter in Ford's *A Single Man* is the acknowledgment of love, not just the validation of sexual desire for "deviant" object choices. Ford's depiction of Isherwood's loving couple—despite being rendered "safe" by having one half already dead at the start of the narrative—has particular historical urgency because same-sex marriage, has, for better and worse, surfaced as the index of equality (this, despite the fact that citizens can still legally be evicted from rented homes or fired from jobs in a majority of states because of their sexual orientation). While many liberals are wary of espousing such "bourgeois" forms of belonging or institutions over freer ways of being, Ford's film is timely *because* it insists that spectators recall the nation's past performances of closeted relationships (not just closeted individuals) in order to consider how to go about revising them in the cultural imaginary.

Playing in Tom Ford's Closet

Before I consider how Ford takes up Isherwood's meanings and transforms them in and for the cinema, I want to briefly look at how the movie was immediately understood, for its reception speaks to the persistence of stereotypes that the film seeks to undermine. In a curious way, Ford's reception mimics that of Isherwood, who was not respected owing to the perceived "lowbrow" nature of his content: "If a writer's themes were Los Angeles, gay life, and alternative religion, then his books were not significant."[4] As we will see, Ford adds to the themes of Los Angeles and gay life a preoccupation with beauty, and his own reception as director suggests that the stereotype of the gay man as aesthete understands a lover of beauty to be shallow, to love only beautiful surfaces, as though surfaces (not ideas, reactions, jokes, and so forth) are the only beautiful objects. Some of the backlash began in the gay community, which disapproved of the advertising campaign that "straightened up" the movie's content by suggesting—according to a heteronormative gaze that projects romance onto a man and woman pictured together—that stars Colin Firth and Julianne Moore play characters that are romantically linked. In fact, the characters did have sex, and Charlotte (Moore) is in love with George (Firth). Ire was heightened when Ford stated that his film was "not a gay film,"[5] meaning that the gay context was simply *there,* and was not the primary catalyst of events.[6] However, Ford's comment was taken as a crass ploy to reach a wider audience. Attacks by those who would have preferred a more orthodox approach to adapting Isherwood's novel grew so strong that Isherwood's partner of thirty-three years and inspiration for the novel, Don Bachardy, publicly defended Ford in an interview for the London *Times.* The interviewer declared, "*A Single Man* is being discussed not as an impressive debut but as a debate on gay politics and the pitfalls of adapting seminal works. Not since Steven Spielberg directed the slave epic *Amistad* in 1997 has a director's identity politics been such a part of a film's buzz."[7]

Upon the film's release, reviewers also saw it through the lens of Ford's gay identity and past as a fashion designer. *Village Voice* critic Scott Foundas's notice is exemplary for circulating stereotypical notions about New York's gays as circuit queens, for instance, when he avers that, for Ford, it is "better to look good than to be good" and likens Ford's style to "Napoleonic gym rats flaunt[ing] their overdeveloped musculature."[8] He proclaims that Ford prefers "extravagant surfaces over the lower depths of meaning and emotion," advising audiences to "think of it as *Vogue Hommes: The Movie*" (Foundas is perhaps alluding to the fact that Ford's partner Richard Buckley, a renowned figure himself, was the former editor in chief of *Vogue Hommes International.*)[9] Stephanie Zacharek of Salon.com decides that Ford is "a designer at heart," while others resort to calling him "fastidious," a term analogous to euphemisms such as "controlling" that plague female filmmakers.[10]

However, conjecture about Ford's commitment to flamboyance has little textual or biographical evidence. Ford moved from Santa Fe to New York in the 1980s to pursue a career as an actor, landing multiple commercial campaigns, and garnering a reputation as "one of the city's great beauties."[11] During this time, he found himself in a circle of artists that included David Hockney, who introduced him to Isherwood; Ford "read everything [he] could find by Isherwood . . . and became a bit obsessed with him" (Sessums, "Tom Ford Tells All"). He decided to take a degree in architectural design from the New School, but, upon graduating, found he wanted to try his hand at designing clothes. He rocketed through the ranks and became famous as creative director of Gucci from 1996 to 2004, taking the house from the brink of bankruptcy to the center of the couture world. Ford then left because he was disinterested in the business demands of maintaining "the first global [fashion] superbrand."[12] He was publicly "out" during the 1980s and 1990s (a crucial time when few celebrities were open despite the reality that, as AIDS descended, "silence equaled death"), and, in 2007, Ford received the Gay and Lesbian Alliance Against Defamation's Vito Russo Award (GLAAD's lifetime achievement award) for his years of cultural visibility and philanthropy.

The insinuation that Ford could not be a fashion designer, gay, *and* intellectually deep was even stronger in gay-oriented media outlets, which resentfully fixated on Ford's good looks to disparage him as a gay "aesthete." One story that circulated widely in online media alleged that Ford called Firth "fat" and told him to lose weight and get a fake tan.[13] Besides its vilifying aims, the piece assumes that choices involving a character's "look" must reflect Ford's personal taste in men. (Even if Ford *did* impress a gossip as rude to Firth, how often is the work of ostensibly straight male directors judged on their rudeness?) In fact, the hero of the novel spends the happiest hours of his day at the gym and makes quite a show of "peeling off his tee shirt" while competitively and erotically outperforming an adolescent boy at sit-ups—quite a feat given that he is fifty-eight (108). The novel is also "about" Los Angeles—in 2003 the *Los Angeles Times* voted it "*the* L.A. novel"—and what is more "L.A." than a tan?

I do not mean to imply that Ford was fanatical about fidelity to the novel, of course. His signature is in every aspect of the film; indeed, it literally appears in the film as he writes and signs a note as George. Isherwood's hero is simply named "George," while Ford's "George Carlyle Falconer" shares Ford's own middle name and the surname of his first lover, well-known illustrator and designer Ian Falconer. His partner of twenty-three years, Richard Buckley, also appears in the film—and in the same shot as Don Bachardy. There are several anecdotes from Ford's own life: for example, one about taking mescaline. In Isherwood's novel, Jim and George share a house offset from the neighborhood by a small bridge. Rather a lot is made of this sagging, isolating stretch; it even plays a key role in their choosing this abode. Ford moves George onto the street—perhaps a picture of the sort of political "tolerance" endemic to Ford's historical generation of American gays that emerged in the 1980s and 1990s. And it seems that once George moves off the island, he must confront the pain of his otherness.

Waking Up

From the movie's first scene, Ford evinces a sophisticated awareness of the means and methods of adapting a novel and of cinema. *A Single Man*, the movie, begins with shots of a naked George drifting in water, then cuts to him visiting the scene of Jim's death, which we realize is a dream when he starts awake in bed. The sleeping George looks dead, and the voice-over plays with the idea of his nonexistence in a reworking of Descartes's cogito straight from the novel: "Waking up begins with saying am and now." When Isherwood's George relates his mental life, it is in the third person, allowing his inner monologue to judge not just his activities but the flow of his thoughts (such as a genocidal fantasy as his mind wanders while driving). Although the book avoids sentimentality, we are drawn deep into George's psychic territory. (Hearing our own voices in our heads as we read his words plays no small part here; it makes his voice just a bit our own, giving a sense of him as an "I," for we cannot hear our own voices any other way.) Ford tells of being moved by the novel's third-person point of view and attests to wanting to suggest that we are "listening to George's soul speak *about* George's earthbound self."[14] However, the source presents just one George to us, though we are acutely aware of the gap between his self-presentation and his private thoughts. As an adaptation, the sense that there are already two Georges (Ford's and Isherwood's) is further complicated by the perception not just of George's body, but of Firth's. What is more, the movie presents us with two diegetic Georges, the one we hear in voice-over in the opening and closing scenes and the one we see and hear for most of its duration.

But the force of Ford's opening salvo is not simply in the voice-over. When George awakens from the gruesome but beautiful vision of Jim's car crash on a snowy road, in which he bends to kiss Jim's corpse, black ink is spilled on the sheets by his hips and stains his lower lip (suggesting the "kiss of death" he has just shared). This image establishes not only that George is a writer and that he writes in his bed, but that he writes *through* his bed, that his bed is a realm of expression. Ford then cuts quickly to a side angle shot of George's body, then to his face, then

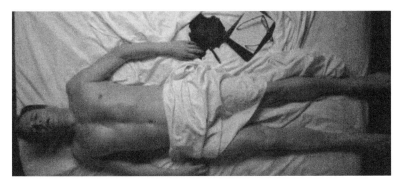

"Waking up begins with saying am and now." Film still from *A Single Man*, directed by Tom Ford.

feet, then face, then hands. By intercutting shots of his face (the locus of subjectivity on-screen) with shots of his corporeal extremities, we see him waking up, becoming painfully conscious of his embodiment in this present: his dream is not reality and Jim is still gone.

The logic of Ford's montage indicates that the dream manifests the ink stain, and we might ourselves awaken to the suggestiveness of this image. Two kinds of "expression," language and semen, come together as the consequences of two ways it is said that repressed content manifests, that is, as two kinds of dreams: the common kind and the "wet" variety. This image of writing with, and, at the same time, as, semen visually puns the term "expression" and suggests that we think of the results of sexual desire and sexuality—in this case, the expression of sexual fluid—as self-expression (even, since George appears alone, as expression of self *to* self). Bringing together instruments of writing, color, and sex under the rubric of expressivity informs us that the conjunction of George's writerliness and sexuality authorizes him to "tell" his story. From the start, then, this is a story of a gay man, a sexual man, and a single man—an argument that such a person can "have" a sexuality (and that it does not only consist of performative acts with others, as some theorists would have it). This may remind us of the novel's cathartic final moment—gone from the film's narrative—in which George conjures up a scenario involving the young men he has met that day and masturbates; he learns that sexual desire is something to be reflected upon, written with the mind and body (identifying the writer with the sexual desirer). Isherwood's George learns to arrive at the little death. Ford's must learn how to achieve the big one.

The Dream Factory

There is clearly a sexual charge to George's dream, and, not surprisingly, given the long-standing analogy between cinema and dreaming, Ford's *A Single Man* self-reflexively considers film's impact on relations of sexual desire and perception. Isherwood's novel is very much concerned with the effects of living in Los Angeles in 1962. Ford amends this to include "the dream factory" as L.A.'s original basis, perhaps most conspicuously via a billboard still from Alfred Hitchcock's 1960 watershed, *Psycho,* of heroine Marion gazing terrified directly forward as she is murdered for being the object of the abject Norman Bates's desire—for any sexual desire for a woman is taboo to Norman (who, in a meta-cinematic move, gazes at her through the frame of a peephole prior to his attack). Our perception of Marion's face perceiving her killer—is it Norman? Us?—is to see her beautiful face *as* afraid, an image of the erotic tension between desire and fear.[15] *Psycho* changed how America thought about looking and sexual desire, bespeaking the anxiety—and consequent titillation—over desire, beauty, gender identity, detection, and visibility.

Marion's face overlooks the scene in which George talks to a handsome hustler (a figure of Ford's creation), Carlos (played by a prominent model in Ford's fashion campaigns). Carlos, cruising the parking lot in broad daylight, seems to be the most "indecent" character in the film—which is also to say, the one with the most mastery over his sexuality. Just as Hitchcock frequently aligned spectators' perspectives with those of his heterosexual male heroes as they gazed at women's bodies, Ford aligns us with George through another series of cuts; we gaze with him at Carlos's beauty in lingering shots of his eyes and lips. But if Norman Bates needed a peephole (which is, *Psycho* suggests, part

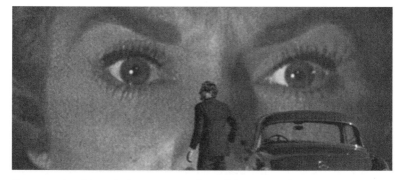

George as the object of Marion's gaze. Film still from *A Single Man.*

of his problem), here none is needed; looking erotically at a man is already taboo. Just stealing glimpses in the context of 1962 is titillating (as when, in another scene in the novel, George leers at two tennis players on campus).

The second cinematic reference I want to spotlight is to Wong Kar Wai's 2000 masterwork *In the Mood for Love*, set in Hong Kong, also in 1962. *In the Mood for Love* formally plays with visibility in various ways; it is full of shadows, smoke, rain: obfuscation so heady that it slows time. There are several subtle allusions to that film in *A Single Man*, including repeated shots of similar-looking clocks and the introduction of characters to the scene via shadows or reflections. But the starkest connection can be heard in the film's score, and in how a beautiful, plaintive leitmotif accompanies slow-motion sequences—a staple trope of Kar Wai. In fact, Ford commissioned *In the Mood for Love*'s composer, Shigeru Umebayashi, to write music for *A Single Man*. Moreover, the narrative of *In the Mood for Love* is also concerned with romance, secrecy, and detection. It follows two neighbors who discover that their spouses are having an affair with each other. The protagonists attempt to learn how such a thing could come to be, and so stage a series of dates, trying to perform their way into understanding adulterous behavior. Events are ambiguous, but it seems that they become overwhelmed by the excitement of this clandestine endeavor, and that they, too, have an affair.

What is especially pertinent about *In the Mood for Love* with regard to *A Single Man* is that the couple's relationship is so romantic *because* it is modeled on the "perverse" affair of their spouses, *because* it is secret, because it is closeted. It reminds us that what one puts in a closet reflects who one is. It is a space to prepare the performance: not outside of ideology or influence, but not quite public yet (like the green room/office that George uses before entering the classroom with, to use Isherwood's phrase, his "psychological makeup" on). From its opening scene, *A Single Man* reminds us that, to a degree, we write the scenes we act out. We may not get to invent the vocabulary with which we script our lives, but to a great extent, we choose our scene partners and are still responsible for delivering our lines correctly. Adopting particular identities is a way of thinking one's self into a way of being, not estranging or distancing oneself from a "proper self" (as involved in the phrase "playing a role"), but recognizing that we *think of ourselves* as being kinds of people, which entails certain beliefs, attitudes, anxieties, and so on.

The specter of secrecy in *Psycho* and *In the Mood for Love* points to a way of interpreting *A Single Man*'s attitude toward sexual identity and cultural visibility. The first time we meet Jim (in flashback), he and George are agreeing to buy their house, which is full of large windows and glass walls. George jokingly wonders if Jim "is ready to live in a glass house," to which Jim responds: "You're the one who's always saying we're invisible." Jim's line is echoed later in the film by Kenny, a student of George's, who, when George protests that he cannot walk back to the apartment naked after a late night swim in the ocean, replies, "We're invisible, don't you know that?"

In the audio commentary for DVD release, Ford underlines this dialogue, claiming that the historical treatment of homosexuals as invisible motivated him to make this film. We might again think of Ford as a member of a particular post-1960s generation of American gays concerned chiefly with cultural visibility and a politics of identity, which held "gay" to refer to a more or less coherent and nonfungible experience. Thus, the film presents three generations of gay identity: Isherwood's George, whose identity was fiercely internal and whose invisibility was taken for granted; Ford's George, who *worries* about his visibility; and the younger generation of Jim and Kenny, who *enjoy* their invisibility, who toy with its boundaries. Carlos even lives off it (and he does not seem to hate his job). In this way, the movie invites us to consider a newly possible gay identity predicated upon not *actually* wanting to live a closeted lifestyle, but wanting the *semblance* of straightness, or at least some control over the *degree* of one's visibility. In the beginning, we suffer with George as he is excluded from Jim's funeral, but now, Kenny revels in his culture's determination to avoid knowledge of his existence.

I want to consider one last filmic reference with this in mind. In a scene full of Freudian imagery, George visits his safe-deposit box deep in a bank vault, where he keeps mementos and totems of Jim. Locked away within the capitalist institution, this evidence of his sexual identity returns dividends *for* being locked away. One of these is a black-and-white nude of Jim. This image is strongly reminiscent of the style of Bruce Weber, known for erotic black-and-whites of men, and to Weber's own influence, German photographer Herbert List. (Although Jim is no bodybuilder, we might also be reminded of the proliferation of physique films and magazines in the 1950s, most notably in L.A. by Bob Mizer.) Weber is the man behind the late-1980s Calvin Klein campaigns and the "look" of the Abercrombie and Fitch clothing brand since the 1990s, which features nude or near-nude young adults. The white, muscular, and shaved body type propagated by these lines has become widely linked with gay visibility in America. And, of course, Ford's identity as

Jim, as George remembers him. Film still from *A Single Man*.

a designer and fashion photographer may play a role in our perception
of this reference.

We might see the photograph as betokening Ford's generation, which
laid claims to visibility. However, this visibility has been taken to task by
the subsequent generation as sedimentation, not valorization. In recent
years, young gays have coined the term "Aberzombie" to refer to a particular "cookie-cutter" "gay look" and books like Dwight McBride's *Why
I Hate Abercrombie and Fitch* have acknowledged the brand's hegemony
while challenging the physical expectations associated with such a narrow definition of male beauty.[16] George withdraws his personal effects
from the bank (he's putting everything in order as he's planning to shoot
himself that evening) and later, Kenny, with whom he has just shared a
late-night drink and a naked swim, finds the photo. Despite their salacious interactions, it is this photographic evidence that solidifies George's
sexual proclivities for Kenny, and he summarily proceeds to offer himself
(also naked) to George.

I don't think it's a coincidence that Ford—expanding Kenny's role in
the novel—represents the younger generation for a 2009 audience by having Kenny invite George to "look first" when he strips on the beach before
proposing sex later (after seeing the photograph). Isherwood's George
recalls a postwar cruising area where homosexuals gathered, one that
suggested the promise of sex before gazing at the other's naked body.
Today, the appearance of social networking Web sites like Manhunt.com
and Adam4Adam.com and smartphone apps like Grindr (which started
in L.A.) have made an enormous impact on gay courtship behavior, and
it is standard in such venues for the image of nakedness to precede sex,

or at least the promise of sex. These popular technologies reverse Isher-wood's order of events by permitting users to play with visibility through options of "public" and "private" photos so that one can unveil one's (constructed) identity with increasing titillation. Visibility becomes a continuum, yet still serves as the matrix along which gay sexual desire is noted and revealed. Similarly, one has only to take the briefest of glances at the flourishing gay porn industry to make out the obsession with bedding "straight" guys (often entailing deception or revenge fantasies), and the longing for the transgressive sex act that relies on the existence of the closet as the major selling point and source of attraction. And, as Linda Williams observes: "If we have learned anything from Foucault it is that discourses of sexuality . . . are forms of publicity in which technologies of print, photo, film, video, and digital forms of pornography have been particularly important."[17] Similarly, that George is played by openly straight Firth may also excite some spectators.

While George's Weber-esque photo signifies one thing to Kenny, it means something else to George. This is how he remembers Jim. We know from a flashback that George took this image in the middle of the desert, at a complete remove from society. This image highlights the film's depiction of their relationship as romantic for being secluded, diverging from traditional schemata of romance. Most famously, in *Deceit, Desire, and the Novel,* René Girard demonstrates the importance of the triangulation of desire in the history of Western literature (which, he believes, reveals the reality of desire). As David Shumway puts it, the "love triangle" is "a convention that is nearly indispensable to the [history of Western] romance and the novel," and Eve Kosofsky Sedgwick views this triangle, which traditionally consists of men competing to win possession of a woman, "as expressing otherwise repressed homoerotic desire."[18] For Girard, desire is "mimetic" as the choice of object the hero comes to desire is not determined by that object itself, but because he learns to imitate a third person, a rival "mediator," to whom his attention is misdirected (Girard discusses love amazingly little and its relation to desire is unclear). If gays have been trying to win paramours away from all of society for so many centuries, how humbling now to face other mortal men.

However, in this idyllic portrait of Jim and George, there is no need for mediation, there is no rival (that is, arguably, save all of society). Theirs is a highly romantic picture of closeted love, a fantasy of being the only two people in the world. Thus, *A Single Man* proffers a gay relationship as a closed circle—a schema visually reinforced by casting, as both men are about the same height and build (they look like movie stars, too). There is never any indication that either Jim or George corresponds to traditional masculine and feminine gender roles (nor is either connoted a "top" or "bottom"), and when we see them meet it is in a two-shot (rather than the shot/reverse shot sequence frequently employed in heterosexual romance narratives). Moreover, telling the story audiovisually requires that we perceive Jim's body and voice in the present before us, rather than filtered through George, as in the book. Seeing and hearing Jim provides access to *his* thoughts and emotions, rather than George's recounting of them, allowing him, too, to be a site of identification. Compared to the novel, the story becomes more *theirs* than strictly George's, inviting spectators to reflect on the depiction of gay *relationships*.

In light of the changing cultural attitudes and new technologies mentioned earlier, the movie arrives when—and for the first time—visibility is becoming an option. Ford's *A Single Man* reveals that with this visibility comes the possibility of real flesh-and-blood rivals—as in the presence of Kenny, the ersatz modern gay figure who "long[s] for the kind of setup" George has. It seems visibility opens the doors to nostalgia for invisibility. In Ford's early 1960s, without a rival, Jim and George find each other *inherently* desirable—a reciprocity viably called love. Neither must pursue nor "win" the other. But despite the timeliness of Ford's promotion of gay love, we should be wary lest his film fool us into a historically problematic longing for a pre-1960s sexual revolution and an overly romanticized notion of carrying on a relationship in private: a closet without suffering.

With this in mind, we might see Ford as faithful to Isherwood's intention of tearing down the closet walls to an extent. In 2009, when, in many areas of the country, gays could be open about their sexual orientation, they still could not have their relationships acknowledged by the nation through the institution of marriage. (In 2013, in *United States v. Windsor,* the U.S. Supreme Court declared unconstitutional Section 3 of the Defense of Marriage Act defining marriage as between a man and a woman.) And there emerged a fascination by gays with what was, for the first time in history, lost: secrecy. This mourning for the taboo nature of sexual encounters threatened to rebuild the closet, and showed that self-respect was not sufficient for social freedom. Gays could respect their own sexual identities privately, and so participate in the maintenance of the closet at large.

In this context, it matters that Ford shows the depth of loss (via suicidal desire) when cultural acknowledgment of one's emotional subjectivity as a lover is withheld. In turn, his invitation to the spectator to acknowledge gay coupledom is progressive. Perhaps this is why Ford could not include one of Isherwood's most poignant aspects of George and Jim's relationship, which had a degree of openness to it. It was loving, yet stable enough to allow Jim to pursue his sexual curiosity outside its confines (not unlike Isherwood and Bachardy's relationship as documented in *Chris & Don: A Love Story*).

Ultimately, though, the cinematic *A Single Man* illuminates how our memory of the closet inflects our attitudes toward it now—and who better understands the function of a closet than Tom Ford? Almost every scene involves the question of the past returning, from the specter of Jim in George's dream to Charlotte reminiscing about England to Carlos recounting his journey to America. Seen from this perspective, Ford *had* to make an adaptation; this form shapes and echoes its content. Thus, despite its differences and 2009-pertinent story, the film version of *A Single Man* directs spectators outward, too, to remember Isherwood, his novel, and the stories we tell about the vicissitudes of sexual identity in the 1960s.

Notes

1. Colin MacCabe, Kathleen Murray, and Rick Warner, eds., *True to the Spirit: Film Adaptation and the Question of Fidelity* (New York: Oxford University Press, 2011), 5. A different version of this essay, "Dying to Love: Gay Identity, Suicide, and Aesthetics in *A Single Man*," was published in *Cinema Journal* 54.2 (Summer 2013).

2. Christopher Isherwood, *A Single Man* (1964; reprint, Minneapolis: University of Minnesota Press, 2001), 47.

3. Harry Benshoff, "(Broke) Back to the Mainstream: Queer Theory and Queer Cinemas Today," in *Film Theory and Contemporary Hollywood Movies,* ed. Warren Buckland (New York: Routledge, 2009), 193. In 2004, Massachusetts became the first state to ratify gay marriage, and, in 2010, the "Don't Ask, Don't Tell" military policy prohibiting homosexuals from serving openly was repealed. At the time of this writing, nineteen states and the District of Columbia offer same-sex marriages. No federal same-sex marriage rights are currently recognized, though this issue seems to be in constant legal flux.

4. Dan Luckenbill, "Isherwood in Los Angeles," in *The Isherwood Century: Essays on the Life and Work of Christopher Isherwood,* ed. James J. Berg and Chris Freeman (Madison: University of Wisconsin Press, 2000), 34.

5. Jeffrey Podolsky, "Tom Ford on *A Single Man*: 'This Is Not a Gay Film,'" *Wall Street Journal,* November 23, 2009.

6. Richard Dyer once commented on two ways to dismiss a gay film: "one is to say, 'Oh, it's just a gay film'; the other, to proclaim, 'Oh, it's a great film, it just hap-

pens to be gay.'" See B. Ruby Rich, "New Queer Cinema," in *New Queer Cinema,* ed. Michele Aaron (New Brunswick, N.J.: Rutgers University Press, 2004), 21.

7. Eric Gutierrez, "Tom Ford Was Right about Isherwood," *The Times* (London), February 5, 2010.

8. Scott Foundas, "Better to Look Good Than Be Good for Tom Ford's *A Single Man,*" *Village Voice,* December 8, 2009.

9. Prominent critics Peter Travers and Roger Ebert are two important exceptions to the critical rule. Travers called Ford "a true visionary," and Ebert did not assume that Ford's George's house and clothes were simply style for style's sake, but understood what they elucidated about character: "[Ford] has been faulted for over-designing the film, but perhaps that misses the point. Perhaps George has over-designed his inner vision." See Peter Travers, *"A Single Man," Rolling Stone,* November 23, 2009, and Roger Ebert, *"A Single Man," Chicago Sun-Times,* December 23, 2009.

10. Like the majority of critics, Zacharek credited Firth for the film's depth. She wrote that "Firth is a triumph of substance over style," and that he is "lovely" and it is "harder to be lovely than beautiful." See Stephanie Zacharek, *"A Single Man:* Tom Ford's shallow but compelling debut," Salon.com, December 9, 2009. Typically, when an actor has been around for decades and suddenly gives an enlightened performance, the director shares credit. For his part, Firth was outspoken about the quality of Ford's direction, repeatedly calling him a genius, and even thanking Ford for his artistic influence when he won his Academy Award as Best Actor the following year for *The King's Speech.*

11. Kevin Sessums, "Tom Ford Tells All," *Advocate,* December–January 2010.

12. Jess Cartner-Morley, "Tom Ford Rewrites Rule Book in Surprise Comeback Show," *Guardian UK,* September 13, 2010. Ford made a surprise return to fashion in 2010 (with looks inspired by *A Single Man*) with a private, no-cameras-allowed fashion show meant to be "a reaction against the mass and rabble that the industry has become."

13. Sarah Lyall, "He Wears a Revealing Sort of Restraint," *New York Times,* December 2, 2009.

14. Tom Ford, audio commentary, *A Single Man* (Sony Pictures, 2010), DVD.

15. Norman Bates is, of course, played by Anthony Perkins, an actor later known for having same-sex affairs and a friend of Isherwood's.

16. See Dwight McBride, *Why I Hate Abercrombie and Fitch* (New York: New York University Press, 2005).

17. Linda Williams, *Screening Sex* (Durham, N.C., and London: Duke University Press, 2008), 241.

18. David Shumway, *Modern Love: Romance, Intimacy, and the Marriage Crisis* (New York: New York University Press, 2003), 45. For a discussion of Sedgwick and Girard, see 238.

7

A Real Diamond

The Multicultural World of *A Single Man*

JAMES J. BERG AND CHRIS FREEMAN

Describing the relationship between novels and history, Jill Lepore suggests that "the novelist is the better historian . . . because he *admits* that he is partial, prejudiced, and ignorant, and because he has not forsaken passion."[1] There is no better novelist-historian than Christopher Isherwood, who wrote passionately and from a highly subjective point of view about the world around him.

Isherwood lived in Berlin in the early 1930s and in Southern California in the 1940s and after. He is recognized as a sharp-eyed chronicler of his time and place. In *Goodbye to Berlin*, first published in the 1930s, he anticipated the severity of that volatile cultural moment. His autobiographical narrator is the "man on the street"—and the streets are foreboding. The war is coming. Isherwood knows it, but many in his milieu do not. Of his landlady, for example, the narrator says, "She will adapt herself to any new regime. This morning I even heard her talking reverently about 'Der Führer' to the porter's wife."[2] Such is the banality of politics.

Thirty years later, Isherwood turned his attention to American culture as he experienced it in Los Angeles. In his 1964 masterpiece *A Single Man*, the protagonist, George, is an intelligent, heartbroken, somewhat cynical mouthpiece for Isherwood. In the film adaptation, as portrayed by Colin Firth, George plays the same function for first-time writer and director Tom Ford. The fashion designer has made the novel look beautiful, and some of the story's record of its time comes through as well.

Ford's film is complemented by an astonishing documentary from 2007. Filmmakers Tina Mascara and Guido Santi brought the story of Isherwood and his partner, the painter Don Bachardy, to life in their award-winning *Chris & Don: A Love Story*.[3] These two films provide a bridge between George's time and our own, in terms of sexual politics and social reality, and between print and visual media. These films do for *A Single Man* what Bob Fosse's *Cabaret* did for *Goodbye to Berlin*—they provide visual representation of a long-ago time and give viewers and readers points of reference for connecting the man, his work, and our times.

Isherwood's narrative style has been called documentary fiction. In *A Single Man,* which takes place during one day, George lives a variation of the author's life. Isherwood was not at that time a single man, having been in a committed relationship with the much younger Bachardy for almost a decade. The novel can be seen as a "what if" proposition: What if something happened to Don; what if Isherwood didn't have a network of gay friends to support him; what if he didn't have a spiritual basis (Vedantic Hinduism) for living his life?

As with any adaptation, there will inevitably be debate about the fidelity of the film to the novel. That is a question for Tom Ford. For academics, there is a level of interest and relevance for both versions of the text, in an extended classroom scene. Indeed, the longest scene in Isherwood's short novel takes place on the campus of San Tomas State College, the fictional locale of Los Angeles State College (now California State University at Los Angeles).

Isherwood wrote *A Single Man* after having spent several terms teaching at various colleges and universities in Southern California. At first he taught courses in the modern novel, but when he accepted a semester position at the University of California at Santa Barbara for the fall term of 1960, he was given a title for his lecture series—"A Writer and His World." He was thus free to talk about his best subject, himself, and the gestation and publication of his own work. Those lectures at UCSB shed light on Isherwood's process as well as his views on teaching.[4]

Two reminiscences of Isherwood's teaching have been published, both of which shed some light on Isherwood the professor. Dan Luckenbill, who retired from the research library at UCLA in 2006, became friends with Isherwood after taking a writing class from him there in 1965. Luckenbill writes: "Isherwood did not lecture in the strict sense. . . . The range of topics was probably staggering for almost anyone attending, let alone those of us who were young students." In preparation for the course, Luckenbill read *A Single Man,* which had just been published. He noted that the cover drawing of the author was by "Bachardy," which sparked the alert student's curiosity (shades of George's inquisitive protégé, Kenny). Luckenbill recalls that he was "startled that I found

Isherwood so attractive and was unable to fit his image with those of persons who shared his age."[5]

Michael S. Harper, the distinguished poet and professor at Brown University, was in Isherwood's first class at Los Angeles State College in the fall of 1959. He describes Isherwood as "no traditional teacher. . . . He maneuvered his bushy eyebrows in expressive wit encouraging us to enter the give-and-take of the classroom." Harper was an outstanding student who was also black and heterosexual; his intense respect and admiration for his mentor provide an inside view of the kind of man Isherwood was in the classroom, a sort of celebrity version of George. Harper believes that Isherwood had a strong but varied impact on a wide range of students. They realized later that Isherwood was "the only one of our teachers . . . who treated us [black male students] like men with no sense of condescension."[6]

More than any other teaching experience, Isherwood drew on his year at Los Angeles State for his portrait of college life in *A Single Man*. San Tomas State College lies at the foot of the San Gabriel Mountains, giving it "something of the glamour of a college high on a plateau of the Andes, on the few days you can see them properly." George likes the neighborhood, "a tacky sleepy slowpoke Los Angeles of the thirties. . . . How charming it is! . . . Mexicans live here, so there are lots of flowers. Negroes live here, so it is cheerful. George would not care to live here because they all blast all day long their radios and television sets. But he would never find himself yelling at their children, because these people are not The Enemy. If they would ever accept George, they might even be allies."[7] This diversity, surely, anticipates the kind of coalition building that almost rejected the anti-same-sex marriage Proposition 8 in California in the 2008 election.

Multiethnic Los Angeles is visible on the campus. But George is almost too much of an idealist—"a man trying to sell a real diamond, for a nickel, on the street. The diamond is protected from all but the tiniest few, because the great hurrying majority can never stop to dare to believe that it could conceivably be real" (48). George, like Isherwood, is appalled by the tyrannical majorities of the world, what Isherwood called "The Enemy." Among these enemies are George's straight-laced neighbors and their obnoxious children; local and national politicians; and even those at the college, which is "a clean modern factory, brick and glass and big windows, already three-quarters built . . . being finished in a hysterical hurry" (42).

Clearly, this is public higher education in California in the 1960s. Inside the classroom, the modern student body has taken shape. The students in George's class represent Southern California's multiracial society, which the rest of the country barely recognized, much less understood. This demographic is one of the things that makes Isherwood's novel both rich with period detail and prescient; for George's classroom will become, over the subsequent years, the predominant model of higher education in the United States: a student body made up of all ages, races, and backgrounds.

While George will have a special bond with Kenny after class and later that evening, in the classroom George's closest ally is Wally Bryant, his "little minority sister" (70). Wally's gayness is a secret seemingly shared between them, perhaps through nothing more than a mutual, unspoken understanding.

George's descriptions of his students are based on their appearances and what to him seem their eccentricities. George sees the Asians (including Lois Yamaguchi, Kenny's girlfriend) as "enigmatic"; he is "intimidated" by the "hypersensitive" Estelle Oxford, one of his best students and a "Negro." Despite the fact that Isherwood's terminology may seem stereotypical or retrograde to twenty-first-century readers, his depiction of minorities in the novel is, we believe, progressive. Isherwood's treatment of the realities of a multicultural, multiethnic campus is similar to his depiction of George's homosexuality: it is not a problem to be solved but a matter of fact. And Isherwood has George deal in a reality that many people of his time were not yet ready for. A year after the novel was published, racial riots broke out in the Watts area of L.A. and, of course, all over the country throughout the decade. The historian-observer in Isherwood tells the truth of his time, as he had before in Berlin in the early 1930s.

Unfortunately, the representation of the college scenes in Ford's adaptation misses an opportunity to portray Isherwood's Los Angeles. The campus community looks white and middle-class—from the faculty in the lounge (which includes a cameo by Bachardy) to the students in the class. Lois Yamaguchi is now a blonde whose only purpose seems to be to show that students smoked in class. The rest of the class is similarly bland, and Wally has been replaced by a respectable-looking white gay couple. The film's campus atmosphere isn't that of a public college or the Los Angeles that Isherwood knew.

The novel's classroom scene centers on a discussion of Aldous Huxley's *After Many a Summer Dies the Swan*. A student asks whether Huxley is anti-Semitic because one of his characters says that "the stupidest phrase in the Bible is 'they hated me without a cause.'" Confronted with this question, George responds with a harangue about racial and ethnic understanding: "The Nazis were *not* right to hate the Jews. But their hating the Jews was *not* without cause. No one *ever* hates without a cause" (69–72). What is astonishing about this part of the novel is that Isherwood anticipates the discourse on diversity in higher education from the last twenty to thirty years. Rather than paper over the differences he sees in the classroom, Isherwood calls for acknowledgment and discussion of diversity. As to the issue of hating without a cause, George says: "A minority is only thought of as a minority when it constitutes some kind of a threat to the majority, real or imagined. And no threat is ever *quite* imaginary. . . . There always is a reason, no matter how wrong it is." George is talking directly about the Jews and blacks present in the classroom, but his subtext includes the gay minorities too. Isherwood's wishful thinking here is for real engagement between people instead of benign tolerance. "Sure, minorities are people—*people*, not angels. Sure, they're like us— but not *exactly* like us; that's the all-too-familiar state of liberal hysteria in which you begin to kid yourself you honestly cannot see any difference between a Negro and a Swede." George wants to get specific; he wants to single out Estelle Oxford and Buddy Sorenson by name, but he does not. "Maybe, if he did dare . . . everybody would embrace, and the kingdom of heaven would begin. . . . But then again, maybe it wouldn't" (71).

A Single Man teaches us an approach to diversity as an opportunity, not as a problem. George's diatribe avoids the piety of "teaching tolerance": "Let's face it, minorities are people who probably look and act and think differently from us and have faults we don't have" (ibid.). It is important for Isherwood that people acknowledge difference and the fears associated with it. To do otherwise would be folly and can lead to violence: "We all keep trying to believe that if we ignore something long enough it'll just vanish." Of course, we know from history that it did lead to violence. Here, Isherwood cautions against the danger of "annihilation by blandness."

Characterized by a stark depiction of contemporary life and modern tensions, *A Single Man* is a valuable book to teach in many contexts: the modern novel, gay studies, Los Angeles and California literature. We have taught the novel on several occasions and find that students respond to the cantankerous George enthusiastically. What seems most challenging for them to imagine, though, is the life of George and Jim as a couple. Because there are few cultural representations to the contrary, students typically think of gay lives in the early sixties as filled with secrecy, shame, and loneliness. But teaching the novel with the documentary *Chris & Don* goes a long way toward solving that problem. The extensive home movies featured in the film show the time and place vividly. The film also shows the life two gay men built together. It portrays what a gay couple endured in midcentury America. The defiance of Isherwood and Bachardy, in contrast to the much more private life of George and Jim, helps students see a broader range of gay experience.

An unexpected aspect of the documentary, though, sheds further important light on *A Single Man,* especially for an audience of undergraduates. In the film, they see Don drawing Chris during his death from cancer at the end of 1985 and in early 1986. What the documentary presents is Bachardy as a "single man," someone trying to continue his life after the death of his longtime companion. The role reversal is instructive and provides, perhaps, a much more faithful adaptation in that sense than Ford could ever have hoped to do.

One student in a literature class at the University of Southern California, for example, noted that having a sense of the relationship between Chris and Don helped him compare their life to George and Jim's life. He got "a better understanding of the period of the novel and of the deep sense of loss that George feels. And while George finds himself almost unable to continue living, the strength of Don Bachardy is felt and appreciated. The story of Chris and Don is one of strength, almost an impossibility, given what they were up against."[8]

It seems to us that a great benefit of teaching a text like *A Single Man* is its historical value—its value as history. It tells some significant truths of its time and place: George's experience and worldview are historically accurate, and Isherwood captured the truth, preserved it, and now we have an informative way to connect mid-twentieth-century life to twenty-first-century life. Isherwood's diamond is worth much more than a nickel. Especially when the novel is read in conjunction with the documentary, we can see and appreciate the value of George's story in our own lives.

Notes

1. See Jill Lepore, "Just the Facts, Ma'am," *New Yorker* (March 24, 2008): 82.

2. Christopher Isherwood, *The Berlin Stories* (New York: New Directions, 1954), 206–7.

3. See chapter 2 in this volume by the filmmakers for further discussion of *Chris & Don.*

4. The lectures have been published in *Isherwood on Writing,* ed. James J. Berg (Minneapolis: University of Minnesota Press, 2007).

5. See Dan Luckenbill, "Isherwood in Los Angeles," in *The Isherwood Cen-*

tury: Essays on the Life and Work of Christopher Isherwood, ed. James J. Berg and Chris Freeman (Madison: University of Wisconsin Press, 2000), 32–33.

6. Michael S. Harper, "Ish circa 1959–1963," in Berg and Freeman, *The Isherwood Century,* 54, 58.

7. Christopher Isherwood, *A Single Man* (1964; reprint, Minneapolis: University of Minnesota Press, 2001), 41–42.

8. From an essay by a student in Chris Freeman's "Los Angeles Stories" class in the fall semester of 2008.

II

THE RELIGIOUS WRITER

During the last few days, I quite suddenly decided to take a stab at my autobiographical book about America. . . . My inspiration is Jung's resolve "to tell my personal myth." Therefore I shall try to dwell only on the numinous, on the magical and the mythical.

—CHRISTOPHER ISHERWOOD, *Liberation*

That Isherwood settled in Los Angeles for the last half of his life is part coincidence, part intention, and part temperament. He originally traveled to L.A. to see the American West after a dismal New York winter, to seek out his old friend the mystic writer Gerald Heard, and to see if he could get work in the film studios. Through Heard, he came to know Swami Prabhavananda. Aside from Bachardy, Isherwood was never closer or more devoted to anyone than he was to Prabhavananda.

The American Isherwood is the Vedantic Isherwood. Isherwood approached Vedanta, at least in the beginning, less as a religion than as a philosophy. "Vedanta philosophy consists of three principles. First, that man's real nature is divine. Second, that the aim of human life is to realize this divinity. Third, that truth is universal."[1] Isherwood believed the first principle because he believed in Swami. He spent the rest of his life attempting the second. His diaries document his ongoing efforts to understand Vedanta and, through Vedanta, to understand the truth of this life.

Nearly all of Isherwood's significant work after 1940 is influenced by his devotion to Vedanta. His very conception of being a writer is influenced by the second principle, the attempt to realize divinity:

It seems to me that the purpose of the art of writing is to understand, to reveal the deeper nature of experience, to make life and its phenomena, and all the human beings and creatures around us more significant. To make our own lives fuller of meaning and thereby to render our whole experience moment by moment more significant than it otherwise would be. (*The Wishing Tree*, 155)

For two decades, Isherwood's attempts to write about religion were primarily in essays and in his translations of Vedanta texts. Not until *Down There on a Visit* (1962) did Isherwood try to write directly about his religion in fiction. Near the end of his life, he addressed it again in his memoir *My Guru and His Disciple* (1980). He mined his diaries for the memoir, trying to have the last word on his relationship with Prabhavananda. He knew there were skeptics, close friends of his who thought his religion so much "heathen mumbo-jumbo" (a phrase Auden once used to describe Isherwood's religion). He was writing with those very people in mind, even as he struggled with his own critical resistance to "religion" and the spiritual life. In his diary, he wondered: "Am I perhaps inhibited by a sense of the mocking agnostics all around me—ranging from asses like [John] Lehmann to intelligent bigots like [Edward] Upward? Yes, of course I am. In a sense, they are my most important audience. Everything I write is with a consciousness of the opposition and in answer to its prejudices."[2]

He struggled with *My Guru and His Disciple* as a summation of his American life and his attempt to realize it through Vedanta. This section of *The American Isherwood* addresses Isherwood's spiritual work through his fiction, his diaries, and his religious writing.

Australian scholar Victor Marsh, author of *Mr. Isherwood Changes Trains* (2010), a book-length study of Isherwood's religious life, takes on the question of "home," one of the most compelling aspects of Isherwood's long life. His quest for a psychic, earthly, and spiritual home was the source of so many relocations, as Marsh calls them, and it was, ultimately, Swami Prabhavananda who helped Isherwood find his "home."

Isherwood found a kindred spirit in Aldous Huxley, one of the most important writers and thinkers of the twentieth century. Huxley's work is revisited in Robert L. Caserio's thoughtful consideration of "mysticism" in the form of the novel. Caserio, an expert on literary modernism and the 1930s in particular, sheds new light on how we understand modernist novels and how they "think." His essay is a rather different take on the same literary relationship addressed by Peter E. Firchow later in this volume. Firchow addresses the Hollywood aspects of this collaborative friendship.

Two of Isherwood's novels from the 1960s—*Down There on a Visit* and *A Meeting by the River* (1967)—are the focus of the next two essays in this section. Rebecca Gordon Stewart, who is based in Scotland, did a great deal of research in the archive as an Isherwood fellow at the Huntington in 2010–11. Her essay considers *Down There on a Visit* in the context of Dante's *Divine Comedy*. Tracing in particular his changing literary selves as Isherwood experiments with narrators and points of view, Stewart's essay describes the journey through Hell and Purgatory over the long time frame of the novel's four episodes.

Paul M. McNeil's consideration of Isherwood's final novel situates the book in a kind of ethics—of sexuality, of brotherhood, and of devotion—and universal truth. McNeil argues that Isherwood had no patience for moral relativism, especially when the well-being of others was involved. McNeil also addresses Isherwood's treatment of bisexuality and fidelity in the novel.

The last two chapters in this section are by scholars who contributed to *The Isherwood Century*. Niladri R. Chatterjee, who interviewed Don Bachardy in our earlier book, here addresses the complex relationship Isherwood had with India. Isherwood's faith—his role as a Westerner deeply involved with Eastern religion and tradition—as well as his "Britishness" put him in a vexed situation. Chatterjee uses Isherwood's diaries and his religious writing to reevaluate the complexities of Isherwood's sense of India.

Italian scholar Mario Faraone surveys and assesses the influence of Isherwood's spiritual devotion to much of his work from the American period. The discipline of devotion and the discipline of writing merge in Faraone's consideration of the central roles religion and spirituality play in the life and work of Isherwood.

Notes

1. Christopher Isherwood, *The Wishing Tree*, ed. Robert Adjemian (San Francisco: Harper & Row, 1986), 42.

2. Christopher Isherwood, *Liberation: Diaries, Volume Three: 1970–1983,* ed. Katherine Bucknell (New York: Harper, 2012), 554.

8

Isherwood and the Psycho-geography of Home

VICTOR MARSH

It is not Home that one cries for but one's home-self.

—CHRISTOPHER ISHERWOOD, *Kathleen and Frank*

Dislocations

When Isherwood arrived in the United States in 1939, he was close to what might be termed a "nervous breakdown." He was already enjoying his first taste of success as a writer, yet fame could not paper over the cracks undermining his sense of security. The crisis was not only psychological in nature; his ontology—his sense of who he was in relation to the wider order of being in the world—had been thoroughly destabilized and he was, in effect, falling apart.

Since May 1933, he and his young German lover Heinz Neddermeyer had been moving restlessly from one European country to another so that Heinz could escape conscription, a desperate five-year period of avoidance that had included an attempt to get his lover into Britain. But Heinz had been refused entry, unable to maintain the fiction of coming into Britain at Isherwood's mother Kathleen's invitation to work as "household help." Their attempts to avoid the inevitable were ultimately frustrated when, in 1938, Heinz was arrested and imprisoned as he crossed the border back into Germany, trying to renew a visa.

Isherwood's father had been killed during the First World War, when the ten-year-old Isherwood was in boarding school, and he was henceforth sufficiently disgusted by nationalist rhetoric to be, in effect, immunized against the patriotic enthusiasm for war, yet war was stalking Europe again. The diaries from this time—1938 in particular—provide a telling portrait of a self in crisis. His disaffection from England and his sense of the suffocating values that country represented to him deepened, and Europe offered no safe haven. He was impressed with the novel by the Austrian writer Robert Musil, *Der Mann ohne Eigenschaften (The Man without Qualities)* and he described himself in the same terms, as a "man without qualities" (or character, or attributes)—a kind of hollow man:

> For the more I think about myself, the more persuaded I am that, *as a person,* I really don't exist. That is one of the reasons why—as much as I'm tempted to try—I can't believe in any orthodox religion. I cannot believe in my own soul. No, I am a chemical compound, conditioned by environment and education. My "character" is simply a repertoire of acquired tricks, my conversation a repertoire of adaptations and echoes, my "feelings" are dictated by purely physical, external stimuli. . . . Der Mann ohne Eigenshaft *[sic]* is never to be trusted.[1]

Isherwood was a man in urgent search of an authentic self, and he relocated often, moving on from situations that suppressed his need to explore new possibilities of being and becoming, and he would revisit his own life experience for reworking into literary "myth." Whether his writings were nominally fictional or autobiographical (he once said he couldn't tell the difference), Isherwood was constantly probing, reflecting, and reinventing versions of selfhood. Even the ostensibly fictional books would be recounted by a namesake narrator. Critics unsympathetic to his quest sometimes take this self-referentialism as a form of egotism, and a superficial reading of the autobiographical approach often conflates this technique with narcissism. On closer attention, however, these simplistic, pseudopsychoanalytic interpretations tend to fall apart.

In his review of *My Guru and His Disciple* for the *New York Review of Books* in 1980, Stephen Spender noted that Isherwood has "often been accused of egotism in his work":

> Yet in the sense in which the word is usually employed this seems to me to miss the point. The self-solidification of the true egotist acts as a wall between him and people. The strident ego sings only its own tune, blocks out the sounds of the others. The Isherwood ego is not of this kind.[2]

Spender reads it, then, in the manner suggested by Isherwood himself:

> It is an acute self-consciousness that makes even his most disinterested actions seem mockery to him. His ego is also an instrument of sensibility

through which the people the novelist observes become transformed into characters in his fiction. (Ibid.)

By the late 1930s, Isherwood was in fact increasingly disgusted with his ego self and its "repertoire of acquired tricks." Recalling his feelings on his departure to America with Auden, he wrote in his diary:

> Why were we going to America? I suppose, for myself, the chief reason was that I couldn't stop travelling. . . . I was also running away from myself: that was why I never stayed anywhere long. I could remain in Portugal, for example, as long as I could believe in an objective Portugal. But sooner or later Portugal would dissolve and reveal itself as the all-too-familiar, subjective "Isherwood Portugal." Then I fled in disgust.[3]

The note of disgust is particularly telling.

Not everyone reads him as sympathetically as Spender. For example, D. S. Savage wrote in 1979 (when most of the oeuvre had been published): "his writing can now be seen to spring from a self-preoccupation of all but narcissistic intensity."[4]

There are critical issues in play here that I believe need to be closely reviewed. If the churches' construction of the homosexual as a religious pariah has faded somewhat from public discourse (which I would dispute), in any case the marginalization had been enthusiastically taken up by psychology, and the psychopathological model carried the baton of stigmatization forward into a "secular" age. Savage's critique was published in the journal *Literature and Psychology*. His credentials appear to lean more toward the literary than the psychoanalytic, but the attempt to thoroughly psychoanalyze writers through their texts was fashionable at the time. This characterization of Isherwood is extant even today, as is obvious from tracking the reviews of Peter Parker's 2004 biography of Isherwood.

Reviewing that biography for the *Irish Times* in 2004, for example, Robert O'Byrne opined that Isherwood "was vainglorious to a ludicrous degree," claiming that "like all self-centred people," Isherwood understood himself very poorly.[5] "Nobody fascinated Christopher Isherwood as much as Christopher Isherwood," O'Byrne continues, arguing that Isherwood's "crystalline prose style managed to conceal that character flaw from readers." He depicts Isherwood as a "fraudulent rebel . . . without much honour or respect."

It is my position that the confusion about identity and the "interest in exploring himself" that O'Byrne found so lamentable was the spur for an interrogation of selfhood that drove Isherwood's writing and his personal journey into Vedanta philosophy and practice with his guru, Swami Prabhavananda. It is that very research which has revived interest in Isherwood today, not only from a queer readership, but also from an audience for whom the problematized self is a critical postmodern issue. Isherwood was later to make great literary use of the trope of the "performing" self, rehearsing different possibilities for identity. But at this early stage, to see himself as the "hollow man" was the beginning of a stripping away of illusions that can (and in his case, did) prepare him for either a psychological breakdown or a spiritual breakthrough (or both). And clearly, by the time he was preparing to leave Europe, it was having a radically destabilizing effect on his psyche.

Isherwood asks himself what his faults are (whether he is a coward, a liar, selfish, vain, and so on) but, in an interesting foreshadowing of his later shift in metaphysics, he sees this as "the interest which *Der Mann ohne Eigenschaften* is bound to feel in his *outward* personality just because he knows himself to have no inner life at all." Parker paraphrases Isherwood thus:

> The style was the man: what else was there? *Der Mann ohne Eigenschaften* is a man without character, properties or attributes, with no recognizable soul, indeed "no inner life at all." (*Isherwood,* 342)

He had begun to see himself simply as a "character" who performed in public—at lectures and readings, when meeting strangers—just as much as he performed on the page. He realizes that to all his friends (save Auden, perhaps) he is a facade, and that he is in danger of being locked into that public persona by his readers.

Behind the performativity, and with no reliable basis on which to form an integrated subjectivity, his feeling of not really knowing himself was acute and deeply felt. Were he content to bluff his way forward, regardless, perhaps Isherwood would deserve the kind of treatment he has often received, but a more thoughtful view might recognize here the origins of spiritual inquiry. Without sincerity there would be no crisis of conscience.

A more insightful and expert reading of "narcissism" can be drawn from the psychoanalyst D. W. Winnicott of the British object-relations school. Winnicott argues that when the environment does not support the developing personality and requires the person to sacrifice his or her own spontaneous needs to adapt to environmental demands, there is not even a resting-place for individual experience and the result is a failure in the primary narcissistic state to evolve an individual. The "individual" then develops as an extension of the shell rather than that of the core, and as an extension of the impinging environment.[6] This reading of narcissism makes it easier to understand Isherwood's increasing sense of unreality and his self-confessed inability to shake off the "performing" self in the early years. Winnicott continues:

> What there is left of a core is hidden away and is difficult to find even in the most far-reaching analysis. The individual then exists by not being found. The true self is hidden, and what we have to deal with clinically is the complex false self whose function is to keep this true self hidden. (Ibid.)

It is clear from the reference to Robert Musil's "man without qualities" that Isherwood was deeply dissatisfied with the "complex false self" diagnosed by Winnicott, and he would go on to make extensive *literary* use of the play of false selves with a more assured handling of the trope as he matured. In the later works (which Savage ignores), the result of his deep inquiry into the nature of what Winnicott calls the "core" is quite discernible, but this had come about through his prolonged study and practice of Vedanta, under the guidance of his spiritual adviser, Swami Prabhavananda, head of the Vedanta Society of Southern California.

The role of the guru within the *bhakti* (devotional) expression of yoga is commonly misunderstood outside of the Vedanta traditions. To fail to recognize, or respect, the focalizing power of the guru–student relationship, as many Western commentators continue to do, is to miss a great deal of Isherwood's process. In *The Tibetan Book of Living and Dying* (1994), Sogyal Rinpoche, who has done much to popularize Tibetan Buddhist teachings in the West, writes insightfully of what he calls "the alchemy of discipleship" and the Western suspicion of "masters."[7] Western thinkers who value their independence rankle at hints of submission in the teacher–disciple relationship, assuming suspiciously that the spiritual preceptor must be intent on rendering the student utterly passive and subject to the guru's will. To the contrary, Rinpoche writes:

> It is essential to know what real devotion is. It is not mindless adoration; it is not an abdication of your responsibility to yourself, nor undiscriminating following of another's personality or whim. Real devotion is an unbroken receptivity to the truth. Real devotion is rooted in an awed and reverent gratitude, but one that is lucid, grounded and intelligent. (*The Tibetan Book of Living and Dying*, 136)

To miss this, at the core of the practice, or to interpret it only suspiciously, is to miss a significant factor in the life, then, and leaves the superficial commentator focusing on externals.

Relocation

Where will a man find rest when he is bored or appalled with his own ego performance? Perhaps we might assume that he would turn to religion. But, disgusted with his Anglican upbringing, Isherwood had decided to quit religion as a young man. Like many others of his generation, he saw himself as an atheist and briefly embraced socialism before taking up a conscientious position as a pacifist. He detested his mother's pious embrace of Anglicanism and was particularly repelled by her class-based snobbery toward Catholics. During his parents' courtship, his father had tried to get his young wife Kathleen interested in theosophy and, after the marriage, resisted her attempts to get him more involved in "public religion."[8] "To Kathleen," wrote Isherwood, "Christianity meant traditional worship publicly shared and church-going was its essential expression" (190). Frank, on the other hand, who had had too much public religion in the army ("to him, church-going was like church parade"), was "temperamentally attracted to Hinduism and Buddhism," notes his son, "because it taught a private religion of self-effort, self-knowledge, and solitary meditation" (ibid.).

Isherwood's failure to connect to the sacred through Anglicanism was not entirely owing to a poor relationship with his mother. Parker has retrieved something of Kathleen Isherwood as a person in her own right, rather than as seen only through the eyes of her older son, but even Parker's favorable characterization of Kathleen suggests why the religion could not be embraced by the son: "Her letters and journals show someone who was in many ways conventional: she was a devout Christian, had a proper respect for royalty, and believed that people should know and keep to their place in the social hierarchy" (*Isherwood*, 10).

The "place in the social hierarchy" for an unapologetic sexual deviant was deep in the closet, as his predecessors J. A. Symonds, E. M. Forster, and even Oscar Wilde had discovered. Isherwood was not prepared to follow that path. To explore the alternatives, he had to relocate to another country (the United States), and to yet another culture's philosophical and religious traditions.

Thomas Merton's characterization of the Anglican church provides an unexpected but useful second opinion in this regard. In his autobiography,

Merton describes his encounter with Anglicanism during a sojourn at an English school—Ripley—where he boarded for two years following an earlier, formative period at a French lycée:

> Prayer is attractive enough when it is considered in a context of good food, and sunny joyous country churches, and the green English country-side. And, as a matter of fact, the Church of England means all this. It is a class religion, the cult of a special society and group, not even of a whole nation, but of the ruling minority in a nation. The thing that holds them together is the powerful attraction of their own *social* tradition, and the stubborn tenacity with which they cling to certain social standards and customs, more or less for their own sake. The Church of England depends, for its existence, almost entirely on the solidarity and conservatism of the English ruling class.[9]

Isherwood's diaries from 1948 record his reading the Merton autobiography with great interest (*Diaries,* 1:407).

Merton's characterization speaks to that complacency with the fundamental classist assumptions of one's social milieu against which Isherwood was reacting. In a very real sense, this style of religion has very much to do with belonging within the context of the network of associations that knit together the kind of social identification wherein religion operates as the instrument of normative social conformity. But this matrix of belonging only served to marginalize Isherwood and was clearly not a path to liberation for him as an unrepentant homosexual.

In his novel *Maurice,* E. M. Forster describes the character of Clive struggling to overcome "the worst crime in the calendar":

> He came from a family of lawyers and squires, good and able men for the most part, and he did not wish to depart from their tradition. He wished Christianity would compromise with him a little and searched the Scriptures for support. There was David and Jonathan; there was even the "disciple that Jesus loved." But the Church's interpretation was against him; he could not find any rest for his soul in her without crippling it.[10]

After rejecting the politics and morality of his mother and his "caste" and, given his rather urgent need for an anchor in a time of great personal crisis, it was unlikely Isherwood would turn to something so pallid as this class-based Anglicanism for his ontological, or metaphysical, reorientation.

After a series of displacements and an increasing dissatisfaction with the performative ego, he needed a radical revisioning of his identity positioning that would allow him to locate what he called the "home self." As he wrote later, "the desire, the *homesickness*, for sanity is the one valid reason for subjecting oneself to any kind of religious discipline."[11] "It is not Home that one cries for but one's home-self," he wrote in *Kathleen and Frank* (285). Elsewhere, I have proposed that the great disillusionment that many gay men go through—alienation from the normative discourses of family, church, and the law—often takes the form of a stripping away of illusions. For some, this can serve as a rite of passage, even an initiation, precipitating profound doubt and a rigorous process of self-inquiry that gives them little peace until they find a resting place—a kind of docking point for their tired and battered subjectivity to reconnect and reformulate. Disillusioned with his home country, separated from his lover, horrified to watch the whole of Europe collapsing into war, he had failed to develop a sense of self that could survive the crisis. Looking back forty years later, he wrote:

> I was empty because I had lost my political faith—I couldn't repeat the left-wing slogans which I had been repeating throughout the last few years. It wasn't that I had lost all belief in what the slogans stood for, but I was no longer wholehearted. My leftism was confused by an increasingly aggressive awareness of myself as a homosexual and by a newly made discovery that I was a pacifist. (*My Guru and His Disciple*, 4)

At first, his search for answers took the form of looking for ways to substantiate his pacifism. This led him to look up a former acquaintance, the writer Gerald Heard, who had moved to Los Angeles at the same time as Aldous Huxley. Heard and Huxley were both involved with a guru, a Swami from the Ramakrishna Order, who was teaching Vedanta practice and Advaita philosophy out of a temple in Hollywood. Isherwood was not a likely candidate for conversion to any form of religion, and neither Heard nor the guru himself was about to try to convert him.

Vedanta teaches that the object of existence is not to "transcend," but to realize what we really are, a realization obtained not though logic but through a process of direct intuition, as modeled by the sages. In the Advaita, or "nondual" form of the teachings, particularly as taught within the Ramakrishna tradition, only Brahman, the supreme principle, has existence, and ignorance ("*a*vidya," as opposed to "vidya") of this reality leads to the erroneous belief that phenomena can exist apart from the Absolute. The idea of the personal self as a "separate" entity, then, is a delusion that produces unnecessary stress and anxiety. For the restless, deluded entity to be brought back into reunion with the One that contains the many, what will be required is a gradual shift in the focal length of habituated awareness, to recover, ultimately, what the poet Rumi terms "the root of the root" of the self.[12] Concomitantly, it will also require a revisioning of previously held notions of identity that grew up in ignorance of the real state of affairs.

In Isherwood's case, we see (as Lisa Colletta points out) that "the confusion, hopes, and fears" of an entire era—the political uncertainties between two major world wars, compounded by a personal crisis of identity—is reflected in the texts.[13] The study and praxis of Vedanta would become one of three major contributors to resolving the psychological and ontological crisis for Isherwood, providing him an unprecedented opportunity (and a challenge) as a student of a profoundly integrative spiritual system: "what Gerald recommended was a practical mysticism, a do-it-yourself religion which was experimental and empirical."[14] Empirical yes, but "do-it-yourself" only in the sense that to embrace the doctrines up front was not an a priori requirement.

Heard understood that it was no use hitting Isherwood with a full-on doctrinal assault. Both he and Swami Prabhavananda respected Isherwood's initial skepticism, emphasizing praxis and firsthand, empirical experience over theory, refusing to even define the nature of the experience encountered there: "Gerald wasn't asking you to take anything on trust. It was essential to try 'this thing' for yourself. If, after a reasonable time, you had found nothing, then you were entitled to say it was all a lie" (*An Approach to Vedanta*, 24). "This thing" became a shorthand reference for what they declined to define.

If he was slow to accept the theoretical basis, Isherwood quickly came to respect and admire the Swami:

> I do not believe in his teachings with the whole of my mind, and I will not pretend that I do, but I have enough belief to make a start. My reason is not offended. My approach is strictly experimental. I will put myself in his hands, and trust him at least as far as I would trust my own doctor. I will try to live the kind of life he prescribes. If, at the end of three or four years, I can conscientiously say that I have done what was asked of me and had no results whatsoever, then I will give up the whole attempt as a bad job.[15]

Theoretical study was not far behind, however. Apart from the empirical benefits of meditation practice, this form of Vedanta—and more important the relationship with the guru himself—came to represent an unexpectedly complete solution to Isherwood's struggle to locate an integrative subjectivity. With his fiction taking a backseat, Isherwood was soon engaged in service projects for his teacher, and in 1944 they published a translation of the Bhagavad Gita together. This was followed by other key texts from the Vedanta tradition (the Shankara in 1947, the Patanjali in 1953, the Ramakrishna biography in 1965). As he said later: "By the time we had finished translating the book I realized that I had been studying it with an ideal teacher and in the most thorough manner imaginable."[16]

Just as he had embraced German, in the 1930s, as a way of rehearsing a new possibility for selfhood, in spite of his initial "prejudice" Isherwood found the "very Indianness" of Vedanta helpful during the 1940s. He was "grateful to Vedanta for speaking Sanskrit," as he put it; he could learn a religion afresh, without the associations carried from the Anglicanism of his upbringing:

> I needed a brand-new vocabulary and here it was, with a set of philosophical terms which were exact in meaning, unemotive, untainted by disgusting old associations with clergymen's sermons, schoolmasters' pep talks, politicians' patriotic speeches. (*My Guru and His Disciple,* 49)

In addition to meditation practices, "seva," or "selfless service," is an important aspect of practice in most spiritual traditions, and service to the guru is something a keen aspirant is glad to offer as intrinsic to the relationship. It is important to keep this in mind when reading Peter Parker's characterization of Isherwood as someone being exploited by his guru. As a form of "karma yoga," service supplements the introspective process of meditation and the devotional relationship with the guru and, as an exercise in selflessness, shifts the focus away from the obsession with ego gratification toward the subtle transformation of subjectivity that results from a realignment of the personal with a deeper "Self."

The Advaita tradition is concerned to construct a nondualistic conception of reality. All forms, including the sense of the personal self, only appear to exist in separation. Even in using terms such as "Param Brahman" for absolute reality, the part of the absolute that exists in every person—the Atman—is construed as not separate from Brahman itself. Given Isherwood's crisis, it is significant that he entered into the study of the key concepts of the philosophy quite thoroughly. To illustrate some of the principles, I will cite extracts from the introduction to their translation of one of the key texts of this tradition, *The Crest-Jewel of Discrimination* (in Sanskrit, the *Viveka-Chudamani*), written by the great eighth-century South Indian reformer Shankara:

> Shankara only accepts as "real" that which neither changes nor ceases to exist. . . . No object, no kind of knowledge, can be absolutely real if its existence is only temporary. Absolute reality implies permanent existence.[17]

The emphasis is on what is "real," in the sense of "unchanging." So the question arises:

> What, then, *is* the Reality behind all our experiences? There is only one thing that never leaves us—the deep consciousness. This alone is the constant feature of all experience. And this consciousness is the real, absolute Self. (*Shankara's Crest-Jewel*, 7–8)

In this context, Isherwood's angst—the disorientation, the psychological restlessness, and the attendant metaphysical or ontological displacement—could be diagnosed as a spiritual crisis that would not be improved by what could only be a futile attempt to stabilize what is *inherently* unstable, fragile, and temporary, even delusional: namely, the separate ego-sense that we call our "self."

According to Buddhist practitioner Peter Conradi, through meditation the practitioner discovers the "flimsy" nature of the self ("as experience, not theory"), coming to the realization "that life is a stream of becoming, a series of manifestations and extinctions," leading to an awareness that the notion of the individual ego is "a popular delusion."[18] Through all the ups and downs of the next four decades, Isherwood made more than a theoretical acquaintance with "the one thing that never leaves us"— Shankara's representation of the "real."

The practice of meditation given to Isherwood by the Swami (known as doing or making *japam*—the repetition of a "mantra," or sacred phrase, with the aid of rosary beads for counting the rotations) was an opportunity for him to dig deeper into the layers of being—into the "deep consciousness" to which they refer in this section—to locate the eternal, unchanging aspect of self, known as the "Atman," which partakes of the very same nature as, and is not separate from, the absolute principle: "Brahman." In this model, "Brahman" represents the formless source of all forms, which are expressions of its own nature, and this includes consciousness itself. To recognize the eternal "Self" not only is the basis for achieving *personal* fulfillment but also lays the foundation for the realization of the matrix of unity underlying all forms: "The Self is everywhere," says the Isha Upanishad. "Whoever sees all beings in the Self, and the Self in all beings, hates none. For one who sees oneness everywhere, how can there be delusion or grief?" This quotation is taken from "What Is Vedanta?" on the Vedanta Society of Southern California Web site, which states: "All fear and all misery arise from our sense of separation from the great cosmic unity, the web of being that enfolds us," citing the Upanishads:

> "There is fear from the second," says the Brihadaranyaka Upanishad. Duality, our sense of separation from the rest of creation, is always a misperception since it implies that something exists other than God. There can be no other.

The Vedanta Society site also quotes Vivekananda, the pioneer figure who first brought the Ramakrishna message to the United States:

> This grand preaching, the oneness of things, making us one with everything that exists, is the great lesson to learn," said Swami Vivekananda a century ago.
> The Self is the essence of this universe, the essence of all souls. . . . You are one with this universe. He who says he is different from others, even by a hair's breadth, immediately becomes miserable. Happiness belongs to him who knows this oneness, who knows he is one with this universe.

Intimately present within each being, Atman is indispensable for consciousness, and is the "real" source of peace and bliss, because its nature is unchanging. The personal self, which is acquired as the outward persona that forms in response to the external world, is subject to change, and is an unreliable basis for stability, happiness, and satisfaction. The goal of spiritual practice is not to destroy that relatively illusory, "false" self—for that is needed to function as the mediator with the changing world—but to shift one's center from close and exclusive identification with it and recover the deepest roots of being within the zone of the unchanging—the eternal, underlying basis of all life and consciousness, the Param Brahman.

As a practitioner of meditation, Isherwood was regularly brought into a close awareness of the condition of his "illusory" mind-self and how far it could bring one away from identifying with the "unchanging." He was not one to pretend to a greater degree of enlightenment than he had actually achieved, and he kept a rigorous record of where he really was, as uncomfortable as that could be.

He once likened the first-person praxis of autobiography to holding a knife in the wound; in other words, far from the kind of self-indulgence of the narcissist, a charge that draws a more insightful reading from Adam Phillips, a psychotherapist from the British object-relations school. His review of *Lost Years* for the *Guardian,* in 2000, recognizes Isherwood's "determination to track down even the most elusive and unappealing aspects of his past in order to understand and honestly portray himself, both as a writer and as a human being."[19] In contrast with the lingering accusation of narcissism, Phillips interprets Isherwood's use of recollection not just as a way to construct the personal myth but as "the best cure for egotism." Phillips observes, astutely, that "we may look better if we rearrange the facts, but rearranging the facts is also moral propaganda" and he recognizes that as a writer, Isherwood was aware of the need for an ongoing "critique of the self-justifying voice."

The "home" that Isherwood sought was located neither back at the family seat in England (nor through regression to the fond memories of his childhood nursery). Nor was it in California, as pleasant as he found that location for more than forty years. Nor was it in his long relationship with the artist Don Bachardy, which carried its own sources of stress. His restlessness was only assuaged as he learned to realign himself with the underlying, all-encompassing ground of being, under the guidance of his patient spiritual mentor.

Notes

1. Peter Parker, *Isherwood: A Life Revealed* (New York: Random House, 2004), 340. For more, see Robert Musil, *The Man without Qualities,* trans. Eithne Wilkins and Ernst Kaiser (London: Secker & Warburg, 1953–54).

2. Stephen Spender, "Issyvoo's Conversion," *New York Review of Books* 27 (1980): 18.

3. Christopher Isherwood, *Diaries, Volume One: 1939–1960,* ed. Katherine Bucknell (New York: Harper, 1996), 4.

4. D. S. Savage, "Christopher Isherwood: The Novelist as Homosexual[ist]," *Literature and Psychology* 29, nos. 1–2 (1979): 77.

5. Robert O'Byrne, "A Fraudulent Rebel," review of *Isherwood: A Life* by Peter Parker, *Irish Times,* June 26, 2004), 13.

6. D. W. Winnicott, *Through Paediatrics to Psycho-analysis: Collected Papers.* (1958; reprint, London: Hogarth Press, 1975), 212.

7. Sogyal Rinpoche, *The Tibetan Book of Living and Dying,* ed. Patrick Gaffney and Andrew Harvey (San Francisco: HarperCollins, 1994), 133–34.

8. Christopher Isherwood, *Kathleen and Frank* (New York: Simon and Schuster, 1971), 167.

9. Thomas Merton, *The Seven Storey Mountain* (1948) (New York: Harcourt Brace Jovanovich, 1975), 65.

10. E. M. Forster, *Maurice* (New York: Norton, 1971), 70.

11. Christopher Isherwood, *My Guru and His Disciple* (New York: Farrar, Straus and Giroux, 1980), 120; emphasis added.

12. Andrew Harvey, *Way of Passion: A Celebration of Rumi* (Berkeley: Frog, 1994), 51.

13. Lisa Coletta, ed., *Kathleen and Christopher: Christopher Isherwood's Letters to His Mother* (Minneapolis: University of Minnesota Press, 2005), xi.

14. Christopher Isherwood, *An Approach to Vedanta* (Los Angeles: Vedanta Press, 1963), 23.

15. Christopher Isherwood, *Exhumations: Stories, Articles, Verses* (New York: Simon and Schuster, 1966), 122.

16. Christopher Isherwood, *Essentials of Vedanta* (Los Angeles: Vedanta Press, 1969), 98.

17. *Shankara's Crest-Jewel of Discrimination,* trans. Swami Prabhavananda and Christopher Isherwood (Los Angeles: Vedanta Press, 1947), 7.

18. Peter J. Conradi, *Going Buddhist: Panic and Emptiness, the Buddha and Me* (London: Short Books, 2004), 49.

19. Adam Phillips, "Setting the Record Straight," *Guardian* online (November 9, 2000), Guardian Unlimited. Accessed 2004. http://www.guardian.co.uk/books/2000/nov/09/londonreviewofbooks?INTCMP=SRCH.

9

Isherwood and Huxley

The Novel as Mystic Fable

ROBERT L. CASERIO

We have yet to settle the role played by novels in Christopher Isherwood's attitudes toward mysticism. His statements about his fiction's relation to religion are not the whole story of the ties that Isherwood's novels—and the novelistic genre itself—might have to mystical experience. *My Guru and His Disciple* is the story of a compromised religious conversion. Isherwood was unable to consummate his relation to Atman—the Reality of the mystics—by becoming a Hindu monastic. When Isherwood in August 1945 ended his two years of protomonastic life, under the direction of Swami Prabhavananda at the Vedanta Society Center in Hollywood, we are told by Isherwood, from the vantage point of 1980, that his leading motive was hope of "a lasting relationship" with William Caskey.[1] The reconstructed diary, *Lost Years,* suggests that multiple erotic liaisons, not just Caskey, motivated the antimonastic turn. But the career of Isherwood's writing was equally strong a motive. In May 1943 Isherwood notes (from the perspective of 1980) that he felt "general anxiety about my future as a fiction writer" (*My Guru and His Disciple,* 124). "Swami didn't tell me *not* to write any more novels," but "took it for granted" that Isherwood would redirect his writing to religious ends.

"The fiction writer was thus being forced to go underground," Isherwood says as he looks back. "But he was determined to survive. . . . He was now a subversive element, whose influence would grow steadily stronger" (ibid., 125). In February 1945 the fiction writer surfaced: beginning work at Warner Brothers, Isherwood became "a screenwriter who happened to be living in a monastery" (185). So, before Caskey, and despite the generation of the novel *Prater Violet* from within the contemplative life of the Center, the novelist enacted an opposition between mystical leanings and novel writing that the film director Berthold Viertel implies in his objection, in February 1943, to Isherwood's preference, as Viertel put it, for "obsolete" Hinduism rather than for "an ivory-tower life of novel-writing" (99). Viertel's antithesis is echoed in the either/or cast of mind—a life of devotion to mysticism or a life of novel writing—that three months later (and in 1945 and in 1980) is reiterated by Isherwood. The antithesis maintains itself. Peter Shneidre, Isherwood's friend and fellow Vedantist, asserts that "religion, practiced in faith, will quickly take a human soul to where literature, even religious literature, cannot follow."[2] Shneidre's assumptions are Isherwood's. In 1966 Isherwood squirms to think of Vedantists reading *A Meeting by the River:* "my translations [of sacred Hindu texts]," his diary says, "must make my novels less, rather than more excusable in their eyes—it isn't as if I didn't know any better!" (*My Guru and His Disciple,* 290–91). One of the memorials of Isherwood's departure from the Center, also from 1945, is Isherwood's essay "The Problem of the Religious Novel." The problem is the difficulty the religious novel gives novelists in representing saint-hood. "The mystical experience can only be written around, hinted at, dimly reflected in word and deed," Isherwood concludes.[3] Attempting to write "around" it, *My Guru and His Disciple* issues out of Isherwood's existential and artistic unease. Impelled by "a transitional stage, between Swami's death and my own," Isherwood's 1970s diaries project "a highly subjective memoir" of Swami, a character "mysterious to me" and hence "a real artistic problem."[4] Because Swami is a "contemplative" rather than an "active" figure, he makes it difficult for Isherwood to picture him even in "a nonfiction novel" (525).

But what if "the problem of the religious novel" is intrinsic to the novel form? Despite the form's apparent secular worldliness, might "the novel" as we have known it be tethered to a contemplative tradition that, however indirectly, links novels to the mysticism that opens upon Reality? Worried about becoming a "self-satisfied 'religious' writer," Isherwood felt progress on *My Guru and His Disciple* blocked. Yet he felt that the block "must be telling me something" (*Liberation,* 554). Was it telling him something he had already told himself? Isherwood was on the verge of turning "the problem" of the religious novel into a point of access in his 1960 lecture "What Is the Nerve of Interest in the Novel?" "However apparently sordid or distressing or tragic or grim the circumstances of a novel may be," the novelist "is also the eternal, who looks down upon everything and enjoys it."[5] He is like a Hindu monk whom Ramakrishna observed coming out of his cell twice a day in order to clap his hands "as though he were a spectator in the theater, . . . as though the whole universe were an enormous . . . performance" (65). Here Isherwood solders the monk and the novelist, uniting them as visionaries. Nevertheless, as *My Guru and His Disciple* makes evident, Isherwood fell away—consciously, at least—from such a unifying perspective. Eight months after completing *My Guru and His Disciple,* he laments, "I don't know what I think of it" (*Liberation,* 627).

Isherwood fell away from a unifying perspective perhaps because of the literary and critical culture out of which he emerged. The worldliness of prose narrative fiction has been taken for granted by literary history. The era of literary modernism is the source of Isherwood's experiments with the boundaries between fiction and memoir, but literary modernism traditionally has been identified with secularism. What we must do, I think, is rescue Isherwood from his unease: a result perhaps of his misrecognition— and literary history's misrecognition—of the novel's place in mysticism. The effort will require a look at religion in Anglo-American modernism, with attention to G. R. S. Mead's modernist journal *The Quest,* one of the transnational conduits whereby Eastern religions, including Vedanta, entered the background that nurtured Isherwood. It will also require fresh consideration of Aldous Huxley's hostility to the novel form. Huxley seems to assign fiction an innate enmity to the knowledge of mystical being: "the Perennial philosophy," as Huxley calls it. Isherwood came to think of Huxley's censoriousness as the symptom of Huxley's being "essentially a square" (*My Guru and His Disciple,* 202). That assessment might have been intensified by Huxley's antinovelistic animus. Did it drive Isherwood to defend the dignity of his novel writing—and simultaneously to assert the antagonism between fiction and faith? Moving against the grain of that antagonism, I propose, is the relation of novelistic form to contemplation rather than to action, and the form's relation to timelessness rather than to history. In this regard, Isherwood's *Down There on a Visit* is a crucial text. Even the restless wandering of that novel's protagonists—a wandering that Isherwood's expatriation in America underwrites—might be tied to mysticism.

Religion in Modernism

Pericles Lewis argues that "the attempt to turn the novel's sociological possibilities toward a consideration of [religion and philosophy] helped the modernists to transform the novel."[6] Henry James, James Joyce, Virginia Woolf, and Marcel Proust sought "a secular sacred," Lewis writes, "transcendent or ultimate meaning to be discovered in this world, without reference to the supernatural"—yet still and all engaged with it (21). They tried (as in Woolf) to turn daily life into a sacred continuum, or (as in Joyce) to convert "mimesis into meaning, metonymy into myth, [in a way] so clearly influenced by religion" (185).

In bringing Isherwood and Huxley into the space of Lewis's argument, I am filling out Lewis's point, but not merely following it. Isherwood and Huxley affirm religion more directly than do the other novelists of the "secular sacred," and they approach more nearly the religious undertow of fiction before modernism. *My Guru and His Disciple* surprisingly revises Joyce's *A Portrait of the Artist as a Young Man:* Isherwood's "portrait," instead of ending with a rebellion against religious feeling, asserts its inescapable value. Huxley's novel *Time Must Have a Stop* (1944) gives no quarter to the reader who thinks to avoid Atman. But the sense of religion (and of morality) in Isherwood and Huxley is oriented toward mysticism; and "mysticism" makes no appearance in Lewis's index, even though mysticism in modernist fiction most encapsulates what he illustrates.

The more one brings forward the mysticism in modernist fiction, however, the more likely one is to feel the temporal designations of literary history slipping from one's grasp. Modernist fiction might best justify its period label insofar as it persistently argues that time must have a stop. Literary historians prefer time and its contexts. Lewis anchors modernist fiction historically by extrapolating dialogues between novelists and modernist-era writers about religion—Durkheim and Freud. There is an arena of dialogue that requires no extrapolation, however: Mead's *The Quest,* a journal of exchanges about religion, philosophy, and the arts that, between 1909 and 1931, included among its contributors William Butler Yeats, Ezra Pound, and Rabindranath Tagore, and such writers on mystical or occult traditions as Jessie Weston, W. R. Inge, Arthur Machen, and Evelyn Underhill. *The Quest* prefigures Isherwood's 1945 edited volume *Vedanta for the Western World.* Its influence, especially through Mead's contributor W. R. Inge, informs the Vedantism of Gerald Heard, who, Isherwood says, introduced Isherwood to Swami, "in the sense that Gerald presented . . . Gerald's image of [Swami], to me" (*Liberation, 525*).

The Quest and Mead's 1913 monograph, *Quests Old and New,* are prime examples of modernist thought that, inspired by mysticism, solicits antihistoricist phenomena. Not that Mead's journal ducks specifically contemporary experience. The numbers for 1915–16 contain "A Modernist's Diary" by Robert Waldron, a Catholic priest who will serve the church no longer, not least because his superiors reprimand him for acquiring books of Eastern philosophy. The diary of this prototype of Stephen Dedalus is historically situated; nevertheless, Mead was committed to extracting from the present and the past an eclectic religious tradition (a Perennial philosophy) that brings together Taoism, Buddhism, Gnosticism, the negative theology of pseudo-Dionysius the Areopagite in the sixth century AD, the twentieth-century Buddhism of D. T. Suzuki, and the modernist philosophers Hans Vaihinger, Henri Bergson, and Rudolf Eucken. It is perhaps noteworthy that Eucken, winner of the Nobel Prize for Literature in 1908, coined the current meaning of "activism."

Balancing temporal and atemporal dimensions, Mead emphasizes points about the relation of mysticism to contemplation and action that it will be useful to rehearse as a preparation for turning to Isherwood and Huxley. Mead argues that Buddhist traditions, at least in their "progressive" wing, neither oppose the world of becoming to Nirvana (or "That-ness") nor define Nirvana as "the annihilation of human aspirations."[7] But although becoming can glimpse Nirvana, Mead points out that direct access to it is the province of mysticism. The mystic mind is more likely than others to accept the way in which That-ness defies language. "Being" is trapped in language, and language is as illusive as selfhood. The idea of a self at the back of consciousness is illusory, but consciousness itself exists. Given the importance of consciousness to That-ness, it is likely that contemplation rather than action has a better chance of grasping Reality.

Mead unfolds the transtemporal mystical inheritance of the modernists Vaihinger, Bergson, and Eucken. He aligns with Buddhist analogues Vaihinger's idea that conscious fictions are "the indispensable foundation" of life, so that Vaihinger can be read as an exponent of "practical mysticism" (249, 260). Mead then represents Bergson's metaphysical flux as, in Bergson's words, "the means of possessing a reality absolutely instead of knowing it relatively" (289): the flux is Bergson's Thatness. But Bergson's flux, and Eucken's activism, suggest to Mead a deviation from older religious quests. He again seeks to fuse the new with the old. To Eucken's insistence that the life of consciousness must be strenuously activist, "as though activity were the absolute" (308), Mead contrasts the more subtle approach to action in Taoist tradition, which holds that "When inaction has been achieved, action results spontaneously and unconsciously to the organism" (38–39). And in response to Bergson's assertions that mobility must be the essence of consciousness, Mead eloquently evokes the contemplation that is "the changeless lord of change" (298). "Bergson himself insists," Mead comments, "on the need of concentrated effort for resisting the current of the habitual in order to arrive at intuition. . . . If it is activism and energism and not quietism that is required, at the same time this energetic effort to withstand the flux of conventional conceptualising is an immobility of its own kind" (298–99).

Huxley's War: Mysticism versus "The Novel"

Isherwood's Introduction to *Vedanta for the Western World* virtually recapitulates Mead's exposition. Equally echoing Mead's adjustment of action to contemplation are back-to-back essays in the volume: Isherwood's "The Gita and War" and Huxley's "Action and Contemplation." Although Isherwood, despite his own pacificism, writes to defend Arjuna's commitment to war, Isherwood describes Arjuna's action as both necessary and illusive: "Attached action binds us to the world of appearance. . . . We live in a delirium of doing."[8] Contemplative nonattachment halts the delirium: "The doer of non-attached action is the most conscientious of men" (364).

The succeeding essay by Huxley proposes that "well-intentioned actions performed by ordinary . . . people, sunk in their selfhood and without spiritual insight, seldom do much good" (367). The way toward good action is defined in the contemporary world in political terms. But "the great paradox of politics," Huxley says, is "the fact that political action is necessary [but] incapable of satisfying the needs which called it into existence" (368). Self-abnegation initiates "the radical transformation of personality" that would be the key to collective transformation. "Only one effective method [for such transformation] has been discovered—that of the mystic" (369). The mystic, whom Huxley also calls "the advanced contemplative" or "the theocratic saint," "mitigate[s] the poisons which society generates within itself by its political and economic activities" (ibid.). "The business of a seer is to see; and if he involves himself in . . . God-eclipsing activities"—political and economic—"which make seeing impossible, he betrays" himself and his fellows (370).

"The theocratic saint" is the figure Isherwood believed could not be represented in a novel—or even in what might be called a nonfiction novel, *My Guru and His Disciple*. Certainly, the life pictured in novels seems a matter of selves and groups untouched by metaphysical dimensions. Isn't immediate praxis what the novel has been about since its famous rise in the eighteenth century, or the seventeenth? However, in the face of Huxley's arguments on behalf of the theocratic saint, novels and the apparent vocation of novelists might rightly wither away. *Time*

Must Have a Stop is the twin in fiction of Huxley's immediately previous wartime book, *Grey Eminence* (1941), a study of the seventeenth-century mystic and diplomat François Leclerc du Tremblay, aka Père Joseph of Paris, the right-hand man of Cardinal Richelieu. The most relevant predecessor of *My Guru and His Disciple* (simultaneously like and unlike it), *Grey Eminence* enlists history to witness the betrayal of mysticism by those "poisons" that apparently have been the nerve of interest in novels.

Beginning as a mystic and ending as a politician, Père Joseph thinks he can fuse the contemplative and the active life. The resulting confusion of religion and state propels the Thirty Years' War, at the cost of eight million lives. Huxley's history of the fusion is polemical in regard to contemporary global conflict. During World War II, Huxley insists, the fascist is not the only enemy. Any politics that is not also what Huxley in *Grey Eminence* calls "goodness politics," modeling its justice on ethical values that are appropriate to individuals and small groups, and taking the Perennial philosophy for its guide, amounts to the fascist within.[9] The fascist has long been within. *Grey Eminence* is published four years short of the conclusion of the new Thirty Years' War that began in 1914. Huxley suggests that the seventeenth-century conflict, the Great War, and the Second World War are simultaneous space-times of aggression and destruction. They suggest that historical action is a shadow play, incapable of redress unless one finds a radical departure from it. The temporal experiments of literary modernism appear to hand Huxley the means of communicating an alternative to the self-stultifying actions of "history" and "politics."

Time Must Have a Stop, the novel that follows *Grey Eminence,* exploits the experiments with time that modernists favor. Set in 1929 in fascist Italy, it evokes the prehistory of the present (and again the simultaneity of eras). In the middle of the narrative, one of its two protagonists dies of a heart attack. Up until that death Huxley has made use of a realistic mode. True to the experimental nature of literary modernism, he then undoes his use. Against the grain of "realism," one-third of the novel's remaining seventeen chapters render the afterlife of the dead man.[10] We follow his conflicts with a Reality that solicits an attention his egoism refuses to give it, on account of his stubborn gravitation toward destructive earthbound attachments.

The other protagonist, an eighteen-year-old poet and nephew of the man who dies, remains alive, but, thanks to *his* egoism, indirectly betrays to the fascist police an Italian pacifist-mystic, who submits to arrest. The novel's epilogue draws the moral lessons. The poet, a maimed veteran of the North African campaign, has not lost habits that duplicate his uncle's limitations. But there has been an advance: he has sheltered the Italian visionary when the latter was released from prison. What the poet learned from the mystic—in effect the lessons of *Grey Eminence*—becomes the substance of the novel's epilogue. An excerpt from the epilogue is the second essay in *Vedanta for the Western World*. It thus might seem that *Time Must Have a Stop* shows the compatibility of novelistic form, especially in modernist fiction's undoing of time, with mysticism. And yet there is also no compatibility, if we are to judge by Huxley's treatment of his protagonists. Whereas Père Joseph treacherously surrenders mysticism to politics and activism, Huxley's poet and his uncle treacherously surrender mysticism to art and poetry. The poetry represents fiction, if only because his poems mirror the novel. He makes up the poems in response to his immediate experiences. The poems thus duplicate what is happening in the prose narrative, as if to remind the reader of the way Huxley is building the fiction in two aesthetic modes. Both modes, as well as the protagonists, thereby are identified as vehicles of the betrayal of the mystic pacifist. Visual art also becomes an accomplice: the young poet's dealings with a Degas drawing lead to the pacifist's arrest.

Huxley's wartime books amount to a mortification of Huxley's identities as a narrative artist and historian. Turning to fiction and history, he gives himself nowhere to rest in either. Should we propose that "the novelistic" exemplifies protomystical meditations and contemplative detachments, *Time Must Have a Stop* resists the proposal, because the proposal is aesthetically oriented. The problem with aesthetic orientation, Huxley's mystic tells the poet, is that aesthetics inhibits knowledge of what there is to know. *Grey Eminence* begins novelistically, with accretions of details characteristic of realism. But Huxley then proceeds to indict the details because they obscure Reality. The indictment arrives via Huxley's criticism of Père Joseph's proto-novel, his epic *The Turciad*, which is set in Heaven, where God exalts France: "a strangely materialistic account," Huxley comments, for "telling the truth about the God whom" Père Joseph "had dimly apprehended in . . . contemplation" (153).

An adequately contemplative mind must be at a further remove from ordinary existence than the art of fiction might ever be. In proposing such a radical remove, Huxley shows how untrustworthy fiction's capacity for didactic exegesis is, and for salutary address to his readers' worldly wills. *Grey Eminence* becomes his platform for teaching the threats to "goodness" politics, and *Time Must Have a Stop* becomes a platform for teaching *Grey Eminence*.

But novels are not as incompatible with didactic exegesis as Huxley insists. The problematic role of discursive exegesis in fictional narrative is as old as "the novel" before the novel, which is to say as old as romance. The question looms in the difference between Chrétien de Troyes's *Percival* (ca. 1190) and the anonymous, Carthusian-influenced *Quest for the Holy Grail* (ca. 1225). The former explains little of the mysteries that its adventures unfold; the latter, in contrast, attaches to every adventure a pedagogical lesson. Another romance, which inspired Père Joseph's childhood, is the sixth-century story of *Baarlam and Josaphat*. This narrative is a Christianized version of the life of Buddha, who is Josaphat, a name resulting from mistranslations of *Bodhisatva*. *Baarlam and Josaphat* is also a quest—of its hero for explanations of the world—but the explanations take the form of reasoned debates rather than of hints, as in *Percival,* or of encyclopedic explanation, as in the other grail story. Such prototypes of the novel form are indissociable from varieties of exegesis.

Reference to the involvement of romance with doctrine means only to point out that where Huxley feeds contemplatively inclined readers with explicit (and therefore, I note, with less than mystical) teaching, he is not out of line with the long history of fiction, any more than he is out of line with modernist novels. Modernist novels often move into the territory of the discursive essay, as in Proust, Thomas Mann, and Lawrence. Also in the modernist line are Isherwood's experiments with biography and autobiography, inasmuch as they transgress generic boundaries: they compound real history, fiction, and teaching. The insistent discursiveness of Huxley's novel is traditionally novelistic.

But whether Huxley is writing fiction or history, there is likely a deeper motive for Huxley's antagonism to fiction. The motive lies in a perplexing of will that is at the heart of the mysticism-directed division between contemplation and action. If will to "the delirium of doing" belongs to the world, can we say that it is will that retreats from the world? How can a will, especially one that belongs to a self that is becoming selfless, either be identified as such, or mobilized, by any teaching? The question has no less relevance to Isherwood's retreat from the monastery than to Huxley.

Answers are made complex by the mystic tradition's "active annihilation of self." An immediate relation to That-ness requires the mystic to alienate himself from the world, from what Michel de Certeau in his great study of mysticism, *The Mystic Fable,* calls "the domain of will, [and of] the ethics of a will to do."[11] The path of alienation is the annihilation of the will, and a consequent contemplative distance from action. One of Père Joseph's teachers describes that annihilation, Huxley says, as living "in the abyss of the divine essence and in the absolute nothingness of things . . . and if at times a man finds himself separated from them (the essence and the nothingness), he must return to them . . . by annihilation." Huxley comments: "The learning to live by constant active annihilation is probably the most . . . exacting of all human tasks; but to those who fulfill it comes the reward that came . . . to all the great mystics; the experience of living simultaneously in time and eternity" (*Grey Eminence*, 91).

Who (or what) is the agent of active annihilation remains a mystery. The Italian mystic in *Time Must Have a Stop* advises the poet to scrutinize all impulses to action. One must calculate the effects of every decision and event. The young poet's inattention to the advice, his disastrous willfulness, results in treachery. But the will that is at issue in the treachery seems different from the will that pertains to the mystic. Because "will" might cover differentiations within mysticism's traditions that are not in our working vocabulary, de Certeau is led to formulate what he calls "the mystic volo" (164). He contrasts its form of "wanting" with modern scientific disciplines, in which "there is no field that is not based on a set of postulates and definitions that are not decisional" (168). But with the mystic, "the will is isolated from any possible knowledge . . . detached from anything known or possessed. . . . This volo, because it has no particular object and clings to 'nothing,' changes into its opposite—not to want anything" (169). In this detachment—another facet of contemplation—"mystic discourse," according to de Certeau, can "open . . . the field of a different kind of knowledge" (172).

The paradox of the involuntariness of will might drive Huxley, in a "decisional" direction, to be didactically overexplicit in his work, even though that decisional explicitness is out of phase with the mystic volo. And it is because aesthetic interest and response might be only a false version of the volo, seducing persons away from ethical astringency, that Huxley presents surrogate artists in his fiction with as much hostility as he can muster. But there is one moment in *Grey Eminence* where, almost without noticing, Huxley allows visual art, history, and an historian's equivalent of fiction to emerge as a willful-will-less consent to the affinities between aesthetic contemplation, the novelistic "nerve of the novel," and mysticism. In a chapter called "Nothing Fails like Success," Huxley prefigures Isherwood's passing formulation, in the 1960 lecture I referred to earlier, of the novel genre's access to mysticism.

Huxley's chapter turns to the etchings whereby Jacques Callot illustrated the war caused by Père Joseph. Calling the pictures "pieces of first-hand reporting," Huxley praises the "complete neutrality" and "imperturbability" of Callot's drawings. Then comes something surprising. Huxley writes, "Callot's art is the aesthetic analogue of the personal conduct of [the mystic] François de Sales, [to] whom it was a matter of indifference . . . whether he was in a state of consolation or desolation" (250). Not that Callot is not distressed by what he reports, but his "imperturbability"— presumably his *mystic* imperturbability, given the reference to de Sales—is in his style. And now Huxley adds "the novelistic" to the interidentification of Callot's visual art with the mysticism of de Sales. "It is as though the theme of *For Whom the Bell Tolls*," he writes, "had been treated in the style of Jane Austen" (ibid.). The very bizarreness of the conflation suggests that Huxley, in the face of pictures of war, suddenly is at peace with the novelistic genre. Is it not the case that the theme of war in *Grey Eminence* is being treated in the style of Aldous Huxley? For Huxley initiates seven pages of description of Callot's pictures as if they were Huxley's narrative itself. An extended ekphrasis merges Callot, de Sales, Hemingway, Austen, and Huxley. And a final merger takes place. Having rendered into words Callot's etched drawing of vengeful peasants thrashing a corpse in exchange "for all the outrages suffered through the long years of warfare," Huxley goes on to describe—with the novelistic license denied to history and nonfiction—what the peasants will do after the pictured scene.

The drawing by Degas in *Time Must Have a Stop* will be a motive for Huxley's condemnation of all the arts and for his insistence on the demanding duties of decisional will. In contrast to the Degas, Callot's drawings inspire Huxley's sudden relaxation, a carrying away of himself into the domain of the volo. In other words, for a moment in *Grey Eminence*, fiction, art, and history are all the same mystic fable, and Huxley's psychomachia is surrendered to a truce.

The Novel's Generic Relation to "Mystic Fable"

Environed by Huxley's books, and by fifteen contributions by Huxley to *Vedanta and the Western World*, it is no wonder that Isherwood, Arjuna-like, reentered the battle of life as a novelist, protecting his métier even if it meant distancing himself from mysticism. Perhaps he needn't have been protective. I propose—if only for the sake of hypothesis—to offer seven specimens of fiction (some mingling summary of events with direct quotation) that might exemplify "the nerve of interest in the novel" in a way that complements Isherwood's writing. The specimens might align the novelist-Vedantist not only with modernism but also with an essential generic lineage. Can such few excerpts illustrate any underlying character that countless novels share? A decidedly skeptical answer is likely. However, if the samples stimulate formulations about what novels are, as a thought experiment about the adequacy or inadequacy of generic identities, it might be useful.

(1) A young woman committing adultery is discovered by her husband. She has never loved him, has even despised him. She challenges him to guess why she married him. Because, he responds, she wanted to be wedded before her younger sister was. "It was true, but it gave her a funny little turn to realise that he knew it. Oddly enough, even in that moment of fear and anger, it excited her compassion."[12]

(2) A king and his adviser come upon a man who has been mauled by a wild animal. The injured man asks for the king's help in exchange for his talent as "a patcher of words." "If in speech there be any wounds," the mauled man says, "I can sew them up, so that no damage results from them."[13]

(3) "Twenty-three years before, he had given up what everybody said was a most promising career in radical politics . . . to retire to Florence. . . . The conscious or unconscious hypocrisy of every form of effective public speaking! The asinine stupidity of that interminable repetition of the same absurd over-simplifications, the same illogical arguments and vulgar personalities, the same bad history and baseless prophecy! And that was supposed to be man's highest duty. And if he chose the life of a civilized human being, he ought to be ashamed of himself."[14]

(4) A Greek and a German fall afoul of each other, in part because of a language barrier between them. They fight, and the Greek permanently disables one of the German's hands. "Aleko didn't make any kind of apology, but Hans found this sincere and therefore preferable. They ended up behaving as if nothing whatsoever had happened." Yet Hans says to a third party: "I don't bear the boy any ill will. But one of these days I'm going to kill him or he's going to kill me."[15]

(5) A father, attempting to protect his son from despair, tells him that "temporary . . . was the saddest word of all there is nothing else in the world it's not despair until time it's not even time until it was."[16]

(6) A young woman's quest, over the course of thirteen volumes of narration, has for its aim communication with "the unlocated being of . . . people . . . and not at all with . . . their busy momentary selves."[17]

(7) "And the boy watched them, not daring/To ask why or to whom/This grail was meant to be served,/For his heart was always aware/Of his wise old master's warnings./But I fear his silence may hurt him,/For

I've often heard it said,/That talking too little can do/As much damage as talking too much./Yet, for better or worse,/He never said a word."[18]

I would call what is characteristically novelistic in these specimens a meditative complex. They each exemplify it not only because they solicit interest, but because they bring interest to a surprised halt. The specimens represent nodes of suspense that absorb, as well as require, heightened contemplation. Even the free indirect discourse in the third specimen exacts a meditative stop by virtue of the truth claim it asserts yet leaves uncertain. Moreover, what is being attended to in each specimen is enigmatic, something hidden as well as obvious—another reason they, and their sources, require halted concentration. The boy in (7) instances a dilemma that is perhaps inextricable from language: language might always say too little and too much. One's attention is at one with language, and is also trying to think it through, or to think through it, to a That-ness of what there is to think about. If the specimens represent characters' actions, or the brink of their actions, the reader's attention is at odds with those acts—and, probably, with acts that the reader will execute when the reading is over.

My description of the specimens draws on quests old and new. "Mysticism" designates the hidden: Nirvana. But, as Mead points out, Nirvana is not discovered by refusing Samsara, the world of self-centered desire, of becoming, inferior to Being. Novels go down into the uproar of becoming, even as they lead one's contemplative self to concentrate on what is above it. Concentration means thought, analytic detachment from what language and action afford mind and self—a glimpse of a background depth, Reality. To be sure, the idea of such a background goes against everything we pragmatically live by. And if there really is such a background, we are likely to see no reason why our customary expansiveness, resistant to halts, can't unite with it. That expansive habit seeks to collapse the distance between contemplation and action. But for Buddhism—as well as for Vedanta—disinterested contemplation is not an all-reconciling merger. The psychology of mysticism, inasmuch as it is illustrated by "Buddha's psychology of desire," as Irving Babbitt puts it in his commentary on the Buddhist *Dhammapada*, seems an "intolerably astringent" discipline.[19] Expansive longing gives nothing up, whereas Buddhist attentiveness renounces everything that is outside its contemplative moment.

In *Sex, Pain, and Time* (1939), Gerald Heard, through whose eyes Isherwood first "saw" Swami, repeatedly cites Babbitt. Babbitt notes that by 1936, the date of his translation of the *Dhammapada,* fifteen different Pali terms had been previously translated as the single English word *desire.* Babbitt and Mead agree that the Buddhist vocabulary for contemplation as well as for desire outdistances Western articulations. If Western traditions lacked such refinements of words and concepts, perhaps the European novel developed to fill the gap. Not intentionally, but gropingly, in order to supply a sense of both the painted veil that those who live call life and its hidden farther side, and, at the same time, to supply an incisive technique for meditation on the veil and what is behind it.

De Certeau suggests that it might be no coincidence that the European novel appears in the seventeenth century alongside a flowering of mysticism. The mystics sought, in exilic migrations, a place apart from wordliness. The causes that produced the quest for a place apart include the splintering of religious sects, the creation of the modern state, and the rise of evidentiary history writing. With the old faith lost, and in the face of the rapid corruptions of the new sects and nations, truth for the mystics seemed alienated from the institutionalized world. "Mystics came to designate what had become separate from the institution" (*The Mystic Fable,* 86). Clinging to a separate truth, the mystic solicited ineffable meanings. If my specimens of the nerve of interest in the novel have merit, what de Certeau implies about the relation of the novel to mysticism is worth mentioning. Historical writing in the seventeenth century, according to de Certeau, superseded the ineffable oral and antidiscursive phenomena on which mysticism depended. Early-modern historians assumed that they were rationalizing and thereby obtaining "the knowledge [that mysticism] expresses without knowing it." In comparison with history, such knowledge was classed as "fable" and "fiction," because, de Certeau writes, "like all fiction, it [was] presumed to mask or to have mislaid the meaning it contains" (12). The novel's seventeenth-century origin— *Don Quixote*—mimes the historian's contrast with the mystic fable. But the contrast meditates on history and mystic fable simultaneously. As a reflex of the historian's conflict with the mystic, the novel form wrestles with the mystic's vision of the illusoriness or hollowness of history and action, and in the development of the genre it subsumes, and extends, the wrestling.

Down Here on a Visit

Isherwood's narratives, whether fictional or "nonfictional," suggest that the novelist, and the readers of fiction whose detachment from life (at least, while they are reading) replicates the novelist's contemplation, are not out of touch with That-ness. The suggestion, however, would seem to happen behind Isherwood's back. One must rely on the tales he tells (and the tale that might be told by the history of the genre). The text that is most telling about the compatibility of mystical religion and the novel is *Down There on a Visit,* especially in its fourth segment, "Paul," which is drawn from Isherwood's years at the Vedanta Center. The bisexual Paul, whom Christopher the narrator, himself erotically ambiguous, takes in as a housemate and a fellow contemplative, appears to be Isherwood-the-author's thought experiment about the relation of eros to mysticism. When Paul's eros becomes especially problematic—he is accused, albeit falsely, of sexual relations with a twelve-year-old girl with whom he has flirted—the religious practice comes to an end. Then Paul, a registered conscientious objector, is assigned to work in a forestry camp, where he becomes a hero—until he steps over the color line. Taking as a buddy a black man, he alienates the camp's racist directors; adding insult to injury, he deliberately makes the directors think that the two men are lovers. He is reclassified 4-F. After the war, Paul drifts back to Europe, resuming a precarious life until his death.

There is no Huxleyan exegesis within the text to explain what Paul means to *Down There on a Visit.* On the surface it seems that Isherwood's treatment of Paul demonstrates how little eros conduces to religious vision. It approximates Huxley's derogation of the sexual liberations of Isherwood's era. Echoing Irving Babbitt too, Isherwood appears to use Paul to reject the expansive version of Buddhism that promises reconciliation between mysticism and the flesh. Projecting himself *as* Paul, Isherwood mimes the erotic impulsiveness that he and others identify as the motive for Isherwood's departure from the monastery.

But it is the light that Paul's case throws on the novelist's relation to the mystic volo, his reconciling compatibility with it, that matters most to any attempt to controvert the critics' (and Isherwood's) stories of incompatible antagonisms. Christopher and Paul's experiment in contemplation fails not because of sex but because of its deliberated willfulness. The willfulness, whether religious or sexual, belongs to the world, not to the volo. But even eros, in its involuntary aspects, checks the will that we identify with directed desire. It is Paul's drifting, his inability to settle into any satisfying location, that comes closest to that space apart, the isolation from institutions, to which de Certeau assigns the mystic. The drifting is also legible as a figure of the indiscernible difference between mystic passivity and directed extroverted action. Did the historical Isherwood choose Vedanta or choose against it? Did he will to suppress his novelistic career or to restart it? The questions presuppose a clarity that personal identity or worldly will and choice—Père Joseph's sphere of action—depend upon, but that a mystical perspective transcends.

The four novellas of *Down There on a Visit* comprise what seems to be a historical novel, chronicling Christopher's life from 1928 into the 1940s, alongside the return of global war. The novellas are disjointed in terms of years, but their disjunction also suggests that they are each equally present—time must have a stop!—by virtue of their being situated in what might be, after all, an illusion of historical temporality. The novellas are also about isolated figures who double, triple, and quadruple each other. Their separate identities are therefore also an illusion. The reader can see, if the characters cannot, that Paul is a likeness of Christopher, but he is also, in a curious way, a likeness of the solitary man, Mr. Lancaster, the focus of the first novella. Such similarities implicitly replicate a "teaching" in the "Epilogue" of *Time Must Have a Stop:* "People love their egos and don't wish to mortify them" (248). But Samsara mortifies them. Lancaster is a typical John Bull but lives, for business reasons, in Germany, where he is increasingly self-enclosed in a defeated existence. When the isolation becomes unbearable, he commits suicide. His solitude, and the nearness to suicide it exemplifies, repeats itself. Christopher rescues Paul from suicidal intentions, as a delayed penance for not rescuing Lancaster. But Christopher's willed worldly actions are no more directed than Paul's drifting. In Christopher's case, in all the cases, ego-identities break down. A matrix of shared being underlies the illusive separateness of personalities.

As that matrix is disclosed, true to the volo, the contrast between voluntary and involuntary "doing" also breaks down. In the years between Mr. Lancaster and Paul, Christopher is involved with a bisexual young German (a proto-Paul) who wants Christopher to rescue him, before the war and then after. Both times Christopher justly refuses, deliberately cutting the boy adrift. But the same cutting adrift, eroding deliberation, awaits Christopher. In the second of the novel's segments, Christopher abandons life with an expatriate friend on a Greek island, in order to return to his native England. The abandonment seems rightly, willfully "decisional"—until Christopher realizes that he can never be at home, not even when he emigrates to the United States. De Certeau presents one of his seventeenth-century mystics as an epitome of the mystic character because he was supremely a nomad. The American Isherwood and the American Huxley also are nomads. America is where both are homelessly at home.

Should that be surprising? Not if the mysterious will that is not ego-driven is not at home in the world, or on the world's terms. The "there" of Isherwood's "down there" is Samsara, lovable yet melancholy because persons are not as historically individualized or as freely acting as they seem. There must be something else, something in contrast to the way in which all selfhoods are the same limitary walls, something in contrast to the transitoriness of "visiting." In regard to this "something else," I note the self-reflexive aspects whereby Isherwood witnesses the way in which the novelistic genre, in its historical unfolding, maintains the mysticism that is obscured by the anticontemplative world of becoming, to which novels are superficially faithful. In "Mr. Lancaster" the eponymous figure is said to live in a romance or an epic, literary forms that are genetic predecessors of the novel; and Christopher, who has just published his first novel, admits that he too, like Lancaster, converts what happens to himself into "epic myth." In the next narrative, "Ambrose," life on a desert island suggests the emergence from epic and romance of the realist novel, starting with *Robinson Crusoe*. The third segment, "Waldemar," includes appearances by "E. M.," a scarcely disguised Forster, the modernist novelist who is said to live by a faith that is not an institutional religion, and also to "live by love, not by will" (175). It is as if in this segment, although it brings private lives closer to global history because it is set in 1938 and is closer to war, E. M. the novelist opens a door out of history into a mystical realm. Then, in "Paul" the eponymous restless quester returns the narrative to the patterning of romance. If Paul misses the mystic grail, and if Isherwood and the others do too, it is not because it is all so hidden. The genre of the novel might not disclose it, but harbors it within.

Notes

1. Christopher Isherwood, *My Guru and His Disciple* (New York: Farrar, Straus and Giroux, 1980), 189.

2. Peter Shneidre, "Christopher under the Wishing Tree," in *The Isherwood Century: Essays on the Life and Work of Christopher Isherwood*, ed. James J. Berg and Chris Freeman (Madison: University of Wisconsin Press, 2000), 227.

3. Christopher Isherwood, *Exhumations: Stories, Articles, Verses* (New York: Simon and Schuster, 1966), 120.

4. Christopher Isherwood, *Liberation: Diaries, Volume Three: 1970–1983*, ed. Katherine Bucknell (New York: Harper, 2012), 554, 526.

5. Christopher Isherwood, *Isherwood on Writing*, ed. James J. Berg (Minneapolis: University of Minnesota Press, 2007), 66.

6. Pericles Lewis, *Religious Experience and the Modernist Novel* (Cambridge: Cambridge University Press, 2010), 5.

7. G. R. S. Mead, *Quests Old and New* (London: G. Bell & Sons, 1913), 67.

8. Christopher Isherwood, ed., *Vedanta for the Western World* (1945; reprint, Hollywood: Vedanta Press, 1971), 363.

9. Aldous Huxley, *Grey Eminence* (New York: Harper and Brothers, 1941).

10. Aldous Huxley, *Time Must Have a Stop* (1944; reprint, Normal, Ill.: Dalkey Archive Press, 1998).

11. Michel de Certeau, *The Mystic Fable: Volume One: The Sixteenth and Seventeeth Centuries,* trans. Michael B. Smith (Chicago: University of Chicago Press, 1992), 155.

12. W. Somerset Maugham, *The Painted Veil,* in *The Maugham Reader* (Garden City, N.Y.: Doubleday & Company, 1950), 50.

13. *The Balavariani (Barlaam and Josaphat),* trans. David Marshall Lang (Berkeley and Los Angeles: University of California Press, 1966), 61.

14. Huxley, *Time Must Have a Stop,* 38.

15. Christopher Isherwood, *Down There on a Visit* (1962; reprint, Minneapolis: University of Minnesota Press, 1999), 104, 106.

16. William Faulkner, *The Sound and the Fury* (New York: Vintage International, 1990), 178.

17. Dorothy Richardson, *Pilgrimage 4* (1938; reprint, New York: Popular Library, 1976), 141.

18. Chrétien de Troyes, *Percival: The Story of the Grail,* trans. Burton Raffel (New Haven and London: Yale University Press, 1999), 103, ll. 3244–54.

19. Irving Babbitt, *The Dhammapada: Translated from the Pali with an Essay on Buddha and the Occident* (New York: New Directions, 1936), 110.

10

Down Where on a Visit?

Isherwood's Mythology of Self

REBECCA GORDON STEWART

In the 1950s, as Christopher Isherwood continued to struggle with elements of *The World in the Evening,* he notes in his "Writing Notebook" that he has a new idea for a story, one that after several years of editing, revisiting, and revising would be published in 1962 as *Down There on a Visit.* Although ostensibly the narrative of *Down There on a Visit* may seem greatly removed from Isherwood's original concept of a "conducted tour" through a Hell-like Purgatory of the "temporarily self-detained" ("Writing Notebook," Huntington Library, CI 1158, 58), an examination of Isherwood's unpublished notes alongside the final novel reveals that many of the themes that formed his original plan of rewriting Dante's journey through Hell and Purgatory as narrated in *The Divine Comedy* in fact have remained at the forefront of this novel.[1] Indeed, within the original dust cover text, which, according to Don Bachardy, Isherwood penned himself, there is an emphasis on Christopher's role as a "Visitor" to a "nether world": "Here are people shut up inside private hells of their own making."[2]

As was true with many of his literary creations, Isherwood searched for a title, considering many, including his frequent fallback of "The Lost" ("Writing Notebook," 59). Other titles considered include "The Shades" (which is the term Dante uses to name his inhabitants of Hell), "The Others" (ibid., 57), and, finally, *Down There on a Visit.* Isherwood talks of the idea that the eventual title is a reference to Joris-Karl Huysmans's novel *Là-bas.*[3] This late-nineteenth-century French novel formed part of Isherwood's writing and naming "because it is partly a novel about hell" ("Writing Notebook," 10). Both *Down There on a Visit* and *Là-bas* are "partly" about hell, and, perhaps more importantly, about finding yourself in reference to this hell.

Indeed, in *Là-bas,* the main character, Durtal, is a writer who, having grown weary of the modern world, has excluded himself from society and has become obsessed with the sadist and Satanist Gilles de Rais.[4] Like the characters of Dante and Christopher, Durtal undertakes a spiritual journey as he researches and writes, which arguably represents Huysmans's own journey back to Catholicism. This narrative is ostensibly a religious quest of self-discovery; furthermore, with its subtitle of "A Journey into the Self," this novel represents Durtal, a thinly disguised version of Huysmans, on a quest to "find" himself in order to return to society.

Down There on a Visit, Là-bas, and *Inferno* can therefore be seen to be connected in style and themes. One notable reason is that they represent narrated versions of spiritual and physical journeys undertaken by their authors. What is prominent in all of these works is the focus placed on finding an identity not only through physical travel—seen in Durtal's journeys around Paris, Dante's movements through Purgatory and Hell, and Christopher's various trips—but also through literature, writing, and theorizing. The role of the writer in all three works is fundamental to all elements of plot and characterization.

The concept of reworking and reimagining Dante's epic poems seems to have attracted Isherwood for several reasons, most notably the emphasis on the individual in relation to a journey that represents a process of self-understanding, a perceptibly Freudian theme, which is largely in keeping with much of Isherwood's literary trope. The journey Dante undertakes in the first and second part of *The Divine Comedy* takes him through the depths of Hell and Purgatory consecutively and back toward Earth. In the *Inferno,* Dante comes forth "to look once more upon the stars" (Canto XXXIV, l. 139), and in *Purgatory* he finds himself "born anew . . . Pure and Prepared to leap up to the stars" (Canto XXXIII, ll. 142–45).[5] As the closing lines of Dante's epic poems emphasize, these are tales of an author's fictionalized travel toward a moment of enlightenment as he emerges once again to see the stars. Indeed, Dante has not merely survived Hell and Purgatory, and arisen once again to see the night sky; the journey that he has undertaken has led to a better self-understanding in reference to his beliefs and his relationship with God: as Dante moves toward Paradise, he is renewed "From those most holy waters," and prepared to face the Glory of God (*Purgatory,* Canto XXXIII, l. 142).

The voyage that Dante's self-imaged protagonist undertakes with his guide Virgil shows Dante his own flaws (in relation to the sinners in Hell and Purgatory) in order for him to gain a better understanding of his faith. The process of self-revelation is interrelated with the narrative of the sinners, and it is this theme that Isherwood concentrates on within his outline of "The Forgotten":[6] the male protagonist who takes on the role of Dante (originally called William, then Peter, and eventually named Christopher) must see the inhabitants of this "Hell" in reference to his own self-imposed "Purgatory" in order to be able to return to "Earth," to return to society a changed individual.

Many aspects were changed as Isherwood worked through "The Forgotten," most notably perhaps the fact that the original was to be set in Mexico, which was to "lend its scenery and cultural aspects 'by courtesy'" ("Writing Notebook," 58). One element remains constant, however: this Purgatory is a personal Hell for the self-excluded and the neurotic. As Isherwood questions "What is 'Hell'?" he focuses on the individual: "Hell is a state of untruth, compulsive behaviour and basic insecurity," rather than the Hell of physical suffering in Dante.[7]

Isherwood's reimagined Purgatory is therefore the self-exclusion of the damned and can be linked to his understanding of psychoanalysis: individuals are unable to see themselves clearly and therefore are powerless to escape their own mental turmoil. As Isherwood summarizes, "nobody in [this Inferno] is permanently damned—only temporarily self-detained" ("Writing Notebook," 58). Isherwood removes Divine Law and emphasizes that these characters have placed themselves within this Purgatory (although arguably there are "devilish" characters who are enablers of these lost souls, seen, for example, in the descriptions of the boys on Ambrose's island as devils and satanic minions).

As Isherwood moves toward a more clearly autobiographical style of narrative, the prominence of a desire to understand oneself remains constant. He manipulates his creation of what I call his "mythology of self" and, with his adoption of "Christopher" as a first-person narrator, he refocuses this parabolic journey through Purgatory and Hell on himself. In *Down There on a Visit* Isherwood highlights the overall themes of this narrative when Christopher talks to Paul about his own spiritual searching: "what else can it be for—except to find out who you really are?"[8] In this section we see that while Christopher may not be able to fully come to terms with his own faith and beliefs, he certainly understands spiritualism in reference to his own identity. In essence, all the travels that Christopher has undertaken have represented a process of self-understanding: the journey toward acceptance and finding out who he is has been at the heart of this novel. Fundamentally, in *Down There on a Visit* Isherwood creates a narrative of inward searching, in order to present an idea of self-understanding, which is consistent with how he

reads Dante's original. The "different episodes in the journey are supposed to parallel phases of [Dante's] life" ("Writing Notebook," 61) and
are linked by a regressive narrative that allows the self-imaged narrator
to deal with these memories.

In discussion of his friend's writing, Stephen Spender claimed that
"Christopher's genius is to be entirely Christopher, and yet, at the same
time to act out roles."[9] This assertion implies that there is some kind
of authentic Christopher; however, to the reader (as distinct from those
who knew him as a friend), there are only the "roles," and the impression
gained from these is that there is a multiplicity of "selves" that change
in time, change as self-images shift, change as intellectual preoccupations
shift, but that also change as a function of literary mode. What makes
Isherwood's self-exploration interesting is that he appears to vary literary
kinds and modes deliberately in order to create the many "selves" that are
comprehended in the name Christopher Isherwood.

Furthermore, the act of writing is presented by Isherwood as part of
the process of growth and self-discovery. As such, Isherwood emphasizes
the idea that the Christopher of old and the Isherwood of now are related and yet not identical. The implied author that narrates this story is
not only older, but vitally wiser, and the act of writing has aided in this
journey of maturation. Isherwood both connects with and removes himself from this character called Christopher by creating a dual character:
Isherwood the writer and Christopher the traveler. This reflects Dante's
own style of presenting himself as two separate beings: poet and pilgrim.
It is also in keeping with previous and subsequent works by Isherwood,
most notably in *Lions and Shadows* and *Christopher and His Kind*. Isherwood presents an intentionally adopted strategy of separating older and
younger selves in order to construct a process of self-understanding and
enlightenment in his writing.

Isherwood's dualistic self-imaged characters are different people owing
to the fact that the younger version is on a journey that the older narrator
has already taken. Isherwood specifically focuses the reader's attention on
these Christophers as being separate in *Down There on a Visit*:

> And now before I slip back into the convention of calling this young
> man "I," let me consider him as a separate being, a stranger almost. . . .
> For, of course, he *is* almost a stranger to me. . . . But *what* I am has
> refashioned itself throughout the days and years, until now almost
> all that remains constant is the mere awareness of being conscious.
> (13–14)

The two Christophers are *linked* by a journey of self-discovery, but time and the journey of self-understanding *separate* them.

This style of a dual narrative highlights the manner in which Isherwood manipulates the form in order to focus all aspects of *Down There on a Visit* on a construction and understanding of self. The narrator sees himself removed from his younger self, and he will not apologize for him, as Isherwood notes in his analysis of writing "Mr. Lancaster" when he considers that "Chris must be more clearly seen, and with less hostility" ("Writing Notebook," 126). However, the narrator does, at times, ridicule the immaturity of the young Christopher, thus emphasizing the difference between the two characters. Christopher, for example, perceives himself as being far more sophisticated than the previous generation, in particular Mr. Lancaster, who epitomizes the "enemy," or "the Others."

Although Isherwood seems to have felt that the use of Christopher Isherwood as narrator and protagonist did not work,[10] he is able to focus *Down There on a Visit* on "the attitudes to life which one individual can hold at different times—disengagement versus engagement" ("Writing Notebook," 63), which is fundamental to the construction of this personalized journey through Purgatory and Hell. This question of engagement versus disengagement and the fluidity of self is a prominent feature of the novel, as can be seen in the opening parts: "Now, at last, I'm ready to write about Mr. Lancaster. . . . I realize I must show how our meeting was the start of a new chapter in my life, indeed a whole series of chapters" (11). As this quotation demonstrates, the novel focuses on the "I": the Christopher that links all four travel narratives. Having changed and matured, Isherwood is "at last" able to engage not only with Lancaster, but also with his younger self as he starts out this "new chapter": a twofold journey that represents Christopher's first encounter with foreign lands as well as Isherwood's literary journey of writing about it.

Indeed, as is often the case in Isherwood's writing, duality is a constant and vital element. In his discussion of re-creating Dante's *Inferno,* Isherwood concludes that Dante and Virgil act as "two halves of the one person" ("Writing Notebook," 60), the two main characters acting as a reflection of each other. In earlier drafts, Isherwood intended to have two characters, a Dante and a Virgil. He talks of the relationship that they have, which "is one of recognition, acceptance and discovery: Virgil is an aspect of [Dante]" (ibid.). Moreover, utilizing themes from both *Inferno* and *Là-bas,* Isherwood consistently emphasizes the idea of an internal struggle. In *Inferno,* Virgil and Dante share thoughts quicker than reflections could in a mirror (*Inferno,* Canto XXIII, ll. 25–27), and

Là-bas is full of references to the idea that man is a dual creature: "the desire for good and the desire for evil simply form two opposing poles of the soul" (108).

As Isherwood moves away from a direct reimagining of Dante and Virgil represented by Peter and Paul in "The Forgotten" and adopts an ostensibly autobiographical representation of a divided self, the role of mirrors and reflections remains paramount. Isherwood consistently concentrates on his own physical image within *Down There on a Visit.* The process of achieving self-awareness is imaged by the use of mirrors. This device can be witnessed in much of his writing: marked examples can be seen in his early novel *The Memorial,* in which numerous characters see themselves in different mirrors, and *Goodbye to Berlin,* where Christopher focuses his analysis of his departure from Berlin away from others and back to himself: "I catch sight of my face in the mirror of a shop, and am horrified to see that I am smiling."[11]

Within *Down There on a Visit* and "The Forgotten" there are many instances of reflections and mirrors. Peter imagines himself as a dangerous enemy of the state as he prepares to cross the border to Mexico in "The Forgotten": "I looked in the glass this morning. It is the face of a successful criminal. Successful criminals have grey eyes and very small ears. Their noses are freckled. They look alert, sincere. Their manner is absent-minded but friendly" ("Writing Notebook," 98). Although surely a fantasy, which is reminiscent of W. H. Auden's Airman in *The Orators,* both the reader and Peter begin to get a better understanding of this man as he constructs an imagined identity.[12]

Moreover, in *Down There on a Visit* the process of "seeing" oneself physically is interrelated with the act of spiritually and psychoanalytically "seeing" oneself, witnessed, for example, in Isherwood's focus on the role of the mirror in the act of remembering in "Mr. Lancaster." The mirror allows the writer to see himself as he was; furthermore, one can "even recall the feelings you had as you were looking at it" (27). This is represented as a regressive mirror that allows the author to access his younger self; it allows Isherwood to analyze himself.

Mirrors are an effective tool in "Ambrose," a section that remains largely true to Isherwood's original concept of creating a Hell for his namesake narrator to travel through. With language and imagery that seem to be directly borrowed from *Inferno,* Isherwood creates a Hell-like island that is inhabited by demons and animals (see 90, 98, and 106 for examples). Leaving Ambrose in his self-exiled Purgatory, Christopher is banished as the one that does not belong and is once again faced by his own reflection. Although initially shocked to see the physical changes on his face, it is in his soul that he sees this biggest change (130). Concluding "I almost ceased being myself" on the island (129), Christopher can never be the same, although he is unable to fully understand the importance of what his reflection means.

As Christopher repeatedly searches for himself through travel, Isherwood manipulates the form of *Down There on a Visit* in order to both construct and present his literary self. A striking example of the way in which Isherwood engages with the autobiographical act is his analysis and representation of a fallible memory. He questions memory and implies that the act of writing is a construction and that what is offered is a version of self that reveals more about the present-day author than about the narrated self. Consistently blurring the distinction between autobiography and fiction in his writing, Isherwood creates and then re-creates a literary mythology where "fact" and "fiction" are deliberately confused. This can be seen in *Down There on a Visit* as Isherwood often questions the reliability of his own memory and the act of recall.

Furthermore, Isherwood's literary act of turning "memory" into "discourse" in order to construct a version of "I" is one that he presents as appropriate to his original imagining of his male protagonist gaining spiritual self-awareness through travel. Both *Down There on a Visit* and *Inferno* can be linked in the way that a truth of self is gained and constructed through parabolic journeys. Both Dante and Isherwood are presenting self-understanding and a process of enlightenment through a description of fictionalized travel.

Despite Dante's inability to recall all that has happened to him—"How I entered there I cannot truly say" (72) and "he said other things, but I forget them" (149)—this character enters into what Philippe Lejeune classes as the "autobiographical pact."[13] The inability to recall in exactitude does not in fact change the "truth" of his narrative of rekindling his faith. Similarly, although Isherwood cannot do more than attempt a total recall, the journey presents a "truth" about the implied author Isherwood.

The outcome of Christopher's journey is undoubtedly a better self-awareness. However, what is vital to the manner in which Isherwood constructs *Down There on a Visit* is the way that Christopher interacts with the lost characters of Hell and Purgatory. When Isherwood was planning the structure of "The Forgotten," he placed a great deal of emphasis on the occupants of his constructed Hell, the individuals who were to inhabit the Purgatory that his self-imaged pilgrim was to visit. Each of these encounters that Peter was to have involved interactions with people who made up the forgotten, the inhabitants of Hell. Adaptations of three of Isherwood's original narratives can be found in *Down There on a Visit:* the cousin from the British Consul becomes Mr. Lancaster; Francis Turville-Petre and his island can clearly be seen to be Ambrose and the trip that Christopher and Waldemar take to Greece; and Paul remains the focal character of the final story. The third story that Isherwood was to include about "the inmates of the refugee hospital" was removed and later Isherwood added "Waldemar."

It is, however, more than the fact that these stories can be seen to deal with the same characters as Isherwood's originally planned "The Forgotten" that convinces me that the themes have remained largely unchanged. All of the principal characters that Christopher comes into contact with represent the lost, the self-exiled, and the damned. Furthermore, through meeting these characters and seeing himself in relation to them Isherwood gains a gradual understanding of self, which thus links this later narrative with his original. Mr. Lancaster, Ambrose, Waldemar, Paul, and, of course, Christopher himself all make up the main list of the shades, although numerous other characters, such as Geoffrey and Dorothy, also inhabit part of the Purgatory-like backdrop to Christopher's travels.

As noted earlier, "Mr. Lancaster" opens with Isherwood's commentary about what this piece of writing is to be about: with the repetition of "I," "me," and the idea that Christopher is ready to "start a new chapter" in his life (11), the scene is set for a spiritual, albeit nonreligious journey of self-discovery. In accordance with the way in which Isherwood originally conceived this text as being a reimagined version of Dante's *Inferno,* there is an emphasis on the idea that this is a "fantasy," an "epic drama" (13), and Isherwood introduces his younger self as the "hero" of this "epic myth" (14). Travel is linked to the desire of the Truly Weak Man to "escape," thus emphasizing that the overall structure of this work is the metaphorical journey as Christopher moves toward becoming a Truly Strong Man. The young Christopher accepts Lancaster's invitation to travel with him because "I would have gone anywhere with anyone; I was wild with longing for the whole unvisited world" (13). The desire to visit the world is linked to the escape sought after by the Truly Weak Man, which Isherwood had previously outlined in *Lions and Shadows.*

Mr. Lancaster too is representative of the Truly Weak Man: just as Edward had foreshadowed the future for Eric in *The Memorial,* Lancaster represents what Christopher could become unless he is able to grow and mature both spiritually and mentally. In the same way that Christopher is accused by Paul, Lancaster represents the "visitor" to Bremen: the house that he lives in, with a few photos scattered around showing that he has even been there, does not suit him and he is not able to make this art-nouveau style home his own. Living in the past and unable, seemingly, to escape from the image of father as hero, an impression often manipulated by Isherwood in his writing, Lancaster seems doomed to remain in this Purgatory that he has created for himself.

Indeed, Isherwood makes a pronounced connection between Lancaster and the shades of the *Inferno*. As Lancaster discusses his own views on writing, Isherwood comments: "it reminded me of the way the dead talk about themselves in Dante" (38). Lancaster takes on the role of one of the dead, a recurring phrase used to describe the different characters that are cast in this role. Ambrose in particular is seen as one of the shades when he excludes himself from society: "After all, lovey, I'm dead and you aren't" (75).

Returning to Lancaster, Christopher seems unable to see him as anything other than the older generation that he is desperate to rebel against: Lancaster's views on Berlin, psychoanalysis, and the "cult" of the war remove him from Christopher's generation. Just as Dante in the early parts of his own journey is unable to see clearly the relevance of what is happening to him, Christopher cannot view Lancaster as anything other than "grotesque" (40). Lancaster has created an "epic song" (57) about his own life and by removing himself from the outside world has barricaded himself in this self-imposed Purgatory. As one of the damned, Lancaster is unable to escape and shoots himself. Christopher, having taken on the role of Dante, was unable to save Lancaster, but there is still hope that he will be able to save himself as he moves on to Berlin.

Notably, Christopher's life in Berlin is not narrated in *Down There on a Visit*, although, of course, readers of *The Berlin Stories* have a version of events in their mind. As Christopher and Waldemar face a frontier in the act of escaping from Berlin, we join our Dante-like traveler again. What appears to be significant is that mirroring his initial desire to escape in "Mr. Lancaster," Christopher is once again playacting in the role of hero "escaping." Here, as with the character that he creates for himself on the *Coriolanus* in "Mr. Lancaster," Isherwood the author, far more than Christopher the pilgrim, understands that the idea of self as hero is false, and this self-analysis represents a progression. As he sits on the train in his "nervous, excited mood" (67), there is a sense that Christopher is unable to see the fact that he is "running away." Unable to analyze this and therefore still taking on the role of political activist who is "escaping the

Nazis" (61), it is obvious to the reader that he has not really changed that much from the boy we met in "Mr. Lancaster."

However, the Christopher who arrives on the island of St. Gregory undergoes an Inferno-style journey toward enlightenment. Although I have been arguing that the themes that Isherwood originally outlined in his diaries and notes can be found in all of *Down There on a Visit*, it is in "Ambrose" that the most obvious connection can be witnessed. Reviewing drafts and notes, the story of the Greek island that Christopher and Waldemar visit is the least changed from original inception through to the published version. Much more clearly than Bremen, Berlin, or Los Angeles, this island represents a physical Hell that traps its inhabitants, although as with all of Isherwood's imagery, it seems inviting and pleasant in the first instance.[14]

There are many references to Hell within this story. It is notable that Geoffrey renames the island "Devil's Island." Surrounded by water that appears comparable to the river Styx as Christopher and Waldemar wait for a boatman to carry them across (83), the island is inhabited by minions and devils. Indeed, all of Ambrose's "boys" are described in ways that imply that they have been cast in these roles: they are "inhumanely destructive" and "cruel" (106). Notably, although they are the devils rather than the damned, as with Dante's Hell, they too are trapped; furthermore, they do get pleasure from others' discomfort and pain, linking them to the devils of the *Inferno* who gain gratification in the sport of torture (Canto XXII). Other residents of the island include a goat that is described in devilish terms: "a lean, black, shaggy-legged devil with goblin teeth and slanting Levantine eyes" (91). Furthermore, the landscape of "lava sharp rocks" (96), the unbearable heat (98), and the hidden flames (106) makes this island physically resemble Hell.

Although Ambrose is the creator of this island, he too is one of the shades. Indeed, he takes on the role of the prominent "lost" male within this story, which is emphasized by the fact that, in his mind at least, he is already "dead." However, Isherwood is clear that the focus of this narrative remains on his namesake narrator. Ambrose's "wonderful degradation" makes the narrator question his own life, focusing this section on a process of self-understanding as Christopher asks "Am I happy?" ("Writing Notebook," 116). Ambrose and Christopher could arguably be seen as Virgil and Dante. Ambrose reflects Christopher as he could become and ultimately tells Christopher to leave: just as Virgil leads Dante back up to the surface of the earth, Ambrose banishes Christopher and sends him back to society.

On this island Christopher comes the closest to losing himself and therefore risks becoming one of the forgotten. He removes himself from society by stopping reading newspapers, thus not thinking about politics and the atrocities that are happening in Berlin (97). Isherwood had always highlighted that the Purgatory of "The Forgotten" and subsequently *Down There on a Visit* is one that is self-imposed and relates to an inability of the damned to connect: the inmates of Isherwood's Purgatory are all "merely suffering from alienation in varying degrees," rather than Dante's classification of sinners ("Writing Notebook," 59). This alienation is certainly appropriate to the description of all the main "sinners" being analyzed here. As Isherwood describes in *Down There on a Visit*, the fact that Christopher is "beginning to live, more and more, in Ambrose's world" (97) means that he must find a way to escape this fate.

Conspicuously, it is as Isherwood narrates his loss of self that he most clearly utilizes his "diaries": the inference with the inclusion of this "unedited" text is that the voice that we are reading at this stage is not privy to the journey into a mental Hell that Christopher must find his way out of. It is significant that Isherwood should incorporate diaries into his narrative as he examines the idea that he is losing himself on this island; with unfinished sentences and fragmented narratives, Christopher the writer seems to be losing his ability to narrate himself (129).

As he departs from the island, initiating the end of Ambrose's romantic fantasy, Christopher's seemingly futile search for belonging continues. Back on the Greek mainland he realizes: "I didn't belong on his island. But now I knew I didn't belong here, either. Or anywhere" (135). Interestingly, Isherwood talks of this in terms of having "failed to make the grade" ("Writing Notebook," 117), which emphasizes the idea that Christopher is desperately seeking a sense of belonging, searching for his homeland. Christopher's sense that he does not belong indicates that he is able to see himself more clearly, as emphasized in the aforementioned mirror scene; however, this is negated by the fact that he is unable to see a way forward—there is still no answer to the question of where he belongs. The magic cast by the exciting quest of forming a foreign colony like "real" explorers has dissipated for Christopher; seemingly unable to find not only freedom in travel, but, more important, a sense of belonging, the next section of this novel sees Christopher once again on a ship, this time returning to England and mother in 1938.

Describing himself as a "boomerang," a being flung from England always destined to return, Christopher asks: "Who throws me? I don't know, and I'm not really interested in finding out. Or am I afraid to?

I refuse to answer that question. All I'll tell you is, I'm spinning" (140). Even as he is returning "home," his mind is still searching for answers to who he is and this is absolutely interrelated to the idea of self as traveler. Although Christopher does not answer the question of "who" throws him, his presentation of self evidently suggests that it is England herself that casts him on his eternal journey: a quest to find a freedom from his class and his bourgeois sensibilities.

"Waldemar" focuses on Christopher's return to London at the time of the Munich Crisis, which Isherwood describes as representing limbo: this can be read to mean that there was "neither peace nor war" ("Writing Notebook," 120), but also relates this narrative once again to Dante's original and demonstrates the way in which the London of 1938 represents Isherwood's modern reimagining of Hell, as Bremen and St. Gregory had previously.

Although Waldemar is cast in the title role of this section of the novel, as well as being the only character other than Christopher to appear in all four stories, he is not the real focus. Undeniably, he does have characteristics that place him in the role of the lost soul, seen in his desperation for escape first with Dorothy as he travels into England and then as he begs Christopher to take him with him to America; however, it is once again Christopher who is at the forefront. There is a real emphasis on an individual that has no faith and Christopher even questions whether he has a soul (142), a question that Durtal also asks in Là-bas as he finds himself on the "threshold" of conversion (16).

However, although there is a sense of a being that is lost in meaningless sex and "slogans" of travel writing, there is an idea that the Christopher of this section is more mature and more able to see himself than the Christophers of either "Mr. Lancaster" or "Ambrose." Realizing that the desire for escape is "futile" (177), Christopher is starting to come to terms with his role in society. Beginning to understand himself in terms of spirituality, faith, and pacifism, the Christopher that leaves for America is able to see himself in reference to the world around him, and although the journey through Purgatory is not complete, as we enter the final narrative, we see that there is hope for Christopher.

"Paul" has been the most discussed section of Down There on a Visit and the one seen as most "spiritual." All of the stories, as I have argued, make up the unified journey toward a self-understanding that is both spiritual and psychoanalytic. This final story, however, undeniably makes the clearest references to Isherwood's actual association with Vedanta and his relationship with Swami Prabhavananda. As such, this story is arguably most relevant to Dante's original work, as well as the story of Durtal's acceptance of faith in *Là-bas*.

Once again, there are several references to the *Inferno;* indeed, the character of Augustus Parr, whom Isherwood based on Gerald Heard, specifically alludes to Dante's work (240). Travel, and in particular a journey of self-discovery, must be undertaken by followers of Vedanta in order to find themselves. With religious language utilized throughout— Paul is a "disciple," the act of "confession" is central to the way in which Isherwood writes, even as he accuses himself of Puritanism—this section focuses on the inner growth required as part of a spiritual journey.

In "Paul," Christopher is forced most clearly to recognize his own role as one of the lost, as someone removed from society. Christopher is accused of merely being a "visitor" by Paul in the final sections of this novel: he is like a tourist who is merely sending postcards from the many places he visits, which are both worldly and spiritual (315). In Isherwood's earlier drafts, this idea was always at the forefront: "Paul says, during the hashish scene, 'you know nothing about what it's like to live in Hell, you've only been down here on visits'" ("Writing Notebook," 62). In all of the episodes of "The Forgotten" and *Down There on a Visit,* the male protagonist is shown to be removed: with his inability to engage with his surroundings as anything other than a tourist, he is both a visitor to and a prisoner of Purgatory. Just as Dante is often judged by the sinners for looking on and not being involved, seen, for example, on the frozen lake in Canto XXXII of the *Inferno,* Christopher too is accused.

An outstanding feature of this, the final story of the novel, is that the narrative should not return to Isherwood's point of view at the end of the book. All the other sections have featured a moment of self-reflection. Here, however, the letter from Ronny describing Paul's final days concludes this narrative. Although it may seem that by not returning to analyze himself in relation to these events Christopher has been unable to grow, it is really the opposite: seemingly, Christopher is able to see himself in reference to these events without having to comment on them. Paul has "suffered the tortures of the damned" (317), and there is a sense that Christopher will be able to learn from his experiences, learn to stop being a visitor and get involved with life. The story of "Paul" is not about good versus evil, but rather focuses on "enlightenment": this is a narrative about learning from experience in order to be able to gain this clarification ("Writing Notebook," 121).

As *Down There on a Visit* concludes, the implication is that "now" Isherwood has a clearer understanding of his standards and prejudices and furthermore that this has been achieved in the process of writing the novel: Isherwood the implied author has performed an evaluation of his younger self and, as such, has managed to escape the pitfalls of Purgatory. As with many of his novels and the "autobiographical fiction" previously published, the overall theme is a process of self-understanding and maturation. Isherwood notes that, as he plans this narrative (which at this stage excluded the story of "Waldemar"), these stories constitute

> three visits to private hells. In the first, "I" has little or no under-
> standing of Mr. Lancaster; who astonishes him by shooting himself
> six months later. In the second, "I" has a warm personal feeling for
> Ambrose but can do nothing for him. In fact, it is Ambrose who, in
> a big-brotherly way, finally advises "I" go back to his own life. In the
> third episode, Paul and "I" have a disciple–teacher relationship. . . .
> But "I" isn't big enough to be a teacher, and Paul backslides. ("Writing
> Notebook," 62)

The autobiographical feel of the novel has led to it being described as a sequel to *The Berlin Stories* (as advertised by Methuen Press, which re-published *Down There on a Visit* in 1999). However, Christopher's journey remains faithful to a nonreligious but nonetheless spiritual journey of self-discovery. Furthermore, while the characters that Christopher meets may find themselves unable to remove themselves from their self-imposed Purgatory, seeing a reflection of himself as he could be allows the narrator to gain a better self-understanding. Christopher goes on many visits in this novel, and, although the places he travels to and the people he meets may form part of his literary autobiography, the manner in which the journeys and people are presented reminds us that where Christopher has been on a visit is the Hell and Purgatory that Isherwood originally imagined. Like Dante, Isherwood the author is able to trace Christopher the pilgrim's journey in order to gain the spiritual insight required for him to grow into the Truly Strong Man.

Notes

1. Throughout his notebooks, Isherwood uses the title of *Inferno* when referring to the writing of Dante that he originally aimed to re-create and reconstruct, which included both *Inferno* and *Purgatory*. Throughout this chapter, I too will refer to *Inferno* when analyzing Isherwood's personalized ideas of Dante's Hell and Purgatory. Notably, Isherwood describes his own narratives in relation to a self-imposed Purgatory, although often he utilizes ideas and images from Dante's Hell.

2. David Garrett Izzo, *Christopher Isherwood Encyclopedia* (Jefferson, N.C.: McFarland & Company, 2005), 209.

3. Stanley Poss, "A Conversation on Tape," in *Conversations with Christopher Isherwood*, ed. James J. Berg and Chris Freeman (Jackson: University Press of Mississippi, 2001), 10.

4. See J.-K. Huysmans, *Là-bas (Down There)* (1928) (Toronto: General Publishing Company, 1972).

5. Dante Alighieri, *The Divine Comedy*, vol. 1, *Inferno*, trans. Dorothy L. Sayers (Harmondsworth: Penguin, 1949), and vol. 2, *Purgatory*, trans. Dorothy L. Sayers Harmondsworth: Penguin, 1955). Although Sayers's translations can arguably be seen as problematic owing to the level of interpretation, Isherwood had copies of her translations and therefore I have used the same editions.

6. Throughout I will refer to "The Forgotten" when discussing Isherwood's original plan to rewrite Dante's *Inferno* as a journey into Mexico.

7. See "[Down There on a Visit]: How I came to write the first draft," Isherwood papers (MS CI 1039), Huntington Library, San Marino, California. I consulted other parts of the Isherwood archive, including "Diary, 1933: Diary of a summer in Greece" (MS CI 2749) and "Visit to Bremen: [diary and short story]" (MS CI 1147).

8. Christopher Isherwood, *Down There on a Visit* (1962; reprint, Minneapolis: University of Minnesota Press, 1999), 210.

9. Stephen Stephen, *Letters to Christopher: Stephen Spender's Letters to Christopher Isherwood 1929–1939*, ed. Lee Bartlett (Santa Barbara, Calif.: Black Sparrow Press, 1980), 11.

10. See, for example, George Wickes, "An Interview with Christopher Isherwood," in Berg and Freeman, *Conversations with Christopher Isherwood*, 42.

11. Christopher Isherwood, *The Berlin Stories* (New York: New Directions, 1954), 409.

12. W. H. Auden, *The Orators: An English Study*, in *The English Auden: Poems Essays and Dramatic Writings 1927–1939*, ed. Edward Mendelson (London: Faber and Faber, 1986), 61–110.

13. See Philippe Lejeune, *On Autobiography*, trans. Katherine Leary, vol. 52 of Theory and History of Literature Series, ed. Paul John Eakin (Minneapolis: University of Minnesota Press, 1989).

14. Christopher Isherwood, *Diaries, Volume One: 1939–1960*, ed. Katherine Bucknell (New York: Harper, 1996), 592.

11

A Phone Call by the River

PAUL M. McNEIL

On November 8, 1940, Isherwood became an initiate of Vedanta, one of the six schools of Hindu philosophy. Under the tutelage of his guru, Swami Prabhavananda, he devoted himself to study and ultimately sealed himself off from the world at the Vedanta Center of Southern California, in an effort to realize the "ideal of moksa, or man's release from his involvement in the phenomenal world and the realization by him of the identity of his essential self with the cosmic reality."[1] This central teaching of Vedanta challenged Isherwood, given his inability to repudiate the physical world. In fact, all the while he was living at the Center and aspiring to become a monk, he repeatedly stole away to have sex with men.

When Isherwood left the monastery in August 1945, he did so "for a reason which had nothing to do with the Vedanta Society"—to pursue a relationship with William Caskey. "I had recently met a man with whom I wanted to settle down and live in what I hoped could become a lasting relationship."[2] Caskey awakened anew Isherwood's yearning for domesticity, a feeling that had largely lain dormant since he had been separated from Heinz Neddermeyer on May 12, 1937.

Caskey also turned Isherwood on. The relationship lasted six years, marked by sex, drunken blackouts, and violence. In April 1951, Caskey brought everything to a head: "I'm not in love with you anymore. I've been in love with you for a long time, but now it's over." The feeling was mutual: "Christopher, at the time, really rather hated Caskey but he wouldn't admit to it." With concessions from both sides, Isherwood moved on: "life with Billy had become unbearable."[3]

For Isherwood, the period from 1940 to 1951 was marked by two experiments, one monastic, one domestic. Both failed. On the one hand,

Isherwood found it constitutionally impossible to devote himself exclusively to life at the Center, cut off from the world and denied the pleasures of the flesh. On the other hand, he failed to create a human relationship that could satisfy him both domestically and sexually. In many respects, throughout the better part of the decade he was living at one extreme or another, devoted to the spirit or mired in the flesh.

When he broke with Caskey, Isherwood reflected back on the period and discovered the need for a middle ground: "there must be no more categorical relationships, as far as I'm concerned. I believe that's what went wrong between Caskey and me, and the Center and me—trying to ensure permanence by getting yourself involved, that's no good. No good saying, 'Now I'm married' or 'Now I'm a monk,' and therefore I'm committed" (*Diaries*, 1:439–40).

Isherwood's final novel, *A Meeting by the River* (1967), explores the very moral challenges Isherwood had glimpsed dimly between 1940 and 1951. The novel is brief; the story line is deceptively straightforward. And yet, from this easy narrative a novel of dazzling complexity emerges.

In a letter from Oliver to Patrick, the reader is introduced to two English brothers. Oliver writes from Calcutta, where he lives "in a Hindu monastery a few miles outside the city, on the bank of the Ganges." Patrick is "in the United States on business," working on a film project in Los Angeles. Oliver has learned from his mother that Patrick plans to travel to East Asia. He writes to preempt a visit to the monastery from Patrick, but also to disclose that he is living as a monk and soon plans to take his "final vows" *(sannyas)*.[4]

In subsequent letters and journal entries, the novel unfolds. Patrick travels to Calcutta, where he visits Oliver through his final initiation. Patrick writes to his mother, reassuring her that Oliver is in good health and well fed, all the while putting a picturesque spin on India. Patrick writes more candidly to his wife Penelope disclosing his suspicions about Oliver's chosen path. And Patrick writes to Tom, a young man back in Los Angeles with whom he is having sex. For his part, Oliver keeps a journal in which he meditates throughout on Patrick's intrusive visit as well as their fraternal relationship, his former and perhaps still abiding love for Penelope, and his present and future life as a monk.

According to Claude Summers, "In its fascinating account of two brothers, apparently polar opposites in temperament and belief, who finally reveal their essential similarity, the novel explores two convergent paths to the goal of self-knowledge and finds an ideal of brotherhood essential to both. . . . It affirms the Vedantic road to enlightenment."[5]

In fact, the novel examines the premise central to Vedanta and first explained to Isherwood by Swami Prabhavanada, that "all religions are
essentially in agreement" because they all lead to "enlightenment" or the
discovery of Truth.[6] The paths are many; Truth is one.

In this reading of the novel, Oliver's conversion is at the heart of the
story. His journal entries tell of the struggles he confronts as he strives
to realize "the ideal of moksa." They also record Oliver's perception of
Patrick's "enlightenment."

Patrick's letters, however, subvert this conventional reading altogether,
telling a different story about a darker side of Vedanta. The letters group
into four categories, each corresponding to a different relationship:
brother–brother, son–mother, husband–wife, man–boy. At play in each
of these letters are rhetorical strategies conceived to establish and preserve the terms of that relationship and to isolate one relationship from
another.

Patrick's relationship with his mother is the most readily accessible.
Mother is an archetype, neither unique nor imaginative. As matriarch,
she corresponds with her children abroad, sharing bits of news about
the family and encouraging the meeting of siblings. She preys upon the
siblings' sense of obligation and pulls the otherwise separated brothers
back together; she has a primal and irresistible coercive power over her
sons. Patrick tells Mother precisely what she wants to hear.

Indeed, the letters to Mother are preoccupied with establishing Patrick's
credibility as a narrator. The first boasts about his power of intuition
("you know my feelings, they're *never* wrong"). The second establishes
Patrick as an eyewitness ("now I can say with absolute authority"). The
third asserts his reliability as a provider of information: "Mother darling,
I'm telling you all this because I know you want to hear everything about
Oliver's life and surroundings. If you found out that I'd withheld some
detail from you just because it is unpleasant, you'd never trust me again,
would you?" (100). In short, Mother can rely on Patrick to tell the truth.

The initial letter to Mother is followed by a letter to Patrick's wife,
Penelope. He opens with an admission that falls shy of an apology: "I'm
afraid I have been bad, not writing to you in all this long while. I know
how you hate phone calls and our last few have been more than usually
unsatisfactory, haven't they?" (42). Patrick has failed to be in touch with
his wife while on business in California, and he has bungled attempts to
communicate with her by phone: "I got an uneasy impression from one
or two things you said that you imagined I was behaving strangely—
being cold or distant. . . . I avoided asking you about this at the time,

for fear I'd only make matters worse, but now tell me, was that how you felt? If it was, you had no reason to, *believe me!* You must admit darling, you sometimes fancy things" (ibid.). Patrick chooses to ignore his wife's feelings when speaking with her on the phone. Rather, he engages her in writing. He prefers written communication, which allows for delayed, deliberate responses that involve reflection, to verbal communication, which demands spontaneity (ibid.).

Why does Patrick delay clearing up a simple misunderstanding with his wife on the phone? Patrick is playing a confidence game *("believe me")* in which he is advantaged by delayed rather than immediate communication.

When writing to his mother, Patrick reports that after having been burdened in L.A. by "tiresome lunches" and time spent with "exceedingly dim stars," he treated himself to "a few days' holiday" in a pastoral setting that is "quite wild and unspoilt." He was awed by the beauty of the natural setting, an "outrageously romantic spot," and thought only of Mother, "wishing you could have been with me with your watercolours" (41). To Penelope, he spins a different tale:

> I even suspect . . . that you feel my staying on in Los Angles these last ten days was unnecessary. . . . Well, yes, it's true that I could actually have left Los Angeles a little earlier than I did, and made the trip to India the other way around, via England, and spent a few days with you and the Children. That sounds heavenly, as an idea, but just consider, darling, what it would have been like in fact, our being together with the prospect of parting again so soon hanging over us all the time. You know yourself, the few times that's happened, what a strain it was and how wretched, and how it makes a sort of tragedy out of something that isn't in the least tragic—as though you and I were desperate lovers in wartime, counting the last minutes of my leave! (42–43)

Patrick has not only "disappointed" his wife, but he had no choice: spending Christmas with his family would have raised expectations that would inevitably be dashed. His choice was "absolutely unavoidable." Patrick's love for his wife and family is steady and enduring, quite different from the passing affection of "desperate lovers in wartime." Patrick's con is complete. Penelope is silenced.

Patrick does not lie to Penelope outright, but he does construct an explanation for his behavior that conveniently overlooks what we know to be true from his letter to Mother—namely, that he managed to "escape for a few days' holiday" prior to his departure from Los Angeles and that his "final memories of California are very agreeable." Patrick is posturing. One story is told to appeal to Mother, another to placate Penelope. In fact, neither is entirely true (41).

The time away from his family in England was neither "absolutely unavoidable," as alleged to Penelope, nor a solitary "holiday," as reported to Mother. Rather, the time was stolen from his family at Christmas in order to fuck Tom: "that afternoon down on the reef at Tunnel Cove, with the air full of spray and the shock of the waves making the rock tremble—no, if I talk about that I shall break the magic. It *was* magic, wasn't it, every time we were together, from the first day that we met?" (48). In this description of "the reef at Tunnel Cove," all of nature is charged with energy: the "air full of spray" and the "waves making the rock tremble." In contrast, the letter to Mother describes Tunnel Cove in static terms; the images are solid, sharp, and fixed: "cliffs towering sheer out of the sea, seals swimming in the coves below, and magnificent tall dark solemn woods in deep canyons" (41).

Patrick is a bisexual. For him, heterosexuality and homosexuality are social conceits to which benefits and liabilities are attached. They are artificial. Bisexuality, to Patrick, is natural, as he explains to Tom: "May I also call to your attention that one of your best-seller American psychologists . . . maintains that man is bisexual by nature and that the homosexual who rigidly rejects women under all circumstances is being just as unnatural and square as the heterosexual who rejects men!" (170–71). Human beings are only true to nature when left free to roam the spectrum of sexuality.

In fact, it is not surprising that in *A Meeting by the River* Isherwood presents his most fully developed bisexual character. Throughout his personal life, Isherwood knew many men who behaved as Patrick advocates, most notably Stephen Spender. "This kind of bisexual interests me a great deal. I have met many of them during my life. I describe another of them in *The World in the Evening*, but the one in *Meeting* is far more convincing, I think."[7] For a man who likes to have sex with men in a world ruled by a "heterosexual dictatorship," marriage is a "kind of fortress."[8] Patrick "sallies forth from the fortress to have adventures. Then he rushes back into it." Unfortunately, the married man's "male lover is left standing in the cold" (Leyland, "Christopher Isherwood Interview," 106). And that is precisely what happens to Tom.

Patrick's next letter to Tom is quite graphic:

> You had read the book and it was you who planned the trip and took
> me there. I love the romantic silliness of your doing it, but at the same

time I can't help feeling, to put it mildly, embarrassed! I mean to say, there I was, taking part for all I was worth in a wild scene of passion—it was one of the most insane things I've ever done. . . . I was imagining in my innocence that you were as completely carried away as I was. You certainly behaved as if you were. And now I find everything you said and did printed almost word for word and move for move in this damned book.

Tommy, please don't think I'm angry or hurt about this or that I feel like the victim of a practical joke. Even if you did stage-manage the whole thing, I know that doesn't mean you were just pretending— I'm certain you weren't. You gave me quite satisfactory proofs that you meant what you were doing, on numerous other occasions! And if you got some kind of private erotic kick out of stage-managing, then all I can say is, I hope you thoroughly enjoyed it. (84–85)

Patrick dwells on the literal ("everything you said and did printed almost word for word") and the pornographic ("a wild scene of passion"). What transpired was a "thing," a physical reenactment of a scene in "the book." In fact, Patrick derived a mildly sadomasochistic thrill out of the encounter. Tom was dominant, getting a "private erotic kick out of stage-managing." Patrick was submissive, "mildly, embarrassed," and "the victim of a practical joke."

Tom, on the other hand, is set up to read the letter differently. He dwells on the implied rather than the literal, the emotional rather than the physical. Patrick is toying with Tom, calling him "Tommy" and playing with language as one might affectionately ruffle the hair of an adorable youth: "It's exactly the sort of wonderful sweet idiotic crazy thing you *would* do" and "I love the romantic silliness of your doing it." For Tom, Patrick is implicitly professing his love. The two were transported mutually—"you were as completely carried away as I was"—and yet we learn that the two are not on equal footing (84–85).

Patrick controls Tom. His next letter opens talking about the act of letter writing: "I haven't written for nearly one whole week!" (129). Once again, Patrick is in charge, using the written word and delayed response as tools with which to manipulate people. As with the letter to Penelope, the letter to Tom is crafted; it is shaped to put Tom in his place and seal his devotion. Patrick proceeds gently, choosing to manipulate and endear rather than demand and alienate. With false modesty he begs forgiveness for his failure to write: "I realize our situations aren't the same. You have the right to expect to hear from me. . . . I know I can't expect to hear from you until I leave this place. . . . I know that a lot of things can keep you from writing often—your job, your classes, people you have to see" (130). Patrick implies that his life is narrow, focused entirely on Tom, whereas Tom's life is broad, filled with obligations and people. In fact, the opposite is true. Patrick's life is large and full; Tom's life is small and sparse. By asserting the opposite, Patrick stokes Tom's affection and blunts the edge of Patrick's real message: Tom is strictly forbidden from writing to him while he is living at the monastery. All correspondence from Tom to Patrick is to be directed to Singapore where Patrick will eventually "walk into the hotel . . . and ask at the desk for my mail and shuffle quickly through it, looking for the letters from you! How many will there be—three, four, five, six? . . . I'll be quite content with only one letter, as long as your love is in it" (ibid.). Patrick's rhetoric is that of a giddy boy; his words are ones that seduce because Tom is just that, a boy smitten early in life. Patrick conjures up an image of a pair of lovers who are on equal footing emotionally when, in fact, Patrick is in control.

The remainder of the letter is an intricate profession of love that tricks Tom into accepting his assigned place in Patrick's complicated life. The opening is bold: "What I want to tell you tonight is this—as far as I'm concerned, our relationship seems to keep on growing stronger and deeper, although we're apart. I mean this literally! It's very strange, something I have never experienced before with anyone" (ibid.). The two have only known each other a short time, during which they simply have sex. Both the reader and Patrick realize that he is speaking "literally" rather than metaphorically when he says that "our relationship seems to keep on growing stronger and deeper." Yet, his language invites a more tender reading, one that stirs the heart rather than, *or as well as*, the loins. And as Patrick's con unfolds, it is that reading that he hopes will preoccupy Tom.

Patrick tells Tom of a dream. Having recently been separated from Tom, Patrick "was feeling awful. I needed you so badly. It was chiefly a physical need, I admit, and it was torture, pure and simple." The dream turned wet, but "this was much more than a dream, it was so intense it was a sort of vision. I mean, there was a burning pleasure and then an utter fulfillment with you. . . . But the whole experience went far beyond just sex, it was actually a glimpse of a life which you and I were living together!" (ibid.). The dream is a romantic cliché; sex ("a burning pleasure") transports two lovers to higher plane ("an utter fulfillment"). Tom no doubt swoons as he reads of Patrick's "vision." Patrick no doubt smirks, hedging his bets. The use of the indefinite rather than definite article suggests that there are many possibilities; if managed properly, Patrick's life can include a doting mother, a prodigal brother, a devoted wife, and a boy toy. Tom, on the other hand, is duped by Patrick into circumscribing his life; for Tom, the world is narrow, filled with transcendent love and populated by Patrick and Tom alone.

In the course of the letter, Patrick cultivates Tom's delusion easily because Tom is vulnerable to Patrick's professed and implied devotion. Patrick's rhetoric takes flight:

> Tommy . . . I'm certain that you could be my brother—the kind of
> brother I now know I've been searching for all these years . . . what
> I want is a life . . . in which two men learn to trust each other so
> completely that there's no fear left and they experience and share
> everything together in the flesh and in the spirit. I don't believe such
> closeness is possible between a man and a woman—deep down they
> are mutual enemies—and how many men ever find it together? Only
> a very few even glimpse the possibility of it, and only a very few out
> of that few dare to find it. (131–32)

Patrick tempts the diminutive "Tommy" with a repudiation of heterosexuality, on the one hand, and with the promise of "true brotherhood," on the other. What Patrick envisions is bold and rare: two men bound together "in the flesh and in the spirit." Together, they can find a love that only "few dare to find."

Having stirred Tom's heart, Patrick sets out to explain how they will carve out a place for themselves in the mainstream. Referring to an earlier letter to Tom in which he argued that the two would "have to be crafty and cunning," Patrick pleads on behalf of candor: "No, we must be absolutely without fear. . . . We must find the time and opportunity to go away, right away from everybody to a place where we can be alone, until we have broken down all the last little remaining barriers between us— we shall discover what they are by degrees, petty suspicions and shames and pockets of false pride. When those are gone we can face other people without fear and let them see us as we are" (133). Patrick and Tom will retreat from society to find the bond that joins, whereupon they will return and be greeted with acceptance.

The argument sways Tom, even though Patrick's conclusion is patently preposterous: "We won't be aggressive, but we won't attempt to hide anything. Then it'll be up to the others to decide how they'll react—accept us or reject us. And, do you know, I have faith that we *shall* be accepted, at any rate by the ones we really care about? I believe that our being together is going to find its place and fit in amongst the other relationships of our lives, without even causing any great disturbance" (ibid.). Given the date of the novel, Patrick's claim, "we won't be aggressive," is political; it refers to the increasingly public clamor for what would become known as gay rights and to Patrick's refusal to lend his voice to the cause. Rather, Patrick hopes to keep his homosexuality private in the truest sense of the word; his ambition is narrow and self-centered, confined to his sexual and emotional life alone. He fears "causing any great disturbance" in that life, and so he envisions a world into which he and Tom can slip unobtrusively as a couple and win the acceptance of "the ones we really care about." Missing from his letter to Tom are the voices of "the other relationships of our lives"—the voices of Mother, Penelope, and his two daughters, all of which would surely challenge Patrick's assumptions.

All three aspects of Patrick's life are in balance—until Tom calls the monastery and hastens the meeting by the river.

Patrick's letter drives Tom into a state of frenzied passion. Left with no choice, Patrick is forced to confess to Oliver, but he does so not as a "brother" but rather as "people do to a priest"—in confidence. He uses hyperbole to keep Oliver from judging him: "Do you think I'm awfully wicked, Olly? Do you think I'm damned?" He vows to fulfill his familial duties and quickly shifts the subject of conversation to Oliver: "He went on, in a tone of gentle, reproachful intimacy, do you know why I made such a point of coming here to see you, Olly—it was because I felt that perhaps you needed to talk to me" (142, 146, 151).

Patrick turns his attention from Oliver to Tom, a loose cannon he needs to contain:

> My dear Tom,
> After our conversation last night, I feel I must get a letter off to you at once. . . . (Perhaps you'll say to yourself, well, if he's in such a hurry to clear things up, why the hell doesn't he telephone me? But I think, if you remember anything about last night, you'll have to agree that just wouldn't be sensible. It would still be impossible for us two to communicate calmly with each other in our present emotional state. We'd only get excited and incoherent and tie ourselves up in further misunderstandings.)

Patrick won't call because he needs to control what is said and to end his relationship with Tom (161).

Patrick's strategy is elegantly multifaceted. First, he emphasizes that Tom was drunk and he himself was angry; thus, much of what was said can be either forgiven or forgotten: "Of course, there's always the possibility that you don't remember what I did say—you certainly were drunk";

"I know I lost my temper last night and said some things I shouldn't have said and didn't quite mean."

Next, he identifies with Tom: "First of all, I want to tell you that I do understand perfectly what made you make that call. . . . Believe me, Tom, there've been many times when I longed to call you." Tom was stirred by the very kind of loneliness that "if one lets oneself brood on it, it distorts everything into a nightmare of isolation and self-pity, until one simply doesn't stop to consider the consequences of one's actions or just doesn't care what they'll be" (161–62). Tom and Patrick are human and both know what it means to be lonely. They differ in their response to loneliness. Patrick is measured; Tom is wild. And while Patrick understands Tom's petulance and so forgives him, he nonetheless chides Tom.

The reproach is gentle; the barb is sharp: "I think very few of us ever take the trouble to visualize what may be going on at the other end of a telephone line" (162). Tom is self-absorbed and blinded to the needs of others. On the surface, Patrick appears to be doing little more than scolding Tom with lowered voice.

In fact, he is accusing him of being prone to the very kind of indiscretion that hurts other people:

> So, I was rattled, I'm afraid, and all the more so because I knew you'd already spoken to my Brother. . . . I'm sure you didn't leave him in any doubt as to what the relations between you and me were. . . . It wasn't very pleasant for me to have to confess to him everything that has gone on between us. . . . But I owed it to him not to spare any details, because of course he may well have to face questions from his superiors. . . . I know that Oliver in his loyalty will do his best to cover up the whole affair and make light of it, even though, as a monk, he will be committing a grave sin by not telling the unvarnished truth. This will cause him great distress. (162–63)

First, Tom's call was an invasion of Patrick's privacy, forcing him to disclose to his brother that which he would prefer to hide. Second, the call put Oliver in a compromising position with his spiritual elders; Oliver will be called upon to answer questions about his deviant brother and in so doing be forced to lie.

Tom's actions "cause . . . great distress." They injure the innocent. And it is this moral affront—namely, harming those who neither provoke nor deserve harm—that Patrick alleges is of greatest consequence: "I don't give a damn about myself. . . . I am only thinking of my Brother. No, that's not quite true—I'm thinking also of the elder monks. . . . It's all very well to be defiant and say that my private life is my own affair. Yes, that's true, but only as long as I keep it private. By letting it become public I force my standards of behavior on them, as it were—and what right do I have to do that? I feel I've abused their hospitality. And that I hate" (164). Patrick dons the mantle of moral authority and judges Tom harshly, contradicting his previously envisioned relationship that is boldly public: "We can face other people and let them see us as we are" (133).

The argument for separating unfolds elegantly. Tom is young and naive: "I shouldn't have been angry with you. How could you have understood this? You are an impulsive creature, Tommy dear. . . . I'm just beginning to realize how awfully young you are, young even for your age. Since last night I see that we do actually belong to two different generations." Patrick's seduction was misleading and cruel: "I began to see our relationship in an altogether different light, and for the first time I feel guilty about it, because I now see that I involved you in something which was far out of your depth. . . . I see now how utterly monstrously selfish my attitude was." Patrick has taken advantage of Tom, a discovered truth that compels the morally "upright" Patrick to act in Tom's best interest rather than his own.

And so, Patrick is honor bound to end the relationship with Tom and assume blame for the damage he has done:

> Oh, it was all my fault, of course. In my eagerness to seem young to you, I instinctively concealed my oldness of spirit, my tiredness. . . . You see, I have been hurt, I don't want to remember how many times, there's no sense in brooding over it. You don't know what it's like, thank goodness, that kind of disappointment in someone which takes the edge off your faith in life. . . . The only way I can repay you is to make sure that you won't ever be disillusioned by me. Somebody will hurt you sooner or later, I'm afraid, because you are so reckless and innocent and loving—but it won't be me, that I can prevent, at any rate. (166)

In itself, Patrick's profession is upright. He accepts complete responsibility for involving Tom in a relationship beyond his emotional years. He steps up to his duty as the elder to set things right. Read in the context of his other letters to Tom as well as his meeting by the river, though, Patrick's mea culpa is a manipulative farce. He heaps blame upon himself in order to create the appearance of moral propriety that conceals what in fact he is doing to Tom, inflicting upon him "that kind of disappointment in someone which takes the edge off your faith in life."

Patrick hopes to slither away. "For God's sake, don't get the suspicion that this is leading up to some dishonest attempt to say goodbye without actually saying it, just to spare your feelings and save me the embarrassment." In fact, Patrick does end the relationship without saying good-bye: "Of course we shall meet again. Only I do think we need a period of separation first, probably quite a long one. We ought not to see each other until we can take each other more lightly." Patrick breaks off with Tom without cutting ties altogether. He deviously drops a crumb into Tom's lap: the hope that they will see each other again one day. And he does so for two interconnected reasons. On the one hand, he hedges his sexual bets—in time, he might be able to return to Tom's bed without engaging Tom's heart ("take each other more lightly"). On the other, he bargains that with that light flickering dimly in the distance, Tom won't do anything rash, like contacting his wife Penelope (166–67).

Patrick appends a postscript to the letter, urging Tom to try his luck with girls: "when someone is—as you must admit you are—such a militant standard bearer in the ranks of the man-lovers, isn't it just possible that his sexual inclinations may be partly prejudice? Steady now, don't start denying this right away! First ask yourself frankly, am I against heterosexual love simply because it's respectable and legal and approved of by the churches and the newspapers and all those other vested interests I hate?" (169). Patrick implies that heterosexuality and homosexuality are social institutions that either advantage or disadvantage. Accordingly, Patrick urges Tom to do as he has done and make the socially acceptable choice of marrying a woman. Doing so would provide him with apparent benefits—children and "the experience of being a father." But, more important, it would provide him with the veneer of respectability that would allow for "greater freedom" to do whatever he wishes unchecked "behind the scenes" (170).

In his celebration of bisexuality, Patrick eschews the categorical in the same way that Oliver did when he rejected the ideal of moksa in favor of a faith that grants the coexistence of the phenomenal and the spiritual and in the same way that Isherwood did in 1951 when he walked away from the Center and Caskey in search of a life that balanced the sexual and the spiritual. In turning their back on the categorical, all three point to a tenet central to Vedanta—namely, the assertion first conveyed to Isherwood by Swami Prabhavananda "that all religions are essentially in agreement." With all paths leading to Truth, the line between right and wrong is fluid; Patrick demonstrates the problem with that fluidity or ethical relativity.

Patrick's final letter to his wife is at once endearing and diabolical. The note opens with a sigh, "Oh, Penny—" and ends with a diminutive cuddle, "Yours sleepily but completely." Patrick bubbles throughout the letter, eager to communicate honestly with Penny: "I don't think I have ever felt a greater need to write to you than I do now—there's so much I want to say. . . . I have a strange, rather exhilarating feeling that I've never understood certain things about myself and my life as clearly as I do at this moment." He celebrates his fraternal bond with Oliver, refusing to sleep as Oliver takes *sannyas*: "I feel I ought not to go to bed, I want to hold my own little private vigil to keep him company!" He speaks of the rituals of conversion only to boast of Oliver's daring and capacity for greatness: "I find this act of his, the sheer courage of it, terribly moving. He's so utterly, almost unimaginably alone in what he's doing—far more so than any lone hero on a battlefield." And he professes a love for Penny that is without boundary (178–85).

But it is in that very profession of love that Patrick manipulates his wife in order to protect himself and secure a license to roam sexually free. Patrick's paean to Oliver culminates with a poetically bold salute: "Dear old awe-inspiring preposterous Olly." From there, Patrick segues into a discussion of love:

> I feel so close to him tonight! And through him I seem closer than ever to you my darling—I mean, I feel such closeness in the thought of us three together. Each one of us will belong to the other two always, even if we never set eyes on Olly again. Do you know, while I've been with him here, I've often found myself wondering what would have happened if he had married you! We have never discussed you, only referred to you and the Children occasionally, and yet, oddly enough, I now know for certain that he's still in love with you. And you once told me that you were still in love with him. Isn't it strange that I can talk about this and not feel jealous? Oh, Penny, how extraordinary men and women are in their dealings with each other! Why do two people choose to live together, 'forsaking all others.' Is it love or need? Is the need to be needed stronger than love? Or does love, in its pure absolute (as in alcohol) form, need no relationships? Do we love Olly because he doesn't need us? I know I need you. I hope to God you need me. (182)

Patrick's argument is crafty. First, he constructs a ménage à trois that defies convention and suggests that marriage can take on many different shapes. Second, he implicates his wife; she is party to his defiance of conventional marriage: "he's still in love with you" and "you were still in love with him." Third, he exchanges love for need as the basis of marriage: "I need you" and "you need me." Conventional marriage rooted in love becomes an abstraction easily dismissed, as Patrick speaks of love in decidedly platonic terms: "pure, absolute . . . form" (181–82).

For Patrick—and allegedly for his wife—marriage is a game. "It seems to me that we only play at 'marriage' for the benefit of other people to reassure them that we're like they are and not freaks" (170). For these very reasons he urges Tom to marry; the institution provides him with the veneer of respectability behind which he can live his life as he chooses. And yet, he cautions, "game-playing can be dangerous, because one may get to take it seriously. There is a danger that even you and I might start believing that I really am your husband. And there have been times, I know, when you have suddenly felt insecure. . . . You've accepted the world's values and allowed yourself to think in terms of 'husband,' 'wife,' married couple, etc. and therefore told yourself that you were being humiliated, betrayed and so forth" (182–83).

So, Patrick begs Penny to "accept me as I am." He continues:

> I shall always return from these idiotic adventures with increased love for you and gratitude—in fact, I can only enjoy these adventures if you'll sanction them! Oh Penny, can't we forget about "marriage" altogether and live in our own special way, the way that's natural to us? Can't I quite shamelessly be the child who keeps running home to you, and who is always thinking of you even in the midst of his play? When I see us in that relationship it's obvious to me that you can be more central to my life than any mere wife could be to any mere husband. . . . (184)
> I am all yours, Penny. Yours and the Children's. Never doubt this. To me you are safety and freedom, both together, and those are the two things I need more than anything else in the world. Only you can give them to me. (184–85)

The two have redefined the terms of marriage, redrawing boundaries in ways that allegedly suit both of them, and yet, given that Patrick is a con artist and a liar, one can't help but question the extent to which Penny acquiesces. In fact, one can only infer from the pleading tone of this letter that Penny accepts Patrick's terms because she is trapped and without choice.

And so Patrick shows himself to be the villain that he is. Assuming that Penelope is complicit, Tom is not. As the letter to Penny draws to a close, he tells her as an aside that she might hear from "a young American named

Tom." Patrick dismisses Tom—"he's terribly disturbed, poor boy, and terribly young"—and claims that Tom misunderstood the nature of their relationship: "We'd had a little interlude of pleasure together, he jumped to conclusions and imagined, I don't exactly know what, that I had somehow committed myself to him. . . . So he might try to make some kind of scene with you and perhaps pretend that I've promised him all sorts of things which I never did or could have" (184–85). Patrick is simply lying. He did boldly profess his love to Tom and extend to him the promise of a future together that defied the boundaries of conventional relationships. In short, he destroyed Tom's innocence, inflicting upon him the very hurt he so aptly described when parting with Tom "as that kind of disappointment in someone which takes the edge off your faith in life" (160).

Patrick's musings on bisexuality and marriage fit into Isherwood's larger, critical examination of Vedanta. Like Oliver, Patrick discards the categorical in favor of the relative. When Oliver redraws the boundaries that circumscribe his faith, though, he does so in the service of living a truthful life that is devoted to the greater good. However, when Patrick redraws the boundaries of conventional marriage and sexuality, he does so in ways that serve himself and harm others. So read, the story of Patrick and Oliver is a meditation on the very endorsement of ethical relativism that is at the heart of Vedanta. Clearly nourished throughout his life by Vedanta, Isherwood nonetheless discovered the perilous ethical position endorsed thereby. *A Meeting by the River* reveals how moral judgment is compromised when right and wrong become relative values, easily manipulated to justify individual action with little regard for the interests or the well being of others.

Notes

1. Mircea Eliade, ed., *The Encyclopedia of Religion,* vol. 15 (New York: Macmillan, 1987), 208.

2. Christopher Isherwood, *My Guru and His Disciple* (New York: Farrar, Straus and Giroux, 1980), 189.

3. Christopher Isherwood, *Lost Years: A Memoir, 1945–1951,* ed. Katherine Bucknell (New York: Harper, 2000), 281; Christopher Isherwood, *Diaries, Volume One: 1939–1960,* ed. Katherine Bucknell (New York: Harper, 1996), 437.

4. Christopher Isherwood, *A Meeting by the River* (New York: Farrar, Straus and Giroux, 1967), 9–10.

5. Claude J. Summers, *Gay Fictions: Wilde to Stonewall; Studies in a Male Homosexual Literary Tradition* (New York: Continuum, 1990), 122.

6. Peter Parker, *Isherwood: A Life Revealed* (New York: Random House, 2004), 386.

7. Winston Leyland, "Christopher Isherwood Interview," in *Conversations with Christopher Isherwood,* ed. James J. Berg and Chris Freeman (Jackson: University Press of Mississippi, 2001), 106.

8. Christopher Isherwood, *Kathleen and Frank* (New York: Simon and Schuster, 1971), 380.

12

"Give me devotion . . . even against my will"

Christopher Isherwood and India

NILADRI R. CHATTERJEE

Honesty is always elusive. The nature of language is such that full expression of oneself in words is impossible. Writers deserve our admiration because they are engaged in a battle that they can never win. They constantly chafe at the boundaries of language. They can only expand the boundaries of language but can never escape it. Partial truths are all that can be eventually put on the page. Christopher Isherwood seems to have attempted all his life to put on the page as much of the truth about himself as possible. However, even now, after all his diaries have been published, unanswered questions remain about certain aspects of his life and work. We are still not in possession of the whole truth about his life and work. Of the many questions that remain unanswered is the one concerning his complicated relationship with India.[1]

One of the most interesting still images of the British–Bengali encounter is a marble frieze in the antechapel of the University College, Oxford that depicts Sir William Jones (1746–1794) in profile, sitting on a low stool, with a sheaf of papers on the writing desk in front of him. Pen poised in his hand, he is in deep conversation with a group of what appear to be Brahmin scholars who are sitting on a much lower platform. The Brahmin scholar closest to him has what looks like a scholarly treatise on his lap. In the background are banana plants. The setting of the scene is meant to be Calcutta in the late eighteenth century. The Brahmins have their heads bowed, and are seated at a much lower level with William Jones looking down on them with majestic benevolence, suggesting that the image partakes of the visual systems of colonial representation where the sociopolitical status of each figure is indicated by how high or low the figure is situated on the canvas or, as in this case, the frieze.

An equally interesting, because contrasting, image is a photograph of Christopher Isherwood (1904–1986), Gerald Heard (1885–1971), and Swami Prabhavananda (1893–1976). This image, from the 1940s, shows the Bengali monk seated in a chair, resplendent in his ethnic garb, while his British disciples are seated on the floor. Isherwood is smiling at the camera. In the background is the exposed brickwork of a wall and a half-visible fireplace, marking the setting as Western. There is an irresistible temptation to read the image as one that captures the postcolonial notion of the empire striking back, especially since the image was made while India was entering its last years as part of the British Empire. The Swami himself may have admitted to such a reading of the image because he was, in Isherwood's words, "at heart . . . still a flaming Indian nationalist, and [got] very heated when British policy [was] discussed."[2] And yet, the relationship between Isherwood and the Swami was conducted on the ostensibly suprageographical, suprapolitical level of spirituality. Unlike William Jones's colonial, Orientalist engagement with India through the metonymic presence of the Bengali scholars, Isherwood's engagement is, as he would dearly love to believe, not with India at all but with a philosophy that the writer strives to detach from the country of its origin. It bothered him deeply that the philosophy he had decided to espouse was produced by a people he perhaps did not hold in great affection.

Isherwood's deep-seated prejudice toward India dates from at least the 1930s. In his short story "The Landauers," published in the spring of 1938 in *New Writing*, he pours his racism into the character of Bernhard Landauer. Writing about the character in *Christopher and His Kind* Isherwood says of himself in the third person, "'Isherwood' stresses the 'oriental' aspect of Bernard. In this case, the epithet seems to refer to the Chinese. But Christopher had a prejudice, at that period in his life, against another Oriental race, the Hindus."[3] He tried to explain his antipathy toward what he called "the Hindus" by saying that the antipathy rose from the "fear of something unknown [that] the Hindus knew; something which he might one day have to accept and which might change his life" (58). But the explanation may not be entirely satisfactory because even after he learned that life-altering thing—by which he clearly meant Vedanta—his self-confessed prejudice seems to have remained surprisingly intact. Even in July 1943 we find him recording in his diary that he had told a fellow Vedantist, "I don't like Indians as a race; Swami is an exception" (*Diaries*, 1:308).

The question arises, then, as to why Isherwood was so prejudiced against Indians. In order to attempt an answer to that question, it may be helpful to look at the life and interests of the person whom he admittedly most hated while he was growing up—his mother.[4] From 1923 until very late in her life, Kathleen Isherwood was more than casually interested in India. Madgie Reid was Isherwood's father Frank's first cousin. She was very close to Kathleen and her sons. Isherwood mentions her in *Kathleen and Frank* as Kathleen's "most devoted friend."[5] She was also member of a group called the British Indian Union. As a result, there are not infrequent mentions in Kathleen Isherwood's diaries of meeting Indians, often in the company of Madgie Reid. Another person Kathleen met frequently was Mamie Tristram. It was through her that Kathleen was exposed to the work of Jiddu Krishnamurti in November 1927, and, on March 31, 1928, Kathleen heard the Indian theosophist speak in London.[6] With her were Madgie Reid, her son Jack, Mamie, and her son Leonard Tristram, who was a member of Krishnamurti's theosophical society. Isherwood could not have been unaware of his mother's close association with those who were friends with Indians living in England. I suggest that as a result of his need to hate Kathleen, he also decided to hate everything associated with her. Because she was associating with Indophiliac people, Isherwood became Indophobic instead.

This Indophobia persisted all his life, raising its head most resolutely on the two occasions that he had to actually travel to India. However, the two visits also tempered his anti-India prejudice, and he did not hesitate to record his admiration as and when anything Indian impressed him favorably. The first visit—November 30 to December 9, 1957—was necessitated by his undertaking to write for Western consumption a biography of Ramakrishna, the nineteenth-century Bengali mystic who was responsible for the modern revival of the ancient Vedanta philosophy. So, the visit was essentially research. The second and, for my argument, more significant visit was between December 21, 1963, and January 8, 1964, as a guest at the celebrations of Vivekananda's birth centenary at the Belur Math monastery, which served as the headquarters of the Ramakrishna Order. In his diary entry of September 25, 1963, he says, "A passionate psychosomatic revolt is brewing in me against the Indian trip. I am almost capable of dying at Belur Math, out of sheer spite."[7] In 1977, Isherwood said in an interview while talking about his meeting Swami Prabhavananda, "I was . . . [a] child of Imperial Britain . . . [and] the Swami, before he became a monk, had belonged to a terrorist organisation against the British. So we were really confrontees."[8]

So, much as one might try to disregard the geopolitical force field in which the apparently spiritual relationship between Isherwood and Swami

Prabhavananda operated, an awareness of his country of origin and its problematic relationship with the country of the other existed at a barely-concealed subdiscursive level in both men. For the Swami, Isherwood was also a prize catch, a famous author, even a celebrity who focused the attention of glamour- and celebrity-fixated America on the hitherto unglamorous Vedanta Society of Southern California in Hollywood.[9] In his eagerness to accept Isherwood as his disciple, the Swami found it easy to even accept Isherwood's homosexuality. For Isherwood to accept the quintessentially Bengali Ramakrishna (1836–1886) was far more difficult. Ramakrishna's sheer Indianness got in Isherwood's way of receiving the nineteenth-century mystic as a biography subject that he could warm to.

But as he started his reading in preparation for the biography, Isherwood glimpsed two possible ways by which he could access the otherwise spectacularly alien Ramakrishna—one that he could acknowledge, another that he could not because he was not writing for his own pleasure but effectively under orders from the Belur Math. The access route that Isherwood could not acknowledge was Ramakrishna's sexuality. As someone in possession of a sexuality that was stridently nonheteronormative, Isherwood was fascinated by Ramakrishna's penchant for gender crossing, albeit as a spiritual exercise.[10]

The access route that he *could* acknowledge was the presence of theater in the mystic's life. Theater was an area of abiding interest for Isherwood since childhood. When he started to write fiction, his characters were often developed by using tropes of roleplaying, playacting, and drama. He could not have failed to notice, for example, that *The Gospel of Sri Ramakrishna* by Mahendranath Gupta (1854–1932) contains two major chapters devoted to Ramakrishna's visits to the Star Theater in September and December 1884, not to mention Ramakrishna's own participation in childhood theatricals when he was growing up. On at least one occasion gendercrossing and roleplaying merged into one seamless performance when the young Gadādhar Chatterjee (as he was named at birth) sneaked into the women's quarters of the local landlord's house dressed as a young woman himself.

Star Theater was the site of a gender-crossing performance that had moved Ramakrishna to a state of ecstasy. It was there that Ramakrishna had been enthralled by the performance of an actress named Nati Binodini (1863–1941) in the role of the young Sri Chaitanya. An incident so rich in the palimpsested performance of cross-gendering and spirituality is obviously too explosive for Isherwood to handle. This incident is mentioned in Isherwood's biography of Ramakrishna, but in retrospect, when the mystic is terminally ill and close to death. Besides, the actress is not named. It is as if Isherwood cannot trust himself to, nor would he have been allowed to, analyze the full significance of Nati Binodini's cross-gender performance and Ramakrishna's deep ecstasy. The Vedanta Society of Southern California regularly published an important journal, *Vedanta and the West*. In that journal's March–April 1963 issue was an article titled "Ramakrishna: 'Patron Saint' of the Bengali Theater" by Mallika Gupta, an American woman married to a Bengali and living in Calcutta. Isherwood met her in late December when he was in India. Isherwood could not have failed to see the article. Gupta not only mentions Nati Binodini in her article but also mentions Ramakrishna's delighted appreciation of the actress when she once visited him at Dakshineswar dressed as a "sahib," a British gentleman. Not only, therefore, does Nati Binodini acquire a special status in Ramakrishna's circle for her gender crossing, but the Star Theater becomes a site where the first such gender crossing is performed. When Isherwood published a chapter from the as-yet-unpublished Ramakrishna biography, in the September–October 1963 issue of *Vedanta and the West,* he declared Ramakrishna "the patron saint of the drama in Bengal."

The full significance of the appellation, however, dawned on Isherwood only when he actually visited the Star Theater in Calcutta on December 29, 1963. Interestingly, he was accompanied by Gupta.[11] Although this was not the same theater where Ramakrishna had watched Nati Binodini's cross-gendered performance—that theater had been demolished in the 1930s and used to be at a place not far from the location Isherwood visited—the theater that he saw had also seen performances by an important thespian who was a dear devotee of Ramakrishna. Girish Ghosh (1844–1912) was the one disciple of Ramakrishna in whom Isherwood succeeded in recognizing a kindred spirit. The fact that Girish Ghosh had performed at the same theater where Isherwood himself was now watching a play must have brought home to him, almost physically, the utility of using theater as a sort of guiding star leading him toward the discovery of a vital connection that helped him consolidate his acceptance of Vedanta and surmount his "Hindu horror."

It must be mentioned that during the 1963–64 trip, Isherwood's negative attitude toward India seems to have evolved into a more measured dislike. He was now willing to find the Belur Math "far more delightful than [he] remembered it" (*The Sixties,* 303). He happily indulged his Orientalism in finding galleys sailing down the Hoogly as if "straight out of Cleopatra's Egypt" (ibid.). While he notes with disapproval that "No one had the least obligation to stand in line and take turns" (305) and feels that he has been "pulled . . . up by the roots, flown . . . all these thousands of miles and dumped . . . down here" (306), he also sees that Bengali hymns to Christ have "the merit of taking Jesus right out of the Episcopalian church and putting him back in the middle of Asia, where he belongs" (307–8). He develops a liking for one Swami Aranyananda, "who is really one of the handsomest boys I have seen in this part of the world" (310). He admits that his biography of Ramakrishna is not really "great" because deep down he resented "the censorship of the Math and Madhanvananda's comments" (311). Isherwood finds the play being performed at Star Theater "sheer Dickens" (316). He begins to realize "how naturally theatrical these Bengalis are, and how unnatural it is for them to put on a ditch-dull show like the Parliament of Religions" (ibid.). Isherwood is impressed by the Ramakrishna Mission's project at Narendrapur and remarks, "It makes you feel that India isn't in such a bad way after all" (320). He seems to have enjoyed his time with the students of Jadavpur University (although he erroneously records the name of the university as Javadpur) where he talked about Huxley (328).

Before leaving India on January 7, 1964, he pays a visit to the room at Belur Math where Vivekananda spent his last days. The prayer he says in that room is significant for its ruthless honesty: "Give me devotion to you, give me knowledge of you—*even against my will*. And be with me in the hour of death" (332; emphasis added). The phrase "even against my will" can be read as an admission of Isherwood's anti-India prejudice. He clearly acknowledges that his prejudice is a problem that he cannot gloss over or take lightly. He must wrestle with it. He understands that it needs to be defeated, overpowered by his devotion to Vivekananda in particular and Vedanta in general. What one also has to acknowledge is that his prejudice was perhaps—as I have suggested—a symptom of his need to oppose his mother, the need to construct an image of himself as a rebel, an iconoclast. The irony is that this need to see himself as a rebel also made it seem necessary for him to become someone with a racial prejudice. This prejudice, unfortunately, aligned him to the British imperialists that he was supposedly rebelling against. The politics of identity formation becomes entangled with the politics of race.

Returning to the two images with which this chapter opens, the critical observer must be struck by the way in which the social iniquity in one image is reversed by the spiritual iniquity in the other. Consciously or not, both the images partake of an almost identical mode of representation and visual signification. Both the artifacts achieve a religio-spiritual overlay—one by virtue of its location inside a place of worship, the other by virtue of its capturing a spiritual teacher–pupil relationship. Although ostensibly neither image foregrounds the politics embedded in the scene

Isherwood and Gerald Heard with Swami Prabhavananda, early 1940s. Courtesy of Don Bachardy.

depicted, it is palimpsestically present in both. Isherwood's acknowledgment of the subdiscursive politics that complicates his cross-cultural journey is, thus, the more significant for his sustained effort at using theater to effect as smooth a crossing-over as the vexed colonial subtext will allow. To call Isherwood a racist would perhaps be an oversimplification of the nature of his attitude toward India. Whatever may have been the amount of negativity in his attitude to India before he came in contact with Vedantism, it must be said that once Swami Prabhavananda entered his life, Isherwood recognized that his negative feelings toward India were a problem and he engaged with it as best he could. One must be reminded of the significance of the prayer that he said in Belur in 1964. He craved devotion, even against his own will. This determination to defeat negativity in oneself is surely an example of the sincerity with which he had espoused a philosophy that was not socioculturally his own.

Notes

1. This is a longer version of an article titled "Guiding Star: Christopher Isherwood's Passage to Calcutta's Star Theater," *ANQ: A Quarterly Journal of Short*

Articles, Notes and Reviews 21.2 (Spring 2008): 61–65. I dedicate this article to my friend Prasun Banerjee, without whose gift of a copy of Isherwood's published 1960s diaries this essay would be incomplete.

2. Christopher Isherwood, *Diaries, Volume One: 1939–1960*, ed. Katherine Bucknell (New York: Harper, 1996), 294.

3. Christopher Isherwood, *Christopher and His Kind* (1976; reprint, London: Methuen, 1985), 58. "The Landauers" was subsequently incorporated into *Goodbye to Berlin* (1939).

4. In the introduction to her edited volume *Kathleen and Christopher: Christopher Isherwood's Letters to His Mother*, Lisa Colletta provides some context for the hostility the son had for his mother: "he preferred to believe in a simplified, more creditable, and more exciting version of his relationship with Kathleen, one in which she never understood him, was always the Other, and always in opposition to him" (Minneapolis: University of Minnesota Press, 2005), viii.

5. Christopher Isherwood, *Kathleen and Frank* (New York: Simon and Schuster, 1971), 463.

6. Kathleen Isherwood's unpublished diaries (1911–13, 1916–48, 1950–52, and 1957–59) are held by the Harry Ransom Humanities Research Center, University of Texas at Austin, as a part of the Christopher Isherwood Collection.

7. Christopher Isherwood, *My Guru and His Disciple* (New York: Farrar, Straus and Giroux, 1980), 258.

8. Peter Burton and Neil Bartlett, *Talking to . . . : Peter Burton in Conversation with Writers Writing on Gay Themes* (Exeter, England: Third House, 1991), 58.

9. Isherwood writes about an incident in early November 1956 involving a young monk who was supposedly "arrested on a morals charge" outside Hollywood High School (*Diaries*, 1: 661). Isherwood praises what he considers to be the Swami's "unworldly . . . rueful worldliness" (while quoting the latter's comment, "Why didn't he go to some bar!").The fact remains that the young monk is not allowed to return to the Vedanta Center at Trabuco (ibid., 663, 667). In fact, it is suggested by the Swami that the young monk should be sent off to India to live at the Belur Math (717). This suggestion seems to me to be a classic case of what Julia Kristeva would call abjection. Because the homosexual is the abject in a heteronormative society, I see the Swami's suggestion as possibly homophobic. One doubts that he would have accepted Isherwood's homosexuality quite so readily had the latter not been the celebrity that he was.

10. For a detailed analysis of the homoerotic component of Ramakrishna's spiritual life, see Jeffrey J. Kirpal, *Kali's Child: The Mystical and the Erotic in the Life and Teachings of Ramakrishna* (Chicago: University of Chicago Press, 1995).

11. Christopher Isherwood, *The Sixties: Diaries, Volume Two, 1960–1969*, ed. Katherine Bucknell (New York: Harper, 2010), 316.

13

Spiritual Searching in Isherwood's Artistic Production

MARIO FARAONE

Floating on a straw is very much like goose-stepping on thin ice: a dangerous occupation that doesn't allow any room for error and offers only a small chance of success. This somewhat curious notion comes from Isherwood's "Afterword" to his pamphlet *An Approach to Vedanta* (1963), and it is appropriate to introduce the main issue of this essay. Isherwood describes the long road that brought him to Vedanta and explains that the contact with Swami Prabhavananda was for him above all a relationship through which he looked for a "still centre" in life and art. He tries to reply to hypothetical questions raised by his readers: "If you were so desperate at the time, what was your conversion really worth? Weren't you simply grasping at the nearest straw? Weren't you in the mood to believe in anyone and anything?" To such questions, he offers the following considerations: "Yes—it is quite true that I didn't enter upon this new phase of my life in a mood of critical objectivity. I wasn't calm. I was deeply dissatisfied. It is arguable that I was ready to clutch at straws . . . if only they could offer me some sense of security." He then concludes, asking his readers to consider: "I am writing these words more than twenty-three years later. Can one keep afloat for twenty-three years on a straw?"[1]

This is a major issue in trying to unravel Isherwood's search for "a new tone of voice" through his American writings. Religious discourse plays an important role in his writings. I think that it is incorrect to state that Isherwood is not able to measure up to his fame of the 1930s after his move to the United States and California's world of cinema and sunny beaches. Rather, initially through Vedantic daily religious chores and rituals, and then thanks to Vedantic thought, Isherwood changes his way of reading the world and himself, which had been the main themes of his narrative. This change is motivated precisely by the need to find a new tone of voice. Isherwood's newfound pacifism and his need to go to California to talk with Gerald Heard and Aldous Huxley, and his living side by side with a plethora of stimulating intellectuals, represent a turning point in his life, a new narrative discourse in his writings, and a major point of reference for the further penetration of Eastern philosophical and religious thought in Western and, above all, American twentieth-century culture.

Isherwood approached Vedanta through Heard's suggestion of meditation and yoga. Meeting Swami Prabhavananda in August 1939 was the beginning of the search of psychological and spiritual balance he subsequently appears to have found. In addition to providing Isherwood with an entirely new faith free from the dogmatic superstructures of the religion of his youth, Swami and Vedanta offered an ideological and personal answer to his vague dissatisfaction with political commitment and public life in the 1930s. In a 1939 letter to Edward Upward, Isherwood declared the necessity for him to be "personal" and to not belong to any kind of movement:

> So what remains for me but pacifism, of some kind? And what revolution can I attempt to promote but a revolution inside myself? . . . Heard . . . sees the only hope for the future in building up a nucleus of psychically-trained leaders who will gradually spread their influence over the world, and become the directors of the new socialism. These leaders will be trained in the principles of Yoga . . . adapted to the needs of the West. . . . Yes, believe it or not, your unlucky Starn has set his feet on the bottom of this crazy goat-track which is to lead over the peaks of the never-never mountains. (Huntington Library CI 122:28)

It is interesting to note the use of terms such as "goat-tracks," "peaks," and "mountains"—metaphors that will appear again at the end of *Prater Violet* (1945), a short narrative tale that provides the first insight into Isherwood's tormented soul: the need to look for a "north-western passage" to overtake the hideous obstacle of personal and artistic sterility and his first novel since his "conversion" to Vedanta.

Therefore, this straw on which he tries to float embodies the ideological justification for his still uncertain pacifism. At the same time, it represents the cornerstone on which to erect the new building, the "American Isherwood," a descendant of the "European Isherwood" who also searched for balance and expression. And Swami—one of the father figures who have symbolized a lot in Isherwood's life—is the perfect kind of life vest to rescue Isherwood from the ocean of despair in which he has fallen: "This is *not* the story of a conversion through intellectual conviction. Is anyone ever convinced of anything by pure reason alone? . . . The right teacher must appear at exactly the right moment in the right place, and his pupil must be in the right mood to accept what he teaches" (*An Approach to Vedanta*, 17).

Vedanta is a powerful tool because it is not an end in itself. Additionally, Isherwood did not see the observation of the various rituals as an obstacle to his understanding of the love message taught by Ramakrishna through Swami's words. As Isherwood states in his 1951 essay "Vedanta and the West," "the God or godlike man whom we worship must not be allowed to come between us and the knowledge that worshipped and worshipper are, essentially, both projections of the one Brahman."[2] In fact, it is the essential nonduality of Vedanta that fascinates and convinces Isherwood that he is on the right track. He appreciates "the practice of mysticism" precisely because through it "the man may directly know and be united with his eternal Nature, the Atman, through meditation and spiritual discipline, without the aid of any church or delegated minister" (66). Meditation, spiritual discipline, deep relationship with Swami, possible mystic perception of the divine: all these succeed in offering Isherwood the path to self-understanding and to obtain liberation through the direct knowledge of God, a target that now and again appears in different forms in Isherwood's essays and narrative writings. These practices continue, with different intensity, all during his life, as his diaries demonstrate. For instance, the practice of meditation becomes part of Isherwood's daily routine as early as the beginning of the 1940s. At first, he is very shy and irresolute, but progressively he becomes more and more confident that meditation about "this Force" will get him out of his psychological and narrative impasse.[3] He maintains this confidence until old age, another period of fears and despair owing to the increasing perception of physical decay and impending illnesses.

The presence, whether physical or spiritual, of Swami and of his teachings are of the utmost importance to grant Isherwood a better understanding of himself, of the world, and of the inner possibilities of his artistic skills. Isherwood often underlines the routine nature of his praying to God: "Every day I manage to tell my beads. . . . I do it without feeling, compulsively, and yet I know that this represents the only thing I have that stands between me and despair. Trust to nothing else—*ever*."[4] And he is very often aware of the fact that his religious life mainly "consists in making japam without the faintest devotion and indeed mostly while thinking of anything else in the world including my resentments. Now and then I get around to asking Ramakrishna to give me devotion 'even against my will.' And this is not shit. I still believe" (*The Sixties*, 291). With time passing, his faith appears to get stronger even if its outward demonstrations become weaker, because the routine practice of *japam* and of repeating his *mantram* are there to remind him that, as much as his moments of despair may be painful, his will to keep on trying is what really matters to let him crawl along a steep but ultimately rewarding path. This is the road map the 1962 namesake narrator in *Down There on a Visit* sets himself to lead a spiritual life together with his fellow traveler Paul: "this was the eve of new life . . . a life of intention . . . we couldn't hope to succeed all the time. But at least we would have each other's encouragement. And, as long as we didn't stop trying, how could we fail?"[5]

Practices and routines are but the structural elements helping Isherwood in his search. The main pillar on which he builds his new life is Swami himself with his sweet and loving disposition and his strong belief in God's existence. Being a disciple of Brahmananda, a direct disciple of Ramakrishna himself, Prabhavananda is a figure of great help for Isherwood from the beginning. Isherwood perceives Swami's close proximity to the original source of God's word, and he understands that he believes in a person who believes in a person who actually had met God himself, or at least one of his avatars. And the existence of God is something whose certainty is taken for granted by Swami's very same faith. In fact, when Isherwood asks Swami, "You're really *certain* that God exists?" Swami replies laughing: "*Of course!* If He doesn't exist, then *I* don't exist" (*The Sixties*, 133). Later, this passage will appear almost verbatim in *A Meeting by the River*. It is a significant part of Isherwood's personal certainty about the existence of God and may be taken together with the well-known statement in *Exhumations:* "After I got to know Prabhavananda, I gradually ceased to be an atheist; because I found myself unable to disbelieve in his belief in God."[6]

Isherwood's acknowledgment of the powerful influence Swami may have on him is almost epiphanic: "I had to say to myself: No, he isn't lying, either to me or to himself. And he isn't crazy. I know this man. He speaks the same language I do. He accepts the same values. If this is true for him, then I'm forced to admit that it must be true for me too" (*An Approach to Vedanta*, 17). Therefore, Isherwood's steadier and steadier belief in Ramakrishna's teachings and in the Vedantic conception of life as something that will grow and be nurtured by Swami's faith is an extremely important issue in his entire American life. Being a father figure and a guru, Swami becomes the essence of Isherwood's will to believe and provides the daily shelter from dreariness, anguish, and uncertainties:

> Watching Swami, bald-headed at the back, huddled before the shrine, I thought, *He's been doing this all his life, he isn't kidding.* Such a tired old sense that life is routine; and yet I could pray to Ramakrishna for devotion, for help at the hour of death, and for Don, all with really quite considerable faith. (*The Sixties,* 278)

It is important to stress the private nature of Isherwood's faith. Cooperating with Swami in several translations of Vedanta's holy texts, accepting Swami's requests of giving public readings to the Hollywood and Santa Barbara communities, and helping him edit the *Vedanta and the West* magazine, Isherwood feels their relationship to be very personal. After Swami's death in 1976, he notes in his diaries the difficulty in feeling any powerful spiritual emanation from Swami Chetanananda, the temporary substitute in charge of the Vedanta Center. Moreover, now and again he reports that he is not inclined to speak about his faith in public: "For me religion must be quite private as far as I'm publicly concerned. I can still write about it *informatively,* but I must not appear before people on a platform as a living witness and example" (ibid., 319). This happens while Isherwood is staying with Swami at Belur Math, during Prema's taking his *sannyas,* a period of extreme spiritual tension and doubts about his own faith and about the outward appearances of being a believer. When in September 1963 he is pressured by Swami to go with him to India to celebrate Vivekananda's centenary, Isherwood feels miserable about it. His reaction against this trip further underlines how to him religion is always something personal, almost entirely confined to his own private relation with Swami (290). He often muses on this, as, for instance, when he feels imprisoned in Belur Math: "Why do I feel such an intense eagerness to leave this place, and this country? I count the days. It *is* an experience, being here. I *am* getting something out of it, I know. And yet I strain like a leashed animal to escape" (313). This also happens when he has to pay religious devotion to other Swamis of the order: though he finds some to be nice and charming, they do not inspire his mind, respect, or dedication. Isherwood feels forced to act against his own will whenever he has to conform to the outward customs and rituals of the religion he has embraced. He often feels "rage against the Parliament of Religions, the Ramakrishna Math, India, everything. This is a very deep aversion which I have been aware of from time to time ever since I first got involved with Vedanta. It has . . . nothing directly to do with Ramakrishna, Vivekananda or Swami" (324).

Nonetheless, Isherwood continuously perceives the necessity of devotion in order to achieve and maintain the human and spiritual balance he is after. Believing in Vivekananda and Vedanta, and asserting it so often in his diaries, is a *mantram* itself, representing the possibility of reaching integrity in his everyday life. On one special occasion, he gets into Vivekananda's room at Belur Math, prostrates and prays to receive devotion and knowledge of the godhead even against his own will, asking this gift to be granted to Don too, and repeating his prayer on the balcony where Swami first met Maharaj. This act of prostration, a visible acknowledgment of his faith, is something important for Isherwood, the rebel writer, and he repeatedly reflects on it, granting a special significance to his doing it for *his* Swami and not willing to do it for other people: "the first time I prostrated before you, that was a great moment in my life. It really meant something tremendous to me, to want to bow down before another human being. And here [at Belur Math] I've been making pramas to everyone . . . And it's just taking all the significance out of doing it" (325). When he sometimes states that "Ramakrishna Math is coming between me and God," he is actually stating that his faith and his beliefs are built on his own personal relationship with Swami and on the perception of Vedanta religion he has attained through such a guru–disciple relationship. Offering the same kind of devotion to everybody in the order, even to another Swami, for Isherwood would simply mean betraying his guru–disciple/father–son relationship, and it would represent coming back to the former institutional religious organization he belonged to by birth, which he so definitely turned from. The act of publicly demonstrating his faith and attending the scheduled religious festivities seems to upset him. He often declares that he feels obliged to attend official *pujas* only in order to please Swami, not because he wants to: "I hate the puja itself as much as ever—no, not hate, but it is quite meaningless to me, with all these posturing women fixed up in the saris. Even Sarada, with her hair loose on her shoulders but oh so elegantly arranged, seemed theatrical" (132).

Prabhavananda's teachings and Isherwood's becoming accustomed to meditation progressively influence his writings and lead him to modify and refine his point of view and, up to a point, to alter and transform his narrative technique. In February 1940 he reports an occurrence he experiences while lying in bed, remembering (or rather, reliving) a 1936 episode sitting in a small park in Amsterdam with Gerald Hamilton:

> Not only did I relive this instant (which was, I am sure, absolutely authentic) but, for a couple of seconds, I actually *was* the Christopher of 1936. I was—and yet I wasn't; because, standing aside from the experience, I was also aware of the present-day Christopher. I can't, of course, in the least describe the difference between the two personalities . . . but . . . I was intensely conscious of it. I could hold the two selves separate, comparing them—and, in doing so, I caught the faintest glimpse of something else—that part of my consciousness which has not changed, which never will change, because it's part of the Reality. (*Diaries,* 1:91)

This perception of the two "Christopher Isherwoods" forming the same Reality is something very similar to what Isherwood writes in *Down There on a Visit,* describing the "double point of view" employed to narrate the four episodes of the novel. The 1962 Christopher, from the height of his maturity, looks affectionately at the various past Christophers whose experiences he is reliving and relating: "And now before I slip back into the convention of calling this young man 'I,' let me consider him as a separate being, a stranger almost. . . . For, of course, he is almost a stranger to me" (13). "Of course" because the 1962 narrator is aware that an entire maturation process has progressively transformed the various Christophers into very different persons, though it is still possible to notice the continuity existing between them: "There has been no break in the sequence of daily statements that I am I. But *what* I am has refashioned itself throughout the days and years, until now almost all that remains constant is the mere awareness of being conscious. And that awareness belongs to everybody; it isn't a particular person." And because of this perception the 1962 Christopher knows that the previous Christophers cannot be entirely ignored, because, after all, they have all been rings of the same evolution chain: That earlier "Christopher . . . is, practically speaking, dead. . . . I can't revitalize him now. I can only reconstruct him from his remembered acts and words and from the writings he has left us . . . but I will try not to [sneer at him]. I'll try not to apologize for him either. After all, I owe him some respect. In a sense he is my father, and in another sense my son" (14). This passage, a very powerful narrative beginning, holds in a nutshell a number of relevant topics: besides showing the significance of Vedanta for Isherwood's narrative growth, it endorses important issues of Eastern thought, such as the theory of multiple lives and of reincarnation.

Some of these issues appear in other American writings: for instance, metempsychosis, the transmigration of the soul into another body, is represented twice in *A Single Man*. The first occurrence is right at the beginning of the novel when George wakes up and gazes at himself in the mirror: "Staring and staring into the mirror, it sees many faces within its face—the face of the child, the boy, the young man, the not-so-young man—all present still, preserved like fossils on superimposed layers, and, like fossils, dead. Their message to this live dying creature is: look at us— we have died—what is there to be afraid of?" (8). If in this occurrence metempsychosis is merely hinted at, it is certainly treated in a more sophisticated manner at the end of the novel. Observing George asleep, the third person narrator asks himself, "is all of George altogether present here?" (155), introducing the metaphor of the pools in the rock by the sea: "Up the coast a few miles north, in a lava reef under the cliffs, there are a lot of rock pools. You can visit them when the tide is out." Each pool is isolated from the others and it would be possible, for the sake of convenience, to call them by name, such as George, Charlotte, Kenny: "Just as George and the others are thought of, for convenience, as individual entities, so you may think of a rock pool as an entity; though, of course, it is not." This "of course" is the hint of the existence of cosmic unity which goes far and beyond *maya,* the cosmic illusion of separation. The rocks isolating the single pools create a universe of protean organism that, carrying on the metaphor of human conscience, the narrator compares to the various values and defects of the single characters, very different from one another but nonetheless coexisting because "the rocks of the pool hold their world together. And, throughout the day of the ebb tide, they know no other." But at nighttime, "that hour of the night at which man's ego almost sleeps" (to quote *Prater Violet*), high tide comes, that is, "the waters of that other ocean, that consciousness which is no one in particular but which contains everyone and everything, past, present and future, and extends unbroken beyond the utter-most stars" (155–56). The creatures living in the isolated pools are rejoined and overwhelmed by the strength of the individual and universal conscience at the same time. Of course, when the tide comes back again, some of these creatures may by chance return to the same pool where they originally were, or may find themselves in another: "But do they ever bring back . . . any kind of catch with them? Can they tell us, in any manner, about their journey? Is there, indeed, anything for them to tell—except that the waters of the ocean are not really other than the waters of the pool?" (156).

The relationship between Vedanta and artistic production is by no means one-way only; rather, it provides a reciprocal steadier ground for spiritual and professional growth. In fact, Isherwood's work as a screenwriter for Hollywood emerges in many of his writings about Vedanta. Very often, as in *An Approach to Vedanta,* he outlines main concepts of Vedanta as an everyday normal conversation about faith issues between a curious newcomer and an already acknowledged believer; and in *Ramakrishna and His Disciples* (1965), the vitality of the characters benefits from Isherwood's skill to sketch scenes and people, certainly a gift he owes to his 1930s writings, but one that gets sharpened a lot both by his living in the Vedanta Center and by working in the movie industry. This idea of writing narrative as a film treatment, therefore privileging a detailed visualization to a plain narration of events, lively dialogue to long descriptions, is a recurring issue in Isherwood's memoirs, above all intermingled with the Vedanta perception of time present as confronted with time past and time future. For instance, while considering a possible story based on the character of Ganymede, he even conceives "a technique of narration—which one could use on many kinds of material, but which would be particularly suitable for retelling classical myths . . . a technique of describing one's effects, telling *how* one would tell a story rather than directly telling it. . . . The narrative has, of course, to be all in the present tense. It's a little like a film treatment, but cornier, artier, more visual" (*The Sixties,* 115–16). Vedanta faith and scriptwriting skill form a powerful joint venture offering Isherwood relief from spiritual emptiness and opportunities to find the "new tone of voice" he is constantly seeking. This seems to be the case also of "The Wayfarer," the 1955 treatment of Siddharta's life and myth, which was never realized as a feature film.[7] In both the treatment and a two-part lecture about it, Isherwood's skill of grasping the spirituality of Siddharta's message and of conveying it through an appropriate dialogue and a high standard of visualization is at work.

Among the various problems a screenwriter may face in adapting Siddharta's myth for the big screen, Isherwood explicitly indicates that to respect Buddhist religious convictions, "you can't show Buddha preaching, you can't show him at all, you can't show him before his enlightenment preaching, and therefore what seems evident is that you have to show the impact of his teaching on later generations, and I think that in fact this film ought to have the nature of what they sometimes call a dramatic documentary" ("Wayfarer"); and that "anything that happens inside people's heads is very bad in the movies, and in some ways, of course, this process of distaste and weariness and disenchantment in life [experienced by Siddharta] is something we have to dramatize step by step." Asking himself "how in the world are you going to convey Buddha's teachings in a manner which is visual as well as something that is just said by the actor," he indicates in the "time question" a possible way out of several problems caused by the original material. In fact, the prophecy about Siddharta leaving his father's palace to travel the world and embrace a religious life if he sees four signs—an old man, a sick man, a dead man, and a monk—is originally without a deadline, which in Isherwood's opinion provides an amount of problems: "Just what exactly did [Siddharta's father] Subhodana think he was going to do? Was he really going to exclude old men, sick men, dead men and monks permanently from his son's life? Was he going to shut his son up in the palace indefinitely?" Isherwood therefore provides his story with a precise deadline: "As soon as the Prince is grown-up I am going to abdicate in my life-time, and leave him to ascend the throne. Then the moment he is king he can go out into the world, he can see everything, because the prophecy will have been proved untrue." By changing this detail of the original story, Isherwood adds to the realism and plausibility of the story itself. And in accordance to the same issue of plausibility, Isherwood provides another departure from the original story by altering the total wickedness of Devadatta, Siddharta's cousin and enemy, for dramatic purposes:

> I've rather departed from the conventional ideas of making Davadatta purely wicked and destructive. . . . If there's one thing more boring than absolute goodness, it's absolute evil, and it's completely unreal in the sphere of drama and too tiresome for words, I think. So, instead of that, I try to make Devadatta the opposite of Siddhartha, and not always, and not invariably his opponent, although he becomes his opponent later.

From these decisions, Isherwood derives other departures from the original story. For instance, the creation of the dramatic pair Devadatta–Arjuna: "What I've attempted to do is to make Devadatta a kind of Othello, and Arjuna a kind of Iago. Arjuna is the little man maliciously advising the tragic hero or villain; he is always prodding Devadatta on and feeding his jealousy, because he hopes to ride to power and influence on Devadatta's shoulders"; the development of the character of Yasodhara, Siddharta's true love and future wife, as an active and willing woman: "In the tradition Yasodhara is represented as being absolutely passive; she's very sweet, she adores him, he leaves her. Nothing could be duller from a dramatic point of view. Now it struck me that obviously Yasodhara has to be much more of a character than she is represented as being, and Swami feels that this is quite all right and permissible"; and, finally, a significant change in Devadatta's inclination toward Siddharta's enlightenment: "According to the legend, Devadatta pursued Siddhartha with his resentment after he became the Buddha, all through his monastic period, and even founded a kind of rival sect. Now it is very undesirable from many points of view to have this, and I think it would have a kind of farcical element and be thoroughly bad." What Isherwood decides to do in this specific case is have Devadatta following Siddharta; meeting all the people he had encountered in his wanderings; meeting Siddharta himself both in the enlightenment episode under the tree and in the epilogue; going through an experience of self-revelation and conversion; feeling the need to join Siddharta's followers, but receiving the task of becoming ruler of the kingdom: "So I thought that was how I would end up with Devadatta. Because it would be a good paradox, the fact that he who had always pursued ambition finally realized it, but in another way and with another philosophy."

It seems evident that the necessities of abiding by the teachings of Vedanta, and of consulting Swami for his approval, are never separate from the dramatic and artistic requirements in Isherwood's decisions. Repeating his *mantram,* making *japam,* realizing *darshan,* performing *pranam* for his guru are far from being a mere straw on which one may float to survive the ocean of *maya* and of despair. There is no superstition in Isherwood's accepting Vedanta and its outward rituals precisely because he believes in the most important issues of Vedanta faith, and this can be inferred from his writings, his diaries, his notes, and his scripts. Now and then he falters in his belief and, as he is temperamental in his artistic production, he is inconsistent in the confidence of his faith, probably like everybody else in the world. But the faith is there and he is much enriched by it, not only because through it he finds solace from anguish and despair, but also because of the human and artistic strength he gains from meeting Swami and from the act of praying. Meditating and praying may be considered the religious counterparts of devising a novel and writing it: a continuous flow of spiritual and artistic energy that goes to and from Isherwood the Vedantist and Isherwood the artist. In 1962, to Isherwood's question about the meaning of praying to Ramakrishna, Swami answers: "It is good both for you *and* for the person you pray for. . . .

You see, when you are speaking to God like that, there are not two people, it's all the same. . . . All that was needed was faith that the prayer would be answered. You don't have to be a saint. If you had faith, then it would be answered. He said this with that absolute compelling confidence of his. He made you feel he was quite sure of what he was saying" (*The Sixties*, 248). Swami's complete confidence obliges Isherwood to believe, because he finds that it is simply impossible for him not to. Furthermore, Isherwood almost always addresses prayers to the achievement of spiritual goals, even if the hint of a material issue is always present:

> There are only two prayers that I keep wanting to pray, and do pray when I think of them. I pray that Ramakrishna may come into Don's life, more and more; so that when he starts losing his looks and getting older, he will have something that really supports him. And then I pray—and this I ought to do increasingly, because it is horribly important—that I may be helped to leave the body when the time comes. (Ibid., 261)

The ideas of death and of preparing himself to die appear in Isherwood's diaries as early as the beginning of the 1960s and return very often. Above all, he meditates on his own fears and on Swami's encouragement to detach from the physical sphere of death through praying. Isherwood is increasingly upset about the idea of decaying, associating it both to physical and mental decadence and to the fear of losing Don's love. He therefore deeply admires Swami's position about the end of life: "On the 11th [of March, Swami] told me that he now feels quite indifferent whether he goes on living or dies. It is all according to Maharaj's will. He is aware of Maharaj all the time. . . . 'You know, Chris, He is everything. Nothing else matters'" (ibid., 357). To this certainty, Isherwood compares his own feelings of being inadequate: "And I, what do I feel? Stupid, dull, unfeeling, fat, old. Utterly unfit to associate with Prabhavananda, or with Don either. A stupid old toad—and not even ashamed of being one. Too dull for shame." He seems still unable to replace the idea of physical disappearance with that of eternal continuity which lies at the very core of the belief he has chosen and accepted. The *maya*, ephemeral and transient external skin of the world, is continuously represented by the often superficial life he leads, and by the cult of hedonism that is worshipped in that same California which provided him the spiritual shelter represented by Vedanta. And it is by remembering and praying to Swami, therefore accomplishing his teachings even if with a certain amount of doubts, that Isherwood faces the final act on the world's stage: "Swami really *is* present within me because

I remember him. Why shouldn't I remember him when I am dying and get strength and reassurance from that memory? In the last analysis, strength and reassurance are all I'm asking for. . . . My memory of this reassurance is gradually getting dimmer, of course. But it is right here inside me. . . . By dwelling on it, I think I can make it last my time."[8]

Isherwood's perception of Swami's sainthood is an epiphany that occurs very early in their relationship and that he often refers to in his diaries. Probably one of the most incisive occurrences is after Swami's recovery from one of his several illnesses: "He looked absolutely marvellous . . . his face seemed to shine with love and lack of anxiety. I thought to myself, I am in the presence of a saint; and I asked Ramakrishna to help me 'through the power of my guru'" (*The Sixties*, 507). It is important to note that as early as 1944, five years after their first meeting, Swami affectionately declares to Isherwood: "I don't want you to leave here, Chris. I want you to stay with me as long as I'm alive. I think you'd be all right, even if you left here. But I want you. . . . I think you have the makings of a saint. . . . I mean it. You have devotion. You have the driving power. And you are sincere. What else is there?" (*Diaries*, 1:352). The issue of sainthood, and of how to write about it, is central to one of Isherwood's unjustly neglected early American writings, "The Problem of the Religious Novel" (1946), in which he tries to point out how the image of the true saint is a difficult one to be dealt with in narrative, because, according to him, a true saint is a simple, humble, average person who shines of inspiration and of holiness in ordinary life. Catching the experience of a saint is to grab a straw in the tempestuous ocean of the soul: "Nothing short of genius could succeed in [rendering] the portrait of the perfect saint. For the mystical experience itself can never be described. It can only be written around, hinted at, dimly reflected in word and deed. . . . Perhaps the truly comprehensive religious novel could only be written by a saint—and saints, unfortunately, are not in the habit of writing novels" (*Exhumations*, 120).

Notes

1. Christopher Isherwood, *An Approach to Vedanta* (Los Angeles: Vedanta Press, 1963), 67–68.

2. Christopher Isherwood, *The Wishing Tree*, ed. Robert Adjemian (San Francisco: Harper and Row, 1986), 63.

3. Christopher Isherwood, *Diaries, Volume One: 1939–1960*, ed. Katherine Bucknell (New York: Harper, 1996), 177.

4. Christopher Isherwood, *The Sixties: Diaries, Volume Two, 1960–1969*, ed. Katherine Bucknell (New York: Harper, 2010), 79–80.

5. Christopher Isherwood, *Down There on a Visit* (1962; reprint, Minneapolis: University of Minnesota Press, 1999), 213.

6. Christopher Isherwood, *Exhumations: Stories, Articles, Verses* (New York: Simon and Schuster, 1966), 97.

7. Christopher Isherwood, "The Wayfarer," unpublished film treatment, Huntington Library (CI 111, 112).

8. Christopher Isherwood, *Liberation: Diaries, Volume Three, 1970–1983*, ed. Katherine Bucknell (New York: Harper, 2012), 686.

III

A WRITER AT ODDS WITH HIMSELF
IN COLD WAR AMERICA

The utter brutality of those cops, the night before last, and my guilt
that I didn't handle them properly—wasn't wonderful and poised and
mature. I ought to have called their bluff, insisted on being locked up,
hired a lawyer, taken the case to the Supreme Court, started a nation-
wide stink. Why didn't I? Because I'm cowardly, weak, compromised.
My life at present is such a mess.

—CHRISTOPHER ISHERWOOD, *Lost Years*

Isherwood's first decade in the United States was dominated by the Second
World War, his discovery of and devotion to Vedanta, and a rather turbulent love life. As the passage above indicates, Isherwood was caught
in a raid on a gay bar in December 1949, at a time when the LAPD was
at its most virulently homophobic. Although he thinks he should have
been braver and more oppositional, the reality is that this was a common experience. His anxiety over the whole situation is suggestive of a
greater sense of tension, and even fear, pervasive among Isherwood and
his fellow queers (Isherwood's preferred term), even as the "homophile"
movement was beginning to take hold in other parts of Los Angeles.
Isherwood's friend and sometime landlady Evelyn Hooker had already
begun her pioneering research, studying gay men to figure out whether
they were pathological. She even tried to enlist Isherwood to coauthor a
book with her, but he decided against it.

In this personally and professionally frustrating period, Isherwood
produced little fiction, though he did publish what may be seen as his last

"English" novel, *Prater Violet* (1945). He experienced a creative drought as he struggled to integrate his new spiritual life with his "Americanizing" self. He had developed his English identity "against" things: his mother, the Anglican church, Cambridge, middle-class respectability. Being against Englishness was not sufficient to the development of an American identity; he needed to "discover a new self here, an American me."[1] As a pacifist, he was against the war when all of America seemed to be for it. He sought the counsel of friends to find out what being a pacifist meant and how it could inform his life. He tried and then rejected the idea of becoming a monk. For a while, he found a place as a conscientious objector working with European refugees in a Quaker hostel in Pennsylvania. He wrote about that experience in *The World in the Evening,* a novel that took him seven years to finish and which is addressed in several essays in this section. It is, in many ways, Isherwood's least satisfying novel—both for himself and for his readers.

Isherwood became an American citizen in 1946, but he spent the remainder of his career becoming an American writer. In the 1940s, he was a Hollywood writer, which sharpened his skills. As he told Stanley Poss in a 1960 interview, "I think what the movies taught me was visualization. Of course the art of the movie is fundamentally opposed to the art of literature, because the fewer words you have in a movie, the better. . . . You do learn a great deal . . . which purely non-dramatic writers simply don't think about."[2] Isherwood's refusal to denigrate or downplay his writing for the screen—his office job—differentiates him from many writers of his generation in Hollywood's golden age.

It wasn't just his writing for pay that got in the way of his fiction in this period, though. As he tried to find his American voice, he struggled with content, form, and style. Much of that agony can be seen in *The World in the Evening* and its painful, protracted gestation. As Katherine Bucknell writes in her introduction to *Lost Years,* a memoir reconstructed from Isherwood's diaries covering 1945 to 1951, "he was never sure of his subject, never sure how to tell his story." He was bewildered by "how to give life to a narrator of whose identity and sexuality he was uncertain. In a sense, Isherwood had come to a deadlock with himself because, for a time, his identity as a writer and his identity as a homosexual were at odds."[3] Isherwood, the autobiographical writer, could not write about himself and continue to skirt the issue of the sexuality of "Christopher Isherwood."

It may come as no surprise that this period was frustrating for a man who tried to make sense of his life in his work and who was openly homosexual at a time when writing frankly about sexuality was not easy. This is the era of Joseph McCarthy as well as iconoclastic younger writers such as Tennessee Williams, whose work was steeped in sexuality but still misty about homosexuality. And Gore Vidal was even more evasive. As we saw in the first section of this book, with *A Single Man*, published a decade after *The World in the Evening*, Isherwood had achieved an integration of his identities, enabling him to write a concise, elegant masterpiece. Love it or hate it, no one would use those words to describe *The World in the Evening*; nonetheless, getting past that difficult birth was necessary torture for Isherwood. The essays in this section of *The American Isherwood* reconsider that novel and other work from the 1940s, 1950s, and 1960s, showing the importance of what Isherwood was working on and of what he was able to accomplish during these not quite "lost years."

This final section includes essays dealing with Isherwood's creative partnerships and friendships. Auden is the writer most closely associated with Isherwood, but their relationship was significantly strained by geography and ideology in their American lives. They had written several important works together, but their paths diverged after their emigration. As Isherwood noted in his diary, "America parted us." They could no longer write together as they had so successfully in the 1930s, and, as time passed, they saw each other less and less frequently.[4]

Edward Upward was Isherwood's first reader for most of his career. Earlier in his life, in England, he worked with Upward on the "Mortmere" stories. After Isherwood moved to the United States, their relationship was mostly conducted by mail. Upward was alarmed by some of the immediate changes he saw in his old friend, and he firmly but lovingly warned him about potential negative consequences of pacifism and mysticism. Benjamin Kohlmann treats this complex friendship through an examination of important letters from the fall of 1939. As we discussed in our introduction to this book, Upward recognized Isherwood's talent and urged him to stay true to it.

In the 1950s and early 1960s, Isherwood worked with Aldous Huxley on several projects. Isherwood had met Huxley years earlier in England, but he sought out Huxley in Los Angeles to consult with him about pacifism. The late Peter Edgerly Firchow's final published essay is reprinted here. In it, he describes how the Huxley–Isherwood friendship allowed them to explore their common interests in Eastern religion, film writing, and the Southern California landscape. While Huxley went further into mysticism, Isherwood was captivated by celebrity, as Lisa Colletta's essay shows. Colletta, who has published a volume of Isherwood's letters with his mother, specializes in the literature of the 1930s and 1940s and on European expatriates in Hollywood. As she indicates, Isherwood's circle of friends in the 1940s is a veritable who's who of Classic Hollywood, and he would continue to travel in that world for the rest of his life. His fiction in the late 1940s and early 1950s, especially *Prater Violet* and *The World in the Evening,* addressed the lure of celebrity as well as the darker side of Hollywood.

The final three essays in the book all consider the place of *The World in the Evening* in Isherwood's canon. S. Hodson, who carefully cataloged the Isherwood archive at the Huntington, shares her intimate knowledge with the writer's process. Her vast knowledge of the intricacies of the archive gives her a unique perspective on Isherwood's life and work.

The McCarthy era, the Cold War, midcentury—whatever you call this period of American literary and cultural history—is usually seen as an era of homogeneity and prudery. However, as writers such as Williams and Vidal were challenging the boundaries of the stage and the screen (to very different effects), Isherwood's novels found a readership through the mass production of pulp paperbacks. Jaime Harker, author of *Middlebrow Queer: Christopher Isherwood in America,* examines Isherwood's reception by readers across the great American landscape as they found him in dime-store paperback racks. Once Isherwood found his American voice and resumed his own iconoclasm, queer readers across Cold War America read his work, welcomed it, and became devoted fans.

Earlier in this volume, Lois Cucullu discussed E. M. Forster's posthumously published gay novel *Maurice* in relation to Isherwood's *A Single Man.* Joshua Adair looks at Forster's landmark novel in the context of *The World in the Evening.* Isherwood was one of a number of friends with whom Forster shared and discussed the manuscript of *Maurice,* which became an open secret in midcentury literary circles. That it would influence Isherwood should come as no surprise, and Adair analyzes the commonalities between the two works. Notably, only one of these novels would be published in the 1950s. The other would have to wait more than fifteen years to see the light of day—after its author died.

Notes

1. Christopher Isherwood, *My Guru and His Disciple* (New York: Farrar, Straus and Giroux, 1980), 4.

2. James J. Berg and Chris Freeman, eds., *Conversations with Christopher Isherwood* (Jackson: University Press of Mississippi, 2001), 8.

3. Christopher Isherwood, *Lost Years: A Memoir, 1945–1951,* ed. Katherine Bucknell (New York: Harper, 2000), xxv.

4. James J. Berg and Chris Freeman, "Auden and Isherwood," in *W. H. Auden in Context,* ed. Tony Sharpe (Cambridge: Cambridge University Press, 2013), 323.

14

Christopher Isherwood and Edward Upward

BENJAMIN KOHLMANN

The story of Christopher Isherwood and Edward Upward's friendship has been told a number of times. According to the most familiar account, both writers shared a period of intense artistic creativity in the early and mid-1920s during which they collaborated on the stories about Mortmere (also known as "the Other Town"), a grotesque fantasy world they had invented during their school days at Repton. Isherwood went up to Cambridge in 1923, one year after Upward, and the frequently violent and sadistic stories about Mortmere came to be modeled increasingly on the academic cosmos of the university town and its caste of rich "Poshocrats." The standard account of Upward and Isherwood's friendship continues by observing that their artistic paths separated in the 1930s, as Upward embraced communism, an espousal that critics usually claim to have had a detrimental effect on the quality of Upward's writing.[1]

This essay reproduces the text of two letters that Upward sent to Isherwood in the summer of 1939. Written six months after Isherwood's departure for the United States, the letters respond immediately to Isherwood's announcement of his conversion to pacifism and Vedanta, two systems of belief whose tenets were fundamentally at odds with Upward's own ideological convictions. The letters can provide the starting point for a more comprehensive assessment of the friendship between Isherwood and Upward after the height of their Mortmere phase in the 1920s. They suggest that Mortmere remained a central artistic reference point for both writers throughout the 1930s and that it helped them negotiate the calls for political side taking that characterized much of the decade. The letters show that both writers continued to invoke Mortmere as a common artistic ground, a field of literary experimentation that they held to be exempt from the extreme political pressures of the 1930s. Even though Isherwood and Upward did not collaborate again on new stories about the Other Town, Mortmere became the fictional terrain on which the terms of their friendship and the shared qualities of their writing could be explored and defined.

The letters also invite a reappraisal of the myth of Upward as an unrelenting communist hardliner. Mainly because of his radical political orientation, "Allen Chalmers," the pseudonym Isherwood, Stephen Spender, and John Lehmann used to refer to Upward in their memoirs, has become the iconic "case history" of 1930s literature.[2] More than any other writer, Chalmers was the figure onto whom politicized authors of the 1930s could project their artistic fears about going over to the Communist Party and whom they could later use to exorcize their own guilt at having sympathized with Stalinist Russia. In the 1960s, John Lehmann scathingly observed that the "imaginative gift in 'Chalmers' [was] slowly killed in the Iron Maiden of Marxist dogma."[3] Many later scholars have uncritically subscribed to this view, and the predominance of Chalmers in the critical narrative about the 1930s has led one critic to ask, "Did Upward himself really exist?"[4] The letters reprinted here provide evidence that the identification of Upward with the communist hard-liner Chalmers is almost absurdly reductive.

Critics have sometimes written about Upward's espousal of communism as though it happened with the abruptness of a conversion.[5] In fact, Upward's was a long struggle for ideological conviction. As Katherine Bucknell has observed, the "important frontier" that Upward needed to cross was the "internal" one "between vision and disillusion, past self and present self, bourgeois self and Communist self, continually rediscovering and reanimating his developing political and poetic convictions and thereby charting the relationship between them."[6] Upward joined the Communist Party of Great Britain on a probationary basis in 1932, becoming a full member only in 1934. The texts reproduced below show that Upward's adherence to Mortmere was more than a transitional phase on his way to a genuinely communist mode of writing. His unpublished diaries likewise indicate that he continued to think about Mortmere throughout the decade, and Upward revisited Mortmere lore on various occasions in his later stories.[7]

Isherwood's novels, while less constrained by self-imposed ideological demands, rarely feature the kind of anarchic literary aggressions that characterized Mortmere. A prominent instance of Mortmere's influence on Isherwood's writing occurs in his second novel, *The Memorial* (1932).

The book's protagonist, a Cambridge undergraduate, expresses the same kind of savage rejection of university life that animated Mortmere:

> Standing there, he enclosed, he enfolded them all in his hatred—the discreet funny dons, telling legends about Proust; the sincere young neurotics, writing each other ten page notes explaining their conduct at a last night's tiff; the hearties, divided between shop-girls, poker and the C.U.I.C.C.U. [Cambridge's Christian Union]; the College servants, so oily in their deference to all these rich young ninnies; the bed-makers, thievish gossipy old hags, who drank as much of their gentlemen's whisky as they dared, and stank so that you could hardly put your nose inside their broom-cupboards after they had gone. And if, at that moment, Eric could have given the order, the Round Church and the Hall of Trinity and King's Chapel and Corpus Library and dozens of other world-famed architectural lumber-rooms of price-less venerable rubbish would have gone up sky-high with enormous charges of dynamite, and the silk-jumpered young gentlemen and dear old professors been driven out of their well-furnished academic hotels at the point of the bayonet.[8]

However, Isherwood was also capable of subjecting Mortmerean satire to critique. His first novel, *All the Conspirators* (1928), was dedicated "to Edward Upward," and it features a character called Allen Chalmers—the first incarnation of Upward's fictional doppelgänger—whose artistic views bear a distinct Mortmerean inflection. At various points in the novel, Isherwood's alter ego Philip expresses disapproval of Allen's aesthetic outlook: "You see it's just this unfortunate craving for the bizarre which handicaps you, every time. What you call interesting is so often merely quaint, or worse," Philip warns his friend in the novel's opening pages.[9] But this quasi-Mortmerean fascination with the "bizarre" also becomes the shared ground on which Philip and Allen's friendship can be reasserted. Reluctantly returning to the stately home of his family, Philip imagines telling his mother "very curtly" that "this house smells of stewed guts." He notes: "The phrase was Allen's. And Philip had now a sudden desire for the company of Allen, user of curt, foul, trenchant phrases which cut like a surgeon's knife into the gross body of vague words and dreamy thoughts which oppressed him" (98). Philip's ventriloquizing suggests another important aspect of Isherwood and Upward's friendship. Isherwood saw Upward, who was one year older, as his artistic and intellectual mentor and as a late-Romantic hero of sorts. As Bucknell has remarked, "Isherwood was drawn to [Upward's] excitability and his athleticism as well as to the morbid turn of his poetry; above all, he was impressed by Upward's rebelliousness."[10] Isherwood's romanticized view of Upward is carried over into *All the Conspirators* and into Isherwood's early autobiography *Lions and Shadows* (1938). In both texts, the "Allen Chalmers" alias is used as shorthand for what Isherwood saw as Upward's deeply ingrained spirit of disobedience, and the name makes particular reference to Edward's cousin Allen Upward, whom Edward revered as a poet and radical freethinker.[11]

Upward was one of the first guru figures in Isherwood's life, and Isherwood eagerly sought out his artistic advice. In the mid-1920s, at the height of their Mortmere phase, Upward discovered the works of E. M. Forster, and in his eyes Forster was to be praised above all for his "tea-table" method of writing: "Forster's the only one who understands what the modern novel ought to be," Upward instructed Isherwood. Instead of "trying to screw all his scenes up to the highest possible pitch, he tones them down until they sound like mothers'-meeting gossip."[12] Yet, while Upward was the one who identified tea-tabling as a technique, Forster's novels had a more instant and sizable artistic influence on Isherwood. As Peter Parker points out, Isherwood's next literary project, provisionally titled "Seascape with Figures" and begun only a few days after he had read *Howards End,* was modeled on Forster's novel.[13] Over the course of the following years, Forster became one of the central literary models for Isherwood—a writer who publicly praised Isherwood's work and whose writings were in turn absorbed by his disciple. By contrast, Upward soon began to voice his doubts regarding tea-tabling, partly because he thought it betrayed the spirit of revolt embodied by Mortmere. In a diary entry from January 1929, Upward notes: "The teatable must go into the fire. It was a justification of my failure to extract myself from a situation which I loathe."[14] However, this wholesale condemnation is immediately qualified in the same entry: "Probably the teatable is the best solution. Be moderate, be mild, condemn nothing and accept nothing absolutely. Yes, but I am only able to adopt this attitude because subliminally I have strong absolute beliefs. Atheism, free love, communism. . . . The teatable denies all absolute names. Don't burn it." Upward's diary entry expresses a deep ambivalence about the method of rhetorical understatement signified by literary tea-tabling. Yet, while Upward's comments mount a defense of Mortmere and of "absolute" artistic rebellion (including his own budding communist "beliefs"), they are also a genuine attempt to understand an artistic position—Isherwood's—that eschewed forms of ideological commitment.

.

Upward's effort to think through the allure of artistic tea-tabling, in spite of his recognition that it was inimical to totalizing systems of belief, is strikingly at odds with the established view of Upward as an inflexible doctrinaire hard-liner. The letters below suggest the close intellectual and artistic bond that continued to exist between Isherwood and Upward well beyond their youthful immersion in Mortmere, and they indicate Upward's willingness to suspend ideological judgment when it came to his friend's artistic views.

Both letters were written in the summer of 1939, following Isherwood's move to the United States. Isherwood had sent a note to his friend Olive Mangeot earlier that summer, informing her of his decision to embrace pacifism and Vedanta. Mangeot passed the letter on to Upward, who noted in his first letter to Isherwood that he was more than "shocked" to discover his friend's apparent "betrayal" of left-wing politics. Upward's first letter to Isherwood expresses his great disappointment at Isherwood's refusal to take political sides, but it also articulates the conditions on which their friendship was premised and on which it might be continued. Upward's phrasing—"you knew beforehand what to expect of me," "I never expected you to become a Marxist"—suggests a realm of familiarity and intimate knowledge that is capable of mitigating the impact of Isherwood's decision. Isherwood's reply echoes the tone of Upward's first letter by presenting his decision to abandon left-wing politics as a logical extension of his earlier artistic views: "That is the way I will always be: personal. . . . I cannot really take sides in any struggle. My only integrity can be to see the members of both sides as people." Isherwood's letter also invokes Mortmere—in particular Isherwood's fictional doppelgänger Starn—as a way of pointing toward shared artistic interests. Upward's reply, sent one month after his first letter, was later described by Isherwood as "a model of charity towards an attitude one can't understand."[15] The letter notably approves of "a Mortmerish (a Yogish) escapism," even as it cautions against propagating Vedanta as a "movement." Turning Vedanta into some form of collectivist enterprise, Upward warns, would "vitiate and debase" its escapist, "Mortmerish" individualism.

In both letters, questions of artistic style overlap with the problem of ideological commitment. In Upward's view, Isherwood's pacifism—and what Upward's first letter identifies as pacifism's ideological blind spots and covert mysticism—put him in dangerous proximity with fascism. Upward's fears were probably triggered by Isherwood's admission one year earlier that he had been susceptible "to the preaching of an

The opening pages of Upward's first letter to Isherwood after the latter had left England for good. Dated July 23, 1939, the letter reproaches the pacifist Isherwood for "betraying" the two friends' left-wing ideals. Reproduced by permission of the Huntington Library, San Marino, California.

English Fascist leader" in the early 1930s (*Lions and Shadows*, 48). As Upward points out in his second letter, viewing "Yoga" as a movement, and thus disregarding its status as a form of radical individualism, "must inevitably help or hinder one or other—but never both—of the two main political forces which are in conflict all over the modern world. And Mortmere—or Yoga—if it became a movement would tend to help fascism rather than communism." As Upward struggles to come to terms with Isherwood's position, he is led to recognize the attraction that forms of aesthetic escapism continued to hold for him. The conclusion at which he arrives—"I respect your refusal. I still have and always will have a foot in Mortmere"—is startlingly at odds with the established critical view of Upward. Paradoxically, these letters show the communist Upward advocating a form of radical escapism that he also finds embodied in Mortmere: "there is only one kind [of pacifism] that I could really respect,

The opening pages of Upward's second letter to Isherwood, dated August 24, 1939. Upward declares that he will "respect [Isherwood's] refusal" of Marxism: "take up Yoga by all means." Reproduced by permission of the Huntington Library, San Marino, California.

the kind . . . that tries always to escape." The letters reprinted below—and the cache of Upward's correspondence held by the Huntington Library— indicate that critics can profitably revisit Upward and Isherwood's friendship. Most significantly, however, the generosity of Upward's intellectual stance and his capacity for self-criticism should give rise to a reappraisal of received critical opinions that have relegated Upward to a particularly dark corner of British literary history.

Upward's two letters to Isherwood were previously presumed lost by scholars, and they are reprinted here for the first time. The manuscript versions of both letters are held by the Huntington Library (CI 2455 and 2456). I would like to thank Kathy Allinson, Edward Upward's daughter, and Sara (Sue) Hodson, curator of literary manuscripts at the Huntington Library, for the permission to reproduce the text of both letters.

Letter One

39 Woodleigh Gardens

S.W. 16

July 23rd 1939

I have seen your letter to Olive. Shocked isn't the word for what I felt when I read it. And the appalling thing is that for all I know you may feel the same about this letter. I don't think so, however, because you knew beforehand what to expect from me.

I wish I could convey what I want to write by grimaces and inaudibilities instead of by crude statements at a distance.

In brief, I feel much as we once imagined one of us would feel if the other turned Roman Catholic.[16] I can't really believe you've done it. At least, I couldn't at first.

I never expected you to become a Marxist. If you had I should have felt slightly embarrassed. Theoretical Marxism is not in your line. Nor is any other theory or system of opinions in your line. Your strength as a writer has always been and always will be in your ability to see and understand persons and things. If you now start foisting a use of the word "crime" in an emotive metaphorical sense when you are professing to make a statement of fact—that is inexcusable.[17] This objection may seem petty, but I think it is fundamental. Pacifist literature is riddled with such wishful inaccuracies, and to such an extent that if you remove them you simultaneously destroy the basic pacifist arguments. Your second statement, that "all violence always punishes itself etc" is more profoundly inaccurate. The biblical "those that take the sword shall perish by the sword" is far nearer to the truth. (Pacifism in my view is a sort of intellectually degenerate Christianity.) Violence, and particularly the most unscrupulous kind of violence, very rarely punishes itself. Hitler I am sure has a perfectly good conscience and if he is unhappy he is made so by the fear that he himself and his movement may be destroyed by someone else's violence. But violence is not always punished even by someone else's violence, and the majority of those that take to the sword do not perish by the sword. The majority of the soldiers who fought in the 1914 war survived it, and very few generals do not die in bed. The statement that "all violence always punishes itself" is purely sentimental and the deliberate exaggeration contained in the words "all" and "always" does not save the statement from being woolly and dead ("quisb" describes it better).[18]

You say also "I can't believe any longer in revolution by force, because I don't think it will ever work out right." Presumably you don't mean you can't believe that revolutions by force have happened in the past and are likely to happen in the future (revolutions and counter-revolutions by force). "Can't believe" really means "can't approve of." You are in fact opposed to revolution, though unlike the fascists you would express your opposition not by using counter-force but by peaceful (diplomatic?) methods. You would take sides with the fascists against the socialists but you would use other methods of attack than the fascists. I am probably doing you an injustice here. But the fact remains that if you wished to be genuinely neutral in any fascist-communist conflict you would have to abstain from expressing your pacifist views, because they would be bound to injure which-ever side you happened to be in closest contact with. A genuinely neutral pacifism I could respect, but it would be very difficult—if not impossible—to arrive at. It certainly wouldn't have a pretentious theory attached to it. It could be summed up in the simple formula: "I refuse to be violent or to submit to violence, and while there is a single country in the world untouched by war I will go there."

You don't think that revolution will ever work out right. Of course it won't. But—as Forster said—"life won't work out." Perfection is a mystical abstraction and will never exist in reality. Pacifism deals always in mystical absolutes. War is Evil: therefore all wars at all periods of history are equally Evil, no matter whether they result in ten hundred or ten million casualties, whether they lead to a hundred years of reaction or make possible a cultural renaissance. War is Evil: there-fore the Chinese and Japanese governments, since both are at war, are equally wicked—and whichever side wins, the result will be absolutely Evil.[19] Good can never come out of Evil, etc. What half-baked trash it is; and I don't think that I am caricaturing it. First you postulate another and call it "Evil," and then you assert quite logically that one can't come out of the other. But reality has nothing to do with absolute Good and Evil. The Chinese are not all good nor the Japanese all bad: nevertheless a Japanese victory would have far worse consequences for humanity than a Chinese victory. The revolution in Russia did not and will never introduce the reign of absolute Good upon earth; but to argue therefore that it would have been better if the revolution had never happened and the Tsar had remained in power is fantastic.

You know that I loathe violence and shall make a very bad revo-lutionary, but I recognise that this is a weakness and I don't try to justify it. My complaint about many "left" pacifists is that they do try to justify themselves. It does not follow that because they have been horrified by the sight of fighting therefore fighting can never achieve anything worthwhile. Russia, in my view, proves the contrary. But since the contrary does not fit in with pacifists' theories they will tell you that the Russian revolution has achieved nothing.

I know that fighting means killing decent fascist boys.[20] It means also that communists will be forced even to kill other communists who have been conscripted into fascist armies. Wars and revolutions never work out neatly with all the blacks on one side and all the whites on the other. But the fact that war is loathsome does not prove that war never achieves anything good. Only in the realm of mystical absolutes where means are rigidly separated from ends can Good never come out of Evil. (According to Marxists the means condition the ends and vice versa. Is it bad to cut a man's flesh with a knife? Yes, if you do it to wound him. No if you're incising an abscess.)

In the Marxist view there are two kinds of war—the reactionary and the progressive. The war of 1914 was an example of the first, and the war of China against Japan is an example of the second. Wherever an oppressed class or nation is fighting against its oppressor there you have a just war, a war in which victory for the oppressed will be of greater benefit to the human race than victory for the oppressor. This seems to me common sense. It is better that the oppressed should obtain their freedom without war if they can, but once war has started it is better that they should win.

If you say that the oppressed can never improve their condition by fighting I answer that we are talking totally different languages.

You say "There must be a positively friendly approach to the other side . . . It isn't practical? . . . If it isn't the Human Race will die out." A friendly approach to which other side? Before you can say this you must take sides, belong to one side or the other. And having taken sides you must faithfully serve your side, not betray it to the other. By all means make friends with the Japanese soldiers, not in order to help them to subjugate China but to persuade them that they ought to refuse to go on fighting in China. (N.B. Chamberlain is on the same side as Hitler and the Japanese generals.)

I don't believe the human race will die out if there is another world war. At worst, the human race cannot murder the human race. The successful murderers must at least survive. The human race will die out when natural conditions on the earth become unsuitable for human life, not before.

You say that you cannot go on hating, because Hate is a blind alley. (All these Capital Letters are symptomatic.) I agree that blind hate, impotent hate, is a blind alley. But where hateful things exist it is right and human that we should hate them, provided our hate does not paralyse us but leads us to try to change those things. Hate without action is as sterile and evil as love without action.

Even the Christians could not do away with hate. They disguised it as Hell.

This is a long letter and I can't tell how you'll take it.

I feel as though I had blown a raspberry in church. For heaven's sake write and let me know the worst. If it is the worst I won't argue any more. I'll only beg you once again—Don't let it get into your writing. That would be the end, perhaps.

As for Wystan, I'm less surprised about him and I think it will do far less harm to his work than to yours.[21] He always was that way. He will still be a good poet but he will never be the poet he could have been. His greatness, it now seems, said goodbye in the magnificent poem at the end of On the Frontier.[22]

Enough, and more.

But I'd like to know briefly how you take all this.

Isherwood replied to Upward on August 6, 1939, apologizing that "what I wrote to Olive was no doubt very muddled and hasty, and full of claptrap words and capital letters which you find only too easy to explode." His sudden notoriety as a writer had "pitchforked me into the limelight as Wystan's second fiddle," and it had led him to "[make] a mess of my leftism." Isherwood confessed that his "laziness, dilettantism and cowardice" meant that he was useless as a political writer (Parker, *Isherwood*, 445). More than anything else, it was Isherwood's willingness to face his own shortcomings as an individual and as a writer that prompted Upward's second letter.

Letter Two

Five Acres
Bransgore
nr Christchurch
Hants
Aug 24 [1939]

Your letter would have melted a heart of stone. I understand all, and I blame only myself—for having momentarily suspected that you had betrayed everything. What you wrote to Olive terrified me partly because it suggested that you were about to join or to allow yourself to be made use of by a semi-political movement, and a movement which I believe to be profoundly wrong. But I recognise now that you will never deliberately do that. However, your letter to me still contains hints that you are looking for a way to reform the world, even if only by changing people's hearts. But there is only one way to reform the world, and that is by first of all changing material conditions, and I believe that in your bones you know it. You refuse to plunge into the horrors through which and out of which this way leads. Very well, I respect your refusal. I still have and always will have a foot in Mortmere.[23] But Mortmere did not try to reform the world. That was its strength. It was wholehearted, not a murky compromise between the real and the ideal. It rejected the real world outright and created a more satisfying imaginary one.

Take up Yoga by all means, provided you take it up in a Mortmere manner, in the manner for example in which we invented one wonderful card game. But if you start converting other people to it you will vitiate and debase it, just as we debased Mortmere when at Cambridge we made Laily read The Horror in the Tower and The Little Hotel.[24] And worse, if you start converting other people. You will be starting a "movement," and a movement—besides vitiating the true quality of Mortmere—must inevitably become mixed up with politics. A movement, no matter whether you intend it to do so or not, must inevitably help or hinder one or other—but never both—of the two main political forces which are in conflict all over the modern world. And Mortmere—or Yoga—if it became a movement would tend to help fascism rather than communism.

I accept the fact that you feel impelled towards some kind of pacifism. But, as I said in my last letter, there is only one kind that I could really respect, the kind that refuses either to do violence or to submit to violence, the kind that tries always to escape. I will never say, as you suggest: "Poor Christopher has become an escapist. He has betrayed us all." You always were an "escapist" (and why be scared of the label? I'd much rather be called an "escapist" than a "pacifist"). Only if you ceased to be an escapist and became the missionary of some utopian doctrine (and an unconscious agent of fascist propaganda) would you betray both yourself and us.

Let your theory, your doctrine, your philosophy, be a Mortmerish (a Yogish) escapism. You needn't mention it in your writings. In fact you will rigidly avoid mentioning it, and for the same anti-quisb reasons that you avoided mentioning in Goodbye to Berlin your motives for going to Germany. But being armed with it you will be able to get on with your writing, will be able to write about what interests you most—real persons and things.

This is the procedure you have followed so far; why not go on with it now?

I wish with all my heart that you and Wystan may continue to "escape." It is important that you should survive. And remember that Milton was not ashamed to ask the captain or colonel or knight at arms to spare his life. Why should you be ashamed to be an escapist?

I have not stated the case as well as I should have liked, but the substance is there. I feel that I shan't have written this letter in vain.

The new crisis is boiling up as I write. If Chamberlain lands us in a war against Germany I shall be opposed to that war. I say this in case my last letter may have given the impression that I should be in favour of any war against the Nazis. If Russia is out of it such a war could only be reactionary, a struggle between rival imperialists, one almost as bad as the other.

If, as the crisis develops, I am ordered back to school to help with the evacuation, Hilda will stay on here with Crumpy.[25]

Please write again soon and let me know more. Address the letter to 39 Woodleigh Gardens.[26]

I have at last started to write something satisfactory again. I have taken nearly two years to find the form I have been looking for, but now I've got it. It's a development of the form I used in my other short prose pieces but it's far nearer to metrical poetry. There are even occasional rhymes.

Lawrie Little is staying with us here.[27] His poetry gets more and more remarkable, and I'm glad to say that he's had some of it published—in New Verse and The Listener.

Hilda sends love.

Crumpy is developing fast. I become more hopelessly devoted to him every day. But the family curse will probably turn him into a crook when he grows up.[28] I enclose a photo of him taken two months ago.

Bye-bye.

Upward continued to occupy a central place in Isherwood's intellectual life, as both writers relied on each other's advice in literary matters. As Isherwood's last diaries from the 1970s and 1980s indicate, he valued Upward's unfaltering commitment to the communist cause because it provided him with a critical perspective on his own life and work. The difficulties Isherwood encountered in writing *My Guru and His Disciple* (1980), the account of his conversion to Vedanta, were because he felt "inhibited by a sense of the mocking agnostics all around me—ranging from asses like [John] Lehmann to intelligent bigots like Edward. . . . In a sense they are my most important audience. Everything I write is written with a consciousness of the opposition and in answer to its prejudices. Because of this opposition, I am apt to belittle myself."[29] As Isherwood noted, his attempts to justify his newly won religious beliefs in *My Guru and His Disciple* and other books was in part a continuation of the conversation with Upward that had taken place in the summer of 1939: "And am I, also, in writing this book, continually making an apology for the subject matter to Edward? Maybe so, and maybe this is as it should be. Most writers about holy men just go ahead, taking their own devotion for granted and not giving a shit how it will impress the unbelievers" (572).

Notes

1. I am grateful to Kate Bucknell for commenting on an earlier version of this essay.

2. Stephen Spender, "The Case of Edward Upward," *London Magazine* 27 (1987): 29–43; John Lehmann, *Autobiography*, 3 vols. (London: Eyre and Spottiswoode, 1955–66).

3. Lehmann, *Autobiography*, 3:244. See also Valentine Cunningham, *British Writers of the Thirties* (Oxford: Oxford University Press, 1988), 213; and Samuel Hynes, *The Auden Generation: Literature and Politics in England in the 1930s* (London: Bodley Head, 1976), 317.

4. Anthony Arblaster, "Edward Upward and the Novel of Politics," in *1936: The Sociology of Literature*, ed. Francis Barker (Colchester: University of Essex Press, 1979), 179.

5. Arblaster contrasts Upward's "leap of commitment" with his contemporaries' "ambiguity" about joining the Communist Party (ibid., 181). However, it is also true that Upward was in part responsible for forging this myth; for example, the ending of his novella *Journey to the Border* (1938) fictionalized the act of "going over" to the Communist Party as a kind of absolute conversion.

6. Katherine Bucknell, "The Achievement of Edward Upward," in *"The Language of Learning and the Language of Love": Uncollected Writings, New Interpretations*, ed. Katherine Bucknell and Nicholas Jenkins (Oxford: Clarendon Press, 1994), 169.

7. Examples are Upward's tale "The Return to Mortmere" (1943; reprinted in *The Mortmere Stories*) and the story "The Scenic Railway" in Upward's eponymous collection of short stories (1997), which invokes elements from the central Mortmere tale "The Railway Accident." Upward's 1963 diary records in a similar mood that "I am tempted back to Mortmere," and the same notebook contains ideas "for a Mortmere novel" (34: August 15, 1963). The bulk of Upward's seventy-six diaries has been in an uncataloged collection in the British Library since Upward's death in 2009; in this essay, passages from the uncataloged diaries are followed by the number of the diary and, where available, by the date of the entry.

8. Christopher Isherwood, *The Memorial* (1932; reprint, New York: Vintage, 2012), 172–73.

9. Christopher Isherwood, *All the Conspirators* (1928; reprint, New York: Vintage, 2012), 9.

10. Katherine Bucknell, "Introduction," in *The Mortmere Stories*, ed. Katherine Bucknell (London: Enitharmon Press, 1994), 9.

11. In a diary entry from 1927, Edward Upward recalled that he admired Allen above all for being "a non-conformist." In Edward's view, Allen's suicide in 1926 turned him into the consummate Romantic hero: "Allen shot himself with an airgun. After all there is power in our blood. We are not all tallow chandlers and cowards. And it was finer in him since he was an old man. To be able to remain unadapted for so long" (December 5, 1927). The surname "Chalmers" was very likely derived from Upward and Isherwood's aristocratic Repton contemporary John Rutherford Chalmers, the author of a youthful play based on Dante, who went up to Oxford but who visited Upward at Cambridge on several occasions. I am grateful to Paul Stevens, archivist at Repton School, and to Peter Parker for help with identifying the real-life Chalmers. For Chalmers's visits to Upward, see Upward's diary entries from November 1924.

12. Christopher Isherwood, *Lions and Shadows* (1938; reprint, London: Methuen, 1985), 107.

13. Peter Parker, *Isherwood: A Life Revealed* (New York: Random House, 2004), 130–31.

14. British Library, Journal by Edward Upward, 1929, ADD 72689 JJ.

15. Christopher Isherwood, *Diaries, Volume One: 1939–1960*, ed. Katherine Bucknell (New York: Harper, 1996), 7. A substantial portion of Isherwood's reply is reprinted in Parker's Isherwood biography, 445–46.

16. At the end of Isherwood's *The Memorial* (1932), the protagonist Eric announces his conversion to Catholicism, an act that has frequently been read as "a mark of failure" (see James Kelley, "Aunt Mary, Uncle Henry, and Anti-Ancestral Impulses in *The Memorial*," in *The Isherwood Century: Essays on the Life and Work of Christopher Isherwood*, ed. James J. Berg and Chris Freeman [Madison: University of Wisconsin Press, 2000], 146–47).

17. The distinction between "emotive" statements and "statement[s] of fact" looks back to I. A. Richards's Cambridge lectures which Upward and Isherwood had attended in the mid-1920s. Upward was profoundly troubled by Richards's claim that there was a distinct realm of emotive (literary) "pseudo-statements," and tried to disprove Richards's theories in his diaries of the 1930s. See also *Lions and Shadows*, 75.

18. As Isherwood explains in *Lions and Shadows*, "quisb" was "a standard word in our [Upward and Isherwood's] vocabulary, correspondingly [sic] roughly to the term 'shy-making,' and 'shaming' later employed by the Mayfair society world" (49).

19. War between the Empire of Japan and China had been officially declared in July 1937. Isherwood later stated that his sojourn in China with W. H. Auden in

1938—recorded in the coauthored *Journey to a War* (1939)—had helped to turn him into a pacifist.

20. Probably alluding to the reason Isherwood later gave for his decision not to fight in the war: "I called myself a pacifist because Heinz, the boy I had lived with for five years during the nineteen-thirties, was about to be conscripted into the Nazi army and I found it unthinkable that I should ever help to cause his death, however indirectly" (*Christopher and His Kind* [New York: Farrar, Straus and Giroux, 1976], 4).

21. Upward had read Auden's unpublished poems in the mid-1920s. In a letter to Isherwood, he commented: "Auden's poems seem fine. Would he be pleased, do you think, if I told him that I thought them infinitely better than Eliot's?" (CI 2356, Huntington Library). Upward recognized Auden's superior qualities as a poet, but, as I argue elsewhere, he felt uneasy about Auden's political and religious views. For more, see Benjamin Kohlmann, "Edward Upward, W. H. Auden, and the Rhetorical Victories of Communism," in *Modernism/Modernity* 20.2 (2013): 287–306.

22. Auden and Isherwood's coauthored play was first produced by Group Theatre in 1938. Upward is probably referring to the final duet of the two star-crossed lovers Eric and Anna, which begins "Now as we come to our end,/As the tiny separate lives/Fall, fall to their graves./We begin to understand."

23. Upward's diary entries from August and September 1939 record that he once more attempted to write "MM [Mortmere] material" (August 23, 1939). This period of renewed Mortmere activity, coming after a hiatus of a few years, coincided with the months during which Upward wrote the letters reproduced here.

24. Laily, the Worm, was a character in the Mortmere stories, representing the social conventions Upward and Isherwood professed to despise. Laily was modeled on a Cambridge contemporary, the history student Smyth (Bucknell, "Introduction," 12). "The Horror in the Tower" and "The Little Hotel" are two Mortmere stories; the former is reprinted in *The Mortmere Stories*.

25. Edward and Hilda Upward's son Christopher, born in 1938.

26. The Upwards' London address. Upward took up a teaching post at Alleyn's School, Dulwich, in 1932; he retired from Alleyn's in 1961.

27. Lawrence Little had been a pupil of Upward at Alleyn's. He went on to write a novel, *The Dear Boys* (1958), and some poetry.

28. Perhaps a reference to the fact that Upward's brother Laurence suffered from schizophrenia. I am grateful to Kathy Allinson for suggesting this possibility.

29. Christopher Isherwood, *Liberation: Diaries, Volume Three, 1970–1983,* ed. Katherine Bucknell (New York: Harper, 2012), 554.

15

Huxley and Isherwood:
The California Years

PETER EDGERLY FIRCHOW

When Christopher Isherwood arrived in Los Angeles by bus from New York in the summer of 1939, his primary concern was to talk to Gerald Heard about his decision to become a pacifist at a time when it looked very much as if a new world war was about to break out. When the long-anticipated war actually erupted only a few months later, Isherwood remained firmly committed to his newfound pacifist convictions, perhaps in part because they had been recently reaffirmed by Heard, but he nevertheless offered to return to Britain to help in some unspecified, nonmilitary capacity. (The British embassy, however, declined the offer.) He also planned to speak on the same subject with Heard's friend Aldous Huxley. Not only were Heard and Huxley fellow British exiles, but both were well known for their public espousal of pacifist views. Like Isherwood, both had also decided to settle in the United States, partly because they liked the mild Southern California climate, but also because they were disillusioned with a Europe that seemed incapable of listening to (their) reason. There was also the additional attraction of a nearby center for Vedanta studies led by a charismatic monk, Swami Prabhavananda, as well as, in Huxley's case, occasional but very lucrative employment with one or another of the Hollywood studios.[1]

It did not take long for Isherwood to decide that he would stay in California, too, at least on a trial basis. (In the event, he stayed for the rest of his life.) Heard and his companion, Chris Wood (also a friend of Isherwood's, dating from his time in London), proved very receptive and hospitable, introducing both him and his then partner, "Vernon Old," to their wide circle of variegated friends, American and foreign. The Vedanta Center and its Swami also proved appealing to the newly reborn (or at least newly refurbished) Isherwood, who was now prepared to look for answers in places he had hitherto neglected. Although Isherwood had not been conventionally religious since childhood, he was predisposed to believing in Vedanta doctrine by his earlier adherence to the ideas and practices of the American psychologist Homer Lane. That is why it proved relatively easy for him to accept a psychosomatic doctrine like that advocated by the Vedanta movement. As late as 1951 he was still endorsing Homer Lane.[2] For a time he even lived as a kind of monk at the Center, and over the course of the next few decades he collaborated with Swami Prabhavananda on a number of translations of Hindu texts, as well as in writing and/or editing, on his own, original material having to do with Vedanta and the West. Like the other contributors to the Vedanta journal, *Vedanta and the West,* including Huxley, whom he asked for essays, Isherwood was not paid; after all, he noted, they wrote "simply because they are interested in Vedanta and are our personal friends" (*Where Joy Resides,* 12).

At this time, Isherwood also met (or met again) a number of the celebrated German and Austrian exiles living in the Los Angeles area, some of whom, such as Berthold Viertel, he had known intimately for years. It was not long before Viertel and he started working together on what was supposed to be a script dealing with Adolf Hitler's life that had been informally commissioned by a producer on the East Coast. In fact, however, as the surviving synopsis now in the possession of the Huntington Library shows, the subject was really the history of the Nazi movement from its supposed origins in the 1914–18 war until about 1940.[3] As it turned out, the film was never made—and in fact Isherwood even lost money resolving various legal consequences arising from having worked on it together with Viertel—but it did lead to useful contacts with film moguls at Goldwyn and Metro Studios, where Isherwood was eventually hired at what struck him (and me too more than half a century later) as a fabulous salary—the equivalent in today's money of about ten thousand dollars a week. These great sums of money did not interfere much with either Isherwood's or Huxley's other writing. For one thing, the stints at the Hollywood studios were intermittent, and for another, both Isherwood and Huxley were generous in letting others share in their bounty. Besides, as Isherwood's friend and occasional resident of Los Angeles, Gore Vidal, once remarked, "those whom Hollywood destroyed were never worth saving" (Vidal, Introduction, *Where Joy Resides,* ix).

Working on scripts for plays and films was something Isherwood was good at and already had a fair amount of experience doing, not only for a lot less money a few years earlier with Berthold Viertel in London (as memorably recounted in his novel *Prater Violet*) but even more notably with his close friend W. H. Auden, with whom he had collaborated on several plays during the 1930s. It should not be surprising, therefore, that, when in the summer of 1940 Frieda Lawrence approached Aldous Huxley about doing an adaptation of *Lady Chatterley's Lover* for the stage, he at first declined to do it himself, but then told her that Isherwood and (probably) Auden might be the right people to undertake the job. "I think we have the right man on the spot," Huxley wrote Frieda in August of that year, "in the person of Christopher Isherwood, who would probably collaborate with W. H. Auden, the poet; Isherwood and Auden have had considerable experience of the stage and have written successful plays."[4] What he did not say, however, was that Auden and Isherwood's most successful theatrical collaboration hitherto had been the very peculiar verse comedy, *The Dog beneath the Skin,* produced in the mid-1930s by the Group Theatre in London. Just how *Lady Chatterley* might fare at the hands of two avant-garde homosexuals who were known as playwrights primarily for authoring the campy *Dog beneath the Skin* was evidently not something Huxley wished to speculate about. He did, however, go on to tell Frieda that he thought Isherwood was "an intelligent writer with a good sense of the theatre and good taste," and that "Auden is a good poet and theatre man" (*Letters,* 457).

Writing about Isherwood and Auden in these glowing terms seems to have kindled Huxley's own enthusiasm for the project, for toward the close of his letter to Frieda he suddenly took back his earlier misgivings and declared his willingness to participate in the dramatization of Lawrence's novel, at least to the extent of making editorial suggestions to the two prospective principals. (Besides writing Hollywood scripts, Huxley had some, though not on the whole very satisfactory, experience with the theater.) He even showed himself willing to initiate his part of the collaboration by making use of one of his most influential contacts with the movie industry, namely, to run the idea past the celebrated producer William Goetz. Despite these early signs of promise, however, nothing ever came of the project. By the time he broached the idea to Isherwood, the latter was already under signed contract with one of the Hollywood studios and unable to find the extra time to undertake a new, major project like this one. What's more, the other proposed principal, Auden, could not even be located—probably because he was at this time in the opening throes of his stormy relationship with Chester Kallman; and another British exile in Hollywood, John van Druten—who later made "Sally Bowles," one of

Isherwood's Berlin stories, into the phenomenally successful play *I Am a Camera*—flatly turned down Huxley's offer to take part in the venture. Still, this largely negative experience did not discourage Huxley from undertaking another collaborative project with Isherwood. Evidently, he really did think very highly of Isherwood's ability (and congeniality), for Huxley had not previously been given to joint projects of any kind, with the notable exception of Gerald Heard—but that collaboration had been limited to a lecture tour in the late 1930s. Huxley and Heard may have collaborated on talks but they never collaborated on anything written. In fact, the voluntarily initiated, collaborated scripts (there would eventually be several) with Isherwood would be the only ones Huxley ever undertook. The first of these—and the only one ever to be published—was *Jacob's Hands,* a "treatment" (the Hollywood name for a preliminary version or summary of a film script), which was eventually "rediscovered" by the actress Sharon Stone some years after Huxley's death in a neglected box in Laura Achera Huxley's garage. This surviving copy of the original typescript had been sent to Huxley by Isherwood not long after all of the former's books and belongings (except for the manuscript of *Island*) had been destroyed in a disastrous brush fire in 1961; evidently, however, by this time Huxley (and Laura) thought so little of it that they consigned it to the relative oblivion of their garage. It was only published in 1998 at the instigation of Sharon Stone when she realized that she would not be able to star in a film in which the protagonist was male and when, in addition, she failed to find financial support to make a film out of the treatment.

This is perhaps the moment to pause and reflect more generally on the highly unusual linkage between Huxley and Isherwood's names. One of the very few academic juxtapositions of these two writers—Michael Rosenthal's 1994 chapter "Huxley, Isherwood, and the Thirties" in *The Columbia History of the British Novel*—observes that, despite sharing some "curious parallels," such as writing for Hollywood studios in 1940 or sharing a penchant for Eastern religions, Huxley and Isherwood were "two very different kinds of writers and human beings whose lives [were] fundamentally studies in contrast." Despite their differences, however, they did come, in Rosenthal's view, to "represent both the post- and pre-war sensibilities of their generation"; that is, both Huxley (after his early satirical fiction) and Isherwood, from the very beginning, had supposedly shared a literary outlook that dismissed the noisy diversions of the present in favor of the apparently unfashionable but really more permanent values of the past. Rosenthal does acknowledge the fact that Huxley and Isherwood "even collaborated on some projects," but he does not go into the specifics of any of those joint ventures. Instead, he goes on to discuss each writer's novelistic production in complete isolation from the other's; first it is Huxley the novelist (or, rather, would-be novelist) and then it is Isherwood the (dyed-in-the-wool) novelist. While it is true that these two distinguished writers may have given their names to a decade, or at least that is what Rosenthal claims, nevertheless, in his considered view, that is about all they really ever had in common.[5]

Or, at any rate, that is all so far as the academic world is concerned, but it was by no means the whole story that was told after Huxley's death to the wider public—especially to the public at large in California or coming originally from the Los Angeles area, who may already have heard tell of the "Aquarian Conspiracy," also the title of a very popular 1980 book by Marilyn Ferguson. The eponymous conspiracy originally concerned a well-meaning group of optimistic intellectuals and scientists who were convinced that they were living at the dawn of a new and better age, the age, as the popular song had it, of Aquarius. The combination of newfound spirituality, improved technology, hallucinogenic drugs, and clean politics would, so Ferguson maintained, usher in a quasi-utopian time of bliss for the whole planet, starting with California. For most of the believers in the Aquarian conspiracy, Teilhard de Chardin was the leading proponent of this blissful world to come, but close on his footsteps was none other than Aldous Huxley.[6]

So at least it seemed at the beginning. Subsequently, other forces began to view the "conspiracy" in less optimistic terms. This was especially true of Lyndon LaRouche's movement that mixed quasi-fascist ideas with egomaniacal self-glorification. For him the Aquarian Conspiracy consisted primarily of a British plot to wage another Opium War, this time not against China but rather against the United States. LaRouche was based in New York, but when, for the purposes of this essay, I searched Huxley's and Isherwood's names looking for connections between the two, one of the sites I happened upon contained an article titled "The Aquarian Conspiracy: Huxley, Isis, LSD, and the Roots of the American Hedonist Culture," which apparently had been written around 1980 by the *Executive Intelligence Review* staff and published in their journal of the same name—the journal which, as it turns out, was Lyndon LaRouche's main outlet for his ideas.

This LaRouchean essay purports to be a kind of hortatory summary of Ferguson's book (it is not), and contains a variety of remarkable revelations about Huxley, claiming, among other things, that he was "posted" as a "case officer" to California in the late 1930s by the British government in order to prepare the United States "for the mass dissemination of drugs." Huxley was particularly well suited for the job because he and his brother Julian had allegedly been trained for it at Oxford by none other than H. G. Wells. Subsequently, Huxley was said to have recruited to the conspiracy such other distinguished, but oddly assorted, fellow literary and political figures as T. S. Eliot, W. H. Auden, Oswald Mosley, and D. H. Lawrence, whose "homosexual lover" he also supposedly had been. By implication, at any rate, this erotic relationship with Lawrence seems to have prepared Huxley for his subsequent encounter in Los Angeles with the "pederast" Isherwood, with whose help Huxley "founded a nest of Isis cults in Southern California and in San Francisco that consisted exclusively of several hundred deranged worshipers of Isis and other cult gods." The two British writers were soon joined in this demented task by none other than Thomas Mann and Mann's daughter Elisabeth Mann Borghese. Together they "laid the foundations during the late 1930s and the 1940s for the later LSD culture, by recruiting a core of 'initiates' into the Isis cults that Huxley's mentors, Bulwer-Lytton, Helena Blavatsky, and Aleister Crowley, had constituted while stationed in India."

In 1952, so the authors of the *Executive Intelligence Review* article inform us, Huxley "returned to the United States from Britain, accompanied by Dr. Humphry Osmond, the Huxleys' private physician. Osmond had been part of a discussion group Huxley had organized at the National Hospital, Queen Square, London. Along with another seminar participant, J. R. Smythies, Osmond . . . advocated experimentation with hallucinogenic drugs as a means of developing a 'cure' for mental disorders." Osmond, however, was not merely Huxley's private doctor; he had also been "brought in by Allen Dulles to play a prominent role in MK-Ultra [the CIA's code name for secret chemical warfare experiments]. At the same time, Osmond, Huxley, and the University of Chicago's Robert Hutchins held a series of secret planning sessions in 1952 and 1953 for a second private LSD mescaline project under Ford Foundation funding."

Huxley, so it would seem, was not just an eminent novelist and all-around guru, he was also a public as well as secret proponent of a pernicious drug culture, even, if one is to believe the claims of the LaRouchean version of the Aquarian Conspiracy, its "high priest." Almost until the day he died, he apparently labored tirelessly in behalf of that conspiracy, not even resting until he had established at Harvard a cult group matching the one of which he was already the leader in California. After his death, it was left to epigones like Isherwood to continue the bad work he had begun, the end of which was already foreseeable in the early 1980s, namely, the downfall of the USA as the leading economic and military country in the West.[7]

So much for Huxley and Isherwood as Aquarians who appear to have been immensely successful in carrying out the peculiar orders of a British government plotting for unknown reasons to do damage to its chief ally. On the more mundane, human level, however, they seem to have been considerably less successful. Certainly, their joint screen treatment of Jacob Ericson's healing hands encountered little encouragement and no financial support whatever from either the British government or, for that matter, from any of the supposedly multitudinous Isis cults they allegedly had founded, perhaps because *Jacob's Hands* had nothing whatever to do with drugs. On the contrary, the work not only turned its back on contemporary urban culture, as embodied by a variety of hucksters and worldly rich people, but it even went so far as to prefer the animal world to the human one, for the story of Jacob and his wonder-working hands is ultimately one that shows why healing the sick is best confined to nonhuman patients, or that, at any rate, seems to have been Huxley and Isherwood's primary intention.

According to Huxley himself, the lack of success of *Jacob's Hands* is attributable to a conspiracy of a very different kind. Writing to Isherwood in July 1944, Huxley told his collaborator that none of the Hollywood studios would touch the script because the powerful and well-organized American medical profession objected strongly to a favorable depiction of someone who was, in their view, nothing more than a quack and faith healer (see *Letters*, 510). In the event, it is perhaps just as well that Huxley and Isherwood's preliminary screenplay met with little positive response among Hollywood producers because, although it is true that it would have made an unusual film—unusual at least in the context of the kind of films that were being made at the time—it is doubtful if that film would have been a box-office success or would even have redounded to the honor of its authors. According to Isherwood's biographer, Peter Parker, *Jacob's Hands* is "hackneyed, sentimental . . . sorry stuff, displaying none of the distinction one might reasonably have expected of such a collaboration."[8] This judgment strikes me as unduly harsh, not only because scripts (and *Jacob's Hands,* let us remember, was not even a full-fledged script, but only a mere "treatment") never do come across as well as fully fleshed-out dramatic presentations, especially when they have been staged or filmed, but also because neither author apparently ever expected (or even wished) to see their treatment published—and certainly not without a lot of additional rewriting having been done to it.

Isherwood and Huxley would subsequently work on other, more fully developed and more commercially oriented subjects, but it is undoubtedly significant that in 1965, only a couple of years after Huxley's death, Isherwood singled out *Jacob's Hands* as the one script he wanted people to know that they had worked on together. He remembered this script better than the others perhaps because the idea for it was evidently based on Huxley's own real-life experience. "At that time he'd moved out to the Mojave Desert," Isherwood recalled at a session at the University of Southern California honoring the memory of his dead collaborator, "and was living at Llano. And there he had been very interested in some of the old desert types who lived out in what was then the wilderness still. And one of them was a natural healer. He used to heal animals who were sick and Aldous was extremely interested in all these subjects. . . . This man used to say that he absolutely refused to heal human beings because the results of healing human beings were incalculable and it might do more harm than good."[9]

As Isherwood notes, this is the kind of subject that Huxley was fascinated by. It was also one that interested Isherwood deeply, largely because it combined an unorthodox quasi-religious phenomenon (Jacob's mysterious ability to heal the sick), something that both he and Huxley were familiar with from their work on and in the Vedanta movement, with the profoundly moral issue of what happens when the sick are actually healed. As such, the subject raised questions that were disturbing not only to the established medical profession, but also to the established Christian religion. Christ, after all, is the archetypal healer who not only cured the sick but even brought the dead back to life. One of the implications of Huxley and Isherwood's script is that he may not have acted well in doing so, an implication that no Hollywood producer at that time would have been prepared to accept, and certainly would not have been willing to put into a film intended for viewing by the American public.

There was also an unacknowledged personal dimension to *Jacob's Hands,* one that seems to touch more obviously on Huxley's life but that also has implications for Isherwood's. Both Huxley and Isherwood were, at least so far as their contemporaneous society was concerned, sick. Huxley's sickness was more conventional, a sickness of the eyes, one that he had suffered from ever since, at the age of sixteen, he had been nearly blinded permanently by an attack of *keratitis punctata,* an illness that in the early years of the twentieth century was inadequately understood and not easily treatable. When Huxley and Isherwood were collaborating on the script of *Jacob's Hands,* Huxley had moved to the Mojave Desert in part in order to be "cured" of the long-standing aftereffects of this illness. Some of his efforts, as well as some of the results of this "cure," are described in his small book on the so-called Bates eye exercises, *The Art of Seeing*. Although there is still some controversy about the practical success of this cure, Huxley himself seems to have been satisfied that, if not actually cured, his eyesight had improved considerably, at any rate to the point that he managed to pass the California driver's license test.

As for Isherwood, his "illness" was that he was homosexual. Although, unlike his friend and sometime collaborator, W. H. Auden, he never underwent treatment for his so-called illness, Isherwood was at this time profoundly conflicted about his sexuality. A good deal of his attraction to the Vedanta movement is in fact attributable to Swami Prabhavananda's tolerance for his sexuality, at least insofar as the Swami did not conceive of homosexuality as any more of a hindrance to spirituality than heterosexuality, but at the same time Isherwood himself sought to heal himself, by meditation and abstinence, of what he evidently thought of as a kind of illness. Later, he would change his mind about this whole aspect of his life and become an active proponent of gay rights, but much time was to elapse before that transformation (or cure?) took place.

Paradoxically, then, both Huxley and Isherwood were intent on curing themselves of 'illnesses' at the very time when they were collaborating on a story in which the notion of a cure was seemingly put into question. As the female protagonist of *Jacob's Hands*, Sharon Carter, whom Jacob had cured of the effects of polio at the beginning of the story, tells Jacob toward the close: "I wish you'd never cured me."[10] She utters this wish because she knows that, although cured of her lameness, she has now succumbed to another, apparently more pernicious disease, one for which there is no cure because, in the final analysis, she does not wish to be cured of it, namely, the disease of American consumerism. Sharon loves Jacob and knows that Jacob loves her, but she also knows that Jacob would never accept for himself (or for those he loves) a life that depended more on materialistic than on spiritual values. She, on the other hand, is no longer prepared to forfeit her creature comforts, even for the sake of Jacob's love. Hence they both agree to a parting of the ways, with Sharon returning to her luxurious surroundings in Beverly Hills and Jacob returning to the simple life of the desert.

It is in the desert that we first encounter Jacob. It is there also that he cures a sickly dog that has been brought to him by an unhappy, quarreling couple from the city. In the "Epilogue" to the story, however, we are told that the couple is no longer quarreling. In curing their dog of its physical disease, Jacob has apparently also cured them of their psychological illness. This "cure" echoes the healing that Jacob had earlier performed on Earl Medwin, an extraordinarily wealthy young man who had been suffering from heart disease for just about all of his life and whose neurotic mother has been pampering him during the whole of that period. With Jacob's help, however, Earl seemingly overcomes his disease, though in fact in the end it turns out that he has only overcome his fear of it. Dying, he is nevertheless filled with wonder and joy, telling an initially doubtful Jacob that he has "cured me—after all." That is, Jacob has cured him, not of his illness ("that doesn't matter") but of "being afraid." At peace with himself, he passes on with an expression of calm radiance on his face (122–24).

It would seem, then, that in this story there are "cures" and there are cures, at least as far as human beings are concerned. The former cures are physical and superficial, whereas the latter are spiritual and profound. While, as in the case of Earl, Jacob's healing hands are sometimes able only to effect a temporary physical cure, we know that those hands have nevertheless succeeded in achieving a permanent spiritual cure. In leaving the reader with this sense of two types of healing, one of which is far more important than the other, Huxley and Isherwood may be saying that their own physical or social ailments are not what really need curing. What really needs curing is not their illnesses (real, imagined, or societal), but their lives. And the same is true, so the implication runs, of us and our variegated physical and social illnesses. What really matters is what happens to the soul, not the body.

What happens in the soul, of course, also takes a lot longer to happen than what happens in the body, as both Huxley and Isherwood knew very well from the long, arduous years they both spent working at Vedanta spirituality. It is for that reason, no doubt, that Huxley in his famous essay on the "Minimum Working Hypothesis" (originally published by Isherwood in *Vedanta for the Western World*) argued that "the temptation to perform 'miracles' should always be resisted."[11] Jacob has tried to resist that temptation, and to some extent he has actually succeeded. Paradoxically, however, it is his very success in this endeavor that allows him to effect a spiritual transformation in his patients instead.

Isherwood and Huxley would go on to collaborate on other film projects, though none was of equal interest and complexity to *Jacob's Hands*. One of those projects, called "The Miracle," involved adapting a play by Maurice Maeterlinck, *Sister Beatrice,* for the cinema. Another, with the working title "Below the Equator," was a story of adventure and corruption set in a South American country reminiscent thematically of Joseph Conrad's *Nostromo* and no doubt influenced also by Isherwood's then recent travels in Latin America, as described in his book *The Condor and the Cows*. (Huxley had also traveled in and written about Latin America, notably in *Beyond Mexique Bay* and in *Eyeless in Gaza*.) Neither of these collaborative treatments has been published, much less made into a film, and neither probably merits publication or filming.

Why, then, did Isherwood and Huxley continue to work collaboratively on uncommissioned film projects? The answer to this question is, on the one hand, easy: money. In 1947, Isherwood received half of a payment of fifty thousand dollars (or at least ten times that amount in today's money) for an original film treatment of what was eventually to be made into a successful film, *Judgment Day in Pittsburgh*. Isherwood had completed this project together with the experienced scriptwriter, Lesser Samuels, who received the other half of the money. (Lesser Samuels was also involved in the later, unsuccessful collaboration on "Below the Equator.")[12] It is clear that Huxley and Isherwood were hoping for a repeat of the lucky hit of *Judgment Day in Pittsburgh*. On the other hand, although money may have been their primary object, it is also clear that they liked each other and enjoyed working together. Huxley also respected Isherwood as a writer, quite apart from his work on film scripts. When he had doubts about the novel that would eventually become *Time Must Have a Stop,* he turned for help to Isherwood, who agreed to come out to stay for several days with the Huxleys at Llano, where he read and advised Huxley about the novel.[13] And when, much later, Huxley ran into difficulties with his last completed novel, *Island,* it was Isherwood whom he asked for help in making the novel more dramatic (*Letters,* 886). Isherwood returned the compliment by including a discussion of one of Huxley's novels in a novel of his own, *A Single Man;* by asking Huxley to lecture to his class at Los Angeles State; by publicly referring to Huxley as a "very good" writer of film scripts; and by unfashionably preferring Huxley's later fiction—the novels Huxley had written since coming to California—to his earlier, European ones. Although never quite equals, Huxley and Isherwood were good friends. Neither ever denigrated the other publicly or privately, fictionally or otherwise—an especially unusual compliment in Huxley's case. Their collaborations unfortunately did not lead to financial or artistic success. The time they spent on those collaborations was not wasted, if only because they helped these two eminent writers to know and appreciate each other more fully and deeply.

Notes

1. This essay was printed in *Aldous Huxley Annual* 7 (2007), reprinted with permission, and is the revised version of a lecture held at the Fourth International Aldous Huxley Symposium in Los Angeles on July 31, 2008. I thank the Huntington Library for a one-month Christopher Isherwood Fellowship in 2006. I also gratefully acknowledge permission granted by the Huntington Library and Don Bachardy to quote from the Christopher Isherwood Papers.

2. Christopher Isherwood, *Where Joy Resides: A Christopher Isherwood Reader,* ed. James P. White and Don Bachardy, Introduction by Gore Vidal (New York: Noonday, 1989), 178.

3. See Christopher Isherwood (with Berthold Viertel), "The Nazi," 1940, box 8, Christopher Isherwood Papers, Huntington Library (CI 90).

4. *Letters of Aldous Huxley,* ed. Grover Smith (London: Harper and Row, 1969), 456; hereafter *Letters.*

5. Michael Rosenthal, "Isherwood, Huxley, and the Thirties," in *The Columbia History of the British Novel,* ed. John Richetti (New York: Columbia University Press, 1994), 746–48.

6. See Marilyn Ferguson, *The Aquarian Conspiracy: Personal and Social Transformation in Our Time* (Los Angeles: Tarcher/Penguin, 1987).

7. "The Aquarian Conspiracy: Huxley, Isis, LSD and the Roots of American Hedonist Culture," *Executive Intelligence Review;* see "The Modern History Project" at http://www.modernhistoryproject.org/mhp/ArticleDisplay.php?Article= AquarianConspiracy; accessed October 16, 2007.

8. Peter Parker, *Isherwood: A Life Revealed* (New York: Random House, 2004), 455.

9. Christopher Isherwood, "An Evening in Honor of Aldous Huxley," University of Southern California, Friends of the Library, with Laura Archera Huxley, George Cukor, and Robert M. Hutchins, Christopher Isherwood Papers (CI 2238), Huntington Library, March 18, 1965.

10. Christopher Isherwood, *Jacob's Hands,* screenplay with Aldous Huxley (New York: St. Martin's Press, 1998) 135.

11. Aldous Huxley, "Minimum Working Hypothesis," in *Vedanta for the Western World,* ed. Christopher Isherwood (1945; reprint, Hollywood: Vedanta Press, 1971), 105.

12. See Katherine Bucknell, "Introduction," in Christopher Isherwood, *Diaries, Volume One: 1939–1960,* ed. Katherine Bucknell (New York: Harper, 1996), xxiv.

13. See Maria Huxley, unpublished letter to Christopher Isherwood, January 30, 1944, Christopher Isherwood Papers (CI 1008), Huntington Library.

16

The Celebrity Effect

Isherwood, Hollywood, and
the Performance of Self

LISA COLLETTA

When Christopher Isherwood settled in Hollywood at the end of 1939, he was aware that the event signaled a change in his writing, as well as in his life. After a difficult move to America and an unhappy few months in New York, he wrote to his mother on December 5, "Slowly, I am getting around to the idea of writing again. But, it won't be anything like what I've done so far. Philosophical, probably, and deeply religious! Very obscure. Full of dreams and visions. It sounds awful, doesn't it? Perhaps it's only a reaction to movie work."[1]

Although Isherwood felt the need to distance himself from his early writing, his fame rested for many years on *Goodbye to Berlin*, those linked short pieces of semiautobiographical fiction based on his life in Berlin in the early 1930s. As Katherine Bucknell has noted, part of their fame is owing to the fact that "they describe a period and place in modern history that has proven to be of incalculable and horrible significance."[2] Bucknell, among others, argues that Isherwood's portrait of Berlin's demimonde and morally bankrupt middle class has generally been read as revealing a cultural condition that somehow explained and even suggested what was to happen in Europe and to the world in the following years. However, as Antony Shuttleworth suggests, in the early critical reception of *Goodbye to Berlin*, it is hard not to miss a certain coolness. Set as it is against the rising tide of fascism in the early 1930s, Isherwood's portraits of crooks, prostitutes, opportunists, and *artistes manqués* seemed rather reserved and noncommittal. The large political events of the day are there in the background, but the focus is on individual betrayals, and it was difficult for some to see just how—and whether—the book engaged with its time.[3]

The famous metaphor for Isherwood's narrative approach is a "camera with its shutter open," which refers to a type of narrator that is passive, recording and not thinking. The claim to being a camera at the beginning of *Goodbye to Berlin* may account for some of the initial suspicion of Isherwood's lack of historical engagement, but I would argue that his objective narrative style reflects a cultural reality of that historical moment that is probably more revealing of the conditions that fostered fascism than a politically engaged narrative reflecting "uncomprehending liberal alarm" might have been (Shuttleworth, "In a Populous City," 151). Of course, a camera is never objective; it is positioned, focuses on certain things and not others, and frames subjects from a certain angle while it omits other events from its field of vision. Additionally, the critical focus on this metaphor ignores the opening lines of *Mr Norris Changes Trains,* which also employs the imagery of sight but in a very different way:

> My first impression was that the stranger's eyes were of an unusually light blue. They met mine for several blank seconds, vacant, unmistakably scared. Startled and innocently naughty, they half reminded me of an incident I couldn't quite place; something which had happened a long time ago, to do with the upper fourth form classroom. They were the eyes of a schoolboy surprised in the act of breaking one of the rules. Not that I had caught him, apparently, at anything except his own thoughts.[4]

William Bradshaw is on the surface one of Isherwood's passive narrators, but these opening sentences do much to explain what kind of observer he is. He filters what he sees through his own experiences, but he is unsure exactly what those past experiences meant or whether what he sees is really at all similar to the experience he remembers. But it is the meeting of the eyes that triggers the encounter, and the shared glance between Bradshaw and Norris is a flirtation. Bradshaw requests a light for his cigarette, the flame flickers suggestively between them, and the rest of the episode plays out as a performance: Bradshaw wants to be entertained on a long journey, and Norris desires to be charming but is unsure of his audience. Seeing leads to performance, and performance is an important theme in the text, as Mr. Norris's desire to charm makes him perilously unknowable and Bradshaw's enacted aestheticism prevents him from seeing the truth of Norris's character. Clearly, Isherwood's most famous work is neither passive nor objective, but engaged in experience in a uniquely experimental way, a way that understands the various ways the self sees, performs, and playacts but refuses or is unable to call those performances to a traditional moral account.

By the time *Goodbye to Berlin* was published in 1939, Isherwood was already making his way toward Southern California, to work in the film business and to record his experiences at the center of a remarkable cultural shift. The climate and culture in Southern California demanded a different kind of lens, but the perspective would always be Isherwood's. As Peter Parker notes, almost everything Isherwood wrote, "even his occasional book reviewing, contains an autobiographical strand."[5] Many scholars have described Isherwood's writing as semiautobiographical, a rather misleading term but one that does get at the fact that Isherwood shows up—in one form or another—in his various works. Whether as William Bradshaw (Isherwood's two middle names) in *Mr. Norris* or as "Christopher Isherwood" in *Prater Violet* and *Christopher and His Kind*, Isherwood made use of himself as a character, even in his nonfiction, in order to frame experience and understand his environment and his observations. Isherwood acknowledges the aesthetic choice in this stance and that his various performances are fundamental to his art: "The main thing I have to offer as a writer are my reactions (these ARE my fiction or my poetry, or whatever you want to call it)."[6]

Given this autobiographical bent, Isherwood was temperamentally unsuited to the kinds of obscure religious works he suggested to his mother he might write. As a novelist with the sensibilities of an autobiographer, he was always creating characters who were versions of himself, who love what he called "playacting, who charm and flirt and reinvent themselves whenever necessary, and as much as possible."[7] He was also what Auden referred to as "that rarest of creatures, an objective narcissist" (Parker, *Isherwood*, 725). These two characteristics give his writing a bracing, nonconfessional honesty and made him the ideal chronicler of moments of collective reinvention. Isherwood had the prefect *subjective* camera eye to capture unsentimentally prewar Berlin and postwar Los Angeles—two cities that celebrated performance and that are at the center of defining moments of the twentieth century.

Isherwood was not the first English writer to go to Hollywood or to recognize that its alluring power would transform, define, and create value for most of the world. Others, such as Gerald Heard, Aldous Huxley, J. B. Priestley, Dodie Smith, and Evelyn Waugh, just to name a few, had different reactions, though.[8] Priestley noted that the cultural impact of Hollywood seemed trivial enough on the surface, but pointed "to the most profound changes, to huge bloodless revolutions."[9] Hollywood's celebration of performance and its mass marketing of value were threats both to America's own democratic values and to those of the rest of the world, as it undermined the individual and turned him into a consumer instead of a worker. Sunset Boulevard seemed at the center of a new way of being, and Priestley is unsettled by the fast pace, "the pretty frivolity," and the promise of anything you want whenever you want it: "Very soon there would be something like this road all over the world, penetrating Africa, glittering across Asia. *Gas, Eats, Hot and Cold Drinks:* something like this would be spelt out, in paint by day, in neon lights after dark, all the way from Shanghai to Capetown" (*Midnight on the Desert*, 86, 88). Isherwood, too, recognized this, and he understood from his experiences in Berlin that small details of life are huge signifiers of culture. Although his initial reaction is not exactly favorable, it isn't as negative as that of many of his counterparts, as he struggles to make sense of California's paradox of abundance and emptiness.

Isherwood arrived in Los Angeles by bus after crossing the vast desert, "quivering in its furnace glare":

> Beyond the desert, the monster market-garden begins: thousands of acres of citrus groves, vineyards, and flat fields planted with tomatoes and onions. The giant billboards appear. The Coca-Cola advertisement: "Thirst ends here." The girl telling her friend: "He's tall, dark . . . and he owns a Ford V8." The little towns seem entirely built of advertisements. Take these away, you feel, and there would be scarcely anything left: only drugstores, filling-stations and unpainted shacks. And fruit; Himalayas of fruit. To the European immigrant this rude abundance is nearly as depressing as the desolation of the wilderness. The imagination turns sulky. The eye refuses to look and the ear to listen.[10]

His perception reflects the uneasy awareness that Hollywood, with its alluring but superficial values, would come to define culture in the twentieth century; however, Isherwood liked to say that Hollywood was a place that required one to "live intentionally"—a place where one had to live purposefully, performatively, precisely because the surrounding culture, indeed, even the landscape and architecture, offered no traditional or stable identity on which to rely. While authors like Priestley write of a "sinister impermanence" in Southern California, Isherwood found Hollywood liberating *because* of its impermanence, which allowed for individual reinvention. However, Isherwood was always a keen observer, and he was aware that impermanence and performance can make very difficult demands on the individual. Although he revels in the lack of history—"The whole place is like a world's fair, quite new and already in ruins"

(*Diaries*, 1:20)—he consistently remarks that a present without depth can be disorienting and life without historical memory can be defined merely by advertisements: "on the hill, giant letters spell 'Hollywoodland,' but this is only another advertisement . . . for a city that doesn't exist" (ibid.). Performance is related to advertising, not just art, and, though this can be liberating, it can also be dangerous, just as it was in Berlin. It is not easy to live among advertisements, and he warns readers that

> to live sanely in Los Angeles (or, I suppose, in any other large American city) you have to cultivate the art of staying awake. You must learn to resist . . . the unceasing hypnotic suggestions of the radio, the billboards, the movies, the newspapers. . . . They have planned a life for you—from the cradle to the grave and beyond—which would be easy, fatally easy, to accept. ("Los Angeles," 161)

If Isherwood understood the allure of performance and was himself a narrative performer and charmer, Los Angeles made him rethink the purposes of self-performance. His early narrators were dispassionate and wryly amused, but the narrators from his American period are less arch. They are also intentional and committed to revealing their thoughts and motives even when performance and charm might actually be the thought and the motive behind their actions. This seems to me to be the main difference between his European and Californian work. Because he began to feel that performance might be the very nature of the self, or, as Adam Phillips remarks, because Isherwood feared that "self-consciousness went all the way down—that unselfconsciousness is something we enact like everything else," he was drawn to the pursuits of yoga and Eastern religion as a seemingly "Californian" way of explaining the emptying out of the self (7). But it is also that same understanding of the performing self that prompted him to leave the Vedanta Center in Hollywood. The selflessness required to be a monk was antithetical to being a writer, and it was as a writer that Isherwood explored the ways in which various selves—both his and others'—performed and reacted to experience, which was the only thing worth writing about.

In Isherwood's diaries and letters from his California period, one sees evidence of his fascination with performance and celebrity, but it is a fascination marked by unease. In fact, his camera eye didn't translate into film work that well; although he saw better than most around him, he was unable to turn that perspicacity into successful scripts. In 1954, he had been working at the margins of the film business without a single big credit to his name when he bumped in to Gore Vidal on the lot at

MGM. Isherwood had just finished a project for Lana Turner in which she would play Diane de Poitiers. As Vidal tells it in his introduction to *Where Joy Resides,* he found the whole idea risible, but Isherwood answered "grimly, 'Lana can do it.'"[11] Although he mock-warned Vidal, "don't be a hack like me," Isherwood found fun in his own situation, even as he hoped that there was something of substance to back up the celebrity and easy money that had come to justify spending any mental energy at all on wondering what Lana Turner might believably say playing a sixteenth-century French aristocrat. But "under cover of being a hack," Isherwood was exploring the spiritual truths associated with performance and reality at the Vedanta Center in Hollywood, and that exploration would forever change his life and his fiction.

Of course, performance is Hollywood's stock-in-trade, so the combination of Isherwood's spiritual quest and his work in the film business seem in some way like two sides of the same coin, and those two interests combined in Isherwood and made him the perfect witness to the Californication of Western culture. If yogic spirituality leads to an emptying out of the self, then so too does Hollywood celebrity—though, of course, in very different ways and with very different results. Both promise a release from the burden of personality, but while Yoga promises transcendence of the self, celebrity imperils the self, constructing it according to easily identifiable, performable, and reproducible gestures that threaten to overwhelm what is unique. The pursuit of enlightenment and the pursuit of celebrity are both associated with California culture. Isherwood was one of the first to grasp how these two intertwined, and his American phase is therefore an extension of his European phase—not a break with it—and it represents his experience of negotiating a spiritual search with his delight in performance.

If the self is defined by various performing selves, at what point does awareness of self-consciousness become only performance? In the 1940s, Hollywood existed on this cultural razor's edge. Filled with European intellectuals and movie people, Hollywood had a brief moment where popular culture engaged the larger questions of philosophy and history, but those complicated pursuits would easily be swamped by the commodifying nature of Hollywood. Isherwood's Los Angeles self was aware that the pressure to be *seen* as something—whether a writer, a lover, a certain kind of character, or just someone in particular—would move questions of being and performing from the realm of aesthetics and philosophy to the realm of advertising, where the self or selves would inevitably be defined by the allure of fame and the power of commerce. His

Hollywood phase therefore reflects the ambivalence of his attraction and repulsion to celebrity, as he begins to understand the necessity of resisting its allure in order to live life—of living *intentionally*—as well as his acceptance that performance is at the root of our understanding of ourselves.

Cultural critic Clive James has noted that the cult of celebrity is a world-conquering ideology, and the perception of this new form of imperialism was evident from Hollywood's earliest beginnings. Adherents of other ideologies, such as Marxism and fascism, saw in film the potential to promulgate other more overtly political doctrines, but it wasn't until they began to understand the real power of the film medium—its *production* of knowledge and subjects, not just its communication of those things—that movies really worked as propaganda. Unlike the theater, where each performance is a unique achievement, film makes a performance and the performer reproducible; it doesn't so much suggest uniqueness and individuality but the *appearance* of uniqueness and individuality, an appearance that can be reproduced and sold to audiences. The power of moving images and their ability to freeze a performance for posterity and reproduce it for millions quickly made actors into celebrities, not for their performances per se, but for *what* they represented—and the *way* they were represented—to the public. Celebrities represent a unique identity and personality, which seem special but also universally attainable. The perfect and infinitely replicated movie star comes to have a nearly divine effect, what Leo Braudy refers to as "the feverish effect of repeated impacts of a face upon our eyes."[12] After repeated viewings, the audience begins to feel as if it really knows the actors and their lives share common interests, feelings, and experiences. As Braudy has noted, however, the larger-than-life glamour of celebrities creates a growing sense of unease for viewers, as they begin to feel that the celebrity's life is somehow more real and meaningful. Thus, audiences begin to look to celebrities for guidance on what to buy and wear, how to behave, and how to live.

For Isherwood, the threat of Hollywood was not so much in the privileging of performance—art has always done that through aesthetics and ritual—but in robbing performance of its power to reveal the complicated truth of experience. Celebrity simplifies rather than complicates; it makes identity easily visible and performable because the identity of the celebrity is composed of shorthand tricks and gestures, which are, as Braudy claims, "easily detachable from whatever substance they once signified," and their personalities, mediated through films and photographs, become collages, "made from fragments of themselves—polished, denatured, simplified" (4–5). Thus, the fragmentation required of film acting extends to the very personality of the celebrities themselves, and because of their role as consumer product, bought and sold by the studio system and consumed by the movie audiences, the erosion of self is a theme that runs through nearly every Hollywood novel, including Isherwood's *Prater Violet, The World in the Evening,* and to some extent *A Single Man,* where the loss of identity is deeply connected to death or mental breakdown.

While writing these novels, Isherwood was not only working on and off for MGM but he was studying the ascetic teachings of Vedanta and mixing with a group of famous and successful expatriates: Huxley, Garbo, the Hubbles, Stravinsky, and the Viertels. Berthold Viertel was the model for *Prater Violet'*s Friedrich Bergmann, a powerful, domineering, and egocentric film director making a rather sentimental film about Vienna at the very moment the Nazis gained near-complete control in Germany. As in *The Berlin Stories,* Isherwood uses the device of a dispassionate narrator commenting on an ironic, charismatic, and ambiguous character, but this time the complicated Bergmann is drawn to the Isherwood character. The narrator comments on Bergmann's dangerous charm, and there are frequent comments from the narrator and others on the idea of "selling out" one's serious talent in the film business. Although *Prater Violet* shares some narrative qualities with *Mr Norris Changes Trains,* the effect is quite different. "It is an insightful account of the human comedy at the center of the movie business," as Stephen Wade has claimed, and it doesn't narratively privilege the role playing and performance as much as it shows the limits of it.[13] As Bergmann's anxiety about the film, the war, and his family mounts, his artistic anger and moral outrage explode, but he is manipulated into continuing with the film. He continues to play the role of gruff, demanding auteur to finish the film, but after the drunken wrap party, where enemies now act like lifelong friends and the moody star Anita exclaims Bergmann's greatness, he has been embraced by the studio system again. Bergmann and the Isherwood character leave the party together and walk through the deserted streets of London, but in this novel we no longer find the cynical distance of the "Isherwood" character, who ended *Mr Norris Changes Trains* with an ironic question. This performance of a version of himself is less arch and more empathetic toward Bergmann and the choices he has made. He ruminates that the late hour is when "a man's ego almost sleeps. The sense of identity, of possession, of name and address and telephone number grows very faint. It was the hour at which man shivers, pulls up his coat collar, and thinks, 'I am a traveler. I have no home.'"[14]

The last few pages of *Prater Violet* are about empathy and the longing for connection, and "Isherwood" refuses to judge Bergmann for his "sellout" that led only to the finishing of a sentimental film about a city that was soon to be ravaged by war and, ultimately, to a new contract in Hollywood. The narrator understands that beneath all the performances—even with those one loves, the J's, the K's, and L's,—"there is the pain of hunger" (125). "Beneath our disguises . . . Mother's Boy, the comic Foreigner with the funny accent," writes the Isherwood character, "we recognized each other and we knew" (127). This ending could only have been written in America, where Isherwood's understanding of identity and performance changed as a result of his study at the Vedanta Center. There, his camera eye looked beneath the surface as well as dispassionately ranging over it.

If Isherwood was always aware that life itself demands a performance, he was quick to see that Hollywood demanded celebrity, something that was even more destabilizing to the individual. He fell immediately under the spell of Garbo, the kind of studio star that has come to represent the very notion of celebrity. He met her soon after arriving in Los Angeles and found her alluring, but he knew immediately that they could not have a real relationship. He wrote to his mother that if Garbo weren't famous, they might be able to be friends, but her fear of being recognized made her histrionically isolated. She was always covering her face with her hands or her hat whenever anyone passed: "It is like going around with someone who is wanted for murder" (*Kathleen and Christopher,* 157). Of course, if Garbo hadn't been famous, she wouldn't have been Garbo, and Isherwood probably wouldn't have found her very interesting. In his diary he is more explicit, of course, and with his keen eye reveals that Garbo's fame has made her a type, always acting, only able to see herself through the eyes of others. Isherwood understood self-performance, but when one lost the ability to see performance from the inside and became able to identify only with the audience, the danger to the self was profound. His account of Garbo at a picnic at Mount Wilson (hosted by the Huxleys that also included Bertrand Russell, Krishnamurti, Anita Loos, and the Viertels) is revealing of the nature of celebrity. Garbo is "Garbo," fulfilling everyone's expectations of her and charming both Isherwood and Krishnamurti:

> She wore the famous straw gardening hat, with slacks, and a tiny patch of plaster between her eyebrows, to prevent wrinkles from forming. She was kittenish, in a rather embarrassing way; and her lack of makeup and general untidiness were obviously calculated. Just the

same, I liked her and felt quite at ease in her company. She climbed
the figtree in the Viertels' garden to get me some specially ripe figs. I
remember how she referred to some business dealings with the studio,
and said that one must always pretend to be a child when talking
to the front office. She had her own kind of little-girl slyness. . . .
Garbo was anxious to meet Krishnamurti. She was naturally drawn
to prophets—genuine and otherwise. Salka said that she was very
unhappy, restless and frightened. She wanted to be told the secret to
eternal youth, the meaning of life—but quickly, in one lesson, before
her butterfly attention wandered away again . . . I held back to the end
of the procession, because I wanted to walk with Garbo. I had drunk
a lot of beer at lunch, and knew no shame. I only wished my friends
could see me. As we started out, Garbo said: "As long as we're on
this side of the fence, let's pretend we're two other people—quite,
quite different." "You know," I announced solemnly, "I really wish you
weren't Garbo. I like you. I think we could have been great friends." At
this, Garbo let out a mocking, Mata Hari laugh: "But we *are* friends!
You are my dear little brother. All of you are my dear little brothers."
"Oh, shut up!" I exclaimed, enormously flattered. (*Diaries*, 1:49–51)

After just one afternoon, Isherwood understands that in addition to her
great beauty, Garbo's allure rests in her constant performance and the
way she embodies and fulfills the desires and expectation of an audience.
Her attraction to spiritual leaders might have been rooted in her celebrity and the search for something that might give her emptied-out self a
spiritual dimension. But Isherwood was quick to see that even that may
have been an act as well.

Her primary appeal might just be her performance of the tragic Hollywood star, and her attraction to spiritual leaders might just have been a
studied aspect of her personality. However, he notes the power of that
performance:

I suppose everybody who meets Garbo dreams of saving her—either
from herself, or from Metro-Goldwyn-Mayer, or from some friend or
lover. And she always eludes them by going into an act. This is what
has made her a universal figure. She is the woman whose life everyone
wants to interfere with. (51)

After knowing her for only a few weeks, Isherwood begins to see the
limits to her personality and that her emotions are mainly a performance.
She is the ultimate movie star, a collection of recognizable, repeatable
gestures. He writes of seeing her on New Year's Day 1940:

Garbo was at tea with us today. I think Peter is right when he says she's "a dumb cluck." She actually didn't know who Daladier was. If you watch her for a quarter of an hour, you see every one of her famous expressions. She repeats them, quite irreverently. There is the iron sternness of Ninotchka, the languorous open-lipped surrender of Camille, Mata Hari's wicked laugh, Christina's boyish toss of the head, Anna Christie's grimace of disgust. She's so amazingly beautiful, so noble, so naturally compelling and commanding, that her ridiculous artificiality, her downright silliness can't spoil the effect. (67–68)

Garbo's effect is really all that matters, as long as she continues to fulfill expectations and desire. The visual world of the movies demands that the most important aspect of a person is made visible. Garbo's effect is Garbo herself, and it becomes impossible to separate the two. The self-objectification of the performer becomes a way of being, and the awareness of the gaze of others engenders a celebrity's very sense of himself, but, as Braudy explains, the "self is validated in recognition but wise to the ways of both inviting and evading performance" (*The Frenzy of Renown,* 570). Isherwood, very early in his Hollywood life, perceived this in Garbo's famous desire to be left alone, and comments that her dread of being recognized is coupled with a perverse desire to draw attention to herself, because if she isn't recognized by others she isn't real to herself. He goes on to describe a scene where they are out for a walk, and she jumps on the top of a fence at the corner of Mabery Road overlooking the ocean and theatrically extends her arms toward the sea. She waves at people on the beach, throws her arms around Isherwood's neck, and then down by the water darts among the waves laughing and gathering foam in her hands until everyone at the shore has recognized her (*Diaries,* 1:68).

The constructed nature of Garbo's personality becomes evident in nearly every entry in his diary that relates to her. At one point he transcribes their conversation as if it were a movie script—full of recognizable characters and bad dialogue:

SHE *(taking my hand, and letting go of it again immediately):* We must not do that. This is New Year's Day. It might become a habit.

ME *(politely):* Well, it would be a very good habit—as far as I'm concerned.

SHE *(in her Hedda Gabler voice):* How can you say that? You do not know me at all. I do not know you. We might make a terrible mistake.

ME *(gallant):* I'm willing to risk that.

SHE *(raising tragic-ironic eyebrows):* Ah! You are a very *brave* young man!

Later, she asks Isherwood about his then lover Vernon:

SHE: And when you came back to New York he was waiting for you? How *wonderful!* Nobody *ever* waited for *me!*

ME *(not knowing how to answer this one):* Look at that bird diving under the wave. What kind is it?

SHE *(the whimsical little girl):* A duck.

ME: And those big birds flying over there?

SHE: *Big* ducks.

ME: They are pelicans.

SHE: *No!* They are all ducks. And the people who live in that beautiful house—they, too, are ducks . . . You know, I am not surprised that people wait for you. You have a funny face.

ME: Thank you.

SHE: Tell me, are you never sad? Never melancholic?

ME: I used to be sad, but I've given it up. *(etc. etc.)* (Ibid.)

The "Chris" of this part of the *Diaries* is a wry observer of the small performances that reflect a larger cultural moment. He reveals his considerable talents of observation and social satire, but beneath the humor lies the unsettling knowledge that Garbo's celebrity precludes her from ever being authentic in the company of others, or at least from understanding her performing self, and understanding the way one performs one's various selves is part of living intentionally. Garbo is so fully "Garbo" that, as Braudy claimed, "the line between self and role, body and identity, being and name" has become completely obliterated (*The Frenzy of Renown,* 570). Hollywood's script for Garbo would soon be a script for her audience, as they too begin to enact the gestures of personality that have been so alluringly presented to them on the silver screen. In *The Berlin Stories,* Mr. Norris had also lost the ability to understand his performing self, and this made him politically dangerous and untrustworthy. In Hollywood, performance can lead to a loss of self-knowledge that is dangerous existentially and spiritually—and perhaps ultimately politically as well, but in Hollywood Isherwood was less interested in politics.

Becoming aware of one's place and of the nature of performance is at the heart of *The World in the Evening,* probably Isherwood's least critically acclaimed work. As Stephen Wade claimed, "The novel is enlightening with regard to the clear need to rewrite and express with new viewpoints much that had occupied his thoughts in the Berlin years" ("Christophananda Writes His Religion," 8). The narrator, Stephen Monk, begins the novel, as many narrators in Isherwood's novels do, with the imagery of sight. At a Hollywood party, Monk catches an image of himself in a mirror wearing his "usual crazy costume . . . [his] masquerade as musical-comedy Hollywood character."[15] However, his flashy white tuxedo and crimson bow tie went entirely unnoticed by the collection of Hollywood phonies, whose lives revolve around being seen and/or talked about. The hosts, the Novotnys, live

> high up on the slopes of the Hollywood Hills, in a ranch-style home complete with Early American maple, nautical brasswork and muslin curtains; just too cute for words. It looked as if it had been delivered, already equipped, from a store; and you could imagine how, if the payments weren't kept up, some men might arrive one day and take the whole place there on a truck, along with Mrs. Novotny, the three children and the Cocker Spaniel. (9)

Of course, the sense of Hollywood being a manufactured place pervades Isherwood's fiction and nonfiction alike, but, in both, the fakeness, while often railed against, offers the opportunity to act intentionally about one's life. *The World in the Evening* is a novel about that kind of intentionality. Monk is defined and constructed by his wives. Elizabeth, his first, explained to him who he was, and Jane, his second, merely uses him as an appropriate companion. He must learn to define himself, and it is the healthy relationship between Bob Wood and Charles Kennedy that suggests an alternative to the empty life he had been living. Joshua Adair has argued that the novel's celebration of a homosexual community that is normal, natural, and authentic is a direct challenge to the superficial, performative values of Hollywood and mainstream America.[16] This is clearly true, as Bob and Charles create a home within the Pennsylvania Quaker community of Tawelfan, a community that accepts them as "wholesome" young men, even if they don't really understand the nature of their relationship (304). Tawelfan—meaning "a place of peace"—is symbolically apart from Hollywood and the spectacular, celebrity values it represents (Wade, "Christophananda Writes His Religion," 8). Hollywood, as Stephen Monk observes, is a place as meticulously contrived as a swimming pool:

> It was brilliantly clean; not one leaf floating on its surface, not one speck of dirt on its tiled floor. God curse this antiseptic, heartless, hateful, neon mirage of a city! May its swimming pools be dried up. May

all its lights go out forever. I drew a deep dizzying breath in which the perfume of star jasmine was mixed with chlorine. (14)

Monk is ambiguous in his sexuality and unsure of the performance that most naturally suits him. Isherwood reflects this struggle by "using motifs of self-reflection . . . related to the various masks and performances that people indulge in as ways to escape from the pains of self-knowledge" (9). In Isherwood's Hollywood novels the theme of self-knowing is always present. It is represented in the struggle between the material world of ambition and celebrity and that of community and acceptance. The symbolism used most often is objects of sight and reflection—cameras, mirrors, swimming pools, movie lights; this, to me, suggests Isherwood's awareness that the artificial glare of Hollywood can illuminate the self or can shine so brightly that only surface traits are seen. One must be awake and purposefully aware under that glare or risk losing any sense of identity and belonging.

Isherwood's awareness of the assault on selfhood did not make him want to leave Los Angeles, though. Instead, he found fertile ground for his spiritual pursuit of self-knowledge, which he pursued through writing about his experiences, but his way of writing about his experiences remained very different from the ways other British novelists wrote about Southern California. For the most part, others responded satirically to the way Los Angeles threatened ideas of the "authentic," and, with the exception of Huxley, who shared Isherwood's desire to shed his past, re-create himself, and pursue spiritual meaning, most British writers eventually left, finding little that was sanguine in a future defined by Hollywood.

Isherwood suggests that even the incredible mansions speak of disappointment and false values. He observes that "many of the houses—especially the grander ones—have a curiously disturbing atmosphere, a kind of psychological dankness which smells of anxiety, overdrafts, uneasy lust, whiskey, divorce, and lies. 'Go away,' a wretched little ghost whispers from the closet, 'go away before it is too late. I was vain. I was silly. They flattered me. I failed. You will fail, too. Don't listen to their promises. Go away. Now, at once.' But the new occupant seldom pays attention to such voices" ("Los Angeles," 159). Isherwood understood the seduction of fame and performance and the psychological anxiety that accompanies it; however, it was the individual's fight against those seductions that made life in Hollywood bracing and full of potential.

Just as he did in *Goodbye to Berlin,* Isherwood's Hollywood writing reveals cultural specifics that speak of much more than their immediate significance. His observant narrators—in both his fiction and his non-fiction, in both Berlin and Los Angeles—are quick to note the various ways people perform and lie to themselves, and he knew that these performances and dishonesties play out on the larger cultural stage. He and the other English people in Hollywood perceived early on that America's celebrity culture would become the dominant way of seeing and assessing value throughout the world; however, Isherwood consistently refuses to judge that culture harshly, from the comfortable position of a moral absolute.

Perhaps Isherwood did write deeply philosophical work, as he told his mother he would, but he certainly didn't do it in a conventional way, nor did he fundamentally break with his past. Instead, he moved the camera to different positions, observing the vanities and petty betrayals of others through the lens of his own performances. His spiritual quest and his semiautobiographical approach to writing allowed him to be as frank as possible about his own and others' inconsistent performances without losing his sense of humor or his novelist's pleasure in those performances. He had a keen eye for the playacting because his suspicion of it is part of his enjoyment of it, and in no other place than Hollywood could he confront that fear and delight.

Notes

1. Lisa Colletta, ed., *Kathleen and Christopher: Christopher Isherwood's Letters to His Mother* (Minneapolis: University of Minnesota Press, 2005), 160.

2. Katherine Bucknell, "Who Is Christopher Isherwood?," in *The Isherwood Century: Essays on the Life and Work of Christopher Isherwood,* ed. James J. Berg and Chris Freeman (Madison: University of Wisconsin Press, 2000), 13.

3. Antony Shuttleworth, "In a Populous City: Isherwood in the Thirties," in Berg and Freeman, *The Isherwood Century,* 150.

4. Christopher Isherwood, *The Berlin Stories* (New York: New Directions, 1954), 1.

5. Peter Parker, *Isherwood: A Life Revealed* (New York: Random House, 2004), 4.

6. Christopher Isherwood, *Diaries, Volume One: 1939–1960,* ed. Katherine Bucknell (New York: Harper, 1996), 365.

7. Adam Phillips, "Knitting: A Review of *Lost Years,"* *London Review of Books* 22.22 (November 16, 2000): 7.

8. See, for example, David King Dunaway, *Huxley in Hollywood* (New York: Doubleday, 1989); H. Mark Glancy, *When Hollywood Loved Britain* (Manchester:

University of Manchester Press, 1999); Sheridan Morley, *Tales from the Holly-wood Raj* (New York: Viking, 1983); Kevin Starr, *Material Dreams: Southern California through the 1920s* (New York: Oxford University Press, 1990); and Lionel Rolfe, *In Search of Literary L.A.* (Los Angeles: Classic Books, 1991).

9. J. B. Priestley, *Midnight on the Desert* (London: Heinemann, 1940), 88.

10. Christopher Isherwood, "Los Angeles," in *Exhumations: Stories, Articles, Verses* (New York: Simon and Schuster, 1966), 157.

11. Christopher Isherwood, *Where Joy Resides: A Christopher Isherwood Reader,* ed. James P. White and Don Bachardy, introduction by Gore Vidal (New York: Noonday, 1989), ix.

12. Leo Braudy, *The Frenzy of Renown* (New York: Vintage, 1986), 6.

13. Stephen Wade, "Christophananda Writes His Religion: Isherwood's Purgatory," *Critical Survey* 13, no. 3 (2001): 6.

14. Christopher Isherwood, *Prater Violet* (London: Methuen, 1946), 122.

15. Christopher Isherwood, *The World in the Evening* (1954) (Minneapolis: University of Minnesota Press, 1999), 10.

16. Joshua Adair, "'Christopher Wasn't Satisfied with Either Ending': Connecting Christopher Isherwood's *The World in the Evening* to E. M. Forster's *Maurice,*" *Papers on Language and Literature* 48, no. 3 (Summer 2012): 302–31. [Adair's essay is reprinted in this volume.—Eds.]

17

A Writer at Work

The Isherwood Archive

SARA S. HODSON

Every collection of personal papers reveals the intangible, subtle aspects of an individual's way of thinking or acting that cannot be discerned through his or her publications or public persona. Christopher Isherwood's archive is no exception. Acquired in 1999 by the Huntington Library from his life partner Don Bachardy, with later additions from various sources, the papers have already seen extensive research use. The four thousand–item collection affords deep insight into every facet of Isherwood's life and writings, including such topics as gay rights, Vedanta, pacifism, Hollywood, and the film industry. This essay will discuss some of the unique and rare elements of the collection and its significance for research, touching on particular sections and items in the archive and what they reveal about Isherwood, his fellow writers, and the matters that meant most to him. The essay will then focus on Isherwood as a writer, and the way his papers reveal his writing craft, using his novel *The World in the Evening* as the prime example. The writer at work will be examined through a look at his drafts of the novel, references to it in correspondence, diaries, and lecture notes, and extensive analytical notes about its creation recorded in Isherwood's "Writing Notebook."

The Isherwood archive presents its own unique representation of its creator. Opening a newly acquired collection is a time of discovery and excitement for archivists, a sort of archival Christmas morning. The initial survey of papers tells us much about the creator, and all that we learn is then bolstered and refined as we venture more deeply into the material. We learn about the person, and about his or her habits of working and ways of organizing (or not) the drafts, correspondence files, documents, and other material. Principles of archival procedure dictate that we rearrange nothing until we have done a complete survey of the collection, in order to ascertain whether there is an existing order that should be retained as evidence of how the creator of the papers thought and worked. If the survey reveals no order, or an order that is inconsistent or unworkable, then the archivist's responsibility is to create an order that will make the papers easily approachable and useful to both researchers and library staff, while referencing the existing order in a way that will enable researchers to understand how the papers were arranged by their creator.

The Isherwood archive presented an unusually tidy and well-organized package for us, revealing his neat and orderly care in looking after his papers. This is in dramatic contrast to many collections we receive, which typically show little or no existing arrangement and in fact often arrive in a state of complete disorder. Moreover, Isherwood had gone through his papers late in his life, adding pencil annotations identifying dates and circumstances surrounding the creation of a given document or draft. Again, this is somewhat unusual, and his notes proved very helpful to us as we processed and cataloged the papers. Very importantly, Isherwood did not rearrange his papers with the intention of helping archivists who would later work with them. Donors often undertake this project, thinking that archivists require or desire the help, when in fact such action actually can make our work more difficult.

Isherwood's orderly files and pencil annotations were quite helpful in enabling us to catalog the collection rapidly. In 1999, when we acquired the papers, we saw the need for speed in processing the collection and making it available soon, as scholars were eagerly awaiting research access. In addition, Isherwood's one hundredth birthday was approaching in 2004, and we wanted to present a major exhibition that year to celebrate the anniversary. Thanks to Isherwood's tidy organization, we were able to assign several people to catalog discrete sections of the collection, helping to speed the process. Ordinarily, one person catalogs an entire collection, for consistency and for familiarity with every aspect of the material. With the Isherwood Papers, several of us worked simultaneously, conferring often and exchanging information about the material and about the people represented, to ensure high-quality and consistent cataloging.

As we worked on the collection, we recognized that it is one of the richest research collections we have seen, and we could readily see that it will support scholarly research for many years to come. One of the most significant aspects of the collection is how it reveals the way Isherwood approached his writing craft, and this essay will explore that question.

For Christopher Isherwood, one of the most autobiographical of writers, his papers hold particular importance for documenting the life that exerted such strong influence on his writings. The collection is rich in both content and formats of material for research. The correspondence files are exceptionally full, with substantial research value. The most extensive series of letters are from W. H. Auden (104 items, 1926–72), Stephen Spender (169 letters, 1929–85), and Edward Upward (302 letters, 1922–85). The correspondence from all three writers provides full documentation of their friendship with Isherwood and of his and their works in progress. Isherwood's relationship with Auden, one of the most important of his friendships, was both complex and integral to the growth of both men as writers and as critics of each other's works. Auden's letters, especially those dating from the 1920s and 1930s, illuminate their collaborations and the extent to which Auden depended on Isherwood to read, critique, and even edit his poetry. Spender's letters comment at length on writers and their works, literature in general, political matters, and his own sexual orientation. Upward reveals himself to be a much less secure writer, relying on his friend for encouragement and support, as he tries to write while teaching full-time.

A remarkable series of ninety-five letters (1932–66) from E. M. Forster, probably Isherwood's most important and valued mentor, touch on his literary efforts and on events such as the bombing of England during World War II. A highlight of this series is the group of letters discussing Forster's reasons for not publishing his novel *Maurice* during his lifetime and for asking Isherwood to oversee its publication after the author's death. Fifty-four letters (1943–65) from Lincoln Kirstein, founder of the New York City Ballet, are especially notable for the correspondence describing his wartime work in Germany as one of the lowest-ranking (private first-class) members of the Monuments, Fine Arts and Archives section of the U.S. armed forces. In 2007, the Huntington purchased seventy-one letters from Isherwood to Kirstein, enabling the library to provide that rare commodity, both sides of a correspondence in one location.

The collection contains smaller runs of letters from many writers and from friends in the film industry and other spheres of Isherwood's life, including Cecil Beaton, Benjamin Britten, Truman Capote, John Gielgud, Alec Guinness, Julie Harris, Gerald Heard, Aldous Huxley, Laura Huxley, Maria Huxley, John Lehmann, Somerset Maugham, Heinz Neddermeyer, Swami Prabhavananda, Dodie Smith, Igor and Vera Stravinsky, John Van Druten, Gore Vidal, Berthold Viertel, Peter Viertel, Salka Viertel, Glenway Wescott, and Tennessee Williams.

A series of diaries documents half a century of Isherwood's life, reflecting the dedication and rigor of his daily writing regimen and offering remarkable insight. His daily diaries have been edited by Katherine Bucknell and published in three volumes, in slightly expurgated form.[1] The original, complete diaries are sealed for a period of time. However, several early diaries are open for research, including a Portugal diary (1935–36), a journal beginning "Holland, Sept. 1, 1935," and the "Diary of a Summer in Greece, 1933." Two remarkable items are the journals that Isherwood and Auden wrote jointly in 1938. Called "Diary of a Trip to Asia," each diary contains their travel and shipboard observations, their experiences in Asia, and drafts of poems by each writer. The trip formed the basis for their 1939 book *Journey to a War.*

Isherwood's family is represented in the collection by both correspondence and diaries. A group of 107 letters (1911–39) from Isherwood to his mother, Kathleen Bradshaw Isherwood, discusses his writing projects and records his reactions to people and places, including his first excited impressions of Hollywood after arriving in 1939. His mother's twenty-nine diary volumes cover the period from 1883 to 1915, a time that included World War I and the death in France of her husband, Frank. An extensive series of 359 letters from Frank to Kathleen deals with his service in the Boer War and in the First World War.

Approximately 1,800 photographs date from about 1895 to 1991. Most of the images are from 1920 to 1985 and depict Isherwood and his travels. Other photographs, including those from 1986 to 1991, portray Don Bachardy and various friends. Several small albums contain pictures from the 1920s, from Berlin in 1929–33, and from Isherwood's wanderings in Europe and the Mediterranean throughout the 1930s. Isherwood appears in many of the photographs, and there are pictures of Auden, Spender, Forster, Heinz Neddermeyer (Isherwood's partner in the 1930s), Gerald Hamilton, and Jean Ross (the inspirations for Mr. Norris and Sally Bowles in *The Berlin Stories*), and others, including a number of unnamed young men.

Beginning in 1939, the great majority of photographs are portraits of Isherwood and, by the 1950s, Don Bachardy, individually and together. Many of the pictures are the work of professional photographers (Patricia York, Carl Van Vechten, Cecil Beaton, Marilyn Sanders, Florence Homolka, and many more). Photographs taken at parties, art openings, receptions, screenings, and other events depict authors Auden, Spender, Gore Vidal, and Tennessee Williams, actors Joan Crawford, Julie Harris, John Houseman, Roger Moore, Paul Newman, and Joanne Woodward, and artist David Hockney. Travel snapshots document Isherwood and Bachardy's trips to Monument Valley in 1953, to Japan, Indonesia, and India in 1957, to Great Britain in 1961, and to Europe in 1970. Audiovisual material in the archive includes several dozen audio recordings (chiefly radio broadcasts and tapes made at home) and a handful of videotapes and films (mostly televised interviews and filmed documentaries). Several boxes of ephemera contain date books, address books, awards, clippings and printed articles by Isherwood, published pieces about him and his writings, published articles about others, and material about homosexuality.

Supplementing the archive of Isherwood's papers is his two thousand–volume library. There are important editions of his writings, inscribed books from Auden, Spender, and others, as well as reference books Isherwood read and used in his own work.

The many literary manuscripts in the archive include Isherwood's writings from every period of his career and encompass all the genres in which he worked. Manuscript drafts, notes, and outlines provide an inside look at the progress and development of his thoughts for his works, plus a vivid sense of the infinite patience and meticulous craftsmanship that he brought to the revising of his writings. For the novel *Down There on a Visit* there are twenty-two separate partial drafts and versions. There are five drafts and sets of notes for *Kathleen and Frank*, as well as four drafts of his autobiographical book *Christopher and His Kind*, along with additional notes and stray pages. Three drafts of *A Single Man* allow researchers to follow its development from its earliest version in 1962, when it bore the title "The Englishwoman," through its change to "The Englishman" later that same year, and finally to the book's final draft as *A Single Man,* dated February 11 to October 19, 1963.[2]

Manuscripts for several of Isherwood's best-known works are not present in the archive. Absent are drafts for his early autobiographical work *Lions and Shadows* and for his comic novel *Prater Violet.* Complete manuscripts are not present for *All the Conspirators* and *The Memorial,* but there is Isherwood's 1957 foreword to a new edition of the former work, and there are partial drafts for the latter. Similarly, *A Meeting by the River* is represented by notes about its revisions but not by a complete draft. A notable absence is any manuscript material at all for *The Berlin Stories,* although the collection contains many references to that work and to Berlin in the 1930s. For example, there are notes and an Isherwood manuscript titled "First Outline for the Book of a Musical Based on Isherwood's *Goodbye to Berlin* and Van Druten's *I Am a Camera*"

(1959), and a screenplay treatment for *Cabaret* written by Isherwood and Bachardy. An important essay titled "Berlin: February, 1952," was written when Isherwood revisited the city for the first time after leaving it in the early 1930s.

Other essays by Isherwood include "My first essay at Cambridge, 1923," a plea for the exercise of free will rather than the enforced prohibition of alcohol. An essay significant for its autobiographical content at a crucial moment in Isherwood's life is "Midnight in New York," composed in his hotel room in late January 1939, upon his arrival in the United States. Apparently feeling himself to be at a momentous transition point in his life, he records his observations about arriving in a new city and nation:

> Well, here you are. Here, for the moment, is your home, your shelter from the night. In your thirty-fifth year, at the age when Dante met the Leopard, when your father got married, this is the place to which thousands of miles of wandering have brought you. Twelve months ago, you were in Hankow, twenty-four months ago, you were in Brussels, thirty-six months ago, you were in Lisbon. This time next year, you will quite possibly be dead. You certainly get around.[3]

The nearly fifty lectures by Isherwood (most dating from the 1960s) provide especially revealing material for research on such topics as his views concerning literature and its place in life, his own approach to writing, and religion in general and Vedanta in particular.

Ten boxes contain scripts and screenplays by Isherwood and others. Examples of his early scripts jointly written with Auden are *The Dog beneath the Skin* and *The Enemies of a Bishop*. Scripts for *Jacob's Hands* and *Below the Equator* represent important collaborations with Aldous Huxley, while Isherwood's collaboration with Bachardy produced scripts for *The Beautiful and Damned, Frankenstein,* and *A Meeting by the River.* In just one of the many connections that the Isherwood Papers have to other archival collections in the Huntington, two more drafts of *A Meeting by the River* may be found in the collection of scripts from the Mark Taper Forum, the Los Angeles theater where the play was produced in 1972. Other scripts include *The Loved One* (written with Terry Southern), *A Christmas Carol,* and *The Adventures of a Black Girl in Her Search for God.*

Among the literary manuscripts by other writers, the poems by Auden form a superb body of research material. In addition to some 175 drafts of poems (both autograph and typewritten, including some unpublished verses, with many bearing Auden's corrections), there is an early note-book in which Auden composed drafts of poems and plays, and which contains laid-in notes by Isherwood. Drafts of more poems by Auden appear in his letters to Isherwood, as well as his replies to Isherwood's comments and suggestions about the verses.

All of the formats described above and represented in the collection provide a rich tapestry of interwoven threads contributing to a full picture of Christopher Isherwood, the man and the writer, and of his place in a wide circle of literary and other friends and acquaintances. The Isherwood portrait that emerges from his papers reveals his relationships with other writers, with Don, and with earlier partners Heinz Neddermeyer and Bill Caskey. The diaries, correspondence, and other materials reveal Isherwood's innermost thoughts about his place in the world, about his spiritual beliefs, his literary hopes and efforts, and his reactions to the people and events around him. From correspondence and other items, we see a generous and humane man who opened himself to help others, whether they were young men troubled about their sexuality or writers struggling over a poem or novel gone wrong.

One of the most important revelations in the archive concerns Isher-wood's writing craft. Through his papers, we see the writer at work, and we can better understand the creation and construction of his literary output. In literary manuscript drafts, in diary entries, in correspondence, in lecture notes, and in his magnificent "Writing Notebook," we see an incomparably patient writer who tirelessly and relentlessly revised, re-wrote, and edited his work until it was exactly as he knew it should be.

Notes and drafts of Isherwood's novels allow us to track the author at work. In addition, there are other formats of material that contain partial drafts and that record Isherwood's thoughts as he imagines, writes, and revises his works. The extensive and varied set of materials representing Isherwood's writing craft is unusually full, more so than in most writers' papers. The archive contains such resources for many of Isherwood's writings, and his 1954 novel *The World in the Evening* can be taken as an example.

This flawed novel that might be regarded as Isherwood's most trou-bled literary progeny, and the notes, drafts, diary entries, correspondence, and other material in the collection, reveal the considerable difficulties Isherwood faced in trying to make the novel succeed as a work of litera-ture. Just conceiving the novel and getting it off the ground presented the writer with such challenges and troubles that even so patient a craftsman as Isherwood must have wished at times to abandon it. In his unpublished diary (Huntington Library, CI 2571), Isherwood notes on April 4, 1947:

> I now have to start thinking seriously about my Quaker novel—called provisionally "The School of Tragedy."
>
> The earlier draft of this novel, which I worked out last year in Santa Monica, won't do at all. The character of Paul, and the story built around him, aren't the proper framework for the things I want to say about religion, pacifism, the problem of minorities, etc. etc. . . . My present intention is to write the whole thing in the third person— maybe through the eyes of a variety of characters.[4]

Isherwood's "Writing Notebook" is an extraordinary, ledger-sized journal in which he records his thoughts, intentions, concerns, successes, and failures in his writing, for both *The World in the Evening* and *Down There on a Visit*. The opening page in the notebook contains the beginning of his first draft of *The World in the Evening*, dated May 8, 1947. This draft consists of just over two chapters before it is abandoned, followed on the thirteenth page of the notebook by the beginning of a second draft, begun on June 17 of the same year. After just three pages, drafts three through six follow, each dated in 1949, and each consisting of just one or two opening paragraphs for the beginning of the novel. There are also several other abortive beginnings for the novel in the notebook, beyond the six labeled drafts.

Isherwood's struggles with the beginning of the novel are apparent throughout 1948 as well, captured in the separate drafts not contained in either his diaries or the "Writing Notebook." There are five partial drafts (CI 1157, 1159-62) dating from 1948, all reflecting his attempts to solve the problem of how to begin the novel.

The successive, abandoned beginnings for the novel continued in Isherwood's diary for 1949. On August 18, 1949, he writes, "Extraordinary difficulty in restarting my novel. The problem of the opening sentence." Then, on December 6, 1949, he laments: "But my novel—that's sitting in front of me again, undented, unformed—like some rubbery bit of material which pops back onto shapelessness the minute you take your hands from it" (*Diaries*, 1:415, 418).

Beyond the troubled beginning of the novel, its construction caused difficulties for Isherwood in other ways, all recorded in the various drafts, diaries, lecture notes, and the "Writing Notebook." One of the biggest problems for Isherwood was the protagonist, who was called Paul, then Charles, before becoming Stephen. While Isherwood had a

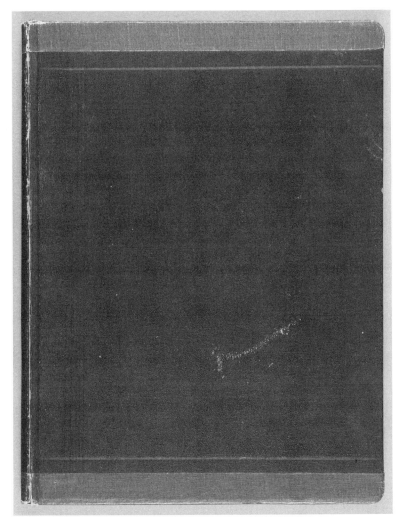

The cover of Isherwood's "Writing Notebook." Reproduced by permission of the Huntington Library, San Marino, California.

sense (a sense that underwent changes, as he repeatedly worked over the novel) about his main character, he had trouble making the final decisions about just who his main character was. In the Diary (CI 2751), he wrote on June 9, 1947, just two months after he started "thinking seriously" about the book:

> Stuck again. After writing a few thousand words, I find it is all wrong—
> every bit of it. The mood is wrong. The tone is false. I'm just not getting
> any place.
>
>   And yet I feel as strongly as ever, that this is a possible novel and
> that something can be made out of it. . . .
>   What is the most important point about Charles?
>   His loneliness. This is a story of loneliness, and this is the problem
> of a lonely man. The novel is about the problems of loneliness. It deals
> with attempted solution—social work, religion, love. It must therefore
> be extremely subjective. Just as much so as if it were written in the first
> person singular.

Isherwood struggled with his character's identity and how closely it should
be based on, or related to, his own persona, the "Christopher" of previous works. In his diary entry for August 17, 1949, he noted, "The great
thing, at the moment, is to restart my novel. 'Stephen Monkhouse' has
got to be me—not some synthetic Anglo-American. The few circumstances can so easily be imagined—his ex-wife, his Quaker background,
etc. But it must be written out of the middle of *my* consciousness"
(*Diaries*, 1:414). However, Isherwood had not yet settled on his protagonist as a version of himself. He realized that he needed and wanted to
create a different character—a fictional character—for whom he would
need to construct a plot, rather than record events from his own life, as
he had done previously. As he wrote in the "Writing Notebook," "Let
me admit: I'm caught in a cleft between my 'Christopher Isherwood'
reportage manner—reporting for the sake of reporting—and the new
manner I'm trying for in this book. I've got to be bold, and not get
scared of having a proper plot. Reportage is a bog in which I'll stick."[5]
His friend Dodie Smith (author of *The 101 Dalmatians*), with whom
Isherwood discussed his novel countless times during its writing, recognized this shift in his approach to the fictional invention and wrote
her reaction to the novel in a letter dated August 14, 1953: "Stephen,
naturally, isn't quite you. He has flashes of you, but you never intended
him to be you exactly."[6]

Years later, as Isherwood looked back on *The World in the Evening*, he
could cast a more dispassionate eye on why the novel gave him so much
trouble and why the finished book was deemed, by himself and by critics,
as less than completely successful. In a lecture about the novel, presented
in Los Angeles on May 11, 1965, Isherwood noted its flaws, including his
difficulties in deciding on the identity of the main character. He remarked
to his audience, "the first of the things that went wrong was to write a

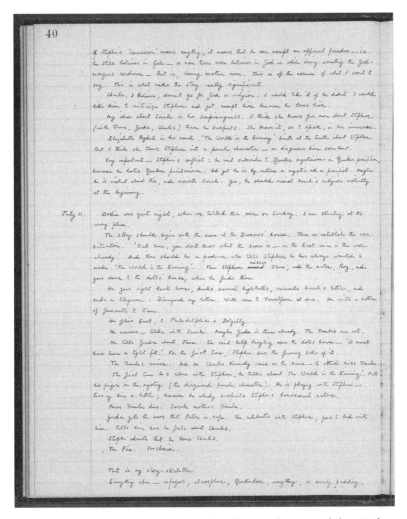

A page from Isherwood's "Writing Notebook" illustrates his "story-skeleton" of
what became *The World in the Evening*, including feedback from Dodie Smith,
author of *The 101 Dalmatians*. Reproduced by permission of the Huntington Library,
San Marino, California.

novel with the 'I' and yet not really know who the 'I' is and not be able
to share in his deepest reactions to things; this always shows."[7]

Directly related to the challenges of creating his protagonist is Isherwood's ongoing dilemma about whether the novel should be written in

the first or third person. The dozen or so drafts of the novel's beginning, both in the "Writing Notebook" and in separate, loose pages, occur in both voices. In the "Writing Notebook," though, Isherwood records his thoughts about the reasons for employing the first or the third person. Early in the notebook, following quickly on the heels of the several draft beginnings, he notes, "The first-person diary style of narration won't do. It somehow destroys Stephen's dignity. He is too self-conscious, too interested in himself. He is enjoying the whole thing too much. This diary-form is coquettish, theatrical, bogus" ("Writing Notebook," 33). Later on (48), he decides that the only way to encompass all he wishes to say in the novel is to use the point of view of various characters, changing this viewpoint as often as he wishes, and including his own as well. He had also explored this notion in his diary, as noted earlier. Still later, he has changed his mind again:

> Well now—suppose we went back to the idea of doing this in the first person?
>
> My argument for this is that now I am revealing a great deal of the story directly, not through dialogue with others. Therefore the objections to First Person Narration cease to obtain. ("Writing Notebook," 71)

In addition to the decisions about the protagonist and voice in the novel, Isherwood analyzed and revised his work in ways that shaped its fundamental focus, direction, and scope. Early on, he sought to tell the story of the Quakers and the European war refugees they sheltered and cared for in Pennsylvania. This would, of course, draw upon his own experiences working with refugees. However, as he struggled with the book and endeavored to shape it into a successful work of fiction, he came to realize that this wasn't the story he was actually trying to tell, that the novel as initially envisioned was too diffuse to gel as a work of fiction. He recognized where the problem lay. He was trying to do too much with the novel and he needed to rein in its scope in order for it to succeed. In his "Writing Notebook," on June 24, 1950, he reflected: "Now I'm becoming very bothered by the large number of my characters. That's because I see the book as a very intricate contraption of plots, sub-plots, motifs, etc. But am I right?" (37). Over time, he knew he was correct to make the novel more focused, that the refugee story, even though it was a tale he wanted to tell, needed to be dropped in order for the novel to concentrate on its protagonist.

Isherwood received an endorsement on his decision to drop the refugee story in the form of his friend Speed Lamkin's pronouncement that the refugee story was "a bore," even as Lamkin gave the book high praise, calling it "the best thing you have ever done."[8] Isherwood reflected on this structural decision in his 1965 lecture on the novel, acknowledging that as he worked on it he grew further and further away from the Quakers and their work with refugees, because he couldn't properly establish the motivation for his main character to go work with the sect. It was too big a story, and the novel was perforce growing away from being the story of Christopher Isherwood and his involvement with the refugee war work and becoming a narrower tale of the protagonist, who was becoming a true fictional character, not the "I" of Christopher Isherwood (Berg, *Isherwood on Writing*, 284).

The "Writing Notebook," an extraordinary record of a writer at work, lengthily, on a troublesome novel, includes not only his own thoughts and concerns about the book, but also a record of the substantial effect of his extended conversations with Smith and her husband Alec Beesley. They were his most frequent sounding board, rereading his drafts, suggesting changes, and providing thoughtful comments on all aspects of the novel. In the notebook, Isherwood writes long notes capturing his conversations with his two advisers. In an entry dated July 11, 1950, he begins:

> Dodie was quite right, when we talked this over on Sunday. I am starting at the wrong place.
> The story should begin with the scene at the Darrows' house. There we establish the war situation. (40)

He goes on with a long, detailed summary of her recommendations and his thoughts about how to implement them. Other entries throughout the notebook similarly demonstrate Smith's and Beesley's comments and Isherwood's determination to work through them. As a record of a writer's ongoing revision of a troubled novel, these passages, together with Isherwood's independent thoughts and worries, are a remarkably valuable resource for research focusing on the process of literary creation.

Isherwood felt enormous gratitude to the Beesleys for all their help, and he thanked them by dedicating the book to them, a gesture that deeply touched them both. In addition, he had the final typescript of the book specially bound in handsome dark green morocco and presented it to the couple. In a further happy association for this final draft, it was typed by Bachardy. The Huntington was fortunate to acquire the bound manuscript in 2003, when it was purchased by the Library Collectors' Council, adding a superb association item to the manuscript material representing the novel.

After flogging on his novel for the better part of seven years, Isherwood at last sent the manuscript off to Random House in late 1953, and, as we would expect, he writes down his thoughts about the strengths and weaknesses of the final draft, noting, "I don't know what the reactions will be to this rewrite, but I feel that now, at last, the book is finished. For better and for worse. Elizabeth ought to be better. I could probably improve her if I did her over. But I shan't, now." From this pensive, weary note, he goes on to say:

> It's strange to have finished. This project has been with me so long. In a way, since 1947—and the other part of it, "The School of Tragedy," remains to be written. Certainly since May 1951. That's thirty months— or twenty-four, if you deduct six months for my time in New York and England. Thirty months to write three hundred pages—ten pages a month! I suppose, with revisions, that's about my usual speed. No wonder I get so little done. (93)

Those final words, showing he has retained his sense of humor despite the considerable and lengthy burden of the novel, bring to an end the section of the "Writing Notebook" devoted to *The World in the Evening*.

Assessment of the novel was mixed, by critics and by Isherwood's friends. From his lecture on the novel, we know that Isherwood himself recognized its weaknesses and imperfections. In the lecture, he lays them out for his audience with a ruthless honesty that is at times painful and nearly brutal to witness. Many of his friends and fellow writers wrote to him in a rather guarded manner, cautiously criticizing the failings they found in the novel but stressing how much they liked specific aspects of it. In these letters, preserved in Isherwood's papers, we see loyal friends seeking to praise where they could but clearly compelled to write honestly of the book's flaws. The critics tended to be less kind, and their reviews often made for uncomfortable reading for Isherwood.

What we can observe about *The World in the Evening*—a conclusion gleaned from Isherwood's notes, drafts, and diary entries, from the "Writing Notebook," from the lectures, and from correspondence—is that the novel is a transitional work in the growth of the writer. In it, he struggled to make the change from his long practice of writing a fictionalized version of his own story, to a new technique of creating a purely fictional work in which the protagonist is an imagined individual, rather than a form of "I," or "Christopher Isherwood." Through all the revising, rewriting, reimagining, and rethinking, Isherwood wrestled with this change, struggling to make the new direction in his writing work in the creation of a novel.[9]

The many varied items in the Isherwood Papers enable us to reconstruct the writer's progress for this novel and for the other writings. From Isherwood's patient, methodical records and drafts, we see his writing craft. The archive of his papers richly supports research on the writer at work, as it supports research on every facet of his life and writings. Scholarly research on the collection has been brisk and fairly constant from the day we opened it. Professional archival ethics regarding patron confidentiality mean that specific scholars and their projects may not be revealed, but researchers have used the collection for all aspects of biographical and critical study. Scholars have studied the multiple drafts of Isherwood's works and have pored over his notes about his writing. They have delved into his lecture notes and into the correspondence files. The correspondence from Isherwood to his mother and the letters between him and Auden are especially rich. Auden scholars have found the drafts of his poems contained in the collection to be particularly useful and rewarding. Researchers have explored Vedanta and its importance in Isherwood's life and have investigated Isherwood as a gay man. The diaries are particularly fruitful and, in coming years, when the sealed diaries are opened, scholars will find much value in them. The Isherwood collection is one of the richest for research that I have seen in many years as an archivist, and it will support research for a long time. The Huntington awards an Isherwood Fellowship annually for research in the collection, sponsored by the Christopher Isherwood Foundation, and scholarly symposia are convened by the library. These programs perform an important role in ensuring that Isherwood scholars will continue to visit the library and that Isherwood scholarship will thrive.

Notes

1. The original diaries that have been published in expurgated form by Katherine Bucknell are present in the Isherwood Papers but are sealed until January 1, 2030, and therefore are not available to researchers. This essay does not include references to or quotations from these original diaries, but only from the published editions, as the restriction on access extends to library staff, as well as to researchers. Thus, I have not looked at, read, or made use of any of these original diaries, as that would constitute a breach of archival ethics. The other original diaries used for this essay are open and available to all researchers, without restriction. See Christopher Isherwood, *Diaries, Volume One: 1939–1960,* ed. Katherine Bucknell (New York: Harper, 1996); Christopher Isherwood, *The Sixties: Diaries, Volume Two, 1960–1969,* ed. Katherine Bucknell (New York: Harper, 2010); Christopher

Isherwood, *Liberation: Diaries, Volume Three, 1970–1983*, ed. Katherine Bucknell (New York: Harper, 2012).

2. [See the essay by Carola M. Kaplan in this volume.—Eds.]

3. Christopher Isherwood, "Midnight in New York," January 1939, Isherwood Papers (CI 1102), Huntington Library.

4. Christopher Isherwood, Diary: 1935–38 and 1947, Isherwood Papers (CI 2751), Huntington Library.

5. Christopher Isherwood, "Writing Notebook," Isherwood Papers (CI 1158), Huntington Library, 38.

6. Dodie Smith, letter to Christopher Isherwood, August 14, 1953, Isherwood Papers (CI 1971), Huntington Library.

7. James J. Berg, ed., *Isherwood on Writing* (Minneapolis: University of Minnesota Press, 2007), 206.

8. Christopher Isherwood, *Lost Years: A Memoir, 1945–1951*, ed. Katherine Bucknell (New York: Harper, 2000), 284.

9. [For other reactions, see the essay by Jaime Harker in this volume.—Eds.]

18

Pulp Isherwood

Cheap Paperbacks and
Queer Cold War Readers

JAIME HARKER

In 1954, after the publication of *The World in the Evening,* Christopher Isherwood wrote Stephen Spender that "I have lots and lots of fan-mail of the type you can guess. I believe if I gave the word, right now, I could start a queer revolution; they are just longing for a Hitler, poor dears."[1] To compare a scattered group of queer readers to Nazis was a particularly unsympathetic rhetorical move in 1954, but Isherwood quickly made it clear that he didn't quite mean it; indeed, the existence of American gay readers both surprised and moved him: "I don't mean that nastily, and I don't really mean a Hitler. Actually, it's heart-breaking, the sense you get of all these island existences, dotted about like stars and nebulae, all over the great black middle west."

When Christopher Isherwood immigrated to the United States, he was determined to reinvent himself as an authentically American author. For fifteen years, he struggled with his new authorial incarnation, and his nearly ten-year struggle to complete *The World in the Evening* resulted in hostile reviews and an unsupportive press. But the response of his readers to *The World in the Evening* was a key turning point in his American career. "The great black middle west" was no longer a blank for him, thanks to gay readers in both rural and urban settings, and it shaped his American authorial identity. Evidence of this relationship comes primarily from preserved letters from readers, which are scattered throughout his correspondence at the Huntington Library. The letters he kept are (with two exceptions) all from men and, of those, a great majority are gay. *The World in the Evening* began what would be an evolving and ongoing correspondence with Isherwood's readers.

A 1954 letter from a Philadelphia bookseller epitomizes the intensity new fans brought to their reading:

> Dear Mr. Isherwood,
>
> It is very early morning and I have just finished reading *The World in the Evening* for the second time. I've been crying like a baby. . . . I want to write feverishly and unashamedly. But I remember Elizabeth being embarrassed by her "fan" mail . . . and I feel an almost belligerent resentment rising at the thought that authors and readers should be cut off from each other by these artificial walls . . . as though we were somehow enemies instead of partners in the act of creation. But dammitall, I can't sleep for talking to you. So here it is! . . .
>
> I have felt your love as though it were directed personally to me. If you had sat down for all the painful, wonderful hours of your creation with only one thought in mind: What [do I] need more than anything else in the world at this time? . . . If this had been your spur and your goal, as perhaps—in a sense—it was, you could not have fulfilled yourself more completely. To fail to return that love with all its overwhelming gratitude would be a most unworthy denial on my part. . . .
>
> If I could think of a word less abused and more beautiful, I would use it . . . but the word *is* Love. Whether you know it or intended it or want it or even understand it, you have drawn together all things I've known and forgotten (including the pain . . . a great deal of the pain) and made them useful to me . . . because I don't think I can ever really hate again—not even myself. . . .
>
> Thank you forever for *The World in the Evening*. (John Collins, CI 747, Huntington Library)

This bookseller reads *The World in the Evening* in ways that have been defined as middlebrow: he emphasizes his emotional experience reading the novel ("I've been crying like a baby"); he identifies with the narrator explicitly and personalizes the story ("I have felt your love as though it were directed personally to me"); he talks about the novel as a model for living, a therapeutic transformation ("you have drawn together all things I've known and forgotten . . . and made them useful to me"); and he emphasizes the symbiotic relationship between reader and writer ("I feel an almost belligerent resentment rising at the thought that authors and readers should be cut off from each other by these artificial walls . . . as though we were somehow enemies instead of partners in the act of creation"). Critics of *The World in the Evening* found it slick, trite, and crass, but many readers found it moving and profound, and they told the author so directly.

While most letters aren't as detailed, many reflect similar sentiments. The emotion the bookseller inspired is also evident in another letter:

> My Dear Mr. Isherwood,
>
> I Love You. Period.
>
> I should like to write a much longer exposition, but frankly I do not feel up to meeting the degree of effort or caution needed to properly justify my "worthiness."
>
> Be it sufficient to note I shall always have a deep and intense personal rapport with your work, your life and, above all, you.
>
> I should like to think one day I might chance to meet you. For now, then, just another "silly boy." (Mark Olson, CI 1844, Huntington Library)

This reader's desire to prove his "worthiness" suggests a nervous suitor, as does his simple, opening declarative statement: "I Love You." The intense emotion Isherwood inspires in his American readers runs directly counter to many critics' dismissal of Isherwood's formal failures. Whatever these critics found wanting in Isherwood's Cold War novels, readers found exactly what they needed.

This reader not only "loves" Isherwood, but he also has "a deep and intense personal rapport with your work, your life and, above all, you," and this identification runs across letters from readers. Another wrote:

> To say that I *am* Stephen would, I suppose, be absurd and presumptuous. At best, I'm Stephen in the first day of the case . . . or perhaps your book is the truck just running me down in the street. I'm certainly not Sarah, or Elizabeth or Gerda or Bob and Charles or Michael . . . or even Jane. They are way beyond me. You have helped make them very real to me. But I have such a very long way to go. (Collins)

Identification marks the readers' intense emotional experience with Isherwood's novels.

His readers identified not only with his characters but with Isherwood himself, believing that they knew him through his novels. One wrote of a later novel:

> With most authors I have great difficulty, either because they are so ceaselessly serious and pretentious as to suffocate lesser souls and make us feel guilty, if we don't like them, of bad taste, even bad faith (Mann and Sartre, in particular—I hope I didn't name your favorite writers), or their novels are so trivial and commercial as to qualify as sophisticated comic books without any pictures. Your books are

an exception to the general rule. I have never felt any didacticism in
them, but always unvindictive truthfulness. (Tom Statham, CI 2225,
Huntington Library)

This reader constructs Isherwood's persona as frank and unpretentious,
equating his narrative persona with himself. Isherwood encouraged such
identification of his narrative persona with himself by making himself
unusually available to his readers. He tried to respond to every letter he
received, and if he didn't succeed, he responded to a remarkable number,
which encouraged additional correspondence. He even invited some of
them to his house. Don Bachardy explained that readers came to the house
often, sometimes making long pilgrimages for that purpose.[2] Isherwood
and Bachardy were always listed in the phone book, and sometimes his
readers would call him up late on a Saturday night, after fortifying themselves with alcohol for courage. He would sometimes talk to them for an
hour. They appreciated his openness, as one wrote:

> Your card was in its tone much more honest and straightforward
> than I had imagined I should expect. . . . When I proudly displayed
> your card to my "colleagues" in one of our local taverns they were
> impressed with the informality and they suggested that I write in
> hopes of getting an answer to something that has been a problem to us
> concerning an experience which we haven't and you probably would
> understand. (Stanley Friedman, CI 879, Huntington Library)

Isherwood's accessibility invited his readers to consider him a trusted friend.

That sense of accessibility inspired letters that went beyond hero worship to casual encounters and the taking of considerable liberties. A teenager pushed this cheeky tone to the limit:

> But don't be hard on Trevor, be hard on me please be hard on me . . .
> pretty please, (UP BONDAGE!!) Well cheeky I got a whole lot of
> answerin' to do after what I've done . . . all over the Atlantic. But
> cutie-pie I'm sure you'll forgive me (wont you just?)
>   Am I an utter fool, who calls me so? No. No I'm not, I'm nice and
> not in the least bit boring (so there.) No I'm not a pretentious poet, I
> write good earthy trash-stuff. But let me tell you sonny, I *respect* them
> having just read Vedanta for the Western World, The Song of God and
> Paddington Bear. You see I'm a sado-intellectuall.
>   It's terry firing to think these words are having themselves read
> by the *greatest* Author (grovel grovel.) It's amazing these words don't
> just fade away into the paper in shame. But no, these are manly words

(Never say die if you can use a lie (KILL KILL) These li'le ol' words
wont be put down. No I say. Women of England say Go-Go. We wont
be sat upon. Well O.K. we will. . . .

   P.S. JOKE (make you laugh) (Jonathan Gear, CI 919, Huntington
Library)

Far from offending Isherwood, the teenager's facetious tone recommended
him because of a shared camp sensibility. He veers from flirting and pan-
dering to criticizing Isherwood, even making fun of himself for being
too praising. This reader was entirely successful in his ploy; he visited
Isherwood in California and corresponded with him for years. That jok-
ing tone earned Isherwood's interest, though many of the teenager's letters
are much more earnest.

   There are also remarkable offerings in the Isherwood archive. One
writer interspersed his eight-page letter, complete with lists of likes and dis-
likes, with beautiful water-color drawings.[3] Another from North Carolina
sent him eight portraits of young men, who identified as straight, with
whom he was having sex. He adds helpfully, "The photos I'm enclosing
are 'introductions' to these boys—for some of them I have naked shots I'd
be happy to send. (Sometimes when I'm knocked over by a guy's looks,
I'd really like to know what his body was like; don't hesitate to ask me
for more photos of any of these guys, or for a different dozen 'samples.')"
(Garth Fergeson, CI 774). The back of each photograph has extensive descriptions of the young man and the sexual acts he enjoys. Here's a sample:

> Rick, Eddie, Terry—Three baseball players, friends of one another and
> good to me. Rick is now married. (photo was taken 10 months ago)
> but even when engaged couldn't get enough blow jobs—would even
> want me to go into the bathroom with him for a minute if his room-
> mate was here. Ideal trade. Terry is called T-Bone by his friends, and
> is our best pitcher. Pitches it to me more often than I can count, and
> enjoys being appreciated for his fine body, dick. Very aloof to people
> (inc. me) at first, but is a hell raiser. In the middle is Eddie, Terry's
> roommate when this was taken. A heart stopper in person. A good
> buddy to me, but not ready for sex. Yet, anyway. Rick knew about
> Terry, Terry doesn't know about Rick (I don't think) and Eddie doesn't
> know about either, which is good. By the way, Rick should be in color,
> because his eyes are startlingly light blue.

This reader's frank discussion of his "trade" with a famous writer is surprising, particularly since he tells Isherwood details that even his own
lovers don't know about each other. But Isherwood's writerly persona

A hand-illustrated fan letter from Craig Makler of Philadelphia to Isherwood, January 15, 1974. Reproduced by permission of the Huntington Library, San Marino, California.

during the Cold War was influenced as much by paperback reprints as by more reputable cloth editions. Isherwood was thus enmeshed in one of the most lucrative and debated movements in Cold War print culture: the "paperback revolution."

In a flirtatious letter sent to Isherwood in 1978, Garth Fergeson of North Carolina goes into great detail regarding his sexual dalliances with the putatively straight men depicted in the photograph. Reproduced by permission of the Huntington Library, San Marino, California.

The rise of paperback books in the United States began with Robert de Graff's Pocket Books in 1939, but the Armed Services Editions created a large market for paperback books during World War II.[4] Other competitors hoped to build on this success: Avon Books, formed in 1941, and Popular Library and Dell Books were issuing paperbacks by 1943; the New American Library (NAL) published Signet Books, which was another important player, as were Ballantine Books and Fawcett Books. Avon won a key court case against Pocket Books in 1944, and postwar paperback publishing became a free-for-all, with high royalties and extensive competition for lucrative paperback titles.

Historians rightly note that this "revolution" was an innovation not of technology but of marketing, because paperback book publishers used magazine distributors, not bookstores, and so were available through drugstores and newsstands. The salacious covers of these paperbacks were the most visible aspect of the paperback explosion in Cold War America. Sex was a recurring theme across genres—gangster, detective, western, romance, science fiction. Michael Bronski notes that pulp paperbacks featured "illegal or taboo sex—adultery, prostitution, rape, interracial relationships, lesbianism, male homosexuality—topics that were, in the words of the cover-copy writers, 'controversial,' 'explosive,' shocking,' and ready to 'reveal the sordid truth in a way you have never read before.'"[5] Cold warrior Malcolm Cowley identified three categories of contemporary fiction: "the Tobacco Road category," "Deviant or Off-Beat Sex (or well-of-loneliness)," and "Proletarian Sex."[6] These salacious covers and narratives prompted police raids, investigations, and congressional hearings.

The Cold War's larger homosexual panic fueled much of this official concern about "deviant" sex, particularly the widespread distribution of "well-of-loneliness" fiction, or what Susan Stryker calls queer pulp, which included paperback originals and hardback reprints. Lesbian pulp has received most of the critical attention, and while paperback originals predominated, some—including Jo Sinclair's *Wasteland* and Patricia Highsmith's *The Price of Salt*—were originally published in hardback. More literary gay novels, reviewed in literary magazines and published by prestige presses, had another (and often much more lucrative) life in paperback reprints, where they were just as trashy as their lesbian sisters. Susan Stryker's collection of gay pulp covers makes this translation clear: pulp versions of *The Well of Loneliness, The Kinsey Report, The City and the Pillar,* and *Other Voices, Other Rooms* made no distinction, in the presentation at least, between literary writers and hacks.[7] This is true even of writers such as Isherwood, Gore Vidal, and James Baldwin, whose literary reputations have survived beyond the 1950s.

To consider queer pulp as part of a larger cultural trend of pulp paperbacks reframes many assumptions about gay life and gay literary production during the Cold War. Queer pulp may have marketed gay life as "shadowy" and marginal, but it was marketed openly, and widely available. Cold War gay print culture was visible, lucrative, and influential, even if it wasn't celebratory. It also contributed to the larger breakdown of cultural hierarchy, in its leveling of literary reprints and paperback originals. It was the threat this lack of distinction posed to Cold War cultural hierarchies that worried cold warriors like Malcolm Cowley, much more so than deviant sex. Cowley's description of a paperback bookstore highlights his concern about discrimination in brow level: "It was rich, random, gaudy, vital, corrupt, and at the same time innocent; it put culture at the disposal of the plain man, even the poorest, for less than the price of a bar whisky; it was impersonal, friendly, egalitarian, and it proclaimed as dogmas its lack of discrimination. 'Here we are,' the books in the big racks seemed to be saying, 'the mud and sapphires of our time, and for one or two pieces of silver you can take your pick of us.'"[8] Isherwood, a self-proclaimed "literary snob," was just as brow-conscious as hypermasculine cold warriors like Cowley; he held a long-standing grudge against the paperback industry for slighting his own carefully constructed literary persona.[9] His struggles to control his own authorial brand came to a head when it came time for Random House to assign the reprint rights for *The World in the Evening*. Although Isherwood preferred the more literary paperback publisher Victor Weybright of the New American Library, the Popular Library was offering double the price. Isherwood's worst fears were realized when he saw the cover of the reprint, which emphasized love triangles and the "decadent" lifestyles of the very rich. A brooding man, hemmed in on two sides by buxom women, graces the cover.

It is impossible to know how many of his readers encountered him in cheap paperbacks, but considering the small print run of his cloth editions and the extensive range of paperbacks, it is likely that those gay readers in "island existences, dotted about like stars and nebulae, all over the great black middle west," read his books in paperback. David Bergman notes that these books "reached a wide spectrum of readers, as well-educated writers were as interested in them as sweaty teenage boys. . . . Both better-educated and less-educated gay readers came together in the reading of pulp."[10] It may have been the medium as well as the message of Isherwood's novels that encouraged such intimacies. The reader from North Carolina provides another, less salacious reason:

> Your writings let me know you by being so personal and by having
> so many places where a perceptive reader can read into a situation

(by your permission, actually by your willing it) more than what you say. . . . The communication I try for in my photos is what I've gotten from you through your books—that is, I think of you as a hero because you celebrate life the way I see it, too, so that I am your distant relation, brother, son, comrade. I can never repay you with words or gifts for all you've given me, without knowing me. And I want you to know *me* a little, not for my ego, but because I do share with you a kind of love, a kind of mutual feeling. An object from you to me (a book, a photo) or an object from me to you (personal photos) is an important sign, a token of shared feeling. (Fergeson)

This reader views the photographs as part of a mutual exchange between reader and writer. In these and other cases, readers pay respect but demand equality, and insist that they have something to give back to Isherwood.

Nowhere is this insistence on equality clearer than in the literary offerings in readers' letters. One titled his poem "Love Letter to Christopher Isherwood":

YOU ARE TOO FOND OF THE EXCLAMATION MARK.
You have never made a sufficient act of contrition
For your sins (who does?). Several of your books are dreadful.
I love you. . . .
Because of your eyes, and because you are hellishly readable:
You draw me on, even at your worst. It won't damn you:
God's not a critic, thank God.
Because you are mistaken and mortal.
Because I loved you before I knew we were both
Homosexual. Because of Sally Bowles. . . .
Yes, because of *Exhumations*, for something
About it has led me to write to you—
Some tone in your voice. Yes, in spite of,
In spite of, in spite of, in spite of—I love you. (Hugh Bragan, CI 654,
    Huntington Library)

He writes a poem in praise of Isherwood, but includes a number of criticisms. Indeed, "in spite of" is the final refrain. Yet, far from being offended, Isherwood kept this letter and continued to correspond with him.

This reader wasn't asking for feedback on this poem, but a number of Isherwood readers did want feedback on their writing. This embedded writing community is one of the most interesting things about readers' letters to Isherwood. Of course, Isherwood met would-be writers through his teaching at California universities, but many readers sent him their literary offerings, particularly poetry and short stories. Isherwood read and responded to a number of these efforts, quite patiently. Some of Isherwood's correspondents eventually went on to become published authors. One, sailor Leo Madigan, author of the immortal *Jackarandy*, took advantage of loosened markets for gay fiction in the 1970s. Even his former lover, architect Jim Charlton, sent Isherwood a novel he had written. Isherwood read it carefully, gave feedback, and used his publishing connections to help Charlton get his novel, *St. Nick*, published in 1981 under the pseudonym Jack Challenge.

Not all of Isherwood's would-be writers were so fortunate, especially those writing before Stonewall. One, author of the self-published *Kala with Poetic Therapy*, wrote Isherwood in 1954 pleading for his intervention, because the U.S. Post Office had declared his book obscene. The author objected strongly to this designation, claiming that "books which really are obscene, e.g., THE NAKED AND THE DEAD, FROM HERE TO ETERNITY (with its frequent use of the word *fuck*), THIS IS MY BELOVED (with its graphic description of an orgasm during intercourse), and other books ad infinitum (some ad nauseum) go thru the mails freely with the Post Office's awareness and blessing" (Isidro de Rieras, CI 764, Huntington Library). He claimed discrimination and asked for Isherwood's help. He included a copy of the flyer that attracted the censors' attention, and this complicated his claim of racial and economic discrimination. Isherwood, of course, could see how the writer made some of his own trouble; his advertisement for the novel began with a bold promise: "My dear Friend: THIS [arrow pointing to text] is the *FIRST PAGE* of the WORLD'S MOST PUISSANT LOVE STORY! ITS KARACHING LOVING SCENES WILL STIMULATE YOU INTO UNLIMITED BLISS." Its subsequent description included numerous typos and often incomprehensible details. Isherwood likely believed this novel to be another kind of trash, but he took the time to discuss his work with him quite seriously. He wrote: "I agree with you that there is nothing in the novel which could fairly be called obscene, according to current standards and the precedents set up by a number of best-selling books in the recent past. . . . But the presentation of the book is another matter. . . . It reads like an advertisement for some kind of aphrodisiac." Isherwood consistently provided this sort of detailed feedback for his correspondents.

Isherwood's patience would seem remarkable, except that readers were treating him as an equal and a friend, and he, in response, treated them the same way, reading their literary efforts as seriously as he read the work of his English friends or his students. He didn't always like his readers' literary offerings, but he responded much as he did to Stephen Spender, Edward Upward, and W. H. Auden. In Isherwood's correspondence with his readers about their writing—much of it gay-themed—he seems to embrace them as fellow connoisseurs of good writing.

In other words, Isherwood's readers behave like fans, as fan studies define them. Henry Jenkins's germinal work *Textual Poachers* argues that fans insist on their right to construct and invent characters, and they resist attempts by the creators of the medium to fix meaning.[11] They identify with characters, invest emotion in them, and very often create their own tributes to these media in fan fiction and discussion boards. Jenkins emphasized the oppositional nature of such fan identity; they reject a subordinate status and impose their own meaning and values. Subsequent fan studies have been more suspicious of this idealization of fans, finding their interests consistent with larger cultural hierarchies. But in the 1950s and 1960s, when Isherwood was first discovering his gay audience, gay and lesbian readers used a variety of print media, popular culture, and fiction to construct oppositional identities. Marilyn Schuster's argument about the lesbian writer Jane Rule's readership is typical, I believe, of this larger focus on the resisting reader: "The negotiation between writer and reader, the bond of reading is always in process, always inflected by the time of place of both writer and reader."[12]

That identity was grounded in an emotional connection that exceeds the acceptable boundaries of highbrow aesthetic appreciation. Indeed, recent fan scholarship emphasizes the role of aesthetics—and the differing understanding of aesthetics—in fan communities. Jenkins discussed the role of emotion in fandom in an online interview, contrasting fan engagement with Bourdieu's notion of aesthetic appreciation:

> Fandom is not about Bourdieu's notion of holding art at a distance, it's not that high art discourse at all; it's about having control and mastery over art by pulling it close and integrating it into your sense of self. And that is an aesthetic transformation, but it's not the way that discourses of high art usually operate, although it is a way individuals talk about their relationship to high art. But you never really see an art critic talk about that moment of passionate transcendence in which they couldn't articulate why they were responding to the music or the painting.[13]

More recent fan scholarship has questioned the deferral of aesthetic issues in fan studies, insisting that connoisseurs of highbrow culture could be considered, profitably, as fans. Jenkins's notion of identification and emotional resonance is also true of middlebrow print culture. Both middlebrow and fan studies emphasize the symbiotic relationship between reader and writer. For gay readers of Isherwood, that relationship was grounded in desire, both its satisfaction and its deferral.

Indeed, what Isherwood gained from his readers was, from his perspective, as valuable as what they gained from him. Although Barbara Hochmann argues that twentieth-century writers resisted readers' desire to equate narrator and author, Isherwood, apparently, never got the memo.[14] His secure place in the literary establishment makes this accessibility even more remarkable. Despite often vicious reviews, his books were always reviewed broadly, and his associations with Auden, Spender, and Forster meant that he could not be simply ignored. That such a writer, accepted (however reluctantly) by a mainstream literary establishment, should be constructing "passionate communities" similar to those of gay pulp writers suggests that our notions of "mainstream" and "oppositional" are not adequate to account for the complex layering and encoding of gay identity during this period.

Don Bachardy understood as well as anyone Isherwood's remarkable availability to fans this way:

> He was always interested to meet people who were interested in what he'd written, and especially if they were young people and especially if they were young men. He identified with young people and to see what their experience meant to them to see if he could identify with it. He was feeding himself as well as being helpful to them. . . . He really was curious about them, especially if they were interested in him, and especially, as I say, if they were young men, then he could really relate to them on the basis of his own experiences as a young man.[15]

Isherwood imagined his relationship with Cold War gay readers as truly symbiotic: he identified with them as much as they did with him.

These extensive encounters with readers had a profound effect on Isherwood's subsequent authorial identity. He expanded his small group of gay writers to include a transnational cast of gay readers, similarly allied against the Enemy. His sixties novels *can* pass but can also be decoded. He turned his own consumption of popular texts, his own fandom, into a source of his own literary production.

Notes

1. Christopher Isherwood, letter to Stephen Spender, July 22, 1954, Stephen Spender collection, Bancroft Library, University of California at Berkeley.

2. Don Bachardy, phone interview with the author, September 23, 2009.

3. Craig Makler, letter to Christopher Isherwood, January 15, 1974, CI 1766, Huntington Library, San Marino, California.

4. John B. Hench, *Books as Weapons: Propaganda, Publishing, and the Battle for Global Markets in the Era of World War II* (Ithaca, N.Y.: Cornell University Press, 2010). For more about paperback books in the United States, see, for example, Thomas L. Bonn, *Undercover: An Illustrated History of Mass Market Paperbacks* (New York: Penguin, 1982); Piet Schreuders, *Paperbacks, U.S.A: A Graphic History, 1939–1959* (New York: And Books, 1981); Allen Billy Crider, ed., *Mass Market Publishing in America* (New York: G. K. Hall, 1982); and Frank L. Schlick, *The Paperbound Book in America* (New York: R. R. Bowker Company, 1958).

5. Michael Bronski, *Pulp Friction: Uncovering the Golden Age of Gay Male Pulps* (New York: St. Martin's Press, 2003), 2–3.

6. Malcolm Cowley, "Hardbacks or Paperbacks?" in *The Literary Situation* (New York: Viking Press, 1955), 122–23.

7. See Susan Stryker, *Queer Pulp: Perverted Passions from the Golden Age of the Paperback* (San Francisco: Chronicle Books, 2001).

8. Malcolm Cowley, "Cheap Books for the Millions," in *The Literary Situation,* 98–99.

9. Christopher Isherwood, *Lost Years: A Memoir, 1945–1951,* ed. Katherine Bucknell (New York: Harper, 2000), 68.

10. David Bergman, "The Cultural Work of Sixties Gay Pulp Fiction," in *The Queer Sixties,* ed. Patricia Smith and Patricia Juliana (New York: Routledge, 1999), 36.

11. Henry Jenkins, *Textual Poachers: Television Fans and Participatory Culture* (New York: Routledge, 1992).

12. Marilyn R. Schuster, *Passionate Communities: Reading Lesbian Resistance in Jane Rule's Fiction* (New York and London: New York University Press, 1999), 14.

13. Henry Jenkins, "Fandom and/as religion?," Intensities interviews Henry Jenkins @Console-ing Passions, University of Bristol, July 7, 2001, http: intenstities .org/Essays/Jenkins.pdf.

14. Barbara Hochmann, *Getting at the Author: Reimagining Books and Authors in the Age of American Realism* (Amherst: University of Massachusetts Press, 2001).

15. Don Bachardy, phone interview with the author, September 23, 2009.

19

Not Satisfied with the Ending

Connecting *The World in the Evening* to *Maurice*

JOSHUA ADAIR

They Hated the Book

Few books have been so poorly received by friends and critics alike as Christopher Isherwood's *The World in the Evening* (1954). Remarkable for its stylistic and thematic departures from his earlier works, the work was almost unanimously dismissed as a failure and continues to be marginalized by critics and readers. Katherine Bucknell's "Who Is Christopher Isherwood?" asserts that "the book is marred both by repressed anger about the difficulties of trying to write as a homosexual and by psychological inaccuracies."[1] This poor evaluation may be the result of a combination of elements: Bob Wood and Charles Kennedy, important secondary characters in the novel, mark Isherwood's first depiction of an overtly homosexual, nonstereotypical couple; the novel itself is not organized around an Isherwood-inspired narrator; and the novel's narrative subtly but radically depicts a prototype of gay community. The novel, I contend, requires reconceptualization to appreciate its value in terms of innovation and for its significant connection to E. M. Forster's *Maurice*. In other words, if we accept Fredric Jameson's assertion that we perpetually read through the lens of prior texts and experiences, then we must attempt to read it as a text apart from Isherwood's oeuvre: as a unique narrative exploring the possibility of forming spaces within society amenable to gay men.

By drawing upon Jameson's ideas, *The World in the Evening* can be situated as a "socially symbolic act."[2] Jameson argues that a text is not just a text; rather, it represents a unique cultural artifact from a specific moment in history that evokes the sociopolitical climate at the time of its composition and suggests social change or the necessity thereof. Jameson argues that all such "cultural artifacts" are informed (either by the author's choice or subconsciously) by the "political unconscious," and the impetus to analyze and attempt to alter the sociopolitical/ideological situation of any society at a given point in history (20). For Jameson, meaning does not exist apart from contextualization. The temptation here is to suggest "historical" contextualization, but, for the Marxist Jameson, history remains largely inaccessible: "history is *not* a text, not a narrative, master or otherwise. . . . It is inaccessible to us except in textual form, and . . . our approach to it and to the Real itself necessarily passes through its prior textualization, its narrativization in the political unconscious" (35). In other words, to grasp any sense of history (however one construes the term) or the past, one must draw upon extant textual evidence. But, as Jameson observes, we cannot read any text without the influence of our experiences, textual and otherwise.

While I fundamentally agree with Jameson's assertions, I would like to propose the possibility of actively choosing to read a text as unique and innovative. To do so, we must resist the temptation to rely solely on familiar interpretive strategies, or to attempt an interpretation heavily schematized by the author's previous works or other novels we've read. What I suggest as an effective alternative approach is to read *The World in the Evening* in a purposeful mode, to understand it as part of a literary tradition dedicated to exploring same-sex attraction and community, but also to recognize its treatment of those themes and issues as a unique (perhaps even singular) contribution to that tradition. As I have suggested, the novel represents a new narrative for Isherwood and for his audiences. Readers' and critics' attempts to contextualize the novel through their experiences of Isherwood's previous work prove fruitless: for the vast majority of the reading audience (at it did at its publication and today), it offers a first glimpse into a community where a gay couple lives with relative openness and success.

While the novel unquestionably represents a departure from Isherwood's trademark strategy of focalizing narratives through the voice of a narrator who is a version of himself, the primary narrative remains fairly conventional in a number of ways. Organized around the experiences of the protagonist, Stephen Monk, the novel traces Stephen's personal development through a series of failed heterosexual and homosexual relationships. Isherwood scholar Claude Summers suggests: "*Evening* traces the journeys of its worldly, self-absorbed protagonist from egoism to spiritual awareness and from world-weariness to commitment."[3] When the novel opens, Stephen is about to leave his flagrantly adulterous wife, Jane. The untenability of Stephen's life in Hollywood with Jane becomes quite clear, so much so that he must flee in order to save himself. After a dramatic parting fueled by violence and infidelity, he returns to his Aunt Sarah, a Quaker living in Dolgelly, Pennsylvania, to reassess his life.

In Pennsylvania, Stephen finds himself in conflict with the tranquil, subdued lifestyle of Dolgelly and contemplates committing suicide. He is a man without a place in the world and apparently always has been. Along the way, we learn that his first wife, Elizabeth Rydal, an acclaimed novelist whose best-selling novel becomes the title of Isherwood's novel, succumbed to cancer some years before. We discover that what seems to have been Stephen's most significant romantic relationships was actually a complex union, rife with difficulty. After being struck by a bus (possibly a subconscious attempt at suicide), Stephen delves deeper into his own tempestuous past while finding himself, somewhat unwillingly, integrating into the social fabric of Dolgelly. A major feature of this integration, and the subject of the more subversive secondary narrative of the novel, is his close friendship with a gay couple, Bob and Charles. They are not the "stereotypical" gay men depicted in much literature at the time: both are masculine, socially and emotionally well-adjusted, and each evinces a strong desire to gain equal rights for homosexuals. Much like Stephen's, the story of Bob and Charles centers on the need for increased self-awareness and the necessity of creating a community for oneself in society.

While the secondary narrative represents a small portion of the overall novel (less than twenty out of 301 pages), this subplot suggests a significant linkage with other literature that imagines community formation or community integration for gay men, as well as an important development in Isherwood's fiction. Isherwood had read *Maurice* in manuscript and discussed it with Forster.[4] The story of Bob and Charles represents a "truly transgressive" narrative space, to use the concept of Marilyn R. Farwell.[5] Such spaces, she asserts, pivot upon conceptions of sameness (similarities in outlooks and goals, as much as the eradication of gender difference and other related binary systems) and can help us understand how counternarratives show us our world in new and challenging ways. Isherwood's *Evening* offers such a narrative; Bob and Charles represent a successful gay couple forging space for themselves in an unlikely community. Both men are well-adjusted, service-minded, and adamant in their desire to garner rights for themselves and others like them. Isherwood refuses reliance upon past stereotypes of gay men presented in literature:

men frequently depicted as weak, depraved, and/or mentally unstable. They are both exemplary in their normalcy; Isherwood bravely circumvents prevailing notions of homosexuality in his depiction of these men and presents characters worthy of respect and admiration. Conversely, Stephen represents the harm inflicted upon individuals quashed by societal standards, made too uncomfortable to express their desires.

The transgression of this narrative space is manifold and bears some close examination before proceeding. First, Isherwood neatly subverts the established norms for a British writer by choosing the United States as the setting for his novel. As an emigrant from England, Isherwood was widely criticized as being unpatriotic and selfish, and endured insinuations of failed masculinity and homosexuality. He understood displacement and disenfranchisement and chose a setting paralleled by his own life experience and the greater freedom he experienced as a homosexual living in the United States. It is also worth noting that while Isherwood's personal freedom always seemed to expand when he left England—either for Germany or for the United States—that freedom also tended to diminish shortly afterwards owing to social and political climate changes. Jamie Carr observes:

> In the increased atmosphere of militancy and conformity imposed in the Cold War era and under McCarthyism, the methods of exclusion of "deviant" others were many: surveillance, arrest, expulsion from jobs, trials, and internment. Those considered unpatriotic or a threat to national security—Communists, foreigners, conscientious objectors, homosexuals—became targets of explicit forms of discipline and punishment.[6]

As the space where Isherwood saw a potential for change, the United States in the 1950s proved as frightening as 1930s Germany and therefore the United States became the perfect setting for a reimagined world.

Isherwood takes this social critique one step further by choosing a Quaker society as the space for his narrative, an unlikely locale for an exploration of gay men creating a community for themselves. However, as Carr observes, homosexuals were not the only group of alienated individuals during wartime: two other important groups were pacifists and conscientious objectors. These groups of so-called deviants were frequently lumped together and treated as unpatriotic, effeminate troublemakers. By aligning these various groups of outsiders, Isherwood makes an important statement about the necessity of minorities finding expression and power by uniting. Finally, rather than selecting an urban environment, as is often the case in gay novels, Isherwood chooses a rural one, a choice at once purposeful and jarring for his readers. The implication of this particular choice may be that our well-established sociogovernmental infrastructure, best evidenced in urban spaces, must be abandoned in favor of starting afresh and abandoning outmoded approaches that lead to the marginalization of many groups in society.

Isherwood's narrative focuses on characters whose sexuality would have been considered aberrant in midcentury America. Surprisingly, though, Bob and Charles are characterized as a fairly average couple encountering difficulties similar to any comparable heterosexual couple. However, Stephen's sexuality appears more complex. While Stephen should be easily categorized as an affluent, white, male, heterosexual protagonist, he confounds these categories by having sexual affairs with men and failing to perform adequately as a traditional husband. Stephen, Bob, and Charles form a narrative about men, their sexuality, and their place in society. Women do appear within this narrative, and while their presence is integral at various points, Isherwood focuses more directly upon men marginalized by society. He never resorts to prevailing stereotypes about homosexuals being mentally ill or effeminate; he draws a community of individuals striving for personal enlightenment despite their heterogeneity. Ultimately, Isherwood's narrative explores how men who do not fulfill patriarchal mandates might find a place within society.

It is this focus on men who do not fit societal stereotypes that allows Farwell's theories to operate effectively here. Whereas traditional Western narrative is structured around dichotomous difference (i.e., heterosexuality, binary gender opposition, good versus evil), Farwell argues that narratives refusing such dichotomies ultimately work to subvert the established order: "Sameness, ironically, undercuts the stark symbolic gender differences which are created in the rest of the text and undercuts the heterosexuality which informs the rest of the narrative" (*Heterosexual Plots and Lesbian Narratives*, 103). By organizing his narrative around three men who do not conform to mandatory patriarchal sexual mores, Isherwood presents readers with an opportunity to experience an innovative narrative that calls into question their own lives and literary experiences.

Only Connect

Before moving into a textual analysis of *Evening*, some historical and biographical Jamesonian contextualization seems essential. At no point during this exploration do I intend to suggest a direct causal link between actual events in Isherwood's life and the features of his work because to do so seems reductive and speculative. However, the relationship between Forster and Isherwood shaped the outlooks of both writers and their artistic choices; thus these influences become avenues for understanding the novel as a text writing back to Forster's *Maurice*.

Forster greatly influenced Isherwood's life long before they met:

> I saw it all suddenly while I was reading *Howards End*. . . . Forster's
> the only one who understands what the modern novel ought to be. . . .
> Our frightful mistake was that we believed in tragedy: the point is,
> tragedy's quite impossible nowadays. . . . We ought to aim at being
> essentially comic writers. . . . The whole of Forster's technique is
> based on the tea-table: instead of trying to screw all his scenes up to
> the highest possible pitch, he tones them down until they sound like
> mothers'-meeting gossip.[7]

Isherwood formally met Forster in 1932. Peter Parker observes: "The lunch took place in Forster's flat at 26 Brunswick Square in Bloomsbury, and Isherwood at once fell under Forster's spell."[8] From then until Forster's death in 1970, the two maintained a warm friendship that often included discussion about their literary pursuits.

During these conversations, a major point of discussion was *Maurice*. Forster had been working on his "gay novel" since before World War I, but he maintained dissatisfaction with the novel as a whole, particularly its ending. Not long after they became friends, Forster shared the manuscript with Isherwood:

> Christopher felt greatly honored, of course, by being allowed to read
> it. Its antique locutions bothered him, here and there. . . . And yet the
> wonder of the novel was that it had been written when it had been
> written; the wonder was Forster himself, imprisoned within the jungle
> of pre-war prejudice, putting these unthinkable thoughts into words.
> Perhaps listening from time to time, to give himself courage, to the
> faraway chop-chop of those pioneer heroes, Edward Carpenter and
> George Merrill, boldly enlarging *their* clearing in the jungle.[9]

Far more than just a well-established author sharing work with a younger, less well-known writer, the exchange of the *Maurice* manuscript created a dialogue between the two men about gay life. Forster insisted that *Maurice* subvert traditional narratives about homosexual men by ending happily; nevertheless, he had difficulty achieving this goal. In *Christopher and His Kind,* Isherwood recalls,

Almost every time they met, after this, they discussed the problem: how should *Maurice* end? That the ending should be a happy one was taken for granted; Forster had written the novel in order to affirm that such an ending is possible for homosexuals. But the choice of a final scene remained open. Should it be a glimpse of Maurice and Alec enjoying a life of freedom, outside the bounds of society? Should it be Maurice's good-humored parting from his faithless former lover, Clive: "Why don't you stop being shocked and attend to your own happiness?" Christopher wasn't satisfied with either ending. (The latter was ultimately adopted.) He made his own suggestions—as did several of Forster's other friends. He loved this continuing discussion, simply as a game. (127)

Forster's willingness to invite criticism about his arguably most personal work impressed Isherwood, who felt that *Maurice* didn't ring quite true. In *A Great Unrecorded History,* Wendy Moffat observes that "*Maurice* was a revolutionary new genre—a gay love story that ended happily. It was Morgan's cri de cœur."[10] For Isherwood, though, gay community looked quite different. His dissatisfaction with the novel's denouement, I argue, does not diminish its impact upon him; rather, this difference in viewpoint suggests that he recognized a jumping-off point from which he might formulate his own version.

As a result, Forster served as both a respected elder and a valued colleague to Isherwood. Isherwood does not so much reject the ideals of *Maurice* as he redirects its energies, infusing them with his own experiences and ideals. He played a pivotal role, in fact, in making certain *Maurice* received mainstream release. "For Isherwood, shepherding Forster's gay fiction posthumously into print was both a sacred trust and a political adventure," Moffat notes. "He believed that publication would give Forster a second life as a pioneer of gay writing" (19–20). Isherwood, it seems, valued the spirit and energy of *Maurice* tremendously; he also recognized the absolute necessity of contextualizing the novel in the time of its composition. At one point, Forster asked Isherwood whether the story "dated," to which Isherwood replied, "Why *shouldn't* it date?" (*Christopher and His Kind,* 126). In other words, Forster's text holds value as a historical document, as the first novel to imagine a community for gay men. When examining a social group's development, timelessness is not necessarily the highest value if one wishes to trace the progression of thought regarding social change. Isherwood noted that he felt *Maurice* "superior [to Forster's other novels] because of its purer passion, its franker declaration of its author's faith" (ibid., 99). I believe the same can be said about *Evening*.

Although Isherwood found both proposed endings to *Maurice* unsatisfactory, he recognized its potential power to inspire new thought about gay men forging community for themselves. Isherwood would carry this awareness with him for the rest of his life. Moffat recounts a meeting in 1970: upon seeing John Lehmann examine his collection of books on E. M. Forster, Isherwood commented: "Of course all those books have got to be re-written," he said. "Unless you start with the fact that he was homosexual, nothing's any good at all" (20). Isherwood's interactions with Forster emphasized the necessity of exploring homosexuality in creating and understanding literature that impacts how all people perceive it. This approach to writing, in turn, ultimately influences homosexuals' place in society and the potential for the creation of a safe space for them. Although Forster's endings might not have rung true to Isherwood, the novel's goal did. This interaction with Forster inspired Isherwood to create his own vision of a community that integrated gay men. Over time, he would become the clear legatee of Forster's efforts in imagining and depicting gay space. James J. Berg and Chris Freeman note: "because Isherwood began to incorporate gay issues into his published fiction, notably in *The World in the Evening* (1954), their relationship began to shift as Isherwood became a mentor figure, with Forster admiring and envying his candor and courage" (*The Isherwood Century*, 5).

Whereas Forster's novel concludes with Maurice and Alec venturing into the greenwood to start a quasi-mythical life of happiness and fulfillment together, Isherwood presents a practical, down-to-earth depiction of two men, Bob and Charles, already living together, having forged a community for themselves in a quaint village in Pennsylvania Quaker country. In contrast to Forster around 1913, for Isherwood in the 1950s, gay community formation is neither magic nor wish fulfillment; rather, such a formation is a mundane (though not dull or unimportant) pursuit with numerous practical considerations.

Pennsylvania Deutsch

In Dolgelly, Isherwood emphasizes creating community wherein all voices are considered and consensus proves fundamental. For this reason, *Evening* presents a gay couple integrating into an established community, rather than starting anew. Rather than choosing separatism, as Forster does with *Maurice*, Isherwood suggests that if gay men are going to secure a place in the world, it must be done *within* society. Bob and Charles actively participate in society and work to change attitudes and perceptions that marginalize them. Staying their ground and fighting is the only option; society, not the marginalized, must change. As Isherwood shows through Stephen, withdrawal from society proves disastrous and potentially fatal. Summers argues, "The lack of community has always been of interest to Isherwood; and he has been particularly concerned with the predicament of one constituent group of 'The Lost,' the homosexual" (*Christopher Isherwood*, 30). Isherwood rejects withdrawal as a solution for his gay characters; for him, social standards must be reformed.

Bob and Charles represent diversity in an unlikely place and the necessity for greater awareness and acceptance of individuals outside patriarchal, hegemonic standards of normalcy. Although Bob has been labeled by Jonathan H. Fryer's unkind critical phrase as "another retarded adolescent fairy," he represents one of the few early positive characterizations of a gay man in fiction.[11] We learn almost immediately that Bob defies stereotypical characterizations: "Bob had an unexpectedly gruff voice which contradicted the delicacy of his face but went with his broad strong shoulders."[12] We discover that Bob is an amateur painter and lapsed Quaker. He proudly declares his belief in God to Stephen, but asserts that he "can't stand the sort of people who do" believe in God (102). In other words, the judgment and lack of acceptance often attendant to Christian belief irritate him. Nevertheless, we learn that he has recently attended a Meeting, leaving us to surmise that perhaps some shred of the Quaker belief system still persists within him.

Stephen's aunt Sarah delivers a clear characterization of Bob:

> He's Luke and Esther Wood's son, from over at New Faith. They were both birthright Friends, such splendid people. Esther was clerk of the Monthly Meeting for many years. They've both passed away, now. Oh, you're just going to love Bob! Such a fine, clean boy. So thoroughly wholesome. (59)

Bob defies gay stereotypes: no neurotic, ill-intentioned pleasure seeker bent on destroying all morality in anyone he meets, he is a nearly picturesque specimen of American masculinity—if one overlooks his homosexuality. Furthermore, he is not rootless, like so many gay men in literature preceding *Evening*: an established community member, he boasts a clearly delineated family history. He also served in the military "and might be going back in the Navy, soon" (103). His willingness to serve in the military demonstrates his bravery and willingness to defend his beliefs. Bob represents a new breed of gay man in fiction. Indeed, the novel narrates uncharted territory: gay men in a successful relationship.

Despite the community's admiration for the couple, Sarah does not fully understand Bob and Charles's relationship: "Those two boys! They're so comical, when they're together, I could laugh myself into a fit! Though, half the time, I really haven't the least idea what they're talking about" (59). While Sarah misapprehends, perhaps willfully, Bob and Charles's relationship, she feels great affection for them: "You should see their house! They've made it so charming, in an informal, masculine way. I always think it's so nice when two men get along together, like that" (60). While she may not completely understand it, Sarah represents a model of tolerance that is still prevalent in society.

Of the two men, the defiant Bob makes a stronger impression. After coming out to Stephen (who already knew), he bursts into a diatribe because Stephen suggests he be less aggressive in declaring his and Charles's homosexuality: "Maybe we should put people against us. Maybe we're too damned tactful. People just ignore us most of the time, and we let them. We encourage them to. So this whole business never gets discussed, and the laws never get changed" (105). This passage elucidates much: Bob's statement establishes his comfort with his sexuality. As Maurice did, he transcends the self-loathing permeating most gay literature to that point. In addition, he's angry about his identity group's treatment by society. He appreciates the kindness shown to him and Charles by the citizens of Dolgelly, but resents the community's inability to confront homosexuality openly. Bob's rage represents an important development for nascent gay community; personal fulfillment proves insufficient, gays must seek equal legal rights. In short, Bob demands safety and equality for himself and his kind, if only by living openly with Charles and evincing a strong sense of self-respect.

One of the most insightful scenes involving Charles underlines the importance of the Quaker's all-inclusive approach to living as a transferable ideal for gay community formation. While Stephen and Charles discuss Bob's conflicted relationship with the Quaker faith and his irritation about Charles's opinions on the topic, Charles announces: "He accuses me of sneering at them. But he's quite wrong. I respect them. And I admire them in a lot of ways. They don't sit nursing guilty consciences, they go right out and work the guilt off, helping people" (109). For Charles, the fundamental tenets of Quakerism represent a healthy approach to life that might improve any community. Like Bob, he favors action and service over guilt-ridden inertia. Two keys to community formation for gay men, Charles suggests, are action and frank, honest dialogue. In this way, Quaker tenets form a framework for the achievement of an inclusive community. After these initial passages, Bob and Charles disappear for many chapters. In the interim, Isherwood focuses upon Stephen Monk and the spectrum of variation inherent in all human relationships. While the tendency in reading Bob and Charles might be to dismiss them as assimilationists, Isherwood makes clear that *all* relationships possess similarities. Furthermore, through the explication of Stephen's relationship history, we come to recognize that the hallmark of relationships is variation; no single model exists and romantic relationships between members of the opposite sex are often as rife with tribulation and dysfunction as homosexual relationships. Heterosexuality frequently fails to stave off infidelity, mental and physical abuse, and general unhappiness, just as it does not ensure the solidification of a well-balanced personal identity or contribution to one's community. Isherwood carefully attacks these long-held beliefs about the institutions of heterosexuality and marriage in order to highlight the possibility of successful romantic relationships of any permutation.

Of all the characters in *Evening,* Stephen emerges as the least stable in terms of personal identity, community identity, and sexual orientation. His narrative foils Bob and Charles's, underscoring the highly functional nature of their relationship while highlighting Stephen's general insecurity. Stephen seemingly personifies the privilege of the American Dream, but from the outset, he possesses little or no sense of self. During the party scene that opens the novel, he thinks to himself, "If you had asked who I was, almost every one of them [the party guests] would have answered 'Jane Monk's husband,' and let it go at that" (5). The actress Jane, Stephen's second wife, dominates his life and sense of self; Isherwood presents her as a stereotypical femme fatale bent on emasculating her husband. Traditional heterosexist narratives invite readers to construe an adulterous wife as evil and her cuckolded husband as victimized. However, Isherwood depicts both parties as destructive, selfish, and cruel; Stephen hates Jane because she outshines, and simultaneously defines, him, and Jane despises Stephen's weakness and acquiescence.

Upon witnessing her infidelity ("Caught. Caught her at last."), Stephen flees the party, leaving Jane forever. Almost immediately, his identity insecurity emerges. While checking into a hotel, he thinks: "After all, I suppose I do actually exist." Through the hotel staff, he finds validation as he imagines they see him as "a real person. All our guests, by definition, are real people" (13). This insecurity is further illustrated by Stephen's final action as he leaves his and Jane's house:

> I came back into the bedroom for my suitcase, feeling weak and shaken and nearly sober. It was then that I remembered Elizabeth's letters. . . . I couldn't leave them alone with Jane. She might burn them. She might even read them. I should have to take them along with me—wherever it was that I was going. (12)

Elizabeth's letters, the remaining emblems of his first wife, shore up Stephen's sense of his pre-Jane identity, an identity developed through Elizabeth herself. Whereas Jane functions as trophy wife with her perfect looks and sophisticated sense of fashion, Elizabeth represented Stephen's search for an intellect-based identity and his need for someone older (twelve years his senior) and wiser to define him.

Throughout the novel, Stephen conjures the deceased Elizabeth either to bolster or to explore his sense of self: "Yes, I admit it, you invented me. Until you'd told me who I was, I didn't begin to exist. I was the most lifelike of all your characters" (19). Once he arrives at Aunt Sarah's, he imagines Elizabeth in his room so that he can analyze his choice to come to Pennsylvania: "In order to hear what Elizabeth would say, I had to make her appear. . . . Closing my eyes now, I willed myself to see the tiny slant-ceilinged upstairs room of our house on the Schwarzee" (42). Even after her death, Stephen avoids relying on his own thoughts or beliefs in order to assess his place in life; he defines himself by his relationships. In a traditionally patriarchal society, Stephen inhabits a feminine positionality as the weaker partner in all his relationships by refusing to forge an identity of his own. He spends his first weeks at Tawelfan rehashing his relationship with Elizabeth, indicating his desire to find a relationship in which he feels a strong sense of identity.

Stephen is an example of what we now call codependency, and his ambivalence about his sexual orientation may be a symptom of that. Although Isherwood initially depicts Stephen as heterosexual, we learn through his musings about Elizabeth that he may be bisexual. When Charles, the local physician, attends Stephen after his accident, a strong homoerotic interest on Stephen's part emerges:

> [Charles] brought a chair over and sat down by the bed, taking my wrist in his big hand. His eyes focused intently on my face, with a delighted amusement, as though my broken thigh in its clumsy cast were a private joke between the two of us. I began to feel pleasantly

passive and cozy and safe. His mere presence was almost hypnotically protective; it made you want to go to sleep. If there was any worrying to be done, I felt, he would take care of it all. (54)

Stephen's near-euphoric submission to Charles clearly suggests more than a comfortable physician–patient relationship. Rather, Stephen gives in to Charles as he succumbs to Jane and Elizabeth. It is this lack of identity in Stephen that Isherwood repeatedly underscores: a society that prohibits a free expression of variations of sexual desire produces stunted individuals incapable of reaching full personal development.

Stephen's nonsexual interactions with Charles might be explained away, but his affair with Michael Drummond cannot. Married and traveling together, Stephen and Elizabeth meet a young man whom they both immediately admire. Stephen recalls:

> I first saw him as he passed our windows, quite near to the shore, in a collapsible rubber boat, bronzed like an Indian and naked except for a pair of very British-looking football shorts. His suntan made his blue eyes pale and vivid and his blond hair seem almost white. He was a strikingly handsome boy with a slim, muscular body, and he paddled with ferocious concentration. (151)

One can hardly miss the erotic intonation to Stephen's observation; he clearly finds the young man physically desirable. We quickly learn that Stephen finds Michael all the more appealing because "he was young enough to accept me uncritically in my new role of the mature married man" (153). Stephen relaxes in Michael's presence, believing that the young man accepts the identity he has constructed via his marriage to Elizabeth. In addition, he can fulfill some homoerotic desires with Michael without actually transgressing any societal boundaries. Before long, though, mutual attraction complicates the relationship; Stephen distances himself from Michael when he believes Elizabeth pregnant, assuming he will have to playact at fatherhood (158). However, the separation does not endure; Elizabeth unexpectedly meets Michael in the Canary Islands a few years later and their acquaintance renews awkwardly (174). The meeting creates tension between the two men: "Michael's tone was impersonal and extremely polite. He would tell us whatever we wanted to know, nothing more" (176). Stephen immediately recognizes something great afoot:

> In spite of themselves, as it seemed, his eyes kept leaving Elizabeth's face and turning to mine. And there was an expression in them which

I couldn't interpret: it was some kind of challenge or question, I thought. As though he were claiming a private understanding between the two of us, from which Elizabeth was excluded. (178)

Stephen feels discomfort at this shared knowledge, particularly after Michael reveals that they did not meet by chance, but that he'd been looking for Stephen (182).

Nevertheless, the two men start spending more time together, reestablishing their mutual attraction. Michael challenges Stephen's sense of self: "Stephen, I can't stand seeing you unhappy like this," implying that he ought not be in a heterosexual relationship (185). Stephen dismisses Michael's concerns, ruffled by his directness. Shortly thereafter Michael and Stephen climb the mountain, El Nublo, in order for Michael to photograph a Nazi flag flying there and remove it. During their trip, Michael reveals his feelings for Stephen and the two enter into a combative relationship phase, although neither seems willing to leave. Stephen behaves as though he's offended by Michael's effrontery, but he continues to flirt, even offering him anything he wants to come down from a steep cliff. Descending from the unsafe cliff, Michael propositions Stephen and his concession takes little cajoling: "Suddenly, I didn't care any more. The problem had dissolved itself in the beer; and now there wasn't any problem at all, no drama, no tenseness. This was all clean fun, I told myself; and it didn't have to be anything more than that" (194). After their night together, Stephen dismisses it saying, "It simply isn't important" (195). In this way, he simultaneously dismisses his desire and reaffirms his identity as Elizabeth's husband. His reaction wounds Michael and their relationship never recovers. Stephen informs Michael, "You don't understand the kind of life I have with Elizabeth. You don't understand any kind of real happiness" (201). At this point, happiness for Stephen means living within societal boundaries, free of homosexual desire. As a result, the quality of all his relationships, including his marriage, deteriorates and his sense of personal fulfillment diminishes. In this way, Stephen represents Isherwood writing back to *Maurice* as he embodies a Clive Durham–type character who values social mandate over personal desire or integrity.

Elizabeth handles the revelation of his relationship with Michael unexpectedly: "Oh darling, please let's be open with each other, now! This may be the first time that it's actually 'happened,' as you call it. But it's certainly been on your mind before. You've wanted it. You've played all round it. Won't you even admit that?" (211). Clearly, Stephen's desire is more of a mystery to himself than anyone else. He refuses to allow his identity to be defined by nonheteronormative desires, even though his relationship with Elizabeth heads in a similar direction; the couple no longer enjoys physical intimacy (ibid.). Ultimately, Elizabeth's unwillingness to hate her husband for his indiscretion leaves Stephen's identity in ruins; because he uses Elizabeth as his mirror, he turns from her when she begins to reflect something he finds unacceptable. In order to escape his fractured identity, he begins an affair with Jane. An American socialite, Jane reestablishes Stephen's sense of self as a heterosexual male, diminishing the self-doubt created by his affair with Michael and Elizabeth's reaction to that infidelity. As we are already aware, that relationship also fails because Stephen refuses to develop an identity independent of Jane. Once he flees Jane, he searches for a new identity, with the help of Bob and Charles and the community of Dolgelly. However, we are not left with a convincing sense that Stephen will come to terms with his identity or move beyond being defined by societal standards of the time. His is the last line of the novel: "I really do forgive myself, from the bottom of my heart?" Uncertain in tone and lacking conviction, Stephen exemplifies for Isherwood the damage inflicted by a society insistent upon dichotomous definitions and rigid standards of heterosexuality.

When Bob and Charles reenter the narrative, Isherwood gives them an encouraging send-off, finding a sure footing for the narrative that Forster never quite achieves in *Maurice*. Bob reenlists, demonstrating his dedication to service and action. In addition, his decision reveals his desire to defend a country unwilling to do the same for him:

> All you have to do is tell them you're queer, and you're out. I couldn't do that though. Because what they're claiming is that us queers are unfit for their beautiful pure Army and Navy—when they ought to be glad to have us. The girly ones make wonderful pharmacist's mates, and the rest are just as good fighting men as anybody else. (281)

Amusingly, Bob sheepishly admits his reenlistment, all traces of his former militancy evaporated: "Bob Wood came around to Tawelfan with the car to pick me up, shortly before supper. He was in his Navy uniform. He grinned at me with the embarrassment almost any serviceman feels on first meeting a friend who has known him only in civilian clothes" (273). This scene marks an important shift in Bob; he decides to live as an example of what a gay man can be rather than descending into bitterness over his disenfranchisement. His embarrassed grin suggests a reversal in his previously cynical attitude toward the country he will defend and a renewed optimism in the possibility of change created through action.

More important, however, is the exchange that follows with Charles. Stephen has been invited to Bob and Charles's house as a dinner guest and the ensuing tableau resembles any marital domesticity. Bob boasts, "Do you know, Steve . . . this is nearly our fourth anniversary? Charles never remembers things like that" (275). A perfectly commonplace observation typical of any couple, by establishing the longevity of Bob and Charles's relationship Isherwood signals to his audience that gay relationships can be both healthy and enduring. A short, playful squabble immediately ensues with Bob and Charles teasing one another about who remembers the events of their relationship accurately. The scene is hopeful and satisfyingly mundane; Bob and Charles are simply another couple (the novel's only successful one) trying to make their way in the world. Bob will go off to fight and Charles will continue to serve the community they both hope to continue to develop as a sanctuary.

An Even World?

Can a marginalized, undervalued novel get a second chance? Is it possible that perhaps rather than representing a sub-par piece of fiction, *The World in the Evening* delivers a narrative outside the established norms of appreciation and criticism? A transformation in how we read Isherwood's novel is absolutely necessary to give it both its proper due and its place within the tradition of gay fiction. If we read, as Jameson suggests, through the lens of prior experience, then we must work to become more aware of this tendency. In so doing, we can create a process of reading and interpretation that facilitates heightened awareness and more insightful critique of our culture. Although such a strategy can never completely escape prior experience, even a small shift in our reading and comprehension strategies allows for the possibility of understanding texts that offer unfamiliar narratives in new and productive ways.

Isherwood's long-standing friendship with Forster shaped his work and worldview in numerous ways, most importantly because their collaboration on the final chapter of *Maurice* helped both men conceptualize gay community formation anew. Although Isherwood disliked Forster's closure of the narrative of Maurice and Alec, I would argue that engagement with that novel helped him write back to Forster's text, altering the depiction of gay communities in fiction and creating another link in the tradition of gay fiction.

Notes

1. Katherine Bucknell, "Who Is Christopher Isherwood?," in *The Isherwood Century: Essays on the Life and Work of Christopher Isherwood*, ed. James J. Berg and Chris Freeman (Madison: University of Wisconsin Press, 2000), 22.

2. Fredric Jameson, *The Political Unconscious: Narrative as a Socially Symbolic Act* (Ithaca, N.Y.: Cornell University Press, 1981), 20.

3. Claude J. Summers, *Christopher Isherwood* (New York: Frederick Ungar Publishing, 1980), 80.

4. [See the essay by Lois Cucullu in this volume.—Eds.]

5. Marilyn R. Farwell, *Heterosexual Plots and Lesbian Narratives* (New York: New York University Press, 1996).

6. Jamie M. Carr, *Queer Times: Christopher Isherwood's Modernity* (New York: Routledge, 2006), 91–92.

7. Christopher Isherwood, *Lions and Shadows: An Education in the Twenties* (1938; reprint, New York: New Directions, 1977), 174–75.

8. Peter Parker, *Isherwood: A Life Revealed* (New York: Random House, 2004), 211.

9. Christopher Isherwood, *Christopher and His Kind* (New York: Farrar, Straus and Giroux, 1976), 126.

10. Wendy Moffat, *A Great Unrecorded History: A New Life of E. M. Forster* (New York: Farrar, Straus and Giroux, 2010), 7.

11. Jonathan H. Fryer, "Sexuality in Isherwood," *Twentieth-Century Literature* 22.3 (1976): 350.

12. Christopher Isherwood, *The World in the Evening* (1954) (Minneapolis: University of Minnesota Press, 1999), 58.

ACKNOWLEDGMENTS

We have been working on Christopher Isherwood together for the better part of the last twenty years. After graduate school, when we both lived in Minnesota, we decided, on a brisk walk around one of ten thousand lakes, to collaborate, something that academics in the humanities don't do as much as we should. That conversation led us to Isherwood, and here we are, happily still hard at work together on our favorite writer. Our first book, *The Isherwood Century: Essays on the Life and Work of Christopher Isherwood,* began at the Modern Language Association in Washington, D.C., in 1996 with a panel called "Christopher Isherwood: Ten Years Gone." Some of the people we met and subsequently worked with on that project include Carola Kaplan, David Bergman, Raphael Kadushin, Sheila Leary, and Claude J. Summers. *The Isherwood Century* won a Lambda Literary Award in 2001, and we had the pleasure of being in Chicago for the ceremony. We shared that evening with Lisa Southerland and with Don Bachardy, whose *Stars in My Eyes* was a finalist in a different category, and our dear friend Dan Luckenbill, who studied creative writing with Isherwood in the mid-1960s at UCLA and spent his career as a librarian at his alma mater. Dan shared many stories with us about his friendship with Isherwood. That intimate knowledge helped us come to a better understanding of Isherwood. Because of his contributions to Isherwood studies, we are honored to make Dan a dedicatee of *The American Isherwood.*

Don Bachardy has been supportive and generous to us since we first contacted him in 1997. His dedication to his partner of thirty-three years is a testament to their abiding love. Knowing Don is as close as we ever got to meeting Chris, but that is awfully close, it turns out. The wonderful documentary *Chris & Don: A Love Story* by Guido Santi and Tina Mascara shows the beauty of this legendary couple, pioneers who lived with and loved each other openly at a time when very few people had the courage and the audacity to do so. Guido and Tina have been friends for a decade, and we are very pleased to include them in this new book, talking about their film and their long, intimate relationship with Don.

Sara (Sue) Hodson at the Huntington Library worked tirelessly to catalog the massive Isherwood collection, and her essay about it sheds light on how the man worked and thought. Her intelligence and acumen inspire us always and rescue us occasionally. Through Sue, we have come to know Steve Hindle, the research director at the Huntington. He recognizes that the Isherwood archive is the twentieth-century jewel in the crown in their holdings and has made it possible for us to work on Isherwood and to bring Isherwood to a broader public. David Zeiberg, the head of the Huntington, has also been a great supporter over the years.

This new book grew out of another MLA panel, in January 2011. "Isherwood in Los Angeles" included talks by William Handley and Lois Cucullu, both of whom are part of *The American Isherwood*.

Doug Armato and the good people at the University of Minnesota Press have done wonders for Isherwood, keeping his books in print in gorgeous editions and publishing scholarly work about him, including Jaime Harker's *Middlebrow Queer*. We are pleased to publish an excerpt of that work here.

We are honored to reprint an essay by the late Peter Firchow and thank Evelyn Firchow and Bernfried Nugel for allowing us to do so. Peter served as Jim's graduate adviser and encouraged his work on Isherwood and Forster. For that crucial support, we dedicate this book to him as well.

Chris Freeman would like to thank his friends and colleagues at the University of Southern California, including Margaret Russett, Larry Green, Joseph Dane, Joe Boone, Michelle Gordon, Dana Johnson, Alice Echols, Leo Braudy, and Richard Fliegel. USC has been a great home to me in my California life. Special thanks to Wendy Davis and Helen Irwin for encouragement, research help, positive feedback, and more. Joe Wittreich and Stuart Curran have been great mentors. Mark Thompson and Malcolm Boyd have given nothing but encouragement and support. Joe Bristow is a new friend and brilliant colleague. Taylor Negron, J. P. Davis, and Jack Larson give me one degree of separation from Christopher Isherwood. Richard Schneider and the *Gay and Lesbian Review Worldwide* have given me a forum to write about Isherwood.

Steve Rohr has been a great friend and associate. And my students, who continue to love Isherwood's work as much as I do, inspire me every day.

Jim Berg would like to thank all the people who made his transition to Southern California possible and even smooth, such as friends Gary Schiff, Gil Diaz, Wade Ellis, Sean Bergara, William Mann, and Casey Strachan. Colleagues and friends at College of the Desert and other California community colleges were also supportive, including Gari Browning, Philip Culbertson, Linda Emerson, Ellen Hardy, and Darlene Romano. Students at California State San Bernardino, Palm Desert Campus, were gracious enough to read *A Single Man* and listen to me postulate about it. My thanks to Fred Jandt and Doris Wilson at Cal State.

CONTRIBUTORS

JOSHUA ADAIR is assistant professor of English and the coordinator of Gender and Diversity Studies Programs at Murray State University. He has published on E. M. Forster's *Maurice,* Beverley Nichols's gardening trilogies, John Fowler's interior decoration, and the house museums of gay men in the United States.

JAMES J. BERG is dean of arts and sciences at College of the Desert. He is the editor of *Isherwood on Writing* (Minnesota, 2007) and coeditor with Chris Freeman of *The Isherwood Century* and *Conversations with Christopher Isherwood.*

JAMIE CARR is associate professor of English at Niagara University, where she teaches literary theory, contemporary Anglophone literature, and literature for children and adolescents. She is the author of *Queer Times: Christopher Isherwood's Modernity.*

ROBERT L. CASERIO, professor of English at the Pennsylvania State University, University Park, coedited *The Cambridge History of the English Novel* and edited *The Cambridge Companion to the Twentieth-Century English Novel.* He wrote *The Novel in England, 1900–1950: History and Theory,* which was awarded the George and Barbara Perkins Prize by the International Society for the Study of Narrative. He is the author of more than fifty essays, articles, and book chapters about English and American fiction.

NILADRI R. CHATTERJEE is associate professor of English at the University of Kalyani, India. A recipient of a Fulbright scholarship and the British Council–Charles Wallace Fellowship, he coedited *The Muffled*

Heart: Stories of the Disempowered Male and was an editor of *American Notes and Queries.* He has contributed to *The Oxford Dictionary of National Biography, The Isherwood Century,* and *The Reader's Companion to Twentieth-Century Writers.*

LISA COLLETTA is professor of English at the American University of Rome. Her research interests include the twentieth-century novel, humor studies, travel and transnational literature, and literary history. Her writing has appeared in numerous journals and essay collections, and she is the author of *British Novelists in Hollywood, 1935–65* and *Dark Humor and Social Satire in the Modern British Novel.* She is editor of *Kathleen and Christopher: Christopher Isherwood's Letters to His Mother* (Minnesota, 2005) and coeditor with Maureen O'Connor of *Wild Colonial Girl: Essays on Edna O'Brien.*

LOIS CUCULLU is associate professor of English at the University of Minnesota. She is the author of *Expert Modernists, Matricide, and Modern Culture: Woolf, Forster, Joyce,* and her essays have been published in journals such as *Novel, Signs, differences,* and *Modernism/Modernity.*

MARIO FARAONE was Christopher Isherwood Foundation Fellow at the Huntington Library in 2009–10 and taught English literature and literature of the English-speaking countries in the Intercultural Studies Department at the University of Trieste and in the universities of Rome, Cassino, Pescara, and Foggia. He has published *Un Uomo Solo,* a study of autobiographical narrative and spiritual renewal in Isherwood's novels, as well as essays on art and politics in the 1930s. Among his other books are *L'isola e il treno,* on the relation between political commitment and art in Edward Upward's work, and *Il morso del cobra,* on Isherwood's artistic reception of Vedanta.

PETER EDGERLY FIRCHOW (d. 2008) was professor of English at the University of Minnesota. He was a prolific scholar of British, American, and German literature, publishing widely on Isherwood, Auden, Orwell, Forster, and Conrad. He is the author of *Reluctant Modernists: Aldous Huxley and Some Contemporaries.*

CHRIS FREEMAN is coeditor, with James J. Berg, of the Lambda Award–winning *The Isherwood Century, Conversations with Christopher Isherwood,* and Lambda Award finalist *Love, West Hollywood.* He teaches English and gender studies at Dornsife College at the University of Southern California.

WILLIAM R. HANDLEY is associate professor of English at the University of Southern California. He is the editor of *The Brokeback Book: From Story to Cultural Phenomenon*; the author of *Marriage, Violence, and the Nation in the American Literary West*; and coeditor of *True West: Authenticity and the American West*.

JAIME HARKER is associate professor of English at the University of Mississippi, where she teaches American literature, world literature, and gender studies. She is author of *Middlebrow Queer: Christopher Isherwood in America* (Minnesota, 2013) and *America the Middlebrow: Women's Novels, Progressivism, and Middlebrow Authorship between the Wars* and coeditor of *The Oprah Affect: Critical Essays on Oprah's Book Club* and *1960s Gay Pulp Fiction: The Misplaced Heritage*.

SARA S. (SUE) HODSON is curator of literary manuscripts at the Huntington Library in San Marino, California. She has written and lectured on Christopher Isherwood and Jack London and is a nationally recognized expert on the issue of privacy in modern personal paper collections. Active in archival organizations, she has been named a Fellow of the Society of American Archivists, the highest award in the profession.

CAROLA M. KAPLAN is professor emerita of English at California State University, Pomona; past president of the Joseph Conrad Society of America; and a faculty member of the Institute of Contemporary Psychoanalysis, Los Angeles. She has written two books on modernist literature, *Seeing Double: Revisioning Edwardian and Modernist Literature* and *Conrad in the Twenty-first Century*. A research psychoanalyst, she is in private practice in Encino, California.

BENJAMIN KOHLMANN is assistant professor of English literature at the University of Freiburg. His essays have been published in *ELH*, *PMLA*, *Modernism/Modernity*, and *Textual Practice*. He is the author of *Committed Styles: Modernism, Politics, and Left-Wing Literature in the 1930s* and editor of *Edward Upward and Left-Wing Literary Culture in Britain*.

VICTOR MARSH is a research fellow in the School of English at the University of Queensland and teaches at Southern Cross University. He is the author of *Mr. Isherwood Changes Trains: Christopher Isherwood and the Search for the "Home Self"* and his autobiography, *The Boy in the Yellow Dress*. He compiled and edited *Speak Now: Australian Perspectives on Same-Sex Marriage*. He also taught meditation on behalf of his guru in a dozen countries in East Asia and the South Pacific.

TINA MASCARA wrote, produced, and directed two independent feature films, *Jacklight* and *Asphalt Stars,* which have been at the Kolkata International Film Festival, the Palm Springs International Film Festival, and the Madrid Film Festival. Her latest documentary (with Guido Santi, with whom she made the award-winning documentary *Chris & Don: A Love Story*) is *Monk with a Camera,* which chronicles the life and spiritual quest of Nicholas (Nicky) Vreeland, a Buddhist monk and photographer.

STEPHEN McCAULEY has written several novels, including *The Object of My Affection* and *Insignificant Others.* He wrote two novels under the pseudonym Rain Mitchell. He lives in Boston and has taught at University of Massachusetts, Harvard University, and Wellesley College. He is associate director of creative writing at Brandeis University.

PAUL M. McNEIL is senior vice dean of the School of Continuing Education at Columbia University. He leads an initiative to develop cross-disciplinary academic programs whose delivery is bound by neither space nor time.

GUIDO SANTI started his career directing short films for Italian television and collaborating with Ipotesi Olmi, a film laboratory coordinated by award-winning director Ermanno Olmi. After receiving his master's degree in film production at the University of Southern California, he produced and directed television specials and documentaries, including *Chris & Don: A Love Story* with Tina Mascara. He teaches film and film history at College of the Canyons in Santa Clarita, California. His latest documentary (with Tina Mascara) is *Monk with a Camera,* about Nicholas (Nicky) Vreeland, a Buddhist monk and photographer.

KYLE STEVENS is the Florence Levy Kay Fellow in Film and the Digital Humanities at Brandeis University. His essays have been published in *Cinema Journal, Critical Quarterly,* and *Film Criticism.* His current research examines psychological realism in the films of Mike Nichols.

REBECCA GORDON STEWART was the Christopher Isherwood Foundation Fellow at the Huntington Library for 2010–11. Her essays on Isherwood have been published in *A/B: Auto/Biography Studies* and *Bloomsbury: Inspirations and Influences.* She is a lecturer at Bath Spa University and in Oxford University's academic exchange program Advanced Studies in England and is researching the influence of D. H. Lawrence on Isherwood's writing.